THE
IMMORTALS
TWO NINES
and Other Celtic Stories

PHILLIP VINE

First published by Pitch Publishing, 2022

Pitch Publishing
9 Donnington Park,
85 Birdham Road,
Chichester,
West Sussex,
PO20 7AJ
www.pitchpublishing.co.uk
info@pitchpublishing.co.uk

A CIP catalogue record is available for this book
from the British Library.

ISBN 978 1 80150 077 7

Typesetting and origination by Pitch Publishing

Printed and bound in Great Britain by TJ Books, Padstow

Contents

John, you're immortal now.

BILL SHANKLY TO JOCK STEIN

Inside the Celtic dressing room,

Estádio Nacional, Lisbon,

25 May 1967

Bill, they're all immortals now.

JOCK STEIN TO BILL SHANKLY

Inside the Pearly Gates,

God's Good Heaven,

Date unknown

To Liz, the love of my life
and
to friends lost, found, and forever:

Eric Brown

Don Fouracre

Simon Norris

Andy Pearce

Connie Rawlinson

Malcolm Sell

Finn Sinclair

Freya Sinclair-Brown

Derek Smith

Sue Smith

These stories are also dedicated to the
millions of Irish men, women, and
children who were the victims of genocide
in the Irish Holocaust of 1845–1850,
and to the immortals of Celtic past,
present, and future.

Heartfelt Thanks

WRITING MAY appear a solitary business but the production of any book is as much a team game as football.

There are publishers, editors, designers, proofreaders, researchers, distributors, bookshops, without whom there would be no book.

So, my heartfelt thanks goes out to everyone at Pitch Publishing whose trust and encouragement and generosity of spirit mean so much to me and whose creativity and professionalism make all things possible.

There is another team, though, that I rely upon at the crucial stage of finalising the text of each book. These are my professional readers whose dedication and intelligence and experience combine to point out both errors of style and of substance in the second draft of my work. Without their critical input and without their creative suggestions, the final versions of my books would be far inferior. Without them, I would be lost indeed.

So, heartfelt thanks go out to these unsung and unpaid heroes: Ishmail Badr; Eric Brown; Pete Murphy; Ray Starling; Des Vine.

I am particularly indebted, however, to my special friend, Eric Brown, the award-winning author of science fiction and crime novels, the best writer I know, who has supported, encouraged, and critiqued my writing for the best part of two decades. Without Eric, I would never have become a published author.

135 Celtic Immortals

1887–2022

In order of appearance in the book

RODDY MACDONALD	Scorer of a winning Old Firm goal in 1979
JOCK STEIN	The original immortal
STEVIE CHALMERS	Scorer of the winning goal in the 1967 European Cup Final
BOBBY MURDOCH	Lisbon Lion
BERTIE AULD	Lisbon Lion
BILLY MCNEILL	Captain of the Lisbon Lions
JOHN CLARK	Lisbon Lion
KENNY DALGLISH	Football genius
BOBBY LENNOX	Lisbon Lion
BOB KELLY	Celtic chairman 1947–1971
DERMOT DESMOND	Current Celtic majority shareholder
THE GREEN BRIGADE	Fans' organisation upholding Celtic culture
PAT WELSH	Fenian activist and Founding Father
TOM MALEY, SR	Founding Father
TOM MALEY, JR	Player in Celtic's first match, 1888
JOHN GLASS	Founding Father
BROTHER WALFRID	Originator of Celtic and the Poor Children's Dinner Table
WILLIE MALEY	Player in 1888 friendly v Rangers; Celtic manager 1897–1943
DR JOHN CONWAY	Founding Father
JOSEPH SHAUGHNESSY	Founding Father
ARCHBISHOP CHARLES EYRE	Catholic Archbishop of Glasgow and Celtic patron
MICHAEL DAVITT	Fenian revolutionary and Celtic patron
NEIL LENNON	Player 2000–2007; manager 2010–2014 and 2019–2021
BROTHER DOROTHEA	Colleague of Brother Walfrid

TOMMY GEMMELL	Lisbon Lion
FERGUS MCCANN	Celtic saviour in 1994
JIMMY GRIBBEN	The man who brought Jock Stein to Celtic
JIMMY JOHNSTONE	Football genius
JIM BROGAN	Celtic stalwart under Stein
JAMES KELLY	First Celtic captain; chairman 1909–1914
CHARLIE GALLAGHER	Celtic stalwart under Stein
JIMMY MCGRORY	Celtic record goalscorer; manager 1945–1965
SEAN FALLON	Celtic captain, assistant manager, immortal
JIM CRAIG	Lisbon Lion
DESMOND WHITE	Celtic chairman 1971–1985
JIMMY FARRELL	Celtic director 1964–1994
CHARLIE TULLY	Football genius
JOE MCBRIDE	Celtic goalscorer 1965–1968
DANNY MCGRAIN	Celtic captain and best full-back in the world
DAVIE HAY	Quality Street member; manager 1983–1987
TOMMY BURNS	Player 1971–1989; manager 1994–1997
PETER LAWWELL	Celtic chief executive 2003–2021
IAN YOUNG	Author of the infamous tackle on Willie Johnston in 1965
JOHN HUGHES	Celtic goalscorer 1959–1971
RONNIE SIMPSON	Lisbon Lion
JOHN DIVERS	Celtic stalwart 1956–1966
NEILLY MOCHAN	Celtic Boot Room stalwart under Stein
BOB ROONEY	Celtic Boot Room stalwart under Stein
JIMMY STEELE	Celtic masseur under Stein
DR JOHN FITZSIMMONS	Celtic doctor under Stein
WILLIE WALLACE	Lisbon Lion
GEORGE CONNELLY	Football genius
HARRY HOOD	Celtic goalscorer 1969–1976
WILLIE ORR	Celtic captain 1904–1907
JIMMY MCMENEMY	Celtic player 1902–1920; assistant manager under Willie Maley
DAVIE HAMILTON	Celtic player during six-in-a-row 1904–1910
ALEC MCNAIR	Celtic player during six-in-a-row 1904–1910
JOHN THOMSON	Celtic goalkeeper, died in action in 1931
JIMMY QUINN	Celtic goalscorer 1900–1915
DAVID LOW	Financial fixer and saviour of Celtic in 1994
BRIAN DEMPSEY	Celtic rebel and ally of McCann in 1994
JOHN KEANE	Celtic rebel and ally of McCann in 1994
KEVIN KELLY	Member of Kelly dynasty at Celtic and member of the Biscuit Tin Board
JACK MCGINN	Founder of *Celtic View*; chairman 1986–1991

TOM GRANT	Member of the Biscuit Tin Board
PHIL O'DONNELL	Celtic stalwart 1994–1999
CELTS FOR CHANGE	Rebel supporter organisation
SAVE OUR CELTS	Rebel supporter organisation
JACKIE MCNAMARA	Celtic stalwart 1995–2005
HENRIK LARSSON	Football genius
PAUL LAMBERT	Celtic stalwart 1997–2005
MARK VIDUKA	Celtic iconoclast 1998–2000
HARALD BRATTBAKK	Scorer of the goal that stopped the ten
ĽUBOMÍR MORAVČÍK	Football genius
CHARLIE NICHOLAS	Football genius
WIM JANSEN	Celtic manager who stopped the ten
JOSEF VENGLOŠ	Celtic manager who signed Moravčík
MARTIN O'NEILL	Celtic manager 2000–2005
GORDON STRACHAN	Celtic manager 2005–2009
CHRIS SUTTON	Celtic goalscorer 2000–2006; media legend
ALAN THOMPSON	Celtic stalwart 2000–2007; assistant to Lennon 2010–2012
JOHAN MJÄLLBY	Celtic stalwart 1998–2004; assistant to Lennon 2010–2014
JOHN HARTSON	Celtic goalscorer 2001–2006
SHUNSUKE NAKAMURA	Celtic stalwart 2005–2009
MACIEJ ŻURAWSKI	Celtic stalwart 2005–2008
ARTUR BORUC	Celtic's Holy Goalie
BRIAN QUINN	Celtic chairman 2000–2007
ANGE POSTECOGLOU	Celtic manager since 2021
GERRY DUNBAR	Editor of Celtic fanzine *Not the View*
MICHAEL NICHOLSON	Celtic chief executive since 2021
SCOTT BROWN	Celtic immortal 2007–2021
KRIS COMMONS	Celtic goalscorer 2011–2017
GEORGIOS SAMARAS	Celtic goalscorer 2008–2014
VICTOR WANYAMA	Celtic stalwart 2011–2013
JAMES FORREST	Celtic immortal since 2010
DAVID MOSS	Celtic scout 2000–2017
JOHN PARK	Head of football development 2007–2016
CHRIS MCCART	Head of youth development under Park
AIDEN MCGEADY	Celtic stalwart 2004–2010
JOHN KENNEDY	Celtic assistant manager under Lennon and Postecoglou
VIRGIL VAN DIJK	Celtic's defensive master 2013–2015
FRASER FORSTER	Celtic's Great Wall in victory over Barcelona
TOM ROGIC	The Wizard of Oz
GARY HOOPER	Celtic goalscorer 2010–2013

KRIS AJER	Celtic stalwart 2016–2021
MIKAEL LUSTIG	Celtic stalwart 2012–2019
MOUSSA DEMBÉLÉ	Celtic goalscorer 2016–2018
RONNY DEILA	Celtic manager 2014–2016
NEIL MCGUINNESS	Celtic scout 2009–2015
JOHN COLLINS	Celtic stalwart 1990–1996; assistant to Deila 2014–2016
LEIGH GRIFFITHS	Celtic goalscorer 2014–2022 and wayward genius
CRAIG GORDON	Celtic goalkeeper 2014–2020
NIR BITTON	Celtic stalwart 2013–2022
KIERAN TIERNEY	Celtic stalwart 2015–2019
JIMMY DELANEY	Celtic goalscorer 1933–1946
CALLUM MCGREGOR	Celtic stalwart since 2013; current captain
SCOTT SINCLAIR	Celtic stalwart 2016–2020
ODSONNE ÉDOUARD	Celtic goalscorer 2017–2021; wayward genius
CHRISTOPHER JULLIEN	Celtic stalwart since 2019
POPE FRANCIS	Celtic supporter; head of Catholic Church
DAVID TURNBULL	Celtic stalwart since 2020
ANDY WALKER	Celtic goalscorer 1987–1991; 1994–1996
ANTHONY RALSTON	A Postecoglou revelation at inverted full-back
LIEL ABADA	A Postecoglou revelation
REO HATATE	Two goals against Rangers in February 2022
KYOGO FURUHASHI	Football genius
GREG TAYLOR	A Postecoglou revelation at inverted full-back
JOTA	A Postecoglou revelation
GIORGOS GIAKOUMAKIS	Leading goalscorer in both Dutch and Scottish leagues
JOE HART	Commanding presence in goal under Postecoglou
CAMERON CARTER-VICKERS	Commanding presence at centre-back under Postecoglou
CARL STARFELT	Commanding presence at centre-back under Postecoglou
DAIZEN MAEDA	A Postecoglou revelation
MATT O'RILEY	A Postecoglou revelation
JOSIP JURANOVIĆ	A Postecoglou revelation
CHRIS FOGARTY	Author of *The Perfect Holocaust*

Personal and Political

I WAS surrounded. How could I have been so stupid?

'Fenian bastards!'

The voices all about me were shards of broken glass.

For a few moments, just after five o'clock on a Saturday afternoon in late October 1979, while walking along London Road in the direction of Glasgow Cross, I felt the greatest fear I had ever known in my admittedly short and sheltered life.

'Roman cunts!'

I had knowingly taken a wrong turning in my life which was about to come to an extremely unpleasant end.

'Find the Fenians, fuck the Fenians, cut the fucking Fenians!'

The voices surrounding me were harsh and full of spit and spleen.

'Fucking Fenian bastards!'

I didn't dare turn my head to look at faces but I could see them in my wild imaginings: close-cropped and sharpened, bony heads, with snarls for mouths and slits for eyes, with pained, pimpled skin, and scowls and frowns for smiles, and rusted razor blades for ragged teeth in open, stinking mouths.

'Cut the Fenian cunts!'

I was shaking like an autumn leaf in the western Glasgow wind.

Underneath my coat was ample evidence I was just such a Fenian these ugly men and boys were hunting. A trembling hand that checked my Celtic scarf – the one with 'PREMIER DIV CHAMPIONS 1979' printed upon it – was hidden from view by my buttoned coat and upturned collar.

'Cut the Catholic cunts!'

Inside my jeans pocket, too, was a cheap memento from Rome: an image of the Virgin Mary that I carried with me wherever I travelled.

I began to pray, 'Hail Mary, full of grace, pray for us sinners now and at the hour of our death.'

My lips may have moved but no sound dared escape my mouth.

I sneaked a look at my closest captors: their boots were for kicking, their bunnets were for slashing, and their faces were twisted visions of hell.

I pondered the powerlessness of prayer.

I seemed to march in unison with these Rangers fanatics. I wondered why, though, they had not pulled at my coat and uncovered my 'Fenian' loyalties. I was not draped in a Union Jack. I was not joining in with their chanting, 'Fuck the Pope! Fuck the IRA! Fuck the Fenians.'

It crossed my mind, for safety's sake, I ought to join their song, 'We are the Billy Boys', but I didn't know the words.

We had been fellow travellers now for maybe ten minutes; we had just passed the Orange Lodge at Bridgeton and, so far so ever so slightly good, I had not yet been uncovered or cut or killed. Was I imagining it or was the crowd about me thinning slightly?

I recalled the ninth-century legend of the Protecting Veil of the Mother of God spread over the city of Constantinople to protect it from enemies at the gates of the city. Had the Blessed Virgin Mary covered me too and saved me from these Protestant barbarians?

I bumped into one of them, stumbled, and was saved from falling by a bearded man wearing a scarf covered in Rangers pin badges.

'Watch it, Jimmy!'

That was all he said. I mumbled, 'Sorry, pal,' by way of an inadequate and fearful reply. He returned to his songs, his racist chanting, and I returned to my fear for my life.

* * *

At the time, I was combining teaching with work as an Irn-Bru salesman.

I was in love with Celtic, watched every match I could afford to attend, and had just witnessed my first Old Firm derby.

It was not a classic game, more perspiration than inspiration, but I could not take my eyes from the action. It was the autumn after Ten Men Won the League, and Billy McNeill's Bhoys were in pole position in the Premier Division after ten games, losing only once at

Morton. In the view from the top, Rangers were nowhere to be seen. The Ibrox side had already been beaten by Partick Thistle, Aberdeen and Kilmarnock.

With 15 minutes remaining, a goalless draw looked odds on in spite of almost constant Celtic pressure. Peter McCloy, the Rangers goalkeeper, was in inspired form. Another corner swung into the Rangers box, however, and this time Roddy MacDonald climbed highest and sent the ball unerringly into the furthest corner of the visitors' goal. Cue an eruption of mayhem and celebration in the West Stand where my seat had cost me £2.60, a large chunk of my commission from my Irn-Bru sales.

After the match, I was carried off my feet by the sway and the surge of the raucous crowd. The jocular, celebratory mood soon darkened, however, as bricks and bottles and stones came raining down from the skies. There was nothing whatsoever that could be done by way of protection as arms were pinioned to sides. People all about me wore bloodied faces. Somewhere to the Barrowfield side of Paradise, Celtic fans broke from the crush, seting off in pursuit of the Rangers fans. I guessed the Ibrox trespassers had run away. At any rate, the bombardment ceased. Faces were wiped clean with bloodstained handkerchiefs and the crowds turned for home, both curses and blessings on their lips. Police were directing Celtic fans in a one-way system away from the city centre. At the time, I lived in Clarkston, and I had no intention of walking even further away from my lodgings. Instead of left, I turned right into London Road.

Within two minutes I found myself surrounded by Rangers fans.

I was naive but not so naive as not to know about razor slashing in Glasgow.

'Fenian bastards!'

How could I have been so stupid, so stubborn?

* * *

I made a deal with the divine. OK, I reasoned, just get me home safe, God, and I'll not miss Mass ever again, and I'll not ever disobey police instructions outside Celtic Park ever again, amen, thank you, God.

By the time I reached Trongate, the Rangers fans mingled with more respectable, less fearsome folks, merged with last-minute shoppers and stragglers heading for home.

I could see Glasgow Cross, and the crowd was thinning. I was safe at last.

It had, however, been a humbling experience. How could I have been so stupid, so arrogant, so naive?

The walk from Paradise to the heart of Glasgow, though, had been an odyssey of sorts, providing an affirmation, a confirmation, and a determination of faith, in both God and in Celtic Football Club. I felt I had escaped a fate worse than death.

After the game, Celtic were one point clear of Morton, four points clear of Aberdeen, and five points clear of Partick Thistle, but these statistics seemed to matter less as I returned, chastened, to my rented room, relieved to have escaped a cutting or worse.

Lessons were learned. God should not be pushed too far, especially as I failed to keep my side of the bargain with regard to Mass attendance. Neither should I wear my favourite tee shirt, the one with the Keep Glasgow Tidy logo, the one with Rangers falling into a council waste bin, except in friendly territory, behind the lines.

That day, too, I understood my passion for Celtic would be no mere love affair but a lifetime commitment.

* * *

If truth be told, though, I fell for Celtic twice. Not that I ever fell out of love with Celtic. It's just that a teenager sometimes enjoys other preoccupations in addition to football.

It was 1967 and I was 15. It was probably the best age for being in love. Everything was so simple then. Light and dark, good and evil, were so much more sharply defined in adolescence.

Inter Milan and the club's infamous manager, Helenio Herrera, were the enemy on that evening of 25 May 1967. Like most of my generation, I was brought up by parents and grandparents in the 1950s who hated former wartime enemies such as the Germans, the Italians and the Japanese. A diet of World War Two adventure story comics reinforced the prejudices. So, Inter were the enemy just because they were Italian.

To add insult to injury, however, the entire world knew that the Inter footballers were both dirty and defensive. Herrera favoured a system of negative football called *catenaccio*, against which it was almost impossible to score. The Italians had been champions of Europe twice in the last three years, only narrowly losing to the fabulous and most famous team in the world, Real Madrid, at the semi-final stage in 1966. Against Celtic on a hot Lisbon night, Inter were considered unbeatable.

This tale really began, though, in 1960, with an eight-year-old boy crying, screaming actually, behind the locked door of his bedroom.

I was suffused with rage and indignation. I had been sent to bed in the middle of a televised football match.

Neither was it any old game of football. It was the European Cup Final, featuring the stars of Real Madrid, already winners of the first four incarnations of the senior European knockout competition, who were locked in mortal combat with the German title holders Eintracht Frankfurt. In the early hours of the evening, I settled to study the grainy, ghostly figures of Madrid and Frankfurt flit across the tiny TV screen. That I might be sent to bed at half-time, that I would be deprived of the denouement of the most exciting moment of my life, never crossed my mind until I heard my mother's voice explode in my ear.

'Time for bed, you!'

I knew Madrid were the best team in the world but I knew, too, that Eintracht Frankfurt had beaten Rangers 6-1 in Germany and 6-3 in Glasgow in the two-legged semi-final, and that had to make them special too.

Neither tears nor tantrums could prevail against my mother's righteous determination. 'I hate you!'

'Just you wait until your father gets home.'

'He is at home, he's in the kitchen.'

It was 2-1 to Real when I was sent to bed. I ran up the stairs, tears and snot dripping from my red face. I slammed my bedroom door as hard as I could, just in time to prevent my mother's hands from beating tattoos about my head.

In the morning, when I discovered the second half had yielded seven more goals and my favourites from Madrid had won by the scarcely believable score of 7-3, I was beyond consolation.

I read that 132,000 had crammed into Hampden Park and that the legendary Ferenc Puskás had scored four times and that his fellow conspirator in goals, Alfredo Di Stéfano, had plundered a hat-trick.

I had missed all of that. I vowed then I would never suffer such humiliation and loss ever again.

* * *

By 1967, I was a veteran of six and a half televised European Cup finals.

After the 1960 final, Real Madrid's potency was spent. More prosaic, more pragmatic footballing forces were unleashed across Europe: Benfica, AC Milan and Inter were teams to be endured rather than enjoyed. I was waiting for the spark of love, for the abandon of carefree, even careless football to return to the European Cup.

I was aware that Celtic had reached the final after ousting the Czechoslovak champions Dukla Prague in the semi-finals, and that they were the first British side to cut so deep into the competition. I had read, though, that Celtic, in the decisive away leg in eastern Europe, had been as defensive, as hard-boiled, as hard-nosed, as ruthless as any of the champions since 1961. It seemed a shame as it appeared a betrayal of the apparent principles of their manager, Jock Stein.

Not that they were given the slightest chance of victory against the apparently impregnable two-time champions, Inter Milan.

There was, though, a whiff of romance about the final: good v evil, light v dark, underdog v invincible. Stein, too, had promised never again to resort to the tactics employed in Prague.

Before kick-off, I harboured, then nurtured, irrational hopes for a Celtic win, just as I dreamed impossible dreams that Lynne Webber from the top deck of the school bus might fall prey to my spotty-faced, bespectacled charms.

I was far from an expert on girls but reckoned I knew most of what there was to know about football. I understood it was out of the question that Celtic might beat Inter but still I hoped. After all, Jock Stein, the Celtic manager, had said, 'We are going to attack as we have never attacked before.'

And they did. I can still see the swirl and the whirl of Celtic forwards pressing ever onwards towards the Inter goal, the cut and the thrust of their movements that sliced and diced the dizzy Italian defenders, the poetry of football played by the team in hoops.

I cried with joy and disbelief as Stevie Chalmers deflected Bobby Murdoch's shot past the Italian goalkeeper, Guiliano Sarti, for the winning goal.

I was in love.

* * *

Celtic, though, was not my first love – that was Cambridge City, at whose Milton Road stadium I saw my first live match, in the company of my wonderful grandfather, against Chelmsford City on a sweltering Bank Holiday in 1959.

Jock Stein, of course, said something similar:

'Unlike many Celts, I cannot claim that Celtic was my first love … but I can say that it will be my last love.'

For Stein to say that in 1955, when still a player for the Glasgow club, and at the end of a season of disappointments in both league and cup, was prescient to say the least.

* * *

From 1967 onwards, my ability to focus on Celtic wavered.

There were no more European Cup finals for the men from Paradise until 1970, so there were no more televised treats to uphold the love affair.

In spite of my volatile teenage emotions, I was devastated when Celtic lost to Feyenoord in the 1970 European Cup Final. For a while I was a jilted lover, let down by the object of my affections. It hurt. It had seemed inconceivable that Celtic might lose this match after triumphing over the English champions, Leeds United, in the semi-final. As improbable, in fact, as Celtic's victory in 1967.

I sulked for so long I missed clear signs of Lynne Webber's interest in returning my affections.

* * *

What I really needed was to fall in love with Celtic for a second time, and that happened at Firhill, Glasgow, on Saturday, 6 October 1979.

When I was offered the opportunity to study and to teach at Glasgow University, I knew this was my once-in-a-lifetime chance to fulfil my dream of watching the men in green and white hoops on a regular basis. It mattered not a jot that I was forced to supplement my income by moonlighting as a sales representative for Irn-Bru. It was worth every moment of trudging Glasgow streets and visiting the corner shops where the fizzy concoction might be sold in order to earn sufficient pennies to watch Celtic at the weekends.

The match against Partick Thistle at Firhill was a 0-0 draw but Celtic's class of '79 swarmed and swirled about the Jags' goalmouth just as the Lisbon Lions had done against Inter Milan 12 years previously. Alan Rough in the Thistle goal made save after unbelievable save, three outstanding ones and seven good ones according to the newspaper report I read the following day. I was in love again and this time there was no falling away, no backsliding, no more backstairs affairs. Watching Celtic on that faraway afternoon was like a confirmation of wedding vows.

I still have the programme for Thistle v Celtic on display on a shelf next to my desk. I keep thinking I'll frame it but I like picking it up and looking inside it too much. I have the ticket too, price £2.20 for a seat in the Centre Stand, together with an admonition to be in my seat 'not later than 2.45pm'.

In fact, I was there moments after Gate 21 opened, soaking up the atmosphere, drowning in the fevered anticipation, reading the programme.

Bertie Auld, a Lisbon Lion, was the Thistle manager. I watched him prowling the touchline, roaring demands for more hunting down of Celtic attackers from his players.

Auld was born just around the corner from Firhill and had been a ball boy there in his youth. In his programme notes he admitted he looked on games against Celtic 'with a certain amount of nostalgia'.

In the Celtic dugout were Billy McNeill and John Clark, two more Lions.

McNeill had been manager at Paradise since Stein's retirement at the end of the disastrous and dismal 1977/78 season in which Celtic won no trophy and in which the club's greatest asset, Kenny Dalglish, was hawked to Liverpool for a mere £440,000. It was a British transfer record at the time but anyone who had watched Dalglish in any of his 338 appearances for Celtic knew the Glasgow club had been robbed.

In his first season at the helm, McNeill led Celtic from nowhere to the title in the closing weeks of the season with a momentous finale at Paradise when Ten Men Won the League by beating Rangers 4-2 having played without the sent-off Johnny Doyle for the last 35 minutes of the match.

In the Thistle programme for the early October 1979 fixture, the only listed Lisbon Lion was Bobby Lennox, who would appear only as a second-half substitute for Vic Davidson.

An article towards the back of the meagre, stapled, 12-page publication was headed 'CAN ANYONE STOP THE GREEN MACHINE?' The odds offered by bookmakers in Glasgow on Celtic retaining their title were as thin as the programme, a miserly 4-9, although the odds on Thistle claiming the Premier League crown were a more generous 666-1. In fact, Alex Ferguson's Aberdeen pipped the East End club to the title by a solitary point and Thistle finished a creditable seventh.

Auld, by the way, performed minor miracles on behalf of the team he had supported as a boy, by keeping the part-time Jags in the Premier League for a memorable five seasons before leaving to manage Hibernian in 1980.

I retain a soft spot for Thistle to this day and always check for their results. The Jags are a club for quirks and kinks and lovely people, desperately few in number, who refuse to give their allegiance to either of the Old Firm clubs in a Glasgow that is either green or blue, Catholic or Protestant, and nothing in between.

I read in the programme that a recent Thistle AGM had proved 'a total disaster' as it was attended by one solitary shareholder.

I felt sorry for them and attended their matches at Firhill whenever Celtic were playing in places too far to follow on my limited Irn-Bru wages.

Still, soft spots and sorrow are not the same as passion. Over 40 years later, the fires of love for Celtic still burn but, for marriages to work and keep on working, there has to be more than the fatal attractions of love at first sight at the Estádio Nacional in Lisbon and second sight at Firhill in Maryhill, Glasgow.

There has to be more than the wham-bam-thank-you-ma'am.

* * *

That vital ingredient for me was the culture and the politics of Celtic.

The purpose and meaning of Celtic sustains me in my support of the club through the periods of loss and disillusion, the times of defeat.

That time, for example, of the failure to achieve the mythical tenth title in a row in 2021. The occasions when the beauty seemed to have been ravaged by time. The times when Celtic's leaders did not seem worthy, seemed to be smaller men than their predecessors.

That was when love needed to be based on solid foundations. And that bedrock, those footings, were primarily political.

* * *

Celtic's very foundation was a political act.

The football club's stated aim of putting food on the tables of the poorest children in the poverty-stricken streets and back alleys of Glasgow's East End was a direct challenge to the politics of stasis, the politics of class warfare in which the privileged classes beat up and exploited the helpless classes of wage labourers and of the unemployed and homeless. Glasgow politics in the latter half of the 19th century was the politics of big fish eating little fish until there were only just sufficient small fry to wait at the tables of the big fish in their big houses.

I was moved, too, by Celtic chairman Bob Kelly's defiance of the Scottish Football Association in 1952 over the issue of the Irish flag flying atop of Paradise. And by Kelly's defiance of the bullying might of the Soviet Union after their invasion of Czechoslovakia in 1968.

I wept with tears of pride as I read Kelly's accounts of Celtic's principled stands in both these instances.

The money men in Celtic's history, however, have always contended with the men of principle and have always threatened to divert Celtic from its political purposes, and from its charitable purposes which, by their very nature, are political purposes.

Today, in 2022, the money men in charge of Celtic, currently led by Dermot Desmond whose worth is valued at more than £2bn, may be permitting Celtic to drift from their core cause, the provision of sustenance to the poorest people of Glasgow.

I say this in spite of the wonderful, but hardly revolutionary, work of the Celtic Foundation. Desmond and his allies are only too well aware of the need for a cosmetic charitable foundation that massages the image of their football club in ways in which the prices of their shares are not diminished.

The tireless political work of the Celtic Green Brigade, a radical supporter group recognised by the football club, their reminders that Celtic is a campaigning football club, a club with socialist and republican ideals, and one in which an Irish identity is still central to the club, is needed more than ever in 2022. The Green Brigade is the conscience of the football club and of the financial institution that underpins the football club.

In his book, *Celtic*, Kelly correctly suggested there were two ways of providing sustenance to the poor denizens of the East End of Glasgow, and one was the pride in seeing their football club succeed on the field of play, while the other was the original charitable provision of food for the poor.

There was tension between these two aims of the Celtic Football Club in 1887 just as there continues to be today. Even though the charitable Celtic Foundation has been provided with an autonomous status, no longer dependent on handouts and hand-me-downs from the football club, the original questions are still asked: should the priorities be footballers' wages or food for the dinner tables of the poor?

It is a balancing act, a tightrope walk. Celtic must beware of the possibilities of love growing cold if the foundations of that love are not sustained. This club from Paradise does not live by football results alone.

* * *

The Immortals, then, is an extended love letter to the love of my sporting life, and I hope and trust the principles on which the football club were founded will remain firmly and staunchly in the centre of midfield of those with power at Celtic Park.

I need this love to last until death us do part.

THE FIRST HALF

The History Bhoys

For it's a grand old team to play for,
For it's a grand old team to see,
And if you know the history,
It's enough to make your heart go,
Oh,oh,oh,
It's enough to make your heart go,
Oh, oh nine-in-a-row, oh

THE 19TH-CENTURY IMMORTALS
1845–1888

1. WELSH AND MALEY

Dublin, in the autumn of 1867, was not a safe place for Irish nationalists, and Pat Welsh, a 19-year-old member of the Irish Republican Brotherhood, was hiding from search parties of the Royal Irish Constabulary, from the patrols of the North British Fusiliers and from friends who might be turncoat informers.

After the military failure of the Uprising in February and March in Killarney and Dublin, after the arrests and sentencing of Brotherhood leaders, after the battle at Tallaght in which 40 lives were lost in the firefight with the Constabulary, and after the arrests and executions of the Manchester Martyrs in November, Welsh felt there was no option left but to seek safe passage on a ship bound for Glasgow. It was why he now found himself hugging the dark and damp of the Pigeon House Fort in the Dublin docks, thinking, if all else failed, if he was uncovered by the authorities, the swirling waters of the River Liffey would welcome him home.

Turning a corner, he saw the dark outline of a soldier, rifle at the ready. Welsh ducked backwards but too late.

'Halt, he who goes there!'

There was no escape. Welsh, though, had assessed the soldier's accent. Just as surely as Pat himself was from County Leitrim, the soldier was from the west, County Clare, if he was not mistaken. Welsh raised his arms in surrender, moved away from his cover. 'You're from Ireland?' he said, refraining from asking the next question. 'Why, if you're from this land, are you in the pay of our overlords?'

The soldier nodded.

'Then, for God's sake help me.'

Welsh moved closer to the soldier who remained silent and with rifle cocked.

'As one countryman to another.'

'You're a Fenian?'

Welsh would not deny a heritage he was proud of but neither would he deny himself the opportunity of escape to a new life across the Irish Sea.

'All I want is to find a ship to take me to Scotland.'

Welsh could see the hesitation in the soldier's lowering, then raising of his rifle.

'My name's Welsh, Patrick.'

He didn't think his name was well known to the authorities. He had not been a leader or an organiser of the attack on the police barracks at Ardagh.

Welsh could see the sergeant's stripes on the soldier's uniform.

Two half smiles emerged on two faces and lit the shadows surrounding them.

'Maley,' the soldier said. 'Tom Maley, from Ennis, and I'll help you if I can.'

Welsh fell to his knees in gratitude.

'You'll give up the revolutionary politics, though?'

* * *

Years later, Welsh had become a prosperous master tailor with a business on Buchanan Street. He had kept his promise to Sgt Maley of the North British Fusiliers. He had become a respectable pillar of the Glasgow Irish middle class.

That is not to say, though, that he did not feel a sense of righteous satisfaction when, in 1878, he heard of the assassination of Lord Leitrim by his tenants. The landlord of his parents in Killargue had been a brutal bully, dividing his time between London society and military service in Leitrim. During the Holocaust of 1845 to 1850, he commanded the local militia and organised the removal of Irish food at gunpoint and its delivery to British ships in Belfast. After the Uprising, in which Welsh had played his honourable part, Leitrim spent much of his time in Donegal arranging mass evictions of tenants and then quelling protests and rebellions against these wholesale clearances of native Irish families.

He was sometimes cheered, buoyed by his past. He could still recite the words that accompanied the establishment of the Provisional Republican Government of Ireland in 1867:

'We have suffered centuries of outrage, enforced poverty, and bitter misery. Our rights and liberties have been trampled on by an alien aristocracy, who treating us as foes, usurped our lands, and drew away from our unfortunate country all material riches. The real owners of the soil were removed to make way for cattle, and driven across the ocean to seek the means of living, and the political rights denied them at home, while our men of thought and action were condemned to loss of life and liberty.

'But we never lost the memory and hope of a national existence ... unable longer to endure the curse of Monarchical Government, we aim at founding a Republic based on universal suffrage, which shall secure to all the intrinsic value of their labour. The soil of Ireland, at present in the possession of an oligarchy, belongs to us, the Irish people, and to us it must be restored.'

Welsh kept in touch with Maley and, in 1869, the soldier, too, decided a new life in Glasgow would be just the ticket, and asked his friend for assistance in return.

Remembering he owed Maley his life, Welsh provided hospitality and introductions to Glasgow Catholic society, to his friends and to his family.

In December 1877, Welsh, a member of the committee tasked with the establishment of Celtic FC, led a delegation from the club to the house of his former soldier friend with the intention of acquiring the signature of his son, Tom Maley, who was already an established footballer, having played for Partick Thistle, Third Lanark, Hibernian and Clydesdale

Harriers. As the Celtic party, including John Glass and Brother Walfrid, were leaving, having been disappointed to find Maley was not at home but courting his future wife, they met Tom's younger brother, Willie. Touched perhaps by divine intervention, the Marist priest and driving force behind Celtic's formation turned to the young man. 'Why don't you come along and sign for us too?'

Glass shrugged his shoulders, as if to say, 'Why not? What's one more among friends?'

Brother Walfrid smiled, reasoning that if the younger sibling signed then the older one would follow suit.

As those who know their history will appreciate, a series of fortuitous synchronicities had combined to bring together some early immortals in the story of Celtic.

* * *

2. THE EARLY IMMORTALS AND IRELAND

Welsh, Tom and Willie Maley, Brother Walfrid, John Glass; all were early immortals. If one man, however, could be considered the architect of the modern Celtic, with its perfections and imperfections, it is Glass.

Like almost all the Founding Fathers – the exception being David Meikleham, a Glasgow shoemaker and a long-standing member of Queen's Park FC – Glass was both Irish and Catholic.

According to Willie Maley, Celtic's first manager, 'John Glass is the man to whom the club owes its existence.'

Glass was born in 1851 in the slums of Broomielaw on the northern bank of the Clyde. His parents had recently fled from Donegal and from the terrors of the Irish Holocaust, caused by the forced removal, at gunpoint, of food from Irish fields by English armed forces. In Donegal, there had been mass burials, and it had been a place where dogs grew fat on corpses. On Aranmore Island, where all its inhabitants starved to death, animals who fed on human carrion were the lone survivors. In Ireland from 1845 to 1850 there were never fewer than 60,000 British agents of enforcement actively engaged in the export of Irish crops.

In 1848, when Glass's parents escaped from these horrors on a steamship bound for the quays at Broomielaw, there were over 73,000 troops and coastguards and police stationed in Ireland, and all were busy about their business of genocide. Sixty-seven regiments of the British army were involved in this crime against humanity.

Glass, like his parents, was a survivor. He worked as a glazier and then as manager of his brother's wood merchant and building business in Gallowgate.

Within the prosperous middle-class section of the Irish Catholic community in Glasgow, Glass met Dr John Conway and Brother Walfrid to discuss the formation of a football club to raise funds for the poor in Glasgow's Irish East End.

Later, Glass became a figure of controversy, leading the way to Celtic's cessation of payments to Walfrid's charity, the Poor Children's Dinner Table, calling his opponents 'soup kitchen cranks' and 'dinner table sore heads'.

Still, though, it is probable that without Glass's hard-headed and brutal commercialisation of the football club, there would be no Celtic today.

Certainly, there would be no successful club, at least not in worldly terms.

* * *

Celtic's original committee, as listed in Willie Maley's *The Story of the Celtic 1888–1938*, comprise the bulk of the Founding Fathers of the football club.

They were: Dr John Conway (honorary president), John Glass (president), James Quillan (vice-president), Hugh Darroch (treasurer), John O'Hara (secretary), Willie Maley (match secretary).

The committee was made up of Joseph Michael Nelis, Michael Cairns, William McKillop, Daniel Molloy, Joseph McGroary, Pat Welsh, Joseph Shaughnessy, John H. McLaughlin, Tom Maley, John McDonald and David Meikleham.

These men, these early Celtic men, were Irish and Catholic – even Meikleham was a devout Roman in spite of his association with the Protestant Queen's Park club – and they ensured that the beating heart of the club would always be found in its Irish ancestry and in Irish politics too.

These men, too, were the cream of the Glasgow Irish diaspora that was the consequence of the Holocaust. They were self-made men, wealthy and assured, middle-class and with varying degrees of social conscience, but all possessed the determination that their project should succeed, and all imprinted their new football club with an indelible identity that was emphasised by the choice of its first patrons, Archbishop Charles Eyre and Michael Davitt.

The first Catholic Archbishop of Glasgow since the Reformation, Charles Eyre was a descendant of the Eyres of Derbyshire whose lands were confiscated in the Henrician purge of recusant Romans in the 16th century.

Davitt was an Irish republican campaigner and activist whose family had been dispossessed by the imperial authorities in 1850 and who arrived in England at four years of age. In 1870 he was convicted of treason and arms trafficking and served seven years in prison. Davitt had planned to attack Chester Castle, steal its store of arms and ship these to Irish freedom fighters via Holyhead but was thwarted by the infiltration of his organisation by police spies.

It says something about the new football club that a man convicted of treason in the courts of the British empire should be invited to become a patron of Celtic. It shouts out loud that, at its inception, in spite of Brother Walfrid's insistence that this was a Scottish and Celtic club, this Celtic Football and Athletic Club was a political institution, a republican and nationalist organisation, a cultural edifice embedded within Glasgow Catholic society, as well as a sporting and charitable institution.

This needs saying and bears repetition. All immortals stand on the shoulders of earlier immortals. If we fail to read our history we risk losing the vision of these men, the panoramic perspective gained from the heights of their achievements.

Without history we are mere mortals. So, before we study the moderns we need to understand the ancients. The true origins of Celtic are to be discovered in the first half of the 19th century.

* * *

3. HOLOCAUST AND SECTARIANISM

No respectful history of Celtic Football Club should begin without contemplation of the horrors of the Irish Holocaust of 1845 to 1850 during which uncounted multitudes – possibly as many as six million men, women, and children – died of starvation and disease in an organised and calculated attempt at genocide perpetrated by English imperialists.

If these brutal facts seem difficult or impossible to believe, it is because there has been a systematic covering up of both bodies, in unmarked graves, and truths. John Pilger, the campaigning Australian journalist, said in 1997, 'The Anglo-American publishing establishment will still kill any book that tells the truth about the starvation of Ireland.' Even in the 21st century, conventional histories of 19th-century Ireland still talk of the Potato Famine or the Great Hunger, as if these deaths were acts of God, beyond the power of man to prevent. Some histories descend further into the depths of deceit by apportioning blame on the stupidity of the Irish, their apparent reliance upon one staple crop of potatoes, or in suggesting it was Irish landlordism that starved Irish peasants. These are both large and powerful lies. The truth is that food in all its rich Irish variety was removed at gunpoint at the behest of absentee English landlords and with the approval and knowledge of London. England's imperial army supervised and enforced this theft and Irish tenant farmers and the surrounding populations were left to starve.

Neither was this genocide an aberration on the part of Ireland's lords and masters. The military conquest of Ireland under the English queen, Elizabeth I, was ruthless and barbaric and, during this war, famine and deliberate starvation became an accepted part of military strategy. In 1574, Edward Berkeley, an English official in occupied Belfast, admitted that, in order to complete the subjugation, the population 'muste be famished'. He concluded his report by justifying this policy of extermination on religious grounds, 'How godly a dede it is to overthrowe so wicked a race … For my parte I think ther canot be a greter Sacrfyce to god.'

Between 1649 and 1654, too, Oliver Cromwell, on behalf of the new English republic, committed further genocidal atrocities, during which around half of the Irish Catholic population was eliminated and many more were sent as slaves to the English colonies in the Americas. During four centuries, according to the dedicated historical researcher Chris Fogarty, 'England turned Ireland into a slaughterhouse of starvelings.' In his book *The Perfect Holocaust*, Fogarty provides irrefutable and detailed documentary evidence to prove the thesis that Ireland was the victim of genocide in the middle years of the 19th century.

Six million murdered Irish sits uncomfortably and unconscionably alongside the six million Jews exterminated in Nazi-occupied Europe between the building of the Dachau concentration camp in March 1933 and the end of World War Two in 1945. Only the methods of execution differed.

* * *

What, though, has this to do with Celtic Football Club?

The simple truth is that without the Irish Holocaust there would have been no football club formed at the inaugural meeting of interested parties in St Mary's Church Hall in East Rose Street, Calton, on 6 November 1887.

In addition to the six million dead, there were at least one million further Irish survivors who escaped from their homeland during the six years of the Holocaust. Most risked the arduous odyssey to North America via the English port of Liverpool. On these voyages there was devastating loss of life, as already hungry and sick Irish men, women and children took passage on notorious Canadian coffin ships on which around one-third of passengers died. One and a half million Irish sought refuge across the Atlantic and one million arrived in Boston, New York and other seaboard cities, to find they had exchanged one form of poverty and destitution for another.

Some 35,000 Irish, however, stayed in Liverpool, making up over 20 per cent of the city's population. Many, too, escaped the ravages of the Holocaust by finding work and accommodation, as well as degrading poverty and prejudice, in the west of Scotland.

During 1848, the average weekly influx of Irish immigrants into Glasgow was over 1,000 people. Between 1841 and 1851 the Irish population in Scotland increased by 90 per cent and one-third of that increase is accounted for by the Irish arrivals in the East End of Glasgow. Irish workers flooded the labour market, eager to take on the lowest-paid work involving the heaviest of manual labour, and happy to accept the most miserable of wages.

These new immigrants faced language problems, as they spoke Gaelic, and prejudice and violence for their willingness to accept payment for their work that undercut the traditional labour markets in the mines, the docks and general labouring. Everywhere the Irish were viewed as drunken, idle and diseased. Typhus was known in Glasgow as the 'Irish Fever' in spite of the causes of this dreaded affliction being unsanitary housing rather than inherent ethnicity.

Naturally, too, there was religious bigotry as well as racial prejudice.

Since John Knox, the firebrand Reformation propagandist, returned to Scotland from exile in Geneva in May 1559 and preached against Catholic idolatry at Perth, inducing Protestant mobs to rampage through Scottish churches destroying all religious images in their paths, Scotland has defined itself as a fundamentally Protestant nation. In 1560, the Scottish parliament renounced the authority of the pope and declared the Catholic Mass illegal. It was a coup of the first order orchestrated by Knox and his military guardians, the Lords of the Congregation, whose foot soldiers' passion for iconoclasm cleansed the altars of Scotland of all things Catholic. The revolution had been remarkable in that it was estimated at the time that a mere ten per cent of the population of the nation was Protestant.

Religious intolerance has continued down the years, through the centuries, and Scotland is still steeped in this foul miasma of sectarianism.

As late as 1923, the Church of Scotland published a pamphlet, *The Menace of the Irish Race to our Scottish Nationality.*

There had been Protestant immigration into Glasgow too, especially in the 1870s and 1880s and especially from the most Orange counties in Armagh. Naturally, the Church of Scotland viewed Reformed Irishmen very differently from the Catholic Irish escaped from the Holocaust.

In the pamphlet, it was claimed, 'No complaint can be made about the presence of the Orange people in Scotland. They are the same race as ourselves and of the same Faith.'

Scots Protestants, of course, are not the sole bearers of bigotry. The sectarian divide in Glasgow is not one-sided. When bigotry is combined with power, however, that is when discrimination is practised and when suffering is imposed upon an ethnic and a religious minority.

Inequalities, too, are the inevitable consequence of a concentration of power. Glasgow in the second half of the 19th century was a city divided and ruled by its prosperous Protestant elite, and its East End, the home of Catholic immigrants, was an overcrowded hellhole of insanitary dwellings and smog-suffused alleyways in which human excrement shared deep puddles alongside acid rain from the skies filled with the pollution from the city's heavy industries.

Ruling classes, in all times and in all places, maintain their grasp on power and privilege not merely by coercion and economic dependency but also by the provision of scapegoats and diversions.

In Glasgow, the Irish immigrants were to blame. They were diseased and dangerous and to be kept in their place. However poor the Protestant workers in the shipyards and mines and factories, at least they were not Irish scum, at least they were not Catholics. The poor white trash of the southern slave states of the USA might have been hungry but at least they were not black. They were the attitudes.

The Roman poet, Juvenal, said of the plebeians in his city, 'Give them bread and circuses and they will never revolt.' In Glasgow, the 19th century and early 20th century city fathers understood only too well that poor Protestant workers had to be appeased. They were given Rangers.

The original football club founded in March 1872 by four young white-collar men was not a Protestant institution. Heaven forbid, but Rangers, in their early incarnation, actually signed several Catholics prior to World War One, including Pat Lafferty (1886), Tom Dunbar (1891–1892), J. Tutty (1899–1900), Archie Kyle (1904–1908), Willie Kivlichan (1906–1907), Colin Mainds (1906–1907), Tom Murray (1907–1908), and William Brown (1912).

Everything changed, however, with the arrival in Govan in 1912 of the Northern Irish shipbuilders, Harland and Wolff. In Belfast, the company operated a strictly exclusionary employment policy: no Catholics. In his book, *The Spirit of Ibrox*, Rangers historian Robert McElroy suggests that a loan by the shipbuilders of £90,000 to their neighbours, Rangers, came with strings attached. The quid pro quo was a promise by the football club to mimic the Protestant-only employment strategy of Harland and Wolff.

Worse, too, was the importation of skilled workers from the Harland and Wolff yards in Belfast. These immigrants were hardline Ulster unionists, loyalists to a man, and dedicated to the supremacy of their Protestant faith, and they became the core of Rangers supporters.

In that same year, too, with the death of the respected and tolerant Rangers chairman James Henderson, and the accession to power at Ibrox of Sir John Ure Primrose, an uncompromising Protestant identity was forged by the Govan club.

The new chairman of Rangers was a notorious opponent of Irish Home Rule and the man responsible for the football club's enduring alliance with freemasonry.

In effect, Rangers had become the home of Conservative and Unionist politics, loyalty to the English empire and its monarchs, and a repository of hatred of all things Catholic and Irish.

Rangers had metamorphosed into the club of the indigenous Scots, a bulwark against the invader, a defender of tradition against the enemies within who would betray the national identity and who would permit the dilution and pollution of the purity of the blood with alien, and especially Irish, immigration. One football club was chosen for this sacred task.

The bastions of the press, too, were on board with this mission. In September 1896, the *Scottish Sport* began describing Rangers as 'Scotia's darling club' and lamented, after recent victories of Celtic and Hibernian over Hearts and Rangers, 'The two Irish teams are at the top of the table. Is this not a reflection on Scotland?'

Cartoons in the *Scottish Referee*, according to historian Bill Murray, routinely depicted Celtic players as possessing 'the dumb look of a creature emerging from a peat bog, while the Rangers equivalent had the noble stature and intelligent eyes of the Aryan'.

As early as 1894, the *Glasgow Observer* reported the abuse of Celtic players by their Rangers peers throughout a match at Celtic Park. 'Fenians', 'papists' and 'Irish' were among the insults but their accompanying epithets were, of course, unprintable in a 19th-century family newspaper.

It was a sad decline from the early, friendly relations between the two clubs in the years immediately after Celtic's formation in 1887. Celtic's first match in May 1888 was against Rangers and the friendly was followed by entertainment in St Mary's Hall in Calton. Both Tom and Willie Maley enjoyed close friendships with Rangers players and these bonds were echoed at board level of both clubs. As late as 1893, for matches in Edinburgh, the two clubs travelled by train together.

By the second half of the 1890s, working-class Protestant Scots were being provided with not only an enemy against which to rant and rail, but also an identity that diverted them from any potential common cause with their fellow poor in Glasgow.

If the Protestant majority living south of the Clyde in Govan were poor and exploited, at least they weren't 'dirty Fenian bastards', 'navvies', or 'tattie-howkers'.

* * *

The purity of the Rangers project was an ongoing priority for decades, taking precedence over football matters at Ibrox from the time of Ure Primrose through to the chairmanship of David Holmes, until the arrival of the iconoclastic David Murray in June 1989.

One curious incident concerns Alex Ferguson, centre-forward and scorer of 66 goals in 98 matches for Rangers from 1967 to 1969. Strangely, the ebullient and bullying striker never played for the club again after a Scottish Cup Final defeat to Celtic in 1969 in which Ferguson was detailed to mark Billy McNeill at corners and in which the Lisbon Lion scored a dramatic opening goal, while his intended shadow had gone absent without leave. Rangers never recovered from this hammer blow and lost 4-0 to Jock Stein's rampant Celtic team.

There may, however, have been a darker reason for Ferguson's demotion to the club's junior side and eventual sale to Falkirk.

At some point, someone somewhere within the bowels of Ibrox discovered Ferguson had married a Catholic. Ferguson denies that his banishment had anything to do with his union with Cathy Holding, but whispers persist to this day.

* * *

This abysmal situation at Rangers continued until July 1989 when the signing of the Catholic former Celt, Mo Johnston, brought an end to exclusionary policies at Ibrox.

Sectarianism, however, was not ended by a stroke of the prolific striker's pen on the contract that made him a millionaire.

On the day of Johnston's transfer, a wreath was laid by Rangers supporters outside the front door of Ibrox; '116 years of tradition ended' was the stark message. The general secretary of the Grand Orange Lodge of Scotland warned, 'There will be an angry reaction.'

As always, it was the economics of the situation that demanded change. Just as in 1912, when Harland and Wolff called the shots, now it was Rangers' desire to participate in a money-making European football league whose constitution would not permit continued bigotry in one of its member clubs.

A deathbed conversion this was not, although the increased debt acquired by Rangers through processing this deal with Johnston was a nail in the coffin of a club that would collapse into bankruptcy in 2012.

* * *

In spite of the cosmopolitan nature of Rangers squads since the David Murray era, the shameful hangover of sectarianism still haunts the club into the 21st century.

The flotsam and jetsam of the past still wash up on Ibrox shores. Much of the club's support is still tribal, still racist, still loyal to the English crown, the Protestant ascendancy and its power brokers in the English Conservative Party that has never done one thing for its white, working-class adherents in Glasgow.

The suffering and martyrdom of Neil Lennon, Catholic and Celtic footballer between 2000 and 2007, and manager from 2010 to 2014 and again from 2019 to 2021, provides all the incriminating evidence necessary for a conviction of the persisting Rangers culture of paranoia and sectarian hatred.

In March 2002, Lennon was forced into retirement from international football for Northern Ireland as a result of death threats from Ulster loyalists prior to a match against Cyprus played at Windsor Park, Belfast. The following year, he was attacked by two Protestant students on the Great Western Road, Glasgow, while in 2004 he was the victim of a road rage incident in the middle of the M8.

In September 2008 Lennon was bottled and beaten by thugs outside Jinty McGinty's pub in Ashton Lane, near to his home in the West End. He was attacked from behind and knocked unconscious before being kicked and punched as he lay on the city street.

The last words Lennon said he heard as he fell were, 'Neil Lennon, you Fenian bastard.'

In January 2011, after threats on his life, Lennon was told by police that it was necessary to place his family and his home in the West End of Glasgow under round-the-clock protection. Lennon's children were escorted to school and their classrooms were guarded by police. Websites sprang up like weeds suggesting that followers should 'Kill Neil Lennon'. In March of the same year, an explosive device intended to do just that was addressed to the Celtic manager at Lennoxtown, the club's training headquarters. It was intercepted by suspicious Royal Mail staff but police admitted that the nail bomb had been put together with the goal of killing or maiming its target.

Similar devices were also posted to Paul McBride, one of Scotland's most prominent and successful QCs, and to Trish Godman, a former

Labour MSP for West Renfrewshire. Neither the law nor politics were professions in which Catholics were accepted with equanimity by the traditional Protestant establishment of Kirk and Tory Party, from whose prejudice the amateur bombers took their lead. A further device was delivered to the Gallowgate offices of Cairde na hEireann, translated as Friends of Ireland. A television news report on the BBC showed one of the convicted pair of bombers wearing a Rangers replica shirt and the other an England football top. Both men, and the minority of the Ibrox club's supporters who still chant 'fuck the IRA', 'kill the Pope', and 'no surrender', are dinosaurs raging against the inevitability of change in Scotland and against their own extinction.

In May 2011, Lennon was attacked in front of 16,000 spectators at Tynecastle, home of Heart of Midlothian, and in front of millions watching on television.

In his times with Celtic, the number of assaults and attempted assaults on Lennon ran into double figures.

It should be emphasised, however, that this ongoing persecution of Neil Lennon no longer had anything to do with the policies or the recent management of Rangers, whose reformation on matters sectarian since the signing of Mo Johnston has been as welcome as it was overdue.

* * *

4. CHARITY MEN AND MONEY MEN

In common with Rangers in 1872, Celtic, 15 years later in November 1887, was founded on specifically non-sectarian lines.

The original purpose of Celtic was charitable. Brother Walfrid, originally Andrew Kerins, a man from County Sligo in the west of Ireland, was the son of a peasant farmer who arrived in Glasgow in 1855 seeking work on the railways. He became a leading light of vision and determination within the Marist Order, and headmaster of the Sacred Heart School in Bridgeton in the East End of Glasgow. He was the driving force behind the formation of a Celtic football club 'for the maintenance of dinner tables for the children and the unemployed'.

Kerins was appalled at the malnourishment of children, at the squalor and disease of the East End slums, made even worse by the loss of businesses and opportunities for employment consequent upon the collapse of the City of Glasgow Bank in 1878 with a liability in excess of £6m. In conjunction with Dr John Conway and the builder, John Glass, Brother Walfrid planned to utilise a new football club to provide sufficient funds to provide 'penny meals' through the auspices of the Glasgow St Vincent de Paul Society.

Brother Walfrid, though, was no mere saintly idealist. His charitable mission was based on hard-headed realism. First, he and his co-worker and fellow headteacher, Brother Dorothea, had watched with interest the rapid growth in popularity of football in Scotland and had discerned its potential for the development and nurturing of a sense of community and of self-esteem in Irish immigrant communities. Exclusively Catholic football clubs had been established in Edinburgh where the early success of Hibernian in winning the Scottish Cup in 1887 was a source of fundamental pride among the Irish community of Little Ireland in the Cowgate, the dark underbelly of the capital city.

Hibernian, incidentally, after their formation in 1875 through the auspices of the Catholic Young Men's Society and Canon Edward Joseph Hannan, who became the club's first manager, suffered from immediate and intense pressure and prejudice. The Scottish Football Association declared no clubs under their jurisdiction should arrange matches against the Catholics from Edinburgh. 'We are catering for Scotsmen not Irishmen' came the portentous pronouncement. Ironically, it was later bitter rivals Heart of Midlothian who defied authority and provided the first opposition for the Hibernian club on Christmas Day 1875.

Irish and Catholic clubs were founded, too, in Dundee, with Dundee Harp in 1879 and Dundee Hibernian in 1909, and in Glasgow, with St Peter's of Partick among a plethora of other sporting organisations, now defunct, that sprang up before Celtic were founded in 1887. St Peter's had actually played Hibs in Bridgeton in September 1886. Brother Walfrid may well have been a spectator.

The two Marist brothers, Walfrid and Dorothea, had the wit and wisdom to envisage the yoking together of this new sport with the opportunities it offered for fundraising for their charity. It was entrepreneurial genius at its finest, incorporating compassion at its heart. The siblings, too, were not unaware of the opportunities offered by football for saving souls. Brother Walfrid, in particular, had been concerned for some time that Protestant soup kitchens were making converts from among his own parishioners.

Something had to be done and, in conjunction with the great and the good – and the wealthy – of Glasgow's Irish community, a meeting was arranged for 6 November 1887 in St Mary's Church Hall.

And the rest, as Celtic people say, is history.

* * *

The formation of Celtic was a political act, an assertion of political will. Feeding starving, malnourished and diseased children with penny meals that also preserved the dignity of hard-pressed parents through the voluntary contribution of one penny was a political declaration of intent, of determination and of self-determination.

It was a direct challenge to a Glasgow society – and to their imperialist masters in London – that permitted and enshrined such poverty within their political institutions and within their economic structures and discriminatory practices.

So, too, was the declaration of 1895 that there would be no tolerance of sectarianism within Paradise.

A proposal was put before the club's committee that there should be a maximum of three Protestant players in any Celtic team. It was decided instead that there should be no restrictions whatsoever. The promulgation was echoed in an editorial from the Catholic newspaper, the *Glasgow Observer*:

'To raise the question of religion is singularly out of place when dealing with sporting matters, and I trust that the last has been heard of it in Celtic circles.'

This tradition, at least, has remained a steadfast core of Celtic's history, although it has proved impossible to entirely eradicate prejudice either from within the higher echelons of the football club or from within the core of the club's support. It took until 1965, for example, for Celtic to appoint its first Protestant manager, and that after great soul-searching by the chairman, Bob Kelly. Among past players, too, European Cup winner and Protestant Tommy Gemmell complained of sectarian abuse from some of his colleagues in his early years at the club. One defeat in the 1950s was followed by dressing room comments about there being 'too many fucking Protestants in this club'. Even in 2021, many supporters mulling over candidates to replace Neil Lennon as Celtic manager were checking credentials in terms of nationality and religious affiliation.

* * *

In 1892, however, when Brother Walfrid was transferred by his order from the Sacred Heart School in Bridgeton to St Anne's School in Spitalfields in the Whitechapel area of east London, some would say that Celtic lost its soul and its conscience.

A living rebuke to soul-sellers and to the harsh realism of the money men within the brotherhood of Celtic's Founding Fathers was gone and lost forever.

First, the generosity of spirit and the helping hands lent by Hibernian to the fledgling Glasgow club were repaid by a ruthless pillaging of their best players by Celtic under the leadership of John Glass and through the illegal means of undercover payments. In August 1888, without the knowledge of either Brother Walfrid or of the club committee, Glass signed eight of Hibs' best players and the Edinburgh club went out of business before the end of that season, although they were quickly reformed, armed perhaps with a less trusting approach to the business of football.

Second, even before the departure of Brother Walfrid, debates were already raging, festering even, within and without the club concerning its nature and purpose. At the annual meeting of members in 1891, two rival parties chose their ground, pitched their camps, set out their battle lines. The *casus belli* was the payment of fees to the club secretary, Willie Maley, but in reality the war was between those who viewed Celtic as a charitable and amateur institution and those who had recently gained the upper hand within the nascent power structures of the club who advocated all-out professionalism.

The amateurs were led by Dr John Conway, the club's first chairman and honorary president, and the man who kicked the first ball at Celtic Park on 8 May 1888 prior to a friendly match between Hibernian and Cowlairs. The *Glasgow Observer* reported, 'Prompt to the advertised time, Dr Conway and Mr Shaughnessy emerged from the pavilion and entered the field, heading the procession of players. The Doctor placed the ball amid the cheers of the spectators, who numbered fully 5,000.'

Conway had worked equally tirelessly on behalf of the poor and diseased in the East End of Glasgow and on behalf of Brother Walfrid's dream of establishing a football club to provide funds for the charity, the Poor Children's Dinner Table. After the match, Conway proposed a toast to 'the Hibernians', and John McFadden, Hibs' secretary, responded by suggesting, 'It would be a sorry day indeed for the Irish in Scotland when residents of one city should act in an unfriendly way towards those of another.' Just three months later Celtic and Hibernian were at war over the poaching of players by John Glass of Celtic and Conway was outraged by this act of piracy and betrayal and strengthened his desire to regain control of the behaviour of the football club he had helped to found.

Neither should it be forgotten that it had been at McFadden's suggestion and insistence in 1887 that Celtic had been formed in the first place.

At the meeting in 1891, Conway's motion in opposition to professionalism was lost by 102 votes to 74, and he was replaced as president by Glass.

When Conway died in 1894 at the age of 35, his passing received no official acknowledgement by the club he had worked so diligently to found and to keep to its original principles.

Three years later in 1897, Celtic became a private limited liability company and, according to company law, such an institution had a duty to maximise profits for its shareholders. A five per cent annual dividend to shareholders had to be paid before any donations to charity could be considered. The Brother Walfrid project was at an end.

Some 5,000 £1 shares were issued by the new company and Glass, described in the accompanying documentation as a 'builder's manager', received 100 shares and an honorarium of £100.

Approve or not of Glass's actions, he was the builder of the modern Celtic Football Club.

* * *

From 1887 to 2022, the debate about the soul of Celtic, its primary purpose, growled and grumbled on, although the power of shareholders enshrined in law and in the family blocks of shareholdings that have controlled the club through most of its history generally ensured the primacy of the service of Mammon over the gentler workings of compassion and charity.

In 1894, the *Glasgow Observer* complained that Celtic had become, 'A mere business, in the hands of publicans and others. Catholic charities get nothing out of the thousands of pounds passing through the treasurer's hands.' The newspaper then posed the question, 'Can we not get a club that will carry out the original idea of Brother Walfrid?' That question was answered finally in 1897.

Into the 20th century, though, the criticism of Celtic's parsimony was still strong enough for Bob Kelly, the controller of his family shares and of those of Mary Colgan of Toomebridge in County Antrim in Northern Ireland, to issue a defence of Celtic morals at the annual general meeting of shareholders in 1960, 'We must come to the conclusion that the club in its present form had over the years done more in the field of charity than it could have done had it remained in its original state.'

Resentment at the takeover of Celtic by wealthy elites and the hijacking of its principles by the power of capital lingered on, however.

The centenary history of St Mary's, published in 1963, suggested that those in charge of Brother Walfrid's former school still burned with indignation and anger at the events of 1897:

'The Penny Dinner Tables lost the financial aid of the Celtic Football Club ... The last contribution to the Poor Children's Dinner Table was made at the AGM of season 1891/92. The committee, after a bitter struggle against the honest element among the team's supporters, got their way at last and turned the club into a business.'

Twentieth-century successes on the field of play were not always matched by charitable endeavour. In 1995, however, the Celtic Charity Fund was established by the football club as a means of 'revitalising Celtic's charitable traditions'. In 2006, the Celtic Foundation began its work of coordination of the club's social, educational, and community work under one umbrella. In 2013, the Charity Fund merged with the Celtic Foundation and much first-class work has been undertaken since then to improve health, promote equality, encourage learning, and tackle poverty in Glasgow and beyond. Many millions of pounds have been raised and distributed to charities dedicated to alleviating the sufferings of those afflicted by the continuing scourges of poverty and blighted opportunity. It is wonderful ongoing work. The sole criticism that might be levelled at all this scurry of 21st-century charitable endeavour is that monies are raised in conjunction with the payment of astronomical salaries to Celtic footballers. The twin obscenities of degrading affluence and degrading poverty sit side by side in the East End of Glasgow.

There is, too, the remaining issue of the ownership of Celtic Football Club. Throughout most of the 20th century, the club has been under the control of family fiefdoms. Lineages of descent and hand-me-down shareholdings have passed from fathers to sons and to grandsons. Where strict family connections were not observed, control of the club was by proteges and by proxies. John O'Hara's 390 shares passed to John Glass, already the owner of over 300 shares, in 1904. Thomas White, a lawyer, was Glass's apprentice and inherited his shares in 1906 at the tender age of 22. Joseph Shaughnessy, another of the club's founders, also died in 1906 and his 650 shares passed to John, his son. In 1931, James Kelly's shares were split between his descendants but his fourth of six sons, Robert, was the anointed one with a place on the Celtic board. James Grant's 800 shares in 1914 were eventually transferred, via his executor, Thomas Colgan, to Thomas Devlin, a trawler owner from Leith. On Colgan's death in 1946, shares passed to his granddaughter, Mary. Tom White died in 1947 and his son, Desmond, joined the board. When Colonel Shaughnessy died in 1953, there remained a triumvirate of power at the heart of the Celtic boardroom: chairman Kelly, Desmond White and Tom Devlin. These three remained in absolute control until the arrival of an outsider in James Farrell, who took up the former Shaughnessy shares in 1964. It was all very incestuous to say the least.

It continued, however, through the Stein years of immortal success and beyond. In 1973, James Grant inherited the shares of his aunt Felicia, who herself had come into her brother Neil's 1,705 fully paid and 1,752 half-paid shares. Neil had in turn acquired his grandfather James's shares. The 19th-century James had been one of the derided Celtic 'publicans' and was an original shareholder. The grandson's shares passed to his son, Tom.

In 1982, Desmond White's son, Christopher, joined the board. Kevin Kelly replaced his uncle Bob on the death of the chairman in 1971. Desmond White died in 1985 and was succeeded as chairman by Tom Devlin.

Eventually, inbreeding of shareholdings causes financial problems and in 1994 Celtic was brought to the edge of bankruptcy, saved only by the infusion of new blood in the shape of the Canadian businessman, Fergus McCann.

* * *

The majority shareholder in 2022 was Dermot Desmond, a businessman and financier, the ninth-richest man in Ireland. He was brought to the club as an investor by Fergus McCann. When McCann left Celtic in 1999, leaving Desmond as the principal shareholder, he told the world that the club was 'in good hands'.

Since then, it is indisputable that Celtic has become a well-run, financially stable institution. This, in turn, has facilitated the nine-in-a-row years of almost unprecedented success.

There is, though, another way, another possibility of another way, of running Celtic.

While footballing success masks the galling reality that Celtic is owned by an absentee landlord with a personal fortune of over £2bn and run from 2003 to 2021 by a multi-millionaire corporate accountant in Peter Lawwell, the failure of the mission to win ten-in-a-row raised further questions concerning Celtic's governance.

The Celtic Green Brigade, the 'ultras' group of fans founded in 2006, outlined plans in 2021 for a crusade to implement eventual fan ownership of the football club. 'Celtic Shared' is a call to arms to return to the original principles of the Founding Fathers, to overturn the decisions of the money men of 1897, the 'greed is good' men who have held sway at Paradise for a century and a quarter and counting. It may be a long road but the journey of a thousand miles begins with the first step.

* * *

It's crucial for Celtic fans to remember and to debate the past and to discover and discuss the future.

This book, however, is unashamedly about the past. We can celebrate the past triumphs of the immortals of the first and second nine-in-a-row successes. Then we can turn our hearts and our hands towards imagining and building a new and brilliant future for our beloved club but one that honours the principles on which it was originally purposed.

The First Nine-in-a-Row: 1965–1974

Foundations

1. JIMMY GRIBBEN

Jimmy Gribben loved nothing better than to be set a task by the chairman, Bob Kelly, or by the manager, Jimmy McGrory.

On this occasion, the Celtic reserve team trainer, factotum and dogsbody, scout, and general fount of football wisdom, was even more animated than usual. As he approached Kelly, he wondered whether he should tug at the man's jacket to gain his attention or tug his forelock to show his respect.

It was almost comical; the little man, the peasant, approaching the tall patrician, the landlord of all he surveyed at Celtic Park. In the end, Kelly turned from his observations of first-team training at Barrowfield, gave Gribben a genial smile and his full attention freely, without the need for the slightest servility.

'Have you found what we're looking for?'

The chairman's voice was mellow as mature wine.

It was late morning in the Glasgow autumn of 1951.

'I've found someone,' the trainer whispered, as if reluctant to share his secrets. Kelly bent his bony body, bowed his head so that he could hear the pearls of wisdom from his retainer's mouth. 'I know someone who will do a job, Mr Kelly, someone who'll fill a hole.'

The chairman unbent his back. 'Good,' he said, 'well done, Jimmy.'

'He'll do a good steady job,' Gribben added, 'maybe not for the first team, but for the club.'

'I'm grateful,' Kelly said. 'Who exactly is it you have in mind?'

* * *

Gribben had been scratching at his memories ever since the chairman told him that Kelly's Kids, the Celtic youngsters blossoming in the reserve team, needed a steadying hand, a wise head, a presence among them to lead them towards maturity, towards performing on the bigger stages, in the First Division.

The trainer dug deep into his memory banks. Eventually, he recalled a story he had heard of a broken nose and a young pitman playing part-time for Albion Rovers.

It was a wet and wintry afternoon at Ibrox, one of those Govan days when night seemed to fall as soon as the sun had supposedly risen behind lowering clouds. Rangers were fulfilling a wartime Southern League fixture at the tab end of 1942 and the club's veteran but fearsome centre-forward, Jimmy Smith, was bossing the Rovers defence with his physical menace. The tale Gribben heard was of a boy, a lanky, bony centre-half, recently signed from Blantyre Vics, who refused to defer to Smith's demands that the defender behave himself and keep well clear of the Rangers man's way. By way of response, the young man twice clattered into Smith's legs, bringing the older figure to the ground. One minute later, the heavy leather football was hoofed high into the thick, drowned air by a Rangers defender and began its downward trajectory towards Smith only yards from the Albion Rovers goal. On such a dismal day, some footballers might have made some token effort to prevent a fifth Rangers goal. This young centre-half, however, whose name was on the tip of Gribben's tongue, was made of sterner stuff, and rose to meet the flying ball. Smith, so it was said, was more interested in revenge than another goal against feeble opponents. His forehead cracked into the Albion defender's face and smashed into Jock Stein's nose.

* * *

'That's his name,' Gribben said to Kelly. 'John Stein from Burnbank.'

The memories returned. January 1949 and Celtic were hosting Albion Rovers. The visitors were compiling a backs-to-the-wall, never-say-die defensive performance, led and marshalled by Stein. The press described the Rovers pivot as heroic. Gribben recalled scribbling the Rovers defender's name in his notebook, deciding it would be no hardship to make the half-hour trip from his home to Coatbridge to watch Stein again.

'He's only got one leg, though,' Gribben told Kelly, and grinned. 'It's as if his right foot's not there.'

Another game, too, played back in Gribben's mind, a reserve fixture against Albion, again at Celtic Park. He couldn't recall the date, but Stein had been up against John McPhail, a Scottish international and a handful and a half on his day, and the Rovers man never gave him a kick or a head of the ball.

'Mind you,' Gribben added, 'Stein's got a hell of a right knee.'

Kelly looked puzzled.

'Look,' Gribben said, 'he can't do a thing with his right foot but, if the ball's in the air, this boy Stein clears it with his knee.'

The two men laughed the laugh of comrades devoted to the same cause, the future wellbeing of Celtic Football Club.

'He'll do a job, Mr Kelly.'

* * *

He knew a player when he saw one, did Jimmy Gribben. He'd been one himself, way back, with St Anthony's in Govan, and with Bo'ness, a tricky, diminutive winger in the mould of his later protege, Jimmy 'Jinky' Johnstone. Gribben played once, too, against Celtic, in November 1927, in the old First Division.

According to 'Waverley', the *Daily Record and Mail* reporter, Gribben was one of the quintet of 'clever' Bo'ness forwards. Celtic won the match 1-0, finishing the season five points behind Rangers in second place, but the report suggested the Celts had been 'in queer street' for much of the second half with the strong wind in their faces and with Gribben running at their defence relentlessly.

* * *

Kelly nodded. He knew a good judge of a player when he saw one. 'Find him then, Jimmy,' he said.

* * *

Stein was in Wales. In 1950, at the age of 27, he had given up the security and the community of Bothwell Pit, and his part-time wage of £10 a week with Albion Rovers, and committed to full-time professionalism with Llanelli of the Southern League.

He was, though, homesick, devoid of familiar comforts. His wife, Jean, was so distressed that Stein had decided to return to working underground at Bothwell.

He was staggered, unbelieving, when Celtic, thanks to Jimmy Gribben's recommendation, came calling for his signature on a contract that would change both his life and the fortunes of the club forever.

* * *

Gribben deserves his place among the immortals of Paradise.

In addition to recommending Stein to Kelly, he was instrumental in persuading manager Jimmy McGrory to take a punt on pint-sized Jimmy Johnstone, who was once described as 'too small to make it big'.

In the programme for Stein's testimonial match against Liverpool in 1978, there was a grainy photograph of a small, smiling man in spectacles and wearing a trilby hat. More significantly, Gribben's left hand was clutching the European Cup won so thrillingly by Celtic in 1967 against Inter Milan. On Stein's return from Lisbon, the manager pushed his way through a throng of well-wishers in the Celtic Park foyer and made his way to the boot room where Gribben was presented with the trophy. In the programme notes, Stein wrote, 'Jimmy was my mentor … No one knew more about football than Jimmy Gribben. He was my friend and my advisor.'

* * *

2. BOB KELLY

It was a midwinter chill of a morning, the sky louring, and the North British Hotel presented visitors with a wry expression in its brickwork, one of disapproval perhaps of the doings of its regular denizens. The hotel's curtained windows were like the closed eyes of conspirators. Secrets might be safe inside but shenanigans might not be countenanced lightly. Its former incarnation as the Queen's Hotel through the Victorian era demanded propriety at the very least from its guests.

The hotel, with its imposing and austere facade overlooking George Square, was the regular location of Celtic board meetings under the chairmanship of Bob Kelly in the 1960s.

The chairman ushered his fellow directors inside. Kelly studied his lined face reflected in the polished oak of the table, saw his white, swept-back hair, and the steel in his eyes, paused for effect, and for renewed courage. 'Well, gentlemen,' he said, 'if you wish for Jock Stein, he is available.'

It was 12 January 1965.

'With your permission, I will open negotiations.'

* * *

Kelly, though, was conscious of his deception.

At no stage during his negotiations with Stein had he consulted with his boardroom colleagues.

He looked around the room, studied faces, familiar and new.

The joker in the pack was James Farrell, appointed to the board on Christmas Eve 1964, a lawyer, an outsider, an addition to the triumvirate of Kelly, Desmond White and Tom Devlin that had ruled Celtic since 1953, since the death of Colonel John Shaughnessy. The colonel was the son of Joseph Shaughnessy, one of the club's Founding Fathers from 1887. Curiously, Farrell was a partner in the Glasgow law firm founded by Joseph, an Irish Scot, a republican, and a defender of miners after the Blantyre Riots of 1887 and of members of the Irish Republican Brotherhood after the bombing of gasometers in Glasgow in 1883.

Kelly hoped for support, for understanding from the newcomer who had argued for the need for a change of management at the football club at the previous board meeting. White, too, was keen on replacing Jimmy McGrory, Celtic manager since the end of World War Two.

* * *

The almost 20 years of McGrory's management had been an era of almost unremitting underachievement, a dark night sky illuminated by occasional lightning flashes of brilliance, false dawns of monstrous disappointments.

There had been the unexpected triumph in the 1953 Coronation Cup in which Celtic defeated Arsenal, the recently crowned English league champions, 1-0; Manchester United, the previous season's title winners, 2-1; and Hibernian, the 1951/52 Scottish First Division champions, 2-0 at Hampden Park before a crowd of over 117,000. In 1951/52 Celtic had finished ninth and in 1952/53 eighth in two dismal league campaign.

In the following season, 1953/54 Celtic won the double of league and cup, presaging a potential for future dominance in the Scottish game which never came to fruition. The 1954 title was the first and last Celtic would win under McGrory.

There had, too, been the miraculous 7-1 victory over Rangers in the 1957 League Cup Final, again raising hopes, soon to be dashed on the rocks of a Heart of Midlothian title triumph in the following season during which the Edinburgh club achieved a record goal difference of 103.

The lows were much more frequent and much more pressing in this post-war era. McGrory was both frontman and fall guy in a football club ruled from top to bottom by Bob Kelly.

There was the final-day avoidance of relegation in 1948 when only a win at Dundee would guarantee them continued membership of the elite level of Scottish football. Kelly's nephew, Michael, later a director of Celtic, said he spent the duration of the match at prayer in St Joseph's Church in Blantyre. The Kelly family's Celtic won 3-2, having been in arrears for much of the second half.

The chairman's post-war priorities were clear when he announced at the end of the 1947/48 season that Celtic was one of only a small number of profitable clubs in Scottish football.

Perhaps the lowest point in these Kelly years came on 15 May 1963 with the replayed Scottish Cup Final, which Rangers won 3-0 to complete their fourth post-war double in a highly competitive era in which Hibernian, Aberdeen, Hearts, and Dundee had also won league titles. Celtic's performance on that day was so dismal that tens of thousands of fans turned their backs on their team and headed for the exits with 20 minutes still to play after Ralph Brand had scored the Ibrox club's third goal. Outside the stadium, scarves were burned and loud and long vocal criticism of the board – and Kelly in particular – was trumpeted outside Hampden Park.

There was tea and sympathy for McGrory. As a player, he might have been the club's longstanding record scorer of 522 goals, but now everyone knew he was Kelly's patsy, too nice a man to discipline Celtic's unruly and inconsistent players. On Cup Final replay day it was Kelly who dropped Celtic's two exciting and potentially match-winning young wingers, Jimmy Johnstone and Jim Brogan. Anger did not even begin to express the frustrations and disappointments of the Celtic support after this humiliation at the hands of their great rivals from across the Clyde.

Neither was this the first or last time Kelly interfered with team selections. There was a famous and unfortunately not apocryphal story from October 1960 when Willie Goldie made his solitary first-team appearance for the Bhoys in a defeat against Airdrieonians. The Celtic team coach was winding its way through the streets of Airdrie when Kelly spotted a young man near the bus stop outside Monklands Hospital. He was wearing a green-and-white-hooped scarf. 'Isn't that one of our goalkeepers?' the chairman asked McGrory. Kelly's voice was loud and conversations and card schools paused and necks craned to see through the stained bus windows and the murky weather. 'It's Willie Goldie,' someone said.

'Stop the bus,' Kelly said. 'Get him on board.'

So impressed was the chairman with Goldie's commitment to the Celtic cause that he told McGrory the young man must be picked to play that day. Goldie was at best the club's third-choice goalkeeper and had only just been signed from Airdrie. Not expecting to appear in the match – he had kept goal for the reserves on the previous evening and then proceeded to enjoy a night out on the town – Goldie was in no fit state to play. When John Fallon, who had been expecting to play, returned to the Broomfield dressing room after inspecting the pitch, he found his boots had been removed and that Goldie was standing there in his goalkeepings kit.

It did not turn out well, as was the case with most of Kelly's interventions. Celtic lost 2-0 after Goldie's two calamitous errors sealed the visitors' fate as they sank to third-bottom of the league. In the words of one reporter, 'Goldie gave away the goals like free soup coupons.'

* * *

By the time of the board meeting at the North British Hotel in January 1965, it was not only league points that were at stake.

Attendances at Celtic Park were alarmingly low, a mere 11,000 turning up for an attractive fixture against Hibernian in March of 1964. Kelly, a stockbroker by trade, a good man with numbers, was sufficiently alarmed to consider the future viability of the club to which he and his family had devoted their lives.

The manager's annual reports, too, made sombre reading. In 1963, McGrory admitted, after the loss to Rangers in the Scottish Cup Final,

'The real issue lay not so much in defeat but in the lack of fight of the team.' One year later, in his 18th report to shareholders, he confessed that he 'could not find words to express his disappointment at not having won a major trophy'. The 1963/64 season saw Celtic finish third in the league with Rangers champions and Kilmarnock as runners-up. There were humiliations, too, in the Scottish Cup, knocked out in the fourth round by Rangers, and in the League Cup, beaten twice by the Ibrox club in the early season group stage, both times 3-0.

By the end of 1964 Celtic were in a slough of despond and slumped in fifth position in the league. On New Year's Day there followed yet another defeat by Rangers, who were severely weakened by injuries to key players Ralph Brand, Jim Baxter and Willie Henderson. Celtic had become mired in mid-table mediocrity.

Even their captain and defensive stalwart since 1957, Billy McNeill, was eyeing opportunities south of the border. Later he admitted, 'I was coming on for 25 and had been at Celtic Park since I was 17. Nothing significant had happened throughout that period and nothing significant looked like happening.' Paddy Crerand, who had joined Celtic on the same day as McNeill, had moved to Manchester United in February 1963, winning the FA Cup in the same year and was on the way to winning a league title in 1965.

* * *

Not all of this was entirely the fault of Bob Kelly, a man who loved Celtic with every fibre of his being. Nevertheless, it was happening on his watch.

'Well, something had to be done,' the chairman confessed. Kelly shifted his gaze from colleague to colleague, from White to Devlin, from Devlin to Farrell, from Farrell to White. Their eyes told him nothing. Kelly had no way of knowing what they had been up to behind his back.

He didn't want thanks for his secret negotiations with Jock Stein but neither did he want prevarication. 'It has to be Stein,' he said, and relief washed over him as he saw heads nod in approval.

* * *

The chairman was steeped in the club, a Celt from the cradle.

His father, James Kelly, had been signed amid great bitterness from Renton in 1888. At the time, the Dunbartonshire side were the unofficial champions of the world having defeated both Preston North End, the English FA Cup finalists, and West Bromwich Albion, who had defeated North End in the final of March 1888. The following season, the inaugural edition of the Football League in England, Preston claimed the title and stayed unbeaten throughout that season in both league and cup. In an age of theoretical amateurism, Kelly had been induced by Celtic to shift his allegiance 15 miles south from Renton to Glasgow's East End, the reward apparently consisting of sufficient cash to permit Kelly to purchase a public house together with a promise of future shares if Celtic were to become a limited company.

Such was the fury at Celtic's bribery of Kelly that several clubs, including Renton, began to openly pursue sectarian employment practices, believing it pointless to employ Catholic footballers as they would have no loyalty if approached by the newly formed and ambitious and ruthless Glasgow club.

James Kelly became Celtic's first captain, and was a pivotal player in the club's early successes in the cup in 1892 and league championship in 1893. After his retirement as a player in 1897, he became a director and then chairman from 1909 until 1914.

In 1902, he became the father of Robert, who would become the chairman of Celtic from 1947 to 1971.

* * *

Bob Kelly was undoubtedly in awe of his father until the latter's death in 1932.

The fourth son of James Kelly, one of ten siblings, Robert Kelly was a footballer himself with Blantyre Celtic and Blantyre Victoria, until he was persuaded to give up the game by his father. It is a curious story related in the son's 1971 book, *Celtic*, and sheds light upon both Bob's principles and his perhaps inordinate and unfortunate reverence for his father. Young Robert had suffered permanent damage to his right arm as a result of being knocked down by a Glasgow tramcar. It was wretched luck but only life-changing when his father intervened and asked him to give up playing football because, he argued, it would not be fair on fellow professionals who might fear for causing the young man further damage: 'Would the average opponent be able to play his natural game when he might have at the back of his mind a worry that he should not have to carry?'

Bob, from that moment, devoted himself to his father's wishes and to upholding James's principles as a shareholder and chairman of Celtic.

'I do not wish to appear boastful,' he wrote, 'when I say that no man in football has received more pleasure from a connection with a club than I have. It was my father – not I – who made this possible.'

In many ways, Kelly's life was saintly and simple. Devotions to his Catholic faith and to his Celtic football team were the twin pillars of his life.

* * *

In the North British Hotel, Kelly's mind wandered momentarily as he watched heads nod in agreement to the appointment of Jock Stein as manager of Celtic.

He thought back to his earlier meetings with the man he was poaching from rivals Hibernian. He recalled stories of derring-do and under-the-counter payments in the days of the Founding Fathers of Celtic, of how John Glass and his colleagues had betrayed the trust of the Edinburgh Catholic club and stole their best players from under their very noses. He thought back to the original Celtic members' pledge to non-sectarianism in their recruitment of players.

Still, though, he worried.

In spite of the inclusivity of Celtic's early history – the club bought in the best players money could buy – and in spite of the clever appropriation of a name that suggested the encompassing of all Celtic nations, the club of the Kelly family had always been supported by a predominantly Catholic and Irish – and generally republican – fanbase.

It was the fact that Stein came from staunchly Protestant stock that worried Kelly now, and it had done since the confidential negotiations with the Hibernian manager had begun. It was why, in their initial meeting Kelly had offered Stein only the assistant manager's position. True, it was also because the chairman was a man who hated to hurt feelings and McGrory's deputy, Sean Fallon, would have expected the manager's job if and when the current incumbent was to be moved to one side. This Protestantism, however, was a real concern. Clearly, Stein was the outstanding candidate for the manager's role – his work at Dunfermline and at Hibs had proved that – but he was a man from Burnbank whose family were all dyed-in-the-wool Rangers supporters and he was a man who would not be able to accompany Celtic players to Mass on matchday mornings. It was why, at Kelly's second meeting with Stein, he offered him a joint managerial role with Fallon.

Stein, though, was a gambling man, a poker player as well as a Protestant, and turned down Kelly's opening gambits as easily as if they had been extra cards offered to a man with a full house. He mentioned an approach from down south, from Wolverhampton Wanderers. He wondered whether Kelly might offer an opinion as to whether he should take the job with the English giants.

In the end, Kelly offered Stein the manager's role and full control, too, over team selection. It was as great a revolution at Celtic as it might be possible to imagine, and Kelly and his fellow directors deserve some credit for looking the inevitable in the face, staring down its eyes, and making peace with change.

* * *

Later, Kelly tried to garner all the credit both for his original appointment of Stein as Celtic reserve team manager in 1957 and for his reappointment as first team supremo in 1965. He professed it to have been the culmination of a long-plotted plan. Stein would be allowed to leave Celtic in 1960 in spite of his revolutionary work with the reserve team, with his proteges breaking through into McGrory's and Fallon's first team. Players including Billy McNeill, Bertie Auld, Stevie Chalmers, John Clark, Paddy Crerand, Charlie Gallagher, Tommy Gemmell, Jimmy Johnstone, Bobby Lennox and Bobby Murdoch all came under the tutelage of Stein.

When McNeill heard of the homecoming of his mentor, Stein, he immediately abandoned plans to leave the club.

Stein, Kelly said, was allowed to leave Celtic on a temporary basis to gain experience at Dunfermline and elsewhere if necessary, before a triumphant return to Paradise. It was nonsense, of course. Just as was the denial of problems with Stein's Protestantism. McNeill himself said, 'Let's not beat about the bush. They were reluctant to give him full control because he was a Protestant.'

Stein's wife, Jean, said, 'John was more or less told by the chairman in 1960 that he had gone as far as he could with Celtic, coaching the second team.'

After all, the reserve team's mentoring was the sole reason he was brought to the club in the first place. On the recommendation of Jimmy Gribben.

* * *

Whether or not any serious objections were raised by White, Devlin or Farrell on that fateful day in January 1965 at the North British Hotel, Kelly had his way and had his man, even if it was the desperation of the club's situation that had driven Kelly to take the risk of appointing a Protestant manager to an Irish Catholic institution.

* * *

Despite his deceit and his dissembling over the Stein appointment, Kelly deserves his place among the Celtic immortals.

On other occasions, he was the man of iron will and unbending principles who stood alone against the prejudice of the powerbrokers of the Scottish Football Association in 1952 and even against the armed might of the Soviet Union in 1968. The flag controversy, originating with the SFA's ordering of the removal of the Irish flag that flew from one end of the old covered enclosure and above Celtic fans congregating in the Jungle section of Paradise, needs to be seen in context.

This particular flag, the tricolour of the newly independent Free State, had been a gift to the club by the first Irish Taoiseach, Eamon De Valera. Since the opening of Paradise, however, the old Irish flag with a golden harp set against a background of emerald green had always been flown. It was a recognition, an acknowledgement, of Celtic's origins in the Irish Holocaust and the subsequent emigration to Glasgow.

The diktat by the SFA had originated in a suggestion by Glasgow magistrates after crowd trouble at the January 1952 derby at Celtic Park, 'The two clubs should avoid displaying flags which might incite feeling among the spectators.' Only Celtic were instructed by the SFA to remove a flag.

The Referee Committee ruled that 'Celtic be asked to refrain from displaying in its park any flag or emblem that had no association with the country or the sport'.

Kelly was still relatively new to power at Celtic, becoming chairman five years earlier on the death of Tom White. In theory, a triumvirate of directors, Kelly, Desmond White and Tom Devlin Jr, were the decision-makers inside the gates of Paradise. All three had inherited shares and power from their fathers. Shareholding systems within privately owned limited companies make both nepotism and patriarchy inevitable. In effect, a combination of his father's shares and his family's assiduously cultivated friendship with the Grants and the Colgans whose 1,100-plus shares were now owned by Tom Colgan's daughter, Mary, who lived in Toomebridge, County Antrim, meant almost absolute power for Bob Kelly.

What now, though, to do with this authority, this responsibility?

Kelly, in addition to his Celtic position, was already president of the Scottish Football League. It would be naive to think he had not also thought of one day wielding power at the SFA.

He discussed the issue of the flag with Desmond White, certainly, but with his ears largely stopped and deaf. Mostly, though, he talked to his dead father, James. Throughout the early years of his life, Bob Kelly had been in thrall to his eminent father, had even given up playing his beloved football at his father's behest.

It had been more than 20 years since James Kelly's demise but still his son would want to do nothing that might make his father less than proud of his son.

When the full SFA council, including Kelly in his role as Celtic chairman, convened to consider its committee's proposal, the result was a threat of 'a fine, or closure of the ground, or suspension or all of those penalties' if Celtic continued to fly the Irish flag and trouble occurred at Paradise.

Kelly had mounted a simple defence based on his opinion, 'Nothing in the rules of football gave the SFA the right to impose such penalties.'

Still, the council voted 26-7 in favour of the motion. Leading the bigots was the SFA secretary George Graham, a member of the Grand Orange Lodge of Scotland and a Grandmason, who Kelly described as 'a much more powerful man in Scottish football than he had any right to be'. Graham's chief ally was the Hibernian chairman Harry Swan, perhaps a man with a long memory who wanted revenge for Celtic's ruthless behaviour in the 19th century when Hibs were supplanted by the Parkhead club as the leading Irish club in Scotland.

Surprisingly, the Rangers chairman John Wilson supported Kelly, although financial self-interest surely played a great part in this unusually comradely behaviour.

Kelly took counsel from both his father and lawyers and stuck to his principles. At the following council meeting, Celtic's 'defiance' was tabled for discussion. 'Anarchy against democratic government' was a phrase bandied about by the Graham clique, apparently without irony.

The council decided 16-15 to extend the threat of suspension from the SFA but support for such a radical move was ebbing away.

The threat, nevertheless, had been real and serious and was only removed once the full financial implications of Celtic's expulsion had belatedly hit home.

In Scotland, self-interest, the power of money, the fear of losing bumper paydays when Celtic came to town, had triumphed over politics in the battle over the flag.

In Glasgow, in 1952, Kelly's strategy of survival won the day, and Celtic lived to fight another day. For many Celtic fans, the chairman's sins of interference in the football of the club and the failure of the football throughout his time in charge until the arrival of Stein is forgiven because of his principled and determined stand over the Irish flag.

For Kelly, though, this was not merely a matter of principle, it was an administrative matter of the SFA's adherence to their own rules. In his autobiography he clearly states, 'My main reason for opposing the ban was not, however, my opinion that the flag was not responsible for sectarian trouble.' Forgive the double negatives. Kelly was a pragmatic politician bent on the survival of his football club, a personal fiefdom he had inherited from his father and which he was resolved to see continue.

Had he not reined in his fierier colleague, Desmond White, who declared Graham, the SFA secretary, would roast in hell for what he was attempting to do to Celtic, 1952 might have witnessed the demise of the club from Paradise to follow the death of Belfast Celtic in 1948. Both clubs were hounded by Protestant-dominated football authorities.

Even so, there are some Celtic fans who might have preferred Kelly to have fought on the principle of the club's right to fly a republican flag if it chose to rather than on a technicality in a rulebook. Prejudice never truly dies.

In its defeat in 1952, bigotry licked its wounds, hid away for a while, shame-faced, not because it was ashamed of its behaviour but because it was ashamed it had not won the day.

In 1972, Glasgow magistrates, in the wake of more mayhem on the terraces, at a time when football hooliganism was rampant across the UK, again asked the Celtic hierarchy, then led by White, to remove the Irish tricolour. Some people, apparently, found it offensive. The persecution, the discrimination, the harassment, erupts from time to time.

The episode with the flag, the attempts at banning Celtic songs, the BBC delight in a Rangers victory, the refereeing biases and, in more recent history, the differential treatment of Celtic and Rangers over breaches in Covid rules, all fit together in a perennial pattern of displays of Protestant power in Scotland.

Soviet power was a different matter entirely.

In protest against the invasion of Czechoslovakia by the USSR and its Warsaw Pact allies, Kelly insisted to UEFA that no Western club should be forced to play against teams from the Soviet bloc of nations. Celtic had been drawn to play Ferencváros, the Hungarian champions. Kelly threatened to withdraw his club from the European Cup. He was accused by some in the upper echelons of the Scottish game of dabbling in politics but, as Kelly and Celtic fans understood, politics was already embedded within the structures of both the SFA and UEFA.

The draw for the first round of the competition was remade and, in protest, representatives of the Iron Curtain nations withdrew altogether.

As Celtic's chairman said, 'There are things for Celtic more important than money.' So, despite his crass and constant interventions in team affairs, sometimes with disastrous results, he was the man who stood up for Celtic's foundational principles.

He was also the man who brought Jock Stein to Celtic, the man who loved Stein, supported Stein, and provided constant companionship, through all of the manager's tribulations as well as his triumphs.

* * *

3. JOCK STEIN

'Morning, Boss,' Stein said.

It was Tuesday, 9 March 1965 when Stein limped through the doors of Paradise as manager of Celtic, and he immediately sought out

Jimmy McGrory, ousted by Kelly and about to begin his stint as public relations officer.

Until the day McGrory died in October 1982 Stein continued to call him 'Boss'. It was a measure of the man that with McGrory he remained unstinting in his humility and generosity.

The Celtic players, too, even those who had never played under McGrory, referred to Celtic's legendary goalscorer and former manager reverentially as 'Old Boss'.

Jimmy McGrory, Celtic's record scorer with 522 goals, might have been resentful about the arrival of this brash usurper whose abilities as a footballer were ordinary at best. Instead, McGrory, when told by Kelly of his changed role within the football club, said, 'Jock Stein is a remarkable man and a man who will give his all for the club, as he has done in the past as player and coach. He has qualities of dedication and determination. He can transform good players into great players. I don't think there is anyone quite like him.'

At the club's annual general meeting in August 1965, McGrory added, 'Had I myself been the chooser of my successor, it would have been Mr Stein.'

Kelly had been worried sick about demoting his idol and replacing him with Stein, but perhaps McGrory had endured enough humiliation in a role he was unsuited to fill. Maybe, too, the constant interference by Kelly in team selections had worn him down. On away days, players waited in shabby dressing rooms with no knowledge of who would be playing and who would be dropped at the whim of the chairman. Eventually, Kelly would appear with McGrory, and sometimes an additional director or two, and they would disappear into the toilet to discuss team selections. When Kelly had decided, McGrory's role was to read out names scribbled presumably on hard toilet paper.

It was no way to run a team, leaving no room for tactical preparation because there was no foreknowledge of player participation. Not that McGrory was interested in strategy and his planning for matches involved nothing but physical work without sight of a football. Since becoming Celtic manager, he had never donned a tracksuit.

To be fair to McGrory, however, this denial of the ball, in order to make players hungry for it on the Saturday, was not uncommon in the 1950s and 1960s.

Kelly said McGrory was 'far too modest and gentlemanly to have made a real success of the job'. In view of this assessment, it beggars belief that chairman and manager shared 18 years together leading Celtic.

McGrory's new role in public relations, which he performed with dignity until his retirement in 1979, was a far cry from his days as a marauding, buccaneering centre-forward for the Celts, when the fans sang his praises from the terracing of Paradise.

> *Tell me the old, old story*
> *A hat-trick for McGrory*
> *A victory for the Fenians*
> *He will carry us through!*
> *He'll carry us through the hue*
> *To beat the bastards in blue*
> *Look forever to McGrory*
> *He will carry us through*

Whatever McGrory's limitations as a manager of Celtic, Jock Stein, though, recognised an immortal when he saw one.

* * *

When Kelly released Stein from his work as reserve team and youth coach at Celtic in March 1960, he neither expected nor suspected his return as manager five years later.

Nor did he anticipate Stein's Dunfermline Athletic would defeat Celtic 2-0 in the replayed Scottish Cup Final of 1961. Kelly, to his credit, was magnanimity personified. 'It's no loss what a friend gets,' he said to reporters. Stein had transformed his charges from a club in danger of both relegation and extinction into debut cup winners and, in the following season, to fourth place in the league and adventures on the grand European stage.

It was no surprise when Hibernian came calling in 1964 and again Stein was successful in raising both the club's league position and profile in world football when his team defeated five-time European champions Real Madrid 2-0 in a prestige friendly. Stein was a rising star in the firmament of football management.

It was Christmas 1964 and Kelly was wracked by indecision, by loyalties to McGrory and his assistant, Sean Fallon, and by guilt from his clandestine meetings with Stein. The Hibernian manager, too, had proved an obdurate negotiator. Something, though, had to be done.

The new year opened with a 1-0 defeat at Ibrox Park. Ongoing indiscipline within the team saw 'Jinky' Johnstone sent off so Kelly, ever the high ground moralist, banned the winger from playing in the team's subsequent match.

The very next day, a measly 13,500 fans squeezed through the turnstiles of Paradise to watch a dismal 1-1 draw with Clyde. As the second half progressed, the home team were increasingly pinned down in their own half with the visitors pressing for a winner on the icy pitch. A continuous chorus of boos and catcalls echoed about the emptying stadium and frozen feet stamped in irate disapproval on concrete terracing and the flooring of the main stand. The final whistle may have been the moment Kelly decided to accede to Stein's demands.

If, however, Kelly had changed his mind in the morning, indecision turned at last to decisive action following Celtic's humbling defeat at Dundee United on the following weekend. A board meeting was called at the North British Hotel for Tuesday morning.

When the Celtic chairman finally made his move, it revealed much about the characters of both Kelly and Stein. If Kelly was stubborn, clinging to his control of all aspects of the club and duplicitous to a degree, in his secretive manoeuvres behind the backs of his board of directors, he met his manipulative match in Stein.

In the autumn of 1964, when Wolverhampton Wanderers sacked their legendary manager since 1948, Stan Cullis, who had led the Molineux club to three league titles and two FA Cups, Stein saw his opportunity and executed a masterplan with dexterity and ruthlessness. The man from Burnbank had no interest whatsoever in moving to England or in joining a club that had informed their manager of his dismissal via a letter with his name scratched from the club stationery. Nevertheless, he contacted his old mentor, Kelly, to ask his advice about the vacancy at Wolves, about whether the chairman thought it would be a good career move for Stein.

Kelly was both galvanised into action, inviting Stein to meet him at the North British Hotel, and duped. As Stein later confessed, he had played the Wolves card in his hand like a master poker player.

When Kelly made his initial offer of the assistant manager's role under Fallon, Stein politely declined and reminded Kelly that he was seriously minded to move to the English Midlands.

It has to be said, too, that Stein was using Hibernian, taking their wages while plotting his next career move and his own financial advancement.

Money and Stein were long-time lovers whose relationship over the years had become a tad one-sided. Stein desired money, respected money, worked damn hard for money, but still real money, serious money, money that would replace his restlessness with security, with peace, eluded him. Money teased Stein to distraction.

He was a gambler from his earliest days. In his teens at Burnbank Cross, he was a runner and a lookout for local bookie Mick Mitchell, who ran his illegal operation with occasional police cooperation. Stein loved a bet and later in life, in Paradise, he and Fallon would spend many an afternoon glued to the television watching the racing. Often, too, the inseparable pair would disappear to Ayr races where the size of Stein's wagers never ceased to shock his more cautious assistant manager.

Stein could be duplicitous too. In his playing days with Albion Rovers, in 1948, when the Coatbridge side were promoted to the First Division, there was a renegotiation of players' wages led by the team captain. Stein assured his colleagues £9 a week was the best they could hope for, and even calmed a dressing room rebellion against the new terms of employment. Stein, though, had negotiated £10 a week for himself in return for a promise to persuade others to accept less.

This is not to be overly critical of Stein. He had worked too many too long days and nights underground in the Lanarkshire mines, seeing men die for their money, to underestimate his privileged position as a football man.

He could at times be extraordinarily generous, treating money as if it were a casual lover rather than a lifetime's romance.

During World War Two, Lanarkshire miners went on strike under the influence of the young firebrand union leader Mick McGahey. Stein gave his £2-a-week wages from Albion Rovers to the strike fund so that he would be no better off than his pitmen colleagues. Later, during the national strike of 1984 and 1985, Stein could be seen cramming bank notes into miners' collection tins.

He never forgot his origins or his debt of gratitude towards his hard-as-miners'-boot-nails upbringing. In an interview with the journalist Hugh McIlvanney, he said, 'Everyone should go down the pit at least once to know what darkness is.'

It was not just the pits, however, that provided Stein with an education in life. His father, George, and his family were Protestant and Rangers diehards, and Stein himself was a fan of the Ibrox club. When the young man showed some footballing ability, a career path was mapped out by George. Blantyre Victoria to Rangers was the plotted pathway to glory. Both teams sported the red, white and blue of Union Jack Protestant patriotism.

Stein was his father's sole son amid a dazzle of darling daughters and George's ambitions for his boy were heightened by the knowledge that Stein provided his only chance to live his own footballing dreams.

Stein, though, signed for Burnbank Athletic, an act regarded by his father as treachery and treason. George tore up the papers and persuaded his son to sign instead for the Protestant Blantyre Vics, but that would be the last time the father imposed his will upon his son.

Whereas James Kelly had suggested that Robert give up the game of football, and found a compliant and dutiful son, George found a son of sterner, rebellious stuff.

Stein signed for Celtic in 1951 and, afterwards, his father never once wished him well. Stein's best friend from boyhood days, too, shunned him for the rest of his life.

* * *

The Celtic manager was not a man for triviality or trappings. He was a hard man and expected and demanded his players were hard men too and, in that pursuit, he curated austerity, created hardship, mental and physical, to build strength of character.

Throughout the Stein era, the club's training facilities were at Barrowfield, half a mile from Paradise. Players changed at the stadium and ran in all weathers down London Road to work on the spartan pitches at Barrowfield. However cold the weather, no tracksuits were permitted.

Stein's own office at Celtic Park, a short pass away from the foyer, was cramped and suitably and impressively frugal.

As for leaving Hibernian in early 1965, Stein was typically hard-nosed. He had done a fine job for the Edinburgh club, leaving them within sight of the top of the league table, even though his last two matches in charge, when Stein's players' minds were distracted by their manager's impending departure, were disappointing defeats against Kilmarnock and Morton. Still, there was sourness and bitterness inside Easter Road at his leaving, as if Hibernian had been used, if not abused, to further Stein's ambitions. His time in Edinburgh looked for all the world like a brief affair, a dalliance.

In Hibs supporters' minds, it brought back recollections of 19th-century humiliations at the hands of a ruthless Glasgow upstart when Hibernian became a recruiting ground for John Glass's Celtic.

Neither Stein nor Kelly gave their Edinburgh counterparts a backward glance.

* * *

On Stein's first day in charge at Celtic, the new manager was calm, collected, and unusually quiet.

Trying to minimise the limp in his gait, he walked from his office to the players' dressing room and told them he expected them to work as hard as he himself would do. There were no volcanic explosions from the new man which some had expected and feared, only that simple demand for commitment.

As the players left for their run to Barrowfield, Stein called for the Celtic goalkeeper, Ronnie Simpson, to stay behind.

Simpson's was a long and winding road of a career, beginning with Queen's Park in 1945. He arrived happily at Hibernian in 1960 via Third Lanark and Newcastle, but four years later found himself face to face with a manager with a reputation for disliking goalkeepers. Shortly after Stein's appointment at Easter Road in March 1964, Simpson made the mistake of asking for a £2-a-week pay rise, and Stein was apoplectic, informing Simpson he would not play again until he dropped his demands.

Simpson refused to train. While Stein approved of striking miners his blessing for footballers who withdrew their labour was another matter entirely. The standoff was resolved eventually when Stein received an offer for Simpson from Celtic. Even then, Stein made sure his was the last word as Simpson swapped Edinburgh for Glasgow.

'If I discover you've been tapped,' the Hibs manager said, 'I'll not rest until I see you and the other club are punished for it.'

One year later, with Stein now in the Celtic hotseat, he spoke again to Simpson:

'Let's forget what's happened between us in the past. This is a new start.'

* * *

It was indeed. The following day, Celtic played at Airdrie and won 6-0. The honeymoon, though, was short-lived.

In the league, Celtic finished the season in eighth place having lost under Stein more matches than they won. Those defeats included humiliating losses home and away to Hibernian, a 6-2 defeat at Falkirk, a home defeat in the Glasgow derby with Partick Thistle, and a thrashing at another of Stein's former charges, 5-1 at Dunfermline.

Only 11,500 watched the final home match of the season.

Kelly wondered if he had made the biggest mistake of his life, whether the disastrous results and attendances under Stein were divine punishments for his disloyalty to McGrory and Fallon, and to the Catholic hierarchy within Paradise.

* * *

There were, however, changes afoot which Stein hoped would come to future fruition. In fact, the new manager was initiating a root-and-branch revolution.

Both training – with a football at last – and tactics were transformed. Players used to running – to Barrowfield, at Barrowfield, and back to Celtic Park from Barrowfield, and then maybe running some more up and down the unforgiving concrete of the terracing steps – were now treated to a tracksuit manager with routines that prefigured what might happen in matchday situations. Tactics were discussed and chalked up on blackboards. John Clark, the Celtic defender, said it was like going back to school and woe betide any player whose attention wandered. Stein's presence was huge and presided over both training ground and dressing room where his banter, his pitman's vernacular, and his encouragement and attention to detail ensured a bond developed between management, coaching staff and players.

Not that Stein ever allowed players to imagine they were his equals. As at Hibernian, the manager immediately asserted his rights to command players' wages. The players, with wins in the Scottish Cup against Queen's Park and Kilmarnock, both occurring before Stein's arrival, were expecting two win bonuses in their first pay packets. When the cash was counted, there was bemusement, followed by dismay and anger. There had to be some mistake. Only one win bonus was to be found. Billy McNeill, the captain, was deputed to see Stein. There had, though, been no mistake. McNeill was dismissed, and Stein hurried from his office, his ankle, damaged in an accidental collision with the Rangers forward Billy Simpson in 1955, causing him to sway and lurch along the Paradise corridors. The door to the dressing room was kicked open and Stein shouted at his cowering charges, 'You were expected to beat Queen's Park, they're fucking amateurs, but you weren't expected to win against Kilmarnock, so that's just *one* fucking bonus you're due.'

It was the beginning of Stein's rule by fear as well as respect – and a grudging love from some of his players. He later admitted that the secret of being a good manager was 'to keep the six players who hate you away from the five who are undecided'.

Sean Fallon confessed that, alongside McGrory, he had not been hard enough on the players.

Stein, though, was not a man either to be ignored or crossed. He wanted and demanded control over everything, even down to the short back and sides haircuts his players sported in his early times at Celtic Park.

He found it difficult to sleep, impossible sometimes, and so found it easy to arrive early and open up at Celtic Park, where he waited impatiently for the players to get to the stadium.

Even when Stein was absent, on scouting missions with Fallon, on race days at Ayr, with Fallon too, his presence still presided over all at Paradise, his shadow lengthening and covering every detail of life at the football club to which he had chosen to devote the rest of his life.

As he had said at that supporters' night in 1955, 'I cannot claim Celtic was my first love ... but I can say that it will be my last love.'

* * *

Stein, however, found his chairman less easy to control.

'There will be no question about it not being Jock's team,' wrote *Evening Times* reporter Peter Pendry, under a banner headline of 'SUPREMO STEIN'. At the morning press conference, the journalist had asked Bob Kelly a straightforward question, 'Will Jock Stein pick the team?' The chairman's answer was equally unambiguous. 'Yes, Jock is in complete charge.'

It was, however, not as simple as that.

Like another Glaswegian autocrat from a working-class family, Alex Ferguson, Stein understood his place in the scheme of things; he knew that deference to superiors was essential at times in his line of business. Just as Ferguson never kow-towed to popular tastes by criticising Manchester United's owners, not Martin Edwards, the local butcher's son, and not the Glazers from far across the Atlantic, so Stein never complained in public about Kelly's continued attempts at intervention in team affairs.

In the past, it was generally reckoned that Kelly's bizarre selections under the management of McGrory had cost Celtic three Scottish Cup finals. In the replayed final in 1955 against Clyde, Bobby Collins, a diminutive creative genius, a right-winger for Celtic but later a midfield creator for Don Revie's Leeds United, was dropped by Kelly, apparently for making an over-forceful challenge on the Clyde goalkeeper in the initial match. Celtic lost 1-0. It was neither the first nor the last time that Kelly's Corinthian attitude would diminish Celtic's chances of winning football matches.

The following year, Jim Sharkey, an elegant inside-forward with imagination and elegance, was dropped from the cup final team to play Hearts, for allegedly drinking too much sherry while at Seamill in the days prior to the game. After the Celts had lost the match 3-1, at Ferrari's Restaurant, Sharkey did drink too much and told McGrory and Kelly in particular to stick their football club up their combined arses. In 1961, there was another replayed final, this time against Jock Stein's Dunfermline Athletic, which Celtic lost 2-0. The omission of the experienced Bertie Peacock was controversial.

The constant interference by Kelly, too, was a major reason behind Paddy Crerand's departure in 1963 for Manchester United. 'You could always tell the day before the match,' Crerand said later, 'whether or not you were in the team. If you happened to pass Bob Kelly in a corridor at the ground and he said "hello", that meant you were picked. If he walked past you without looking your way, you were dropped.'

Stein was to find Kelly's constant visits to the dressing room just before kick-off an ongoing irritant. Sometimes, too, the chairman would demand the dropping of a player.

It was not until the end of January 1966 that the issue of control of team selection was finally settled.

Celtic, after 31 hours of tortuous travelling across Europe, eventually arrived in the Georgian capital of Tbilisi where they were due to play the second leg of their European Cup Winners' Cup tie against Dynamo Kiev, whose home stadium was snowbound. Towards the end of a tetchy 1-1 draw that would see Celtic progress to the semi-finals of the competition, Jim Craig, the right-back, clashed with Kiev's left-winger Vitaliy Khmelnytskyi. Fists were raised and both players were sent off. It was a scrimmage and nothing more and the Celtic defender felt it had been the Ukrainian who had been the aggressor.

'The winger,' Craig claimed, 'punched me after I mistimed a tackle and I chased after him and gave him a mouthful. The referee sent me off as well and I hadn't touched him.'

Kelly was outraged by Craig's behaviour and demanded he apologise, which he refused to do. In an echo of the McGrory era, the chairman demanded that Stein drop the unrepentant Craig for the following game against Hearts. The manager sought out the player in the team hotel and said, 'You'll have to apologise to the chairman.' 'For what?' Craig asked. 'For being sent off,' Stein replied, and turned away.

In the dressing room at Tynecastle, half an hour before kick-off, the Celtic team was read out by Stein. No explanation was given to Craig for his omission.

In the Heart of Midlothian stand sat Desmond White, Kelly's fellow director, who demanded of Craig the reason for his not playing. White was incensed when told by Craig he thought it was due to a lack of apology to the chairman.

At the next board meeting, White insisted that Kelly should keep his word to Stein and stay clear of any further interventions.

Finally, the manager had total control of team affairs at Celtic.

* * *

4. SEAN FALLON

Stein was not one to whom delegation of responsibility or sharing of secrets came easily or naturally.

When he signed a playing contract with Celtic in December 1951, it set him on a soloist's journey. Crossing the great divide between

Protestant Burnbank and the Catholic East End of Glasgow was seen by family and friends as a great betrayal. In his heart of hearts, it must have seemed something similar to himself. From that moment, he was swimming against a dark tide that made him a loner and a man who did not sleep at night. It was a sacrifice of unfathomable depths. He joined Celtic because the club had offered him and his beloved wife, Jeanie, a way out of misery in Llanelli, and a way forwards without descending deep into the Lanarkshire pits once more.

As a manager, at Dunfermline and at Hibs, he had been a sole trader, reliant on his own vision, his own determination and imagination, and he had been a great success.

Still, he was more than pleased to see his old buddy Fallon when he returned to Paradise in 1965.

* * *

Fallon arrived at Celtic in March 1950 from Glenavon FC, a dream come true for a Sligo boy steeped in the romance of Celtic folklore, the traditions of charity and of sweet and flowing and adventurous football. The reality was somewhat different.

At the end of the previous season, the novice-chairman, Bob Kelly had said, 'We have the players but it appears we haven't got a team.'

Fallon arrived to find a club riven with cliques, drinkers and non-drinkers, Scots and Irish, hardened and cynical pros and new arrivals. The newcomer was teased unmercifully about his Sligo accent. In addition, he had to contend with Charlie Tully's company on his passage across the Irish Sea. McGrory had tasked the mischievous winger with ensuring Fallon arrived safely in Glasgow. The young defender's first obstacle to overcome after signing for the Hoops was to stay sober in Tully's company. When his guide asked Fallon what he wanted to drink and the new Celtic man replied, 'Lemonade,' Tully said, 'Don't tell me you're one of *those*!' Fallon said later, 'Charlie's tipple was always the same – a beer and a half of whiskey – and I had no idea how he managed to put so many of them away. I must have had about 14 lemonades keeping pace with him.'

On top of it all, Fallon scored an own goal on his debut against Clyde in a 2-2 draw. The Celtic goalkeeper, John Bonnar, described the scene, 'I'm organising the defence. Sean's on the front post. I tell him,

"Anything your height, Sean, you head it." Over comes the ball. Sean puts it straight in the net. Lovely header! McGrory himself couldn't have done better!'

The fact that he survived his early homesickness, his disastrous debut, and a career-threatening ankle injury, to earn the nicknames of 'Mad Monk' and 'Iron Man', tells everything about Fallon's strength of character.

It helped his assimilation into the team that he performed heroics at the heart of Celtic's defensive efforts in the Scottish Cup Final victory over Motherwell in 1951. David Potter, in his book *Celtic's Greatest Games*, wrote that Fallon and his fellow full-back, Alex Rollo, 'kicked everything that came over the halfway line – paper bags, stray dogs, trainers and their own men included. The wind didnae even get by them.'

By then his teetotalism – which would later help bond him with Stein – was accepted by team-mates as a source of his strength.

As for his ankle injury, Fallon simply went on a pilgrimage to Station Island in the middle of Lough Derg where St Patrick, it was said, experienced visions of hell on his way to converting Ireland to Christianity. 'All I did was pray and fast,' Fallon said. 'I starved myself for three days.' The ankle never troubled him afterwards.

* * *

When Stein arrived in 1951, Fallon was a rock in Celtic's first team.

The Irishman was now one of the old hands but he remembered his own earlier difficulties and sought out the new man.

Stein was an unknown at the time and his arrival from non-league football hardly caused ripples of excitement within or without the dressing room. Celtic sat 12th in the league at the time and facing the prospect of another relegation battle. There were still divisions within the team, now including undercurrents of resentment among some Catholic players at their Protestant peers. It was mostly repressed but the idol of Paradise, Charlie Tully, once explained a defeat by Rangers by suggesting that 'there were too many Protestants in this team'.

Fallon recalled Stein being taken to the reserve team dressing room on his arrival. 'I'd never even heard of him,' he confessed.

Tully, when told the new defender was 30 years of age, said, 'That old fella could be my grandfather.'

Fallon and Stein, however, became inseparable, both at the heart of Celtic's first team defence and at the heart of their social lives outside of football. 'Anyone he didn't kick, I did,' Fallon joked.

After the football, there was Ferrari's Restaurant where the friends – also including Bertie Peacock who had befriended Fallon on his arrival in Glasgow – talked tactics and how Celtic might be changed, improved.

In December 1952, when Fallon was appointed club captain, he was asked to name his deputy. Instead of choosing Bobby Evans, a Celtic stalwart since 1944 and a great on-field organiser and fierce competitor, and instead of selecting his closest friend Bertie Peacock, Fallon picked out Stein, a bit-part footballer with only one foot and a knee to play with, and who had been at Paradise for less than a year.

McGrory's captain had just proved himself one of Celtic's greatest spotters of talent in the history of the club.

* * *

So, when Stein returned to Celtic as manager, there was already an unbreakable bond with Fallon.

It didn't matter to Fallon that Stein had taken *his* job, the position that Kelly had earmarked for him for so long. All that mattered was that Fallon knew the chairman had appointed the right man, that their respective strengths would complement one another just as they had on the battlefields of play. They would be companions in arms, and they would be all right.

'Leadership,' Fallon said, 'is very, very important at a football club, and Jock was a born leader.' Stein, in his turn, now recognised the necessity of partnerships, first with Kelly, and now with Fallon. 'A job is easy,' the new manager said, 'if you're working with people you can depend on.'

Stein understood he could be at times impetuous, at times unpleasant. Time and time again, Fallon would prove to be good cop to the manager's bad cop. Fallon's arm around a player bawled out by Stein would prove invaluable over the years. Later, Stevie Chalmers described his manager as 'a tough man, very often hard to deal with', and admitted, 'Most of the players were frightened of him.' By contrast, Fallon was 'a fatherly figure', someone the players felt they could always approach when in need of a friendly word. Joe McBride, part of the Lisbon Lions' squad for the European Cup Final of 1967, said Fallon had a 'sixth sense' for spotting demoralised and disgruntled players in need of consolation and a positive word.

In the early months of Stein's tenure at Celtic Park, Fallon made a series of timely interventions. At the end of the 1964/65 season, the new manager planned a clearout of players he deemed surplus to requirements. 'Our players have had their chance,' he said after the humiliating 6-2 defeat at Falkirk. Twelve days later, on 26 April, Stein attended a board meeting with a list of players he wanted out of Celtic Park including John Hughes, Charlie Gallagher, and 'Jinky' Johnstone. It was Fallon's role to change Stein's mind.

Johnstone knew who he had to thank for his continued role at Paradise. 'Sean had a wee soft spot for me,' he said. 'If I was ever looking for a wee bit of comfort, you could be sure that Sean would take me to the side and give me a bit of insight.'

Sometimes, Stein needed a strong and honest dissenting voice.

* * *

Fallon, too, had laid many of the foundation stones that would become Stein's glory and memorial. All of the immortals of the Stein-Fallon era – bar Willie Wallace signed from Hearts in December 1966 – were already inside the gates of Paradise before the legendary manager's arrival in March 1965. They merely awaited the touch of iconoclastic genius that Stein possessed and which Fallon complemented with his own wit and wisdom and sheer dependability.

There were the Kelly Kids who Stein himself had coached and nurtured during his spell as reserve team trainer. Of the Lisbon Lions, Bertie Auld, Stevie Chalmers, John Clark, Tommy Gemmell, Jimmy Johnstone, Bobby Lennox, Billy McNeill and Bobby Murdoch were all part of the Kelly youth policy from the 1950s.

Fallon, too, played a major role in developing and transforming many of these players' careers. Auld, for example, was a Fallon signing during the interregnum between the McGrory and the Stein eras.

According to McGrory, now watching events from his office in charge of publicity, Auld's return from Birmingham City in January 1965 was 'almost as significant as that of Jock Stein a few months later'.

There is some controversy over Auld's signing. In Archie Macpherson's biography of Stein, he states categorically that the Hibernian manager 'engineered everything' from his Edinburgh base. Brian Wilson, the author of an official history of Celtic and a former non-executive director of the club with access to past boardroom minutes, said, 'It was Fallon who persuaded McGrory and Kelly that he should travel south to bring Auld back from Birmingham City for an £11,000 transfer fee and, for the player himself, the deposit on a house in Glasgow.' Stein, in fact, had counselled against the return of Celtic's prodigal son. Fallon and the Hibernian manager had stayed in constant touch since Stein's departure for Dunfermline in 1960. Stein had warned Fallon about Auld. 'You're signing trouble there,' he had said.

Whatever the truth, it was undeniable that Auld became the creative heartbeat of Stein's nine-in-a-row immortals and remained so until his departure for Hibernian in 1971.

Fallon also signed the Lisbon Lions goalkeeper Ronnie Simpson, a shrewd capture from Hibernian for a bargain basement £2,000. Simpson, the man who had dared to ask Stein for more and been frozen from the first team as a result, went on in 1967 to win the European Cup and both Scotland's Player of the Year award and his first international cap at the age of 36.

Later, Fallon was responsible for the signatures of Kenny Dalglish – a fanatical Rangers devotee – and Danny McGrain, both indispensable members of the Quality Street Gang who took on the mantle of Celtic heroes once Stein began to break up the Lisbon Lions team.

Stein's assistant was far from being Stein's shadow or Stein's stooge. Credit is due to the Celtic manager for his delegation of duties to Fallon, not something he initially found easy. The assistant manager's book of contacts and his transparent honesty and strength of character in dealing with people from all walks of life proved crucial in maintaining a constant supply of talented youngsters to replenish the Celtic ranks.

'When it came to going out to a player's house and talking to the parents, there was no one better,' McGrain admitted. 'Sean's blarney, his whole relaxed, reassuring demeanour, would put anyone at ease. I'm sure he charmed a hundred players and their parents like he did with me and my mum and dad because he was just someone you immediately trusted and warmed to. Everyone could see the kindness in Sean.'

Fallon had the gift of an eye for players that Kelly and Stein both relied upon. With Dalglish, for example, the scouts and management at

Rangers had decided the boy lacked pace but Fallon saw, as he put it, that 'he was fast in the head'.

Later, too, Fallon's signings included Lou Macari, recommended by a bookmaker; Davie Hay, a tip from a priest; and Tommy Burns, endorsed by a car dealer.

Everyone trusted Fallon and, without him as his faithful ally, it is doubtful Stein would have become the legend and the fairytale winner of nine-in-a-row. Often forgotten, too, is the fine job of caretaker manager Fallon did during that month and a half between McGrory's shift upstairs to the press office and Stein's arrival from Hibernian.

By the time of Stein's arrival on 9 March 1965, Fallon's charges had put together a run of six successive victories, including an 8-0 demolition of Aberdeen, a Scottish Cup quarter-final victory over Queen's Park – the one for which Stein decided a win bonus was inappropriate – and a double over the eventual champions, Kilmarnock.

What might have happened if the original plan of Bob Kelly to replace McGrory with Fallon had come to fruition?

* * *

With typical modesty, Fallon understood there were aspects of Stein's character – his anger, his volatility, his need to control – that the assistant manager could never have replicated. Fallon recognised, too, that these ingredients were essential to Stein's recipe of success.

'I knew at the time,' he said later, 'a lot of my work was going unnoticed by most people, but I wasn't in the job for recognition. I was there to do my best for Celtic.' That Sean Fallon did until his brutal sacking by Desmond White in May 1978.

The Stein-Fallon axis was the rock on which Celtic dominance of domestic football for the nine years 1965 to 1974 – and the conquest of Europe in 1967 – was built.

Its only parallel in the world of football was the teams created in England at Derby County and at Nottingham Forest by the prodigious partnership of Brian Clough and Peter Taylor. Interesting, too, that here Clough was the public face, the celebrity, and Taylor was the stabilising influence, the worker behind the scenes, the talent scout supreme.

The truth is neither Stein nor Fallon – and neither Clough nor Taylor – could have achieved their immortal accomplishments without the other.

Stein accepted as much when he said, 'Our success comes from the feeling of everyone working with each other, everyone helping each other.'

Fallon was the soul of Celtic Football Club, something that never went missing while he was employed within the gates of Paradise.

After Fallon's dismissal, he was denied a promised testimonial by White. His monumental contribution to the club he loved throughout his life was recognised, however, when Fallon was invited by Neil Lennon and the Celtic hierarchy to Flag Day in 2012 to celebrate his 90th birthday. As Peter Lawwell, Celtic's then chief executive, said, 'Sean embodied all that is good about Celtic: its values, its roots in Ireland; its pride in Scotland; its competitiveness; its sense of fair play; its decency; its leadership … You look at Sean as a player, a coach, an assistant manager, and he was someone who would always make you feel proud … to be a Celtic fan.'

The First Nine-in-a-Row: 1965–1974

Turning Points

1. FIRST LOVE, FIRST SUCCESS
24 APRIL 1965
SCOTTISH CUP FINAL, CELTIC V
DUNFERMLINE ATHLETIC

Success breeds success. Winning is a habit and winning trophies is the best kind of winning habit.

Stein knew that but wasn't sure Kelly quite understood that winning was even more important than playing the game.

While he was happy to spend hours chewing the football fat with his chairman – and his assistant manager – Stein knew too that talk was cheap.

At Dunfermline, his first battle as a manager was to avoid relegation. Within ten seconds of his debut in the dugout, Stein's new club had scored against Celtic and were on their way to a 3-2 victory. Six wins from six games saved the Pars from the drop and, during that sequence, Stein displayed all of his revolutionary dark arts of scheming and manipulation. He had assessed the upcoming game against Kilmarnock as pivotal to his club's chances of survival. Willie Waddell's Kilmarnock were to play Clyde in an FA Cup semi-final which necessitated the rearrangement of the league fixture against Dunfermline. Against the wishes of his club's hierarchy, Stein persuaded Waddell to agree on a Monday-night match. As Stein put it, 'Kilmarnock would either be high after winning, low after a defeat, or worried about a replay. Anyway … we would play them while their concentration was low.' A 1-0 win for Stein's club duly ensued and relegation was avoided.

Within 13 months of his arrival, Stein had his first trophy at Dunfermline, a 2-0 triumph over Celtic in a replayed Scottish Cup Final.

Now, four years later, Stein faced Dunfermline in the 1965 final as the new manager of Celtic, and he knew only too well its significance for his future at Paradise.

Celtic had not won a Scottish Cup since 1954. Their last major trophy had been the miraculous League Cup victory over Rangers to the tune of 7-1 in 1957.

For Celtic supporters, the charms of dining out on this spectacular success eight years ago had begun to pall.

By hook or by crook or whatever it took, for Stein, winning against Dunfermline was all that mattered.

* * *

Celtic's opponents at Hampden Park were a fine side, curated and crafted by Stein himself. Dunfermline had been chasing a league and cup double, eventually losing the 1964/65 league title, finishing third, only one point behind both Kilmarnock and Hearts. A 1-1 draw at East End Park with St Johnstone on the previous Saturday had proved fatal.

The disappointment may have darkened their preparations for the cup final. Alex Ferguson, the Pars' leading goalscorer, was dropped for the big game after missing chances against the Saints. Stein was never a man to worry too much about the opposition but he must have permitted himself at least a hint of a smile when he heard the news Ferguson was not to play. In fact, in the final match of the league season on the Wednesday evening following the final, the future Rangers striker, and future manager of Manchester United, was reinstated in the Dunfermline team and scored in a 5-1 rout of Celtic.

Stein was never happy to lose but still permitted himself a wry smile when he considered what might have occurred in the final had Ferguson been selected to play.

In his three seasons with Dunfermline, Ferguson scored 90 goals in 136 appearances. Stein's successor in the Pars' dugout, the managerial rookie Willie Cunningham, had revealed his hand of cards and held back his ace.

Still, Dunfermline were a strong favourite with the bookies to lift the cup for the second time in their history.

Neither team's build-up to the big occasion was ideal. Dunfermline lost the league title and Celtic lost the match before the final, 2-1 at home to Partick Thistle. In his programme notes for the game against the Jags, Stein vented his displeasure at his new club's recent performances, 'Our own staff of players have had their chance – there can be no justified complaints if we seek to strengthen our team. And this is going to be done irrespective of what happens within the next week or two. This will not make pleasant reading – it is not intended to do so.' Stein's patience, always in short supply, was exhausted.

Inconsistency of performance had been the bane of the new manager's life so far at Celtic Park.

Earlier in the month, he rejoiced in the dominant performance in a 4-0 victory at Hibernian and tore out hair by the handful when defeated 6-2 at Falkirk. Stein was in no mood for compromise and a clearout of players he regarded as dead wood and those talents who burned bright one week and dimmed the next was imminent.

It is easy to look with hindsight and from the lofty heights of Stein's later achievements and forget the troubled days and weeks leading up to the cup final against Dunfermline.

Lose, as universally predicted, and Stein might have found one too many enemies in the boardroom.

* * *

The Hampden Saturday was bathed in spring sunshine and Stein was smiling as the players boarded the bus from Largs.

Perhaps he was convinced his broadside against the players in the programme notes and his anger in the dressing room after the midweek defeat by Thistle would have restored the squad's motivation. Stein was always better with sticks than with carrots. On the other hand, maybe the manager was smiling, singing almost, as a result of his cunning tactical tweaks to the Celtic formation and his mind games with the media concerning team selections.

All five forward positions were switched. Bertie Auld, nominally a left-winger, was given licence to roam wherever he felt he might best influence the game. Billy McNeill, stalwart centre-half, was encouraged to trespass beyond the confines of his own half of the field, to provide an additional attacking option at set pieces. This was revolutionary stuff from Stein, heresy to the orthodoxy that defenders should only defend. The final masterstroke from the new manager was to move Bobby Murdoch back from the inside-right position within the forward line to right-half where he excelled immediately.

Hampden was crammed with an officially announced 108,000 spectators although more realistic estimates suggested as many as 135,000 fans, mostly Celtic, were in attendance.

Dunfermline, in their traditional black-and-white-striped shirts, kicked off into a strong headwind, beginning the match at a high tempo, and deservedly took the lead in the 16th minute when the Celtic goalkeeper John Fallon misjudged a high ball caught in the gusting, eddying wind. The ball fell to Dunfermline's winger, Jackie Sinclair – later to play top-flight football in England with Leicester City, Newcastle United and Sheffield Wednesday – whose shot was deflected into the path of Harry Melrose, a stalwart of Stein's former side, who turned the ball cleverly into the unguarded Celtic goal.

For the next quarter of an hour, the Glasgow team struggled to hold and retain possession, and faced a confident Dunfermline XI exhibiting their neat and effective style of football that had been well schooled by their former manager.

Gradually, Celtic began to work their way back into the match and, just after the half hour, Charlie Gallagher unleashed a furious shot from so far out it looked as if it had to travel from Glasgow to Fife. The Dunfermline crossbar quivered and time stood still as fans watched breathless with either fear or excitement. Only Bertie Auld seemed alive to the potential of the situation, racing in from the edge of the penalty area to head the ball home.

Among the Celtic support squeezed on to the uncovered and vertiginous terracing behind the Dunfermline goal, joy was unconfined.

Two minutes before half-time, however, John McLaughlin, a former Stein signing from Millwall, just relegated from England's third tier of football, sent a long, low shot skimming like a stone from beach to sea. Fallon scrambled across his goal line but was unable to prevent the ball from finding its target in the corner of the net.

At the interval Stein was calm, reassuring, yet his desire to win was an electric current travelling from the positive manager to players who were all too often negative, sometimes, switched off altogether. Stein determined that the second half of this match would be the last chance for many of his charges. In spite of the moderating influences of both

Fallon and Kelly, Stein had made up his mind already on many of the players who had blown hot and cold since his arrival. 'Jinky' Johnstone, who had played against the Jags in midweek, would play no part in this cup final, and would play no part in Stein's planned revival of the East End club. The diminutive winger was inconsolable. 'They're going to let me go,' Johnstone told friends while attempting to staunch floods of tears. Both Motherwell and Tottenham Hotspur had already made inquiries and had not been rebuffed by Stein.

At half-time, Fallon had been expecting to play the good cop to Stein's bad cop and was surprised at his boss's calm demeanour. If Celtic failed to turn around the deficit, he anticipated an unpleasant hour or two in the company of Stein and Kelly. The assistant manager was surprised Stein indulged the chairman in his desire to chew the football fat at the conclusion of every game. Fallon, though, had determined on one more attempt to save Johnstone's career at Celtic Park. A come-from-behind cup triumph might put his boss in a more amenable frame of mind.

'Don't worry,' Stein told his charges as they tightened their bootlaces in preparation for a return to the field of play. 'Just keep on plugging away and the rewards will come.'

The blustery spring wind was in Celtic faces as the second half commenced. It had been a dereliction of duty on the Glasgow team's part to fail to take advantage of the wind at their backs in the opening phase of the game.

The second equaliser arrived in good time after 52 minutes. A Bobby Lennox cross from the left wing skimmed the surface of the Hampden turf and Auld was waiting at the far post to tap the ball into the net.

In response, however, Dunfermline attacked in wave after wave, and the turning point of the match came when John Fallon arched and twisted backwards to save a fierce shot from the Pars' right-winger, Alex Edwards.

After a Dunfermline goal was disallowed, disillusionment seeped into the bones and hearts of the Fifers and, in the 81st minute, their worst fears were realised.

A perfect inswinging cross from a corner was provided by Charlie Gallagher and McNeill's forehead made perfect contact with the ball.

The Celtic centre-half had run 30 yards deep into the Dunfermline danger area in order to meet his date with destiny.

For seconds that seemed like minutes as time stretched towards eternity, Hampden's huge amphitheatre was stunned into silence, as if McNeill's header was too much to take in, as if the meaning of this winning goal was expanded along with time and space in a universe inflating too quickly to comprehend.

Then came the roar, the bedlam, the wild rejoicings, and the future. At the other end, Fallon swung like a human pendulum from the crossbar of his goal. John Clark, moved from half-back by Stein to sweep up problems behind McNeill, noticed the badge of honour blood on his shirt, the result of a nose injury sustained in the heat of the battle.

Celtic became the first team in the history of the cup to win after twice falling behind. It had been won, according to Raymond Jacobs in the *Glasgow Herald*, through the 'old-fashioned virtue of unwavering determination'.

For Stein there would come a time for pretty football, but not just yet.

Auld, Sean Fallon's signing, and scorer of two goals, said the image of the celebrating crowd was 'ingrained in my heart'.

Stein admitted afterwards, 'It wouldn't have gone as well for Celtic, had they not have won this game.'

* * *

Adjacent to the Central Hotel, where the post-match party was being held, a small man with spectacles descended from the team coach. In his arms was the cup Celtic had just won.

His name was Jimmy Gribben and he carried the silverware from bus to hotel lobby, pausing briefly to raise it over his head for the adoration of the gathering crowds of fans.

'You'll be here as long as I am, Jimmy,' Stein whispered in his ear.

Inside and outside of the hotel both fans and players continued to party long into the Glasgow night.

* * *

For those with sufficiently clear heads the following morning, the *Express* noted that 'Parkhead was Paradise once more'.

Sean Fallon, at home and at peace at last, sighed with relief that there would now be no wholesale clearout of the players he loved.

Bob Kelly bathed in the warm glow of vindication, permitted himself the luxury of consideration of the possibility that there might be no more abuse hurled in his direction from Celtic supporters weary at the lack of success, weary at the ongoing domination of the Paradise boardroom by his family.

'It's your triumph, too, Boss,' Stein said to McGrory. 'They're your players, you know.'

Kelly approached Stein, considered a small reprimand concerning some of the robust tackles perpetrated by some of the Celtic footballers, but thought better of it.

* * *

2. THE TACKLE
23 OCTOBER 1965
LEAGUE CUP FINAL, CELTIC V RANGERS

It was not something Sean Fallon would have done. Neither was it something Kelly would have countenanced had he known of Stein's determination to target Rangers with a brand of physicality that trespassed on the bounds of assault.

Stein had achieved his initial target. In April 1965 he had reacquainted Celtic with the joy of victory, with the triumph of achievement, and he had done so by preaching the virtues of discipline and dedication.

Even in his own estimation, his imaginative training routines, his tactical intelligence, were lesser components of his masterplan than the inauguration of a thoroughgoing Protestant work ethic throughout the football club.

Celtic had won their first trophy since 1957 but had not yet defeated Rangers in a game that really mattered.

Inside the new manager's psyche there already burned a fire whose flames had been fanned by his shunning by childhood friends in Burnbank, and by his own father's refusal to concede defeat in his Protestant ambitions for his son.

It hurt Stein that George had never once wished him good luck either as a player or now as manager of Celtic. It was this wound, this pain, that gave Stein his cutting edge, his monstrous desire to overturn the natural order of matters football in the city of Glasgow.

Jim Craig, a Celt on amateur terms at the time of Stein's arrival, said his manager 'detested Rangers'. Craig suggested that Stein's obsession with beating Rangers was because he had 'crossed over'. There was nothing so republican, so Celtic, than a former loyalist, a former bluenose.

* * *

Celtic had given best to Rangers, and had surrendered even in the eyes of many supporters, since the heady days of the double of 1954.

Since then, the Ibrox club had won six league titles, four Scottish Cups and five League Cups. Celtic had won just three League Cups, a tournament considered by many Scots to be little more than a worthless bauble. Celtic had won fewer than a quarter of the Old Firm derbies and, in the early years of the 1960s, the East End club were burdened by an inferiority complex to match their underachievement. Sometimes, that sense of subordination was laughed off by players who had been permitted to indulge in dilettante behaviour both on and off the field of play. As Stein said on his arrival from Hibernian, 'I'm tired of hearing about Celtic's potential, Celtic's bad luck, Celtic's missed chances.'

Stein revealed to Sean Fallon shortly afterwards, 'It's Rangers I'm after, and a league title after 12 lost years.'

The first opportunity to challenge Rangers' pre-eminence, aside from an encouraging but unimportant win in the Glasgow Cup six days after the Scottish Cup triumph, was a league game at Ibrox in September 1965.

Stein was disappointed and apoplectic after a routine Rangers victory in which Celtic had attacked and the team in blue had defended as well as scored one more goal than their opponents. Nothing much, it seemed, had changed.

The next chance to overturn the old order would come in the League Cup Final in the following month.

The seeds of Celtic's performance that autumn day at Hampden may have been sown in the away dressing room at East End Park on the Wednesday after the Scottish Cup win over Dunfermline. As fate would have it, the fixture list provided the Pars with an early opportunity for revenge which they took to the tune of a 5-1 humiliation of the visitors. The Celtic players trooped from the pitch, hangdog looks aplenty, but not one suspecting what awaited them. After all, they had won the cup only a few days previously, and that evening's debacle was last-game-of-the-season unimportant.

Bobby Lennox reported that 'the walls of the stadium must have been shaking' as Stein let rip with foul-mouthed tirades and with individual eviscerations of each player's lack of character, lack of backbone. 'We were like jelly,' Lennox added. From that moment, Stein ruled by fear.

Sean Fallon could pacify, and could talk tearful players round if he wished, but Stein would not countenance another performance without heart, without sinew, without mental steel.

The calm, urbane persona the manager had adopted before the Scottish Cup Final in April had disappeared. In the week leading up to the League Cup Final in October, players had to deal with a tense and tetchy manager, one who prowled the corridors of Celtic Park by day and hotel corridors at Seamill by sleepless night after sleepless night. His assistant, Fallon, said Stein knew Rangers' players, their strengths, their weaknesses, better than they knew themselves. 'He had eyes in the back of his head, he had spies, he had gossipers, he just drew on everybody.'

On the day of the final, Stein talked of the first 50-50 ball. 'Win it,' he growled. 'Just fucking win it.'

He took Ian Young, the Celtic right-back, to one side. 'Sort Johnston out first chance you get.' Willie Johnston was Rangers' left-winger and a key man in their attack.

* * *

The Tackle occurred in the very first minute of the game.

The ball found its way out to Rangers' left touchline where Johnston anticipated control and swift movement towards the Celtic goal. He had not reckoned on his direct opponent's fast and scything challenge that bypassed the football and almost cut the winger in half. 'Your first tackle has to make a difference,' Stein told Young as he left the dressing room. It did. Players paused while Johnston lay on the turf. It was as if Young had assassinated his rival in a play of brutal power politics. When Johnston rose to his feet, he was booked for his pains by referee Hugh Phillips, along with Young, but Johnston played no further significant part in the game.

At half-time, with Celtic two goals to the good thanks to a penalty double from John Hughes, Stein reprimanded Young for his reckless tackle:

'You were lucky, son, you could have been sent off.'

Hypocrisy was not a characteristic notably associated with the Celtic manager but Stein had made it abundantly clear that any reduction of his team to ten men had to be compensated by the wiping out of an important player from the opposition.

Young later said he regretted his assault on Johnston for the rest of his life. It is hard, though, to imagine Stein feeling any contrition. For him, winning was a matter of life and death, but winning against Rangers was even more important than that.

Neither would many Celtic fans have shared any remorse with their solid, if unspectacular, right-back who became a cult hero on the terraces from that moment onwards.

The tackle was a statement, loud and clear, that a new Celtic was emerging, one that would no longer be bullied by their great rivals, one that would never again give occasion for their supporters to turn their backs on their team as they had in the replayed cup final of 1963.

In spite of a Young own goal when a shot from Rangers captain John Greig was palmed away by Ronnie Simpson on to the defender's face and into the net, Celtic held on to their victory with a calm and assured defensive display that frustrated and disconcerted their rivals in equal measure.

The headline writer in the *Glasgow Herald*, however, described the match as 'An Orgy of Crudeness'. In his match report, Raymond Jacobs suggested, 'When Celtic meet Rangers the meek do not inherit the earth; and war correspondents, rather than sports writers, should be despatched to these violent fronts.'

Stein did not care. Even Kelly, in spite of his protestations to the contrary, probably did not care. He could at last envision a future in which he was no longer subjected to abuse every time he made his way to his seat in the directors' box.

* * *

It had, though, been a close-run thing.

History hangs in perpetual balance, depends on myriad moments of chance, when alternative universes are still open for business.

Perhaps, in some alternative, but equally real, time and place, Jim Forrest, the Rangers centre-forward, takes at least one of the two simple chances he creates for himself by bamboozling Billy McNeill with his pace and trickery. Both opportunities occurred before Celtic opened the scoring.

Maybe, in the 18th minute, Ronnie McKinnon, the Rangers defender, does not experience a moment of madness and raise his hand to push away a John Clark free kick. Maybe John Hughes misses the resultant penalty anyway. Ten minutes later, conceivably, the referee decides Davie Provan's mistimed tackle on Jimmy Johnstone is unworthy of a second penalty. Maybe the Rangers goalkeeper, Billie Ritchie, makes stronger contact with the ball sent spinning into the corner of the net by Hughes. Maybe Ian Young is sent off because of The Tackle.

In the real world, however, Celtic were two goals in front and the League Cup was theirs to throw away, something which the team of McGrory and Kelly might well have done. As Stein said afterwards, 'It would not have gone so well for Celtic had we not won today.'

* * *

When any era of dominance, whether of a sporting or of a political nature, begins to crumble, inevitably, some people are minded to violence.

With the Rangers players in their Hampden dressing room, and with Celtic parading their trophy around the perimeter of the pitch, some Ibrox fans climbed barriers and assaulted players and staff.

Young was struck and knocked to the ground as was the Celtic trainer and former player, Neilly Mochan. Fortunately, celebrating Celtic fans were models of restraint. The Scottish correspondent of *The Times* recalled an occasion in 1909 when both Celtic and Rangers fans rioted and burned goalposts and turnstiles at Hampden after the 36th Scottish Cup Final ended in a 2-2 draw.

Stein was relieved to see all his Celts return safely to the dressing room. He permitted himself a smile. Later, he would burst into song.

In his younger days, Stein had performed in the miners' welfare social clubs. 'Old Scots Mother of Mine' was a favourite. Nowadays, Stein sang everywhere, and the song was often Sinatra's 1964 hit, 'The Best Is Yet to Come'.

* * *

3. THE END OF THE IRON CURTAIN
3 JANUARY 1966
LEAGUE DIVISION ONE, CELTIC V RANGERS

If Sinatra was Stein's favourite, he loved, too, Danny Kaye's song, 'The Ugly Duckling', so often played on the BBC Light Programme's *Children's Favourites* by Uncle Mac, Derek McCulloch.

It brought him to the edge of tears.

He thought of that song as he plotted the next phase in his masterplan for Celtic: to turn his cup-winning ugly ducklings into beautiful swans that would not only win but win by playing free-flowing and attacking football.

By the turn of the year, after Celtic's 8-1 demolition of Morton on Christmas Day, it was nip and tuck at the top of the league. On the same festive day, Rangers had thrown away the opportunity of a clear lead heading into 1966 by losing at home to Dunfermline. The Ibrox club clung to top spot by the narrowest of margins, a superior goal average of 3.57 to Celtic's 3.53.

On New Year's Day, Rangers returned to form by thrashing Partick Thistle 4-0 and Celtic continued their unbeaten run of 13 league games with a 3-1 away victory at Clyde.

It was perhaps of some significance that the only Celtic defeat so far had come in Govan in September. That match attracted a huge, uncountable crowd. The Ibrox turnstiles were closed 25 minutes before kick-off but still spectators poured in through breached gates and over walls. The result, 2-1 to the home side, seemed to hinge on a strong wind which favoured Rangers in the first half and an injury to McNeill just as Celtic began a wind-assisted second-half rally. It was a scrappy, though thrilling, match, full of blood and thunder tackling.

Stein was distraught. It was nine years without a Celtic victory at the home of their deadly rivals.

* * *

The day of the return fixture dawned with a heavy frost and a rock hard playing surface at Paradise. At 1pm, an hour before the planned kick-off, the bulky figures of the referee, Tiny Wharton, and Stein appeared from the dressing rooms to inspect the pitch. Stein's limp appeared particularly noticeable. It was as if he were gesticulating with legs as well as hands in his attempts to persuade Wharton to allow the game to proceed. Garden forks were found and were prodded and poked into both goalmouths and centre field. Eventually, the two men shook hands in agreement.

No Rangers representative was present in these discussions. Scot Symon, who had been the Ibrox manager since the summer of 1954, and who was 11 years older than Stein and more than a generation behind his rival in terms of his approach to training, tactics, and the use and abuse of psychology, had missed a trick through his absence.

When the players appeared, Celtic's were wearing sandshoes and were keeping their feet far more easily than their traditionally shod opponents.

Fog, too, was hovering around and about the ground, an unwelcome and uninvited guest that would press its presence on its unwilling host before the start of the second half.

The game really should not have been played. Partick Thistle's home match, across Glasgow in Maryhill, was postponed. It was Stein's force of personality alone that ensured the agreement of Wharton.

It was Stein's faith, too, in the players he was moulding, that carried the day. Most managers, with his captain McNeill absent injured, would have been only too pleased to have the match postponed. Stein, though, was a force of nature in these early years as manager, utterly unopposable.

He was a betting man without fear, always ready to pluck another card from the dealer, to double his stakes at the racetrack and at the football, and, in doing so, transform outsiders into favourites.

Some of this rubbed off on his players, just enough, as it turned out, to transform ugly ducklings into swans.

* * *

By half-time, Stein's gamble looked to have failed. In spite of incessant Celtic pressure, in spite of a Rangers team hardly able to keep their balance on the treacherous surface, the Ibrox side were a goal to the good. Within two minutes, a shot from their inspirational right-half John Greig hit McNeill's replacement, John Cushley, and rebounded to Davie Wilson, who slotted the ball past Simpson in Celtic's goal.

It was the same old story of glorious failure. Some of the Celtic players may have been praying for the fog to come to their rescue, for it to descend so thickly that even Stein's powers of persuasion would be insufficient to prevent the game's abandonment. The second half, however, told a revolutionary story.

Since the end of World War Two, Rangers' success was built upon their defensive formation known as the 'Iron Curtain' and named after the defensive military line built across central Europe by the Soviet Union. Their legendary manager, Bill Struth, had won four league titles, four Scottish Cups and two League Cups between 1946 and his retirement in the summer of 1954. Symon had continued to build the Ibrox club's successes on similar foundations, winning six league championships, four Scottish Cups and four League Cups since his first trophy success in 1956.

The rocks at the heart of this system ten years later were McKinnon and Greig and both were outstanding throughout most of the new year match at the frozen Celtic Park. If Celtic were to overtake Rangers at the top of the league and stay there, the Iron Curtain had to be parted and thrown open so that the light of Stein's fluid, attacking football might shine and triumph.

The equaliser arrived five minutes after the restart. Tommy Gemmell crossed from the left wing, Joe McBride dummied, and Stevie Chalmers drove the ball into the back of the net.

Celtic took the lead with a little over 20 minutes left to play, when Charlie Gallagher's corner was glanced home by Chalmers.

In the 74th minute, John 'Yogi' Hughes slipped through the encroaching fog, skated over the icy ground, and skipped past a stumbling Davie Provan, who was enduring a nightmare match, and cut the ball back to the edge of the six-yard box where Gallagher was waiting to strike Celtic's third goal off the underside of the crossbar. With ten minutes remaining, Jimmy Johnstone touched a free kick to McBride who played a square pass towards Bobby Murdoch. Just in time, the referee opened his legs wide to let the ball through, and Celtic's right-half crashed his shot past Billy Ritchie in the Rangers goal.

Surely, nothing could now prevent joy unbounded and bliss beyond compare at Paradise. Some Celtic supporters, however, those of a glass-half-empty and a fearful persuasion, were pointing accusing fingers at the roils of fog swirling across the field of play.

On the rare occasions Rangers had ventured across the halfway line in the second half, it was impossible to see their players from behind the

Celtic goal. Likewise, Rangers fans interviewed after the game said they had seen none of the opposition's goals, and only guessed at the scoreline from eruptions of noise at the further end of the stadium.

Would Tiny Wharton abandon the game at this late stage? In the event, just before the 90 minutes were up, Johnstone's shot from distance rebounded from the foot of a post and Chalmers netted from the rebound and claimed his hat-trick and possession of the match ball.

Ritchie would have seen nothing of Johnstone's original shot, blinded by the fog, as the fifth goal was followed swiftly by the final whistle.

The result was an utter humbling of Rangers from which they were to struggle to recover for years ahead.

It was the beginning of the end for Scott Symon in the Rangers dugout and the very end of football's notorious Iron Curtain.

* * *

As for the development of Celtic's style of football under Stein, a report card at the end of the autumn term of 1965 might have shown 'satisfactory work and progress' but, after the new year fixture at Paradise, those assessing Stein's team might have amended earlier comments to something like 'signs of imagination and excellence'.

For individuals, too, men such as Chalmers, who had been the butt of cruel jokes and savage abuse from discontents on the terraces at Celtic Park, there was redemption and vindication. Murdoch and Gallagher were also gaining recognition and appreciation from fans who had previously reserved their judgements. Hughes, infuriatingly inconsistent, had been a world-beater in the new year match.

Improvements in individuals and improvements in teamwork were all a result of the demonic bullying perfectionism of a man called Stein. 'Not too bad this afternoon,' he said after the humbling of his opponents.

It was left to Sean Fallon, after Stein had left the dressing room, to tell the players, 'What the boss really means is you were bloody sensational today.'

In the silence that followed the players' raucous shouts of joy and exultation, Stein's tuneful voice could be heard in the corridor outside:

'Still it's a real good bet, the best is yet to come.'

There was merit, too, in the big man's optimism. Celtic's margin of victory – 5-1 – was the widest over their traditional rivals since September

1938 when they won 6-2 with that day's hat-trick hero Malky MacDonald, who later managed Scotland for two matches in 1966.

Celtic's unbeaten run now stretched to 22 matches and they were two points clear of Rangers with a game in hand.

A first league title since 1954 was theirs to lose.

* * *

Lose it, though, they nearly did, and in cavalier fashion that had Stein arriving even earlier at Celtic Park after sleepless nights, that had him prowling the stadium corridors like a hungry ghost, that had him gambling harder on the horses, that had him seeking solace in Sean Fallon's friendship, and even had him turning to Bob Kelly for pearls of wisdom.

Distracted perhaps by barely believable European adventures behind the Soviet Iron Curtain, Celtic lost in January to Aberdeen and Hearts, and in February at Annfield, the home of Stirling Albion. A recovery of form in the spring combined with a disastrous March 1966 for Rangers in which the Ibrox club failed to win a single match and lost at Falkirk and Dundee United left Stein and his team on the brink of triumph as April turned to May.

The First Nine-in-a-Row: 1965–1974

The Championships

1. ONE-IN-A-ROW
7 MAY 1966
LEAGUE DIVISION ONE,
MOTHERWELL V CELTIC

The initial championship in Celtic's first nine-in-a-row was won on a sunny May afternoon at a packed-to-the-rafters Fir Park, Motherwell, and, with a last-minute goal in the last match of the season, needs to be set in context.

In truth, Celtic had not been a dominating force in Scottish football since the days before and during World War One. Yes, the Parkhead team won occasional league titles after their 15th triumph in 1919 but, as the 1965/66 season opened with a 4-0 thrashing of Dundee United at Tannadice, their total of championships stood at a miserly 20.

Five leagues in 45 years. By contrast, the number of league titles won by Rangers stood at 32.

Throughout those long lean years, Celtic were akin to a box of fireworks left over from the previous year and kept in a damp cellar. A rocket or a banger or two provided occasional flashes of brilliance, moments of sound and fury – the 7-1 League Cup win in 1957 against Rangers was the brightest spark of all – and there were innumerable false dawns when the blue touchpaper was lit and the firework flamed all too briefly with solitary championships in 1922, 1926, 1936, 1938 and 1954, but these years were times of damp squibs and of frustration and fickle form.

Since their last title, won in 1954, Celtic had been a shambles of a football club. There was some reassurance for supporters in the team's image as a freewheeling rattle bag of mercurial talents especially when compared with the stern and frowning disciplinarians of Rangers, replete with their Protestant work ethic, and their stubbornly tedious winning habits. Still, though, fans of the East End club had to rely on distant memories most of the time. Stories of the great League Cup rout of Rangers in 1957 were told and retold in Glasgow pubs and on the banked terraces of Celtic Park, in default of present success. Dreams were childish delusions.

In the post-war East End of Glasgow, in times of rationing and poverty, in times of slum clearances and gang violence, the diet of Celtic's supporters was thin gruel. Like Oliver Twist, fans asked for more, but they were beaten and sent back to the workhouse for more punishment.

In season 1963/64, Rangers secured a second domestic treble and, in the process, defeated Celtic five times out of five.

The Celtic manager throughout these years of dearth and drought was Jimmy McGrory. In his 20 years in nominal charge – though with only limited authority as Kelly was chairman for 18 of those years – the club legend won just one league championship, in 1954.

It is a testament to his abilities and accomplishments as a player that McGrory is still revered at Celtic Park.

Between 1923 and 1937 McGrory scored 522 times for Celtic, including 55 hat-tricks and one haul of eight goals in one match against Dunfermline in 1928. He is Celtic's record goalscorer and – statistically – the greatest striker in British football history.

Not all illustrious footballers, however, make successful managers. He was too nice a man to provide Celtic with strong leadership. He disliked and avoided conflict, kow-towing to his chairman, and allowing players to indulge in a culture in which they played when they felt like playing, and this, too, in days when 'player power' was a phrase yet to be invented. Paddy Crerand, who left Celtic for Manchester United in 1964, and who had watched enviously as the young Jock Stein coached the Celtic reserve team, said, 'Jimmy just didn't do discipline.'

To many Celtic fans awaiting the commencement of another new season of fresh hopes in August 1965, there was optimism as, in Stein's two months in charge at the fag-end of the previous season, the new man had not only won the Scottish Cup, beating Dunfermline 3-2, the club's first senior trophy since 1957, but had also defeated Rangers 2-1 in the Glasgow Cup semi-final.

To more cynical observers, however, the crushing defeats in the league championship against Falkirk, Partick Thistle and Dunfermline in April 1965 were evidence of a continued wayward and wilful streak in the players at Stein's command.

It was encouraging, therefore, but no more than that, when Celtic won their opening game of the 1965/66 league season 4-0 at Dundee United.

Still, though, to all but children who had never known dashed hopes and the disasters of the preceding generations, glasses raised in East End pubs and clubs on that Saturday evening were almost all half empty rather than half full.

That is, until the best beer began to talk its talk later in the evening, by which time Jock Stein was the Lord Jesus Himself who could walk on water, who could turn dross and disappointment into cups and league titles, and the goalscorers that day were honoured as heroes in tuneless songs and in the wisdom of last-orders whiskies.

For the record, the legendary strikers of footballs that glorious day were Divers, McBride, Young and Gemmell.

John Divers was the privileged scorer of the first goal in the first match of the first nine-in-a-row. On one less happy occasion, he was the man disciplined by Bob Kelly for forgetting his boots when due to play Hearts in August 1963. He was also the great nephew of the Celtic legend Patsy Gallacher, who scored 195 goals for the green and whites in 464 appearances between 1911 and 1925. Divers scored 110 goals himself and is entitled to both affection and respect among Celtic supporters past and present and deserves more than the footnote in history status that is his more usual fate.

Joe McBride, Jock Stein's first signing, from Motherwell for £22,000, was the scorer of the second goal in Celtic's first nine, a shot screwed into the net from 12 yards from an excellent pass from Steve Chalmers. It was McBride's first of 31 goals scored in that celebrated season. He was the joint top goalscorer in Division One alongside a certain Alex Ferguson, who then plied his trade with Dunfermline Athletic. Stein's predecessor, McGrory, later named McBride 'the best Celtic centre-forward I've ever seen play'. Certainly, in this season, he was all but impossible to contain inside opposition penalty boxes. There were complaints – someone once said 'all that McBride does is score goals' – but then some people are never satisfied.

The third goalscorer against Dundee United was the full-back Ian Young, who slotted home from the penalty spot after Bobby Lennox had been brought down by the close attentions of both Tommy Millar and Don Mackay. Two months later Young earned enduring fame as he set the tone for Celtic in the League Cup Final against Rangers with The Tackle on his opposing winger, Willie Johnston. Young had given due notice Celtic would no longer be the paper tigers of Glasgow derbies.

The final goal was a screamer from Celtic's other full-back, Tommy Gemmell, who returned a weak defensive clearance with interest from 20 yards. One report suggested Gemmell 'surprised even himself' by the success of his speculative shot. His goal at Tannadice Park was one of 63 the marauding defender claimed for Celtic. Famously, he is one of only two British defenders to score in two European Cup finals. Phil Neal scored for Liverpool against Borussia Mönchengladbach in 1977 and against Roma in 1984 and Gemmell's goals came in Celtic's 1967 win against Inter Milan and in the defeat against Feyenoord in 1970.

Sadly, Gemmell, in his autobiography, *Lion Heart*, revealed that both he and Ian Young, both Protestants, had been on the receiving end of sectarian abuse from a handful of team-mates who were keen on establishing an all-Catholic team during the 1960s. Names were not named but when Gemmell's book, ghosted by Graham McColl, appeared in 2005, it gave pause for thought once more concerning the delays to Jock Stein's appointment in 1965. Maybe it was the Celtic players who Kelly was concerned not to offend by appointing a Protestant.

* * *

Early optimism, however, already dented by defeat at Ibrox in September, was tempered further during a dismal home draw with Partick Thistle in November in which a former Celt, Jim Conway, scored a deserved equaliser for the Jags after Bobby Murdoch failed to clear the ball decisively.

Raymond Jacobs, preaching caution in the *Glasgow Herald*, did little to lift the mood of disillusionment descending on the Celtic support: 'When Mr J. Stein took control of Celtic in the spring he inherited a group of players wedded to a style of strong running, spirit, and stamina. He has appreciably changed none of these elements or their practitioners. His achievement has been to impose on them consistency of performance.'

Jacobs was an astute observer of all things Celtic and it was interesting his downplaying of revolutionary changes by Stein and also fascinating to note from his report how far Celtic still had to progress under their new boss:

'Even the most successful theme requires variations, otherwise movements become no more effective than telegraphed punches.'

He even singled out Billy McNeill, future captain of the Lisbon Lions, who ended his career with 822 appearances for Celtic and 31 major trophies for his club as player and manager, for criticism, saying the 'instability of Celtic's defence derived almost entirely from McNeill's lack of confidence'.

By the end of Christmas Day 1965, however, Celtic fans were beginning to believe in Santa Claus as they tucked into their turkeys. Rangers had suffered their first league defeat of the season, 3-2 at home to Dunfermline, and Celtic had beaten Morton 8-1.

What was now needed was a victory over Rangers in the traditional new year derby and, when it came, joyously so in the bleakest of midwinter settings, fans from the East End and beyond began to believe.

The overturning of the Glasgow supremacy of Rangers had been achieved, first by determination and tackling of unparalleled ferocity in the League Cup victory, and now by imaginative, adventurous, high-speed creativity that would be a mark of Stein's Celtic over the forthcoming years.

Celtic's attempt to win their first league title since 1954 was almost derailed by the second leg of a European Cup Winners' Cup quarter-final inside the Soviet Union against Dynamo Kiev. The match prior to travelling east was lost 3-1 in Aberdeen and brought to an end a run of 24 competitive games without defeat. The flight to Tbilisi was bedevilled by diplomatic incidents at the height of the Cold War – and by chairman Kelly's insistence on using Aer Lingus in spite of the USSR having no diplomatic relations with the Irish Republic – and the journey time was a gruelling 31 hours. The match itself was exacting and exhausting although ultimately triumphant, a 1-1 draw securing Celtic's passage to the semi-finals. Delays and detours on the return leg of the journey meant the team did not arrive back in Glasgow until 11pm on Friday with a league game against Hearts in Edinburgh just 16 hours away. It was lost 3-2 and Celtic's lead over Rangers also disappeared.

When Celtic stunned Rangers early in the new year, they were two points clear of their rivals with a game in hand. Afterwards, the Ibrox men won back-to-back away matches against St Johnstone 3-0 and Stirling Albion 2-0 followed by successive home victories over St Mirren (4-1) and Hibernian (5-1). Celtic, by contrast, had won three and lost two. Their lead had disappeared once more and, with it, their place as favourites for the league title.

On Saturday, 26 February, both rivals looked to have comfortably winnable fixtures. Rangers duly thrashed Hamilton Academical 4-0 to extend their winning sequence to five. Celtic's game was against Stirling Albion, then fourth from bottom of the 18-team Division One. Albion, wearing striking tangerine jerseys and stockings, looked like Orangemen from the days of King Billy, in stark contrast to Celtic's Irish green and white.

The home team, kicking uphill on their sloped pitch in the first half, played like soldiers from the Battle of the Boyne too. By half-time there had been no goals. During the interval, Stein ordered his troops to shoot on sight, but it was the Binos who scored the only goal of the match seven minutes from time. Three consecutive surrenders for Celtic on the road and glasses in East End drinking houses were now no longer merely half empty. It was all over for yet another season of disappointments and dismal failures.

The month of March, however, told a different tale. Both Glasgow teams worked their way to the Scottish Cup Final but Rangers failed to win any of their four league matches and, after a 3-2 victory at Parkhead over St Johnstone on 12 March, Celtic reclaimed top spot in the league championship. It was an astonishing collapse by the Ibrox club.

In East End Catholic churches, in the parish of St Anne's in particular, candles were lit in thanksgiving for answered prayers and Masses were offered for the future success of Celtic and the players. Just as Celtic had been founded in 1887 to 'put food on the tables of the East End poor', St Anne's had been formed two years later to serve additional needs of the Irish poor including a children's refuge and hostel.

For Rangers to lose 3-2 at Falkirk might be regarded as misfortune; to draw at home to Hearts and away at Kilmarnock looked like carelessness, but to lose, in addition, at Dundee United, just had to be divine intervention.

Celtic, meanwhile, followed up their win over the Saints with a 7-1 victory at Hamilton, a draw at Firhill against Partick Thistle, and a further emphatic 2-0 win at Kilmarnock.

By the end of April 1966, Celtic were level on points with Rangers, but topped the Division One table on goal average. The Hoops had two games to play and their fierce city rivals only one. A win against Dunfermline on Wednesday, 4 May would probably be sufficient to claim a first championship since 1954.

If, however, Rangers were to beat Clyde at Ibrox, and if Celtic were to lose to the Pars, all bets would be off. Clyde were mid-table at best but Dunfermline were one of the best teams in the land, in fourth place in the league table, one point behind third-placed Kilmarnock and with a game in hand. The Pars had won the Scottish Cup as recently as 1961, beating Celtic 2-0 in a replayed final, and in the previous season they had been favourites to beat the Hoops in another final confrontation but eventually lost 3-2. There was, too, the Jock Stein connection. It was Celtic's current manager who had transformed Dunfermline from relegation candidates to challengers at the top table.

Nerves were frayed, fingernails bitten to the quick, as fans flocked to Celtic Park, edged through the turnstiles, and lit cigarettes as they found places on the packed terraces.

Only 10,600 souls arrived at Ibrox, suggesting little faith in their chances of overhauling their rivals from across the Clyde, but the Light Blues edged ahead after six minutes through Jimmy Millar from a cross by Willie Henderson, 'maintaining to the last their admirably persistent challenge', as was reported in the *Herald*.

Soon, too, just before the half hour, Dunfermline took the lead at Celtic Park. The heavy leather ball 'trundled' past Ronnie Simpson in the home goal. Silence and disaffected disbelief reigned in the Jungle and elsewhere in Paradise. Five minutes later, however, Bobby Lennox equalised, heading the ball out of the Pars goalkeeper's hands. By half-time, news had filtered through to both stadiums. Rangers were two goals to the good – their second strike scored by David Wilson – and would return to the top of the table if the 1-1 scoreline stayed the same at Celtic Park.

Celtic, in the second half, attacked, and then attacked some more. On the hour Lennox took aim at the whites of Dunfermline's Danish goalkeeper's eyes, and Bent Martin parried the ball, but only as far as 'Jinky' Johnstone, 'cool as the inside of a refrigerator' as the *Evening Times* dubbed him, who flashed a right-footed shot on the run, and Celtic held the lead, both in the game and in the close-run race for the league title.

Before the final whistle, John Clark, who was outstanding throughout the match and the entire season, headed a goal bound shot off the line with Simson beaten.

That Rangers won 4-0 now mattered hardly at all. For Celtic to fail now required them to be beaten by the same scoreline by Motherwell the following Saturday. They did not.

In fact, they defeated the Well by a single goal. As Raymond Jacobs of the *Herald* put it, 'In the last minute of the last game of the last day of all, Lennox scored the goal.' Jim Craig marauded forwards, overlapped Johnstone, took the ball to the byline, and turned it back to cross the path of Lennox, who swept home from close range. Celtic were champions.

In the sunshine of the love of the majority of the 21,000 crowd at Fir Park, Simson, the veteran goalkeeper, was carried shoulder high from the field of play, and no one would leave the stadium until Jock Stein appeared to receive the acclaim of the crowd.

Celtic were worthy champions. At one point Rangers were seven points ahead, yet the men from Celtic Park never buckled, never stopped believing in impossibilities. They overcame crushing disappointments too, in losing to Liverpool in the semi-final of the European Cup Winners' Cup and to Rangers in the Scottish Cup Final. They had scored 106 goals and conceded a mere 30. They had played by far the most enterprising and imaginative football in Scotland.

One-in-a-row!

* * *

2. CELTIC'S *ANNUS MIRABILIS*
1966/67

It was an incomparable season. During the rights of passage of 1966/67, Celtic won every competition they entered: in chronological order, the League Cup in October 1966, the Glasgow Cup in November 1966, the Scottish Cup in April 1967, the league championship and the European Cup, both in May 1967.

In the process, Stein's immortals scored a barely credible 196 world record-breaking goals.

* * *

Immortal Moments

1. THE AMERICAS

Even before the first competitive fixture of the new season, Stein had a feeling. Something was so right in Paradise it could not be contained but had to be expressed in football of sublime exuberance.

And in words, too. Stein said to his players during pre-season training, 'I think we could win everything in front of us.' And then he said it again and again until it became a mantra as well as a promise of success. For words of predictive understatement Stein's 'I think this could be a season to remember' would take some beating.

Somehow Stein's prophecies never became hostages to fortune.

* * *

The manager had planned well, prepared well and, above all, he had rewarded the championship-winning players with a summer tour which incorporated the delights of Bermuda, New York, San Francisco, Los Angeles, Vancouver, Malibu Beach, Broadway, Disneyland and Niagara Falls.

Stein remembered the close bonds of the players in Celtic's double-winning side of 1953/54 – which he had captained – and it was something he wanted to recreate.

He wanted to be part of that too. Somehow, at least in the summer of 1966 and throughout the subsequent season, Stein managed to remain the unpredictable disciplinarian and father figure to young, sometimes wayward men, while leading the community singing parties on tour and in post-match dressing rooms and communal baths.

Kelly was beginning to understand the gem he had appointed as only the fourth manager in Celtic's history.

'He has his own methods of coaxing and cajoling – aye, even of bullying and reading the riot act,' the chairman wrote in his autobiography. At the same time, however, Kelly added, 'I have never known a manager so close to his players as Jock or one who can read them like a book.'

The tour was a great success. The team remained unbeaten in 11 matches and scored 47 goals. There were two defeats of Tottenham Hotspur who had just finished third in the English First Division and who would later in the season win the FA Cup by beating Chelsea in the 'Cockney Cup Final' of 1967. Bobby Lennox called it 'the greatest trip ever'.

Stein's assistant manager met Bruce Forsyth in Bermuda, the entertainer entrusting his girlfriend, the former Miss World, Ann Sidney, to Fallon's care while he played a round of golf.

By the end of the American adventure team spirit was sky high and, with their manager's predictions ringing in their ears, the players returned to Paradise with a thumping 4-1 win over Manchester United in a prestige friendly on 6 August.

Somehow, the Celtic players managed to love Stein as well as hate him. Key, though, to their success was their absolute belief in him.

* * *

2. CELTIC V BAYERN MUNICH
8 JUNE 1966
KEZAR STADIUM, SAN FRANCISCO

With just two games left to complete the American tour, Stein and his warriors flew in from Vancouver, determined to remain undefeated.

The five-week expedition, though, had been tiring as well as riotously happy. The scheduling of matches, as well as training and partying, was unrelenting and involved travelling vast distances across the North and Central American continents. Both Johnstone and Young had flown home from Canada to tie nuptial knots. Stein's men, too, were bruised and weary from the constant football, having left Glasgow a mere five days after winning the league title at Fir Park, Motherwell.

With two-thirds of the match against Bundesliga club Bayern Munich played, Celtic were 2-0 down.

Since Young's tackle in the League Cup Final of 1965, however, there had been steel as well as silk about Celtic's football.

After 75 minutes, Lennox picked up a loose ball on the edge of the Bayern box, and gave the Munich goalkeeper Fritz Kosar no chance of saving. It was the Celtic forward's 19th goal of the tour.

The Germans, however, were a rising force in European club football. One year later Bayern would defeat Rangers 1-0 in the 1967 Cup Winners'

Cup Final. They would not surrender meekly in this tour match and would not give up their lead without a fight.

Shortly after Lennox's goal, the Bayern full-back Adolf Kunstwadl landed a haymaking punch on Steve Chalmers's mouth and, when the Scot retaliated, a brawl involving most of the players and many from the surrounding crowd ensued. Stein and Fallon entered the fray, albeit with peace-making intent, but the match was held up for seven minutes.

When play resumed, much to Celtic's joy, Joe McBride saved the day with an 82nd-minute equaliser.

In the final match of the tour, with only 12 remaining fit players to choose from, Stein's men beat Atlas from Guadalajara, Mexico, with a solitary goal by Charlie Gallagher two minutes before the final whistle.

Two days later, after a day's relaxation and shopping in New York, a united and jubilant Celtic squad returned to Prestwick Airport where they were greeted by celebrating fans from Paradise.

Stein had achieved what he set out to do.

In addition, he had experimented with a revolutionary new team formation. Out went the traditional 2-3-5 and in came 4-2-4.

* * *

3. RANGERS V CELTIC
GLASGOW CUP, IBROX, 23 AUGUST 1966

Celtic's return to competitive football began with League Cup wins at Hearts, 2-0, and at Celtic Park, 6-0 against Clyde and 8-2 against St Mirren.

The style of the victories had been cavalier and freewheeling. Up next, however, was the forever acid test, against Rangers.

None of what had gone before – the 10-1 and 11-0 friendly successes in Bermuda and in Hamilton, Ontario, and the 4-1 win against Manchester United, or the group stage victories in the League Cup – would matter one jot if Stein's merry men failed to confirm their superiority in the Glasgow Cup.

In its earlier incarnation, this competition was regarded as equally important as the league championship and Scottish Cup and, in fact, predated the formation of the Scottish Football League by three years.

The inaugural final of the Glasgow Cup came in 1888 when Cambuslang beat Rangers 3-1.

The old competition's fame and fortune were now fading but still an official attendance of 76,456 crammed into Ibrox Park to witness this match in the opening round of the cup. In the event, Rangers were humiliated in their own stadium.

McNeill, nominally a centre-half but seemingly everywhere in Stein's fluid 4-2-4 system, found himself cutting inside from the left wing and latching on to a free kick from Gallagher, lost possession, regained it with a timely tackle, and lashed the ball between Ritchie's legs and into the Rangers goal.

It was a hammer blow to the Ibrox men who had started the game with confidence and attacking intent.

Although Lennox later scored a brilliant hat-trick in Celtic's 4-0 win, the hero of the match for Celtic was their veteran goalkeeper Ronnie Simpson, the man Stein had hounded from Hibernian.

In that opening five minutes, when Rangers' football flowed like an incoming tide, Simpson made two crucial saves. First, he dived bravely at the feet of the onrushing Jim Forrest. The centre-forward who scored 145 goals in 163 games for Rangers disentangled himself from the morass of bodies and gestured angrily in frustration. Two minutes later, Willie Johnston found himself with only the Celtic goalkeeper to beat but Simpson anticipated the winger's shot and saved at point-blank range. Captain McNeill calmly patted his goalkeeper on the back as if to say, 'You're only doing your job but you're doing so well, pal.'

Lennox's goals were evidence his scintillating form on the Americas tour had not deserted him. Just after the half hour, saw the Celtic forward receive the ball 25 yards out, turn and simultaneously throw the entire Rangers defence off balance. His shot cannoned into the back of the net from the underside of the crossbar. Later, in the 81st minute, Lennox took advantage of John Greig's misjudgement of a high bounce and slid it past Ritchie from six yards. Clear evidence of how much this match mattered to Rangers can be seen from the length of time their captain lay on the Ibrox turf, refusing to raise his head, acknowledging his guilt. Two minutes later, Auld's pass found Lennox on the left wing. He cut inside and sent a low, skimming shot inside Ritchie's near post.

Stein was in a jovial mood in the dressing room. Afterwards, he joined Kelly and Fallon, who were singing the praises of Bobby Lennox. 'Ach,' Stein said, 'it all depended on Murdoch and Auld in midfield.'

The newfangled 4-2-4 system was working a treat.

* * *

4. CELTIC V RANGERS
LEAGUE DIVISION ONE
CELTIC PARK, 17 SEPTEMBER 1966

The league campaign opened one week earlier with striking wins for both members of the Old Firm. Rangers dismantled Partick Thistle 6-1 at Ibrox, while Celtic cruised to a 3-0 win at Clyde.

The highlight of the second round of league matches was an early clash between the Glasgow giants at Paradise where a capacity all-ticket crowd of 70,000 awaited the arrival of the gladiators.

In the very first minute, Celtic stamped their authority on the game with a classic interchange of passes between Hughes and Lennox and a final ball to Auld whose finish consummated earlier teamwork. Three minutes later, the match was to all intents and purposes over as Murdoch met a cross from the left on the volley and, when the ball rebounded from a Rangers block on the 18-yard line, the midfielder coolly chipped it into the top corner of Ritchie's net.

The Ibrox club reacted with both fury and persistence, strong-arm methods and outdated tactics from the Iron Curtain days, long punts forward from defence, hit and hope, smash and smother.

Seven Celtic players were injured in the furore but still the Parkhead club were comfortable winners, sitting back in the second half, strolling about the pitch, stroking the ball from player to player, and ensuring the humiliation on this occasion was not about such base merchandise as mere goals.

A 2-0 win for the Bhoys and a winning margin that might have been larger. Still, the contrast could not have been greater, bludgeon against rapier, as the *Herald* reporter judged it.

A whirlwind of rational revolution was well under way at Celtic Park. In comparison, the last knockings of an 'ancient regime' were clinging to superstition and rigid structures at Ibrox.

Stein was thinking, planning his way to immortality.

* * *

5. THE LEAGUE CUP FINAL
CELTIC V RANGERS
HAMPDEN PARK, 29 OCTOBER 1966

Perhaps it is unfair to characterise Rangers as a monolith of conservatism in the months following their defeat by Celtic in the previous year's League Cup Final.

In the summer of 1966, while the Celts were on tour, the Rangers chairman John Lawrence and his manager Scott Symon were plotting big-money signings in response to Celtic's league championship.

First to arrive was Alex Smith from Dunfermline, a player Stein knew well from his time at East End Park. The record for a transfer fee paid by a Scottish club was broken in order to acquire Smith's signature on his contract; £55,000 was serious money in the 1960s. Shortly afterwards, Dave Smith was signed from Aberdeen and another £50,000 disappeared from the Ibrox coffers.

It looked, too, from Rangers' performance in this cup final as if Symons or his assistants had been working on the training ground. In spite of falling behind to a stunning Lennox goal in the 20th minute, Rangers produced a workmanlike and organised performance of attacking intent that deserved more than a narrow 1-0 defeat.

Celtic received criticism from their fans for resting on their laurels once they had taken the lead, but it is possible they had no choice, such was the surprising quality of Rangers' play.

In the final analysis, the game proved that Celtic could defend in depth as well as attack in waves. Both Simpson and McNeill were towers of strength and even Johnstone was to be found in his own penalty area dribbling round Rangers' forwards and taking pressure from Celtic's defenders.

Goals from both sides were disallowed by referee Tiny Wharton and there were misses aplenty by the Ibrox forwards, as many as there were occasions of heroic defending.

With just over ten minutes remaining, Willie Johnston's pass found Alex Smith with Simpson beaten and an open goal to aim for. Incredibly, Smith stumbled over the ball which meandered towards the goal line. Just in time, Willie O'Neill, Celtic's left-back, scrambled the ball to safety, and became the hero of the hour and another immortal.

Celtic's defending had been mostly sensible and crafted from determination and composure and skill but luck, too, played its part in the making of legends.

* * *

6. THE TURNING OF THE YEAR: THE LEAGUE CHAMPIONSHIP RACE

By the end of November 1966, the battle for the Division One title was either a two-horse or a three-horse race. Celtic, unbeaten, had claimed 23 points from 12 games. Rangers, unbeaten except for defeat by Celtic, possessed 20 points from 12. And a coat-tails-hanging Aberdeen had played 12 with 18 points. December, though, was a time for giving, both presents at Christmas and points to opponents throughout the month. Aberdeen lost 1-0 at Falkirk, Rangers lost 3-2 at Dunfermline, and Celtic drew 0-0, away at Kilmarnock, the only time Stein's men failed to score in a league game all season, then 1-1 at Aberdeen.

With the arrival of the last day of the year, in spite of those dropped points, Celtic had pulled five points clear of their Glasgow rivals, aided by a postponement of Rangers' Christmas Eve fixture.

On 31 December 1966 it was Glasgow versus Dundee, with Rangers at home to the Dee and Celtic at Tannadice against United.

The Ibrox club could only manage a 2-2 draw and Celtic, despite leading 1-0 and 2-1, lost their unbeaten seasonal record in a 3-2 defeat.

All thoughts of Celtic coasting to a second consecutive league championship while focussing efforts on a European Cup campaign were put to one side and odds-on bets were off. It might now be nip and tuck for the remainder of the season.

The fact that the traditional New Year's Day Old Firm fixture was postponed only added to the tension spreading on both sides of the Clyde.

* * *

7. THE SCOTTISH CUP
BERWICK RANGERS V RANGERS
CELTIC V ARBROATH
28 JANUARY 1967

Celtic were taking the Scottish Cup seriously as always. Stein took his charges away to Seamill for a three-day preparation camp prior to the game against Arbroath and organised a full 11-a-side practice game on their return on the Wednesday.

The north-east team might have been in Division Two but were making a determined drive for promotion, missing out eventually by a single point to Morton and Raith Rovers.

How could the Celtic manager not be in earnest about this fixture after his pointed pre-season comments about winning everything? He hammered home the point with clenched fists and harsh voice: there must be no embarrassing slip-ups on Saturday. He picked his strongest available side.

Of the future Lisbon Lions, only Johnstone and Lennox were missing, the former with an ear infection and the latter with a problematic ankle, and Gallagher and Hughes were no shabby or callow replacements.

In the event it was easy, with the Celts two up before 20 minutes had elapsed through an opener by Murdoch and a screamer of a second from Gemmell from 20 yards out that left the Arbroath goalkeeper, Jim Williamson, helpless in its wake. Chalmers and Auld completed the rout with the third and fourth goals.

While these comparatively serene proceedings were unfolding, however, there were seismic events taking place across the border at Shielfield Park in Berwick-upon-Tweed.

Berwick Rangers were relative newcomers to the Scottish Football League, having been accepted as members only in 1955. Since then the only English club playing in Scotland had settled into a pleasant anonymity and mediocrity and at the time of the meeting with Glasgow Rangers were tenth in Division Two.

Their one collision with back-page headlines in the Glasgow press had occurred in May 1964 when Rangers attempted to steamroller a reconstruction of Scottish football which would have resulted in the expulsion of Berwick and four others from the Scottish Football League. Eventually, with the intervention of Celtic's chairman and that of the Court of Sessions, Rangers' proposal was overturned.

There was, therefore, bad blood spilled all over the fixture when the draw for the first round proper of the cup was made.

Berwick had fought through two preliminary rounds, beating Vale of Leithen 8-1 and Forfar Athletic 2-0.

Rangers' team contained nine full internationals, Berwick's 11 part-time professionals. The outcome, a 1-0 win for the underdogs, was described by Rangers captain John Greig as 'probably the worst result in the history of our club', and by the reporter for *The Scotsman* as 'the most ludicrous, the weirdest, the most astonishing result ever returned in Scottish football'.

The scorer of the Berwick goal, Sammy Reid, was back at work on Sunday morning in an engineering yard, making up for time off in the previous week when his club's manager, Jock Wallace, had demanded extra training prior to the cup match.

Kelly, Stein, Fallon and the Celtic players smiled at the news of the result. Two Rangers forwards, Jim Forrest and George McLean, never played for Rangers again.

The psychological blow to Rangers was severe and reminders of this result still send shockwaves through the club to this very day.

It was advantage Celtic, too, in their pursuit of two-in-a-row.

* * *

8. GLASGOW WINTER, GLASGOW SPRING

By the close of January 1967, Celtic led the Division One table by five points, albeit having played one more game than Rangers and with an inferior goal average due to the tightness of the Ibrox club's defence. A second consecutive league championship, though, was in Celtic's surely safe hands and flying feet.

If the East End club, however, imagined their Govan rivals would be daunted or diminished by their shock cup exit in England, they were sorely mistaken. After the Berwick horror show, Rangers won nine league matches in a row. Celtic, perhaps a tad complacent, possibly a further tad distracted by European adventures and a continuing romance with the Scottish Cup, dropped a crucial point in a 1-1 draw in February in Stirling.

By the end of March, in a two-horse race, it was tight once more. Both Glasgow clubs had played 29 matches and Celtic had 52 points to Rangers' 50.

On April Fools' Day, with Celtic engaged in a Scottish Cup semi-final against Clyde at Hampden, Rangers had the opportunity to return to the top of the league for the first time since the good old days of Protestant dominance.

At Ibrox, they were beaten 1-0 by Dunfermline Athletic. Monday's headline in the *Herald* proclaimed 'the end of Rangers' challenge'. Allowing for journalistic licence it did appear so, although premature celebrations in Glasgow's East End were tempered by experiences of past failures and by the knowledge that Celtic were still only two points clear. In addition, the Bhoys would face fixture congestion as the season progressed, whilst Rangers would play only Saturday to Saturday.

According to a 'Special Correspondent' in the newspaper, 'nothing would go right' for Rangers against the Pars. In the 51st minute Alex Edwards, a player Stein had given his debut five days after his 16th birthday in February 1962, floated a corner into the Rangers box. Waiting there was Hugh Robertson who battered the ball through the thick of the confusion of defenders and past goalkeeper Norrie Martin.

On that same day, Celtic also failed to score, but eventually reached a third successive Scottish Cup Final by beating Clyde 2-0 in the replayed semi.

By the end of April, Celtic had not only won the Scottish Cup by beating Aberdeen 2-0, but had also established a position of dominance in the battle for the league crown.

After Rangers' insipid draw at Dundee, Celtic needed a solitary point to be champions once again. It was theirs to lose now.

* * *

9. CELTIC V DUNDEE UNITED
WEDNESDAY, 3 MAY 1967

Some 44,000 Celtic souls arrived at Paradise for this rearranged fixture, postponed from the weekend because of the club's appointment with Aberdeen at Hampden.

At half-time the Bhoys were leading 1-0 through a penalty won by Lennox and slotted home by Gemmell. During the interval four ball boys trotted around the perimeter track and two lucky youngsters were chosen to carry the Scottish Cup aloft to the accompaniment of ringing cheers. Celtic were not playing well, but well enough, surely, most thought, on that cold midweek evening.

The second half, however, would not conform to expectations, to the will of the assembled masses. In the 54th minute, Billy Hainey, the United inside-forward, rounded Simpson to calmly plant the ball in the back of the Celtic net. The crowd sighed and a collective moan of disappointment rolled about the stadium. Still, though, a draw would be sufficient.

Spirits rose, and soared just after the hour when Willie Wallace sped between a dithering United goalkeeper and his ponderous centre-half to steal the ball and slot it home.

Seven minutes later, however, it was the Celtic defence's turn to play the children's party game of musical statues. A corner was swung in and centre-froward Dennis Gillespie, the Arabs' centre forward, was the only person still moving when the music stopped. The ball sped from his forehead into the back of the Celtic net.

The goal made it 2-2, but that would still turn the trick.

Three minutes later, nerves were raw among both players and supporters as Hainey slipped the ball to John Graham who beat Simpson at the goalkeeper's left-hand post.

Unless Celtic could equalise in the final 20 minutes, the champions would need to rely on taking at least a point from their great Glasgow rivals at Ibrox in three days' time.

In truth, the players huffed and puffed but could not blow the Dundee United house down. Both Lennox and Wallace had chances but were denied by an inspired performance by Sandy Davie in the Arabs' goal.

By the end of the evening, Celtic, with two games left, had 55 points. Rangers, in second place, with just the Old Firm derby to come, had 54 points. Goal average, after an accumulation of Celtic goals and Rangers' poor form in April, had swung narrowly into the East End club's favour by 3.4 to 3.1.

During the entire 1966/67 season Celtic had lost just three competitive matches. One defeat was to Vojvodina, the champions of Yugoslavia, in Novi Sad in the first leg of the European Cup quarter-final, and the other two in the league championship, both to Dundee United.

Now the Parkhead men had to avoid defeat one more time.

* * *

10. RANGERS V CELTIC
SATURDAY, 6 MAY 1967

The day dawned dour with grey-black clouds scudding across the Glasgow skyline, embracing the tops of tenements as they passed.

Fans woke to heavy rain, drowning rats in cellars, sourcing weak points in roof defences, turning roads to rivers, and Ibrox into a mud and water beach.

Wild electricity dropped from the heights of the heavens, shorting domesticated circuits, dancing with devils, defeating the city's transport system with traffic lights stuck on red and with underground trains stuck in tunnels.

Fans cursed as plans to descend on Ibrox with springtime joy and horns and rattles and optimism were put on hold. Each bucket of rain was an omen, an inexplicable message from the gods.

Surely, with a league championship to be decided, with both Rangers and Celtic having European finals to look forward to, Celtic against Inter Milan and Rangers against Bayern Munich, surely this could not be the end of the world promised in the *Book of the Apocalypse*.

Catholics and Protestants alike turned to prayer, to do deals with their respective gods: please let the game go ahead, please let Celtic – or Rangers – win today.

Still, though, the rain descended in biblical proportions.

* * *

Those that can do, those that could, descended on Ibrox Park with 78,000 turning up as opposed to the expected 90,000. Many fell foul of the weather and of the failed Glasgow transportation system. Rangers fans congregated, bedraggled, but under cover.

Celtic fans sang in the now merely torrential rain on the uncovered terracing of Ibrox. It was a minor miracle but the game was on. The play, though, was as grim and gradgrind as the weather. Tackles were as heavy as the incessant downpour. The leaden leather ball stuck in the glue of the mud.

In the 41st minute there were shifts in the tectonic plates that layered this football match. Dave Smith meandered near the left touchline, the ball never far from his boots, peering all the while through the murk and mire of the rain, looking for an opening in the Celtic defence. Like Moses approaching the Red Sea, he suddenly saw a dry passage and pitched the ball forwards to meet a crazy, angled run from right-half Willie Jardine, who controlled the ball, regained his balance, and shot from 25 yards into the top corner of Simpson's goal.

Suddenly, the pouring rain really hurt, really mattered to the soaked skins of the Celtic support. Within 60 seconds, however, Celtic were level.

The ball arrived in the Rangers box via a lofted free kick from Murdoch and it bounced and bobbled and begged to be cleared by the Ibrox men's defenders who hacked and missed several times before Lennox latched on to the elusive football and scrambled a misplaced shot against the post. Johnstone gleefully turned in the rebound.

The troops trudged off at half-time, desperate for tea and sympathy. There would not be much of the latter from Stein, however. This mattered to the Celtic manager, this mattered more than life itself.

The second half began with the men in green and white hoops attacking with power and renewed energy. Chalmers's shot was turned away by a defender's stray leg, Auld clipped a shot just over the bar, and Gemmell scorched a drive held at the second attempt by Martin.

Pressure told and, in the 74th minute, Johnstone scored the goal of his lifetime. He received the ball from Chalmers's throw, set off, jinking all the way, towards the Rangers goal, evaded a wild tackle by centre-half Ronnie McKinnon, veered left, and cracked in an unstoppable shot from all of 25 yards.

Some prayers were answered and some denied, it seemed. The rain continued, meanwhile, oblivious to the gods.

In the next quarter of an hour or so, however, the worst and the best of football and its supporting casts were on display.

When the implications and the realities of Johnstone's second goal had taken root in the fevered minds of some Rangers fanatics, trouble spilled from the covered terraces. Bottles were thrown on to the pitch, and messages of hate were shouted as Celtic waited to take a corner. Fans climbed barriers, invaded the pitch, and the referee stopped the game.

The rain continued, unconcerned and after two minutes, which seemed longer, order was restored. Roger Hynd scored an equaliser, that saved pride, but little else and Celtic were champions for the second season in succession.

At the final whistle, both teams' players fell into each other's arms and embraced like boxers at the end of a bruising battle decided, not by a knockout, but on points.

The men from Paradise became the only club in modern Scottish football, since the inception of the League Cup in season 1946/47, to win every competition entered. It is true that Rangers won trebles in 1949 and in 1964 but in neither of those seasons did they also take home the Glasgow Cup, won on both occasions by Celtic, beating Third Lanark 3-1 in 1949 and Clyde 2-0 in 1964.

In addition, on 25 May in Lisbon, the Celtic immortals won the European Cup, becoming the first British side to lift the trophy.

Symons's Rangers lost their European Cup Winners' Cup Final 1-0 after extra time to Bayern Munich. Although the Ibrox men finished the season empty-handed in terms of trophies, it is worth recalling that they were a fine side in their own right, much underestimated and unappreciated by their supporters whose obsessions with their rivals' achievements soon led to their manager's brutal sacking in November 1967.

* * *

Some weeks earlier, too, on Saturday, 15 April, sandwiched between Celtic's European Cup semi-final first leg against Dukla Prague and a crucial league match at home to Aberdeen, Scotland had become unofficial world champions by beating England 3-2 at Wembley. Four Celts, Simpson, Gemmell, Wallace and Lennox, played in that stirring and dominant victory and Lennox scored the second goal.

To cap it all, in early June, Celtic travelled to Spain to play in Alfredo Di Stéfano's testimonial match and beat the then six-times winners of the European Cup with another Lennox goal.

It was the icing on the best cake in the world.

* * *

Immortal Men 1966/67

Of course, this season was the Stein show, the singing, the kicking open of dressing room doors, the seat-stealing from Helenio Herrera in Lisbon before the European Cup Final, the planning and the plotting, the ranting and the raging, and the peace that passed all understanding at the final whistle.

Stein, though, was no longer the loner. Without the awaydays at Ayr races with Fallon, without the post-match meals with Kelly and Fallon, without the to and fro of ideas buffed and rebuffed in restaurants, maybe the serial successes of 1966 and 1967 might not have come to fruition.

There were others too.

Much is made of Bill Shankly's fabled Boot Room at Anfield in the 1960s. The Liverpool manager who was to anoint Stein as immortal in 1967 arrived from Huddersfield Town in December 1959. His Boot Room, where beer-loosened tongues devised tactics, consisted of Reuben Bennett, who had managed Dundee to two League Cup wins in seasons 1951/52 and 1952/53, Bob Paisley, a player with Liverpool before World War Two, and Joe Fagan, a former Manchester City player and trainer with Rochdale.

Celtic's equivalent of Liverpool's think tank or brains trust consisted of Stein, Fallon and Neilly Mochan, though alcohol was neither needed nor permitted by the teetotal Stein.

* * *

1. 'SMILER' NEILLY MOCHAN

Mochan was the third man in this influential triumvirate of power. 'Smiler', as the diminutive trainer was affectionately known, arrived at Celtic Park in May 1953 from Middlesbrough, and was an immediate success.

Curiously, his first four games for the club were all played at Hampden Park. His debut came in the Glasgow Cup Final when Queen's Park were defeated 3-1 and he scored twice. He also played in the three Coronation Cup matches, victories over Arsenal, Manchester United, and Hibernian in the final, scoring a stunning volley against Matt Busby's team and a trademark 35-yard cannonball for Celtic's second goal against the previous season's Scottish league champions.

Stein, a team-mate in those days, always referred to the Coronation Cup victory as 'Neilly Mochan's final'.

As a player, Smiler was a hard-running, hard-shooting left-winger or centre-forward. He scored twice in Celtic's 7-1 League Cup Final victory at Hampden in 1957. In all, there were 111 goals in 268 appearances.

He is one of a handful of players to score hat-tricks both for and against Celtic. In September 1950, the Parkhead club played host to Morton and Mochan scored three for the visitors including a decisive goal in the 85th minute in a 4-3 thriller.

More palatable history for Celtic fans include Smiler hat-tricks against Airdrieonians in the double-winning season of 1953/54, against Clyde in the Glasgow Cup in 1955, and five goals against St Mirren in the Cup in 1960.

By the time of Stein's return to Celtic as manager, Mochan was assistant trainer, but was promoted by the new manager in the summer of 1965. Stein's instructions were clear. He demanded that Mochan make Celtic the fittest team in Europe and the proof of that pudding came when Stein's team not only played Inter Milan off the park but they ran them off it too.

Equally as important, however, was Mochan's role as intermediary between the management duo of Stein and Fallon and the players. Bobby Lennox described Mochan as a 'buffer'. If Fallon was good cop to Stein's bad cop, Mochan was the runner between the two worlds at Parkhead. Sometimes he would warn the dressing room of the impending arrival of an irate Stein. On other occasions, when Fallon was ensconced with Stein in the manager's office, it would be Mochan's shoulder on which players would cry and complain. Journalist Archie Macpherson said that Mochan 'brought a touch of humanity to the dressing room'.

He was Stein's go-to-dogsbody, though no less respected because of that. His work ranged from guarding the door against late-arriving journalists at press conferences to transforming Jim Craig's boots just before the European Cup Final after Celtic had signed a footwear deal with Adidas. 'For fuck's sake, Jim,' Mochan railed, 'you're the only player in the fucking team wearing those boots. Now I've got to find black paint to get rid of the Puma flash and white paint to put in the Adidas marks.'

There was undoubtedly something of the master and servant, upstairs, downstairs relationship between Stein and Mochan.

Smiler was a greyhound man whereas Stein preferred the blue bloods of the sport of kings. Still, he had not done too badly for a grandson of Donegal where the Irish Holocaust had raged at its most intense just 120 years earlier.

Mochan was Stein's first-team trainer throughout the first nine-in-a-row years and one of the true immortals.

Of the planets that orbited Stein's sun, Kelly was closest, Mercury or Venus, Fallon was his Earth, and Mochan was his Mars, all integral parts of his inner solar system.

The rest of Stein's satellites were further out, although, Jimmy Gribben, for example, moved closest to the sun at trophy times, when Stein remembered his dues and his debts.

* * *

2. BOB ROONEY

Bob Rooney was the physiotherapist at Celtic throughout Stein's years at the club and a vital component of the backroom team. Mostly, Rooney was out in the asteroid belt with the Celtic players, but sometimes he was invited by the boss to come close. It was nothing to do with the football but everything to do with the racing on TV. Fallon would gather the gang of four: Stein and himself, Mochan and Rooney. Usually, they met in Rooney's treatment room in the bowels of Celtic Park and, when the door was shut, it stayed shut until after the last race. If there was a big meeting televised, Cheltenham or Aintree, Rooney and co would go upstairs, trespass on Kelly's territory, indulge in his hospitality, in order to further minimise the chance of disruption.

* * *

Without those times of relaxation with colleagues who became pals for the duration, Stein might well have been dead long before his collapse pitchside on international duty with Scotland in 1985.

The manager's mental states, his sometimes violent mood swings, his sleeplessness, were all well hidden from the public. Stein was a man stressed to stretching point throughout his managerial career and the only time he unwound was while watching the races. For some, Stein's wagers on horses would have increased the pressures of life but for the Celtic manager, win or lose, it was a form of release that kept him sane and maintained his sometimes precarious hold on the land of the living.

Stein, aware perhaps of the urgent necessity to relieve some of the pressures, delegated unpleasant jobs to members of his staff.

Fallon drew most of the shortest straws. Stein's assistant manager was responsible for so much it might have broken a less loyal man. His boss was a poor administrator and had the grace and the good sense to acknowledge it. In consequence, Fallon, in addition to scouting duties, attending race meetings duties, and bridge-building duties between Stein and the dressing room, also took care of the business of arranging Celtic's foreign travel, players' contracts, and their ticket allocations.

The most unpleasant duty of all, however, was releasing players who had not made the grade. As Fallon stated, 'It was by far the worst job I ever had to do. I would never sleep a wink the night before I had to do it.'

* * *

3. JIMMY STEELE

Further out still, in the planetary orbits around Stein, was Jimmy Steele, the honorary fifth member of the backroom team.

If ever a man deserved the title of immortal it is Steele. This man worked for Celtic as masseur, unpaid and on call, for almost half a century. More important, perhaps, than the physical ministrations he offered to the playing staff at Celtic was his regular dressing room presence.

If Steele had not been a magical medical man he could easily have stepped on to any stage and succeeded as a stand-up comedian. He was a born raconteur with the gift of twinkling eyes and a smile always on the point of breaking into laughter. Many times Fallon or Mochan would report to Stein that the dressing room needed a lift and 'get Steelie' was the inevitable recommendation.

Moreover, Steele understood Stein, and the manager's craving for peace that could only come, momentarily, from winning football matches, but more importantly, at least for Stein's mental wellbeing, from playing the horses.

The fact that Steele was a fellow punter was crucial in his relationship with Stein.

In times, too, when sectarian strife was never more than a kiss from a blade away from the streets and terraces of Glasgow, Steele was a force for peace and reconciliation. His work, unpaid of course, for the Scottish Football Association as masseur and joker to the national team, brought him into regular contact with the leading members of the Ibrox dressing room. It is a fitting tribute to Steele that he was loved by John Greig, Ronnie McKinnon and Willie Johnston every bit as much as by the denizens of the dressing room at Celtic.

* * *

4. DR JOHN FITZSIMMONS

One final indispensable member of Stein's backroom team was Dr John Fitzsimmons, close enough to the manager to be photographed next to the boss on the steps of the aircraft taking Celtic to the European Cup Final in 1967. Fitzsimmons knew his football as well as his medicine, having played five times for Celtic in the 1930s. He had been spotted by manager Willie Maley when playing in an amateur match between St Joseph's and

St Mungo's. He was not quite good enough to claim a regular place in the first team but left Paradise in the summer of 1938 to play for Alloa where he scored 22 league goals for the Wasps in only 28 appearances.

Fitzsimmons became Celtic's doctor in 1953 and was on call for Stein throughout the glory years of the first nine-in-a-row.

* * *

5. BILLY MCNEILL

Stein was blessed with both able lieutenants and with invaluable conduits between his office and the dressing room but without his captain, Billy McNeill, he might still have been lost.

The fates of manager and skipper seemed inextricably entwined. Both played for Blantyre Victoria in their formative years – as did Kelly, too, of course. This feeder club for Rangers somehow managed to produce two Celtic managers and a chairman.

McNeill was originally brought to Celtic's attention by the club's captain in the 1950s, Bobby Evans, but it was Stein, in his capacity as reserve team coach, who made the final recommendation to Kelly after seeing the young centre-half perform well for Scotland schoolboys against England in 1957.

He was signed for £250 from the Vics and became one of that talented group of young footballers trained by Stein and known as Kelly's Kids.

He made his Celtic debut at the age of 18 in a League Cup tie won 2-0 against Clyde. A report in the *Evening Times* described him as a 'steady pivot'.

On the training pitch at Barrowfield, Stein experimented with extraordinary tactics. McNeill, for example, was encouraged to abandon his defensive duties at crucial moments and join the forwards in the opposition penalty area. Ball after ball in training was crossed and aimed at McNeill's head.

Years later, the constant repetition of this manoeuvre bore fruit eight minutes from time in the 1965 Scottish Cup Final victory, and again in the European Cup quarter-final win over Vojvodina Novi Sad in March 1967 when McNeill headed home a last-minute goal from a Gallagher corner to take Celtic into the semi-finals.

When Stein left to manage Dunfermline in 1960, McNeill was distraught. But it was Stein's return to the club in 1965 that prevented McNeill from heading south to England.

Bill Nicholson, the legendary Spurs manager, had been desperate to sign the centre-half as a replacement for the veteran Maurice Norman. McNeill could have quadrupled his wages to £100 a week if he had moved but preferred to stay in Glasgow under the tutelage of Stein.

Money was never the biggest issue with McNeill although it certainly loomed larger with some of his team-mates.

As captain, he was deputed, once again, to ask Stein for wage rises on return from the successful tour of the Americas in summer of 1966.

A nervous McNeill explained the desire of his colleagues for an uplift in their basic pay consequent upon a triumphant tour which followed on from a famous cup win against Dunfermline.

'Fuck off,' Stein said, and indicated by hand gestures that his captain should leave his office before it was too late.

It was as if the manager had been asked to put his hands into his own pockets and give his players money that would have been more wisely placed on the winner of a big handicap at Ayr.

McNeill was not only embarrassed at his failure to win his friends more money but was ashamed he had not put up a fight. He could not return to the dressing room immediately so he retired for 15 minutes to the toilets to give the impression he had tried long and hard to negotiate with Stein.

The captain need not have been shamefaced as he was not alone in receiving short shrift when money was in question.

Bobby Lennox admitted he was petrified by Stein. 'There it is,' Stein said, and shoved a contract across the table at his star striker. 'Just effing sign it.'

Dictatorships are almost always the most efficient and cost-effective ways of running football clubs. So Stein was loved, hated and feared in almost equal measure.

To Celtic's greatest manager, it probably didn't matter which emotion predominated among his playing staff. He knew well enough that success was sufficient for loyalty.

He understood, though, what a man as well as a player he had in McNeill, his indomitable captain and deputy on the field of play. 'What makes a great player?' Stein's question was rhetorical. 'He's the one who brings out the best in others and, when I'm saying that, I'm talking about Billy McNeill.'

It was another measure of Stein as a man, this readiness with McNeill, with Fallon, with Gribben, to acknowledge his indebtedness to others, his dependence on them for the successes he enjoyed.

Over the course of 18 seasons, McNeill, the man the fans called Cesar, made a grand total of 822 appearances for his only professional club.

The pinnacle of his career was leading Stein's Celtic to European Cup glory. At the final whistle in Lisbon, the manager headed on to the pitch and embraced first Ronnie Simpson, and then McNeill, the architect and cornerstone of so many Celtic victories.

* * *

3. *THAT* TEAM, TEN SECONDS TO GO, AND THREE-IN-A-ROW
1967/68

Perhaps the saddest thing about winning everything is that there is nowhere else to go, except perhaps downhill.

Stein said, after the European Cup triumph, that his team would never be beaten. After Bill Shankly, Stein's friend and manager of Liverpool, had anointed Stein with immortality in the Celtic dressing room on that night in Lisbon, Stein had pronounced immortality on his players by telling Shankly on the bus back to the hotel, '*That* team will never be beaten.' Later, he repeated the exact same words to Bertie Auld.

Of course, Stein may have been thinking already about changes required to his squad in order to maintain Celtic's place at the pinnacle of both Scottish and European football. He may have meant *that* particular gathering of 11 players would never be beaten.

In fact, he was wrong. That precise team played eight more games together and were beaten by Dynamo Kiev at Parkhead in September 1967 in the opening match of their defence of the European Cup.

* * *

Not only were Celtic unceremoniously dumped from the European Cup by the team from the Soviet Union and defeated by Racing Club in the infamous Battle of Montevideo, but Stein's team also surrendered their hold on the Scottish Cup in a 2-0 home defeat by Dunfermline.

To be fair, the men from Paradise did retain both the League Cup with a 5-3 final victory over Dundee, and the Glasgow Cup with an 8-0 victory over Clyde.

There was, too, the not insignificant matter of attempting to retain the league championship and winning the title for a third season in succession.

By the turn of the year, Celtic seemed to be sleepwalking to disaster. It was as if the players were struggling to come to terms with fame and fortune, with returning to the bread and butter matters of winning mundane football matches.

Not only had they lost their European title but they had lost their tempers in South America and had fallen behind Rangers in their quest for a third successive league title. Their great rivals had defeated Celtic 1-0 at Ibrox in September and in the subsequent league match had allowed St Johnstone to escape from Parkhead with a 1-1 draw. In early December, too, Dundee United, Celtic's sole nemesis from the previous celebratory season, managed a draw at Parkhead.

The net consequence was that when the return Old Firm game was played at Celtic Park on 2 January 1968 the Ibrox team were two points clear at the top of the table.

A win was essential if the champions were not to be accused of being one-season wonders, chokers on success. The match was all-ticket with Celtic Park's capacity capped at 75,000.

Simpson had suffered injuries to his ribs and an ankle in the previous day's 3-2 victory over Clyde at Shawfield. John Fallon would replace the veteran in goal.

Other Lisbon Lions were missing too: Jim Craig, Willie Wallace and Stevie Chalmers. The times they were a-changing.

Twice Celtic took the lead. The opening goal was a lucky one, Auld's free kick on 18 minutes deflecting into the net via Rangers defender Sandy Jardine. With 12 minutes remaining and the Glasgow rivals deadlocked at 1-1, Jim Brogan's pass found Murdoch inside the Ibrox men's penalty area. The Celtic half-back turned on a sixpence and fired an unstoppable shot into the roof of the net. The majority of the Paradise faithful believed their team would be returning to the summit of the league table.

Fallon's second blunder of the game, however, came in the 88th minute. Willie Johnston's shot in the 55th minute had squeezed between the Celtic goalkeeper's knees. Now Kai Johansen shot from distance and the ball somehow squirmed through Fallon's gloved hands and passed beneath his diving body.

After a 2-2 draw Rangers remained two points clear of Celtic and, with no more Old Firm games to come, the destiny of the league championship was still in their hands.

If some of Celtic's old guard was changing, however, there had been a thorough revolution across the river in Govan.

In the previous summer, Davie White, with only one year's experience in management at Clyde and without playing experience except at the same club, was appointed assistant to Scot Symon and, on 1 November 1967, Symon was sacked and the callow White was installed in his place. Might the master, Stein, be able to outwit the novice, White, in the remaining months of the season?

Stein was prepared, if necessary, for ruthless and radical reconstruction of his European Cup-winning side. He had already promoted Brogan from the youth setup and in February he replaced the injured Auld with Charlie Gallagher who became the conductor of Stein's evolving orchestra for the rest of the season.

Through the remainder of January – after the draw with Rangers – and through February and March, Celtic went on a run of 11 successive league victories including a 6-1 away win in Perth against St Johnstone when Lennox scored four goals.

Rangers, though, matched Celtic win for win through that late winter and early spring. Time was running out for the hunters to catch the hunted.

White was showing no signs of weakness under pressure. It was, though, in the Rangers boardroom where cracks began to appear in the Ibrox facade.

Under the leadership of John Lawrence, Rangers' actions had already suggested consternation. The sacking of Symon, an Ibrox stalwart under Bill Struth, and the winner of six league titles, five Scottish Cups and four League Cups, a man who had played both cricket and football for his country, smacked of panic. It also smelled of cowardice as Lawrence sent an accountant to communicate the bad news to Symon.

In February 1968, too, Lawrence perpetrated a PR disaster of gargantuan proportions that allowed Stein and Celtic to retain the highest of moral grounds.

Citing fixture congestion, Rangers withdrew from the Glasgow Cup when drawn to play Celtic at Ibrox in the next round. Not only was the decision criticised as a snub to the city of Glasgow but it also seemed as if the club had no stomach for another battle with their great rivals. Stein observed the shenanigans and smiled.

Ironically, the problems Rangers feared of too many matches in too few days were soon solved by their defeats by Hearts in the Scottish Cup and by Leeds in the Inter-Cities Fairs Cup.

Then on a bitter night at Tannadice, at the beginning of April, Rangers played out a dreary and dismal 0-0 draw and Celtic were now only a single point in arrears.

Two weeks later, while the team from Paradise were cruising to an 8-0 victory over Clyde in the Glasgow Cup at Hampden, Rangers, possibly unnerved by Celtic's proximity in the league table, possibly undermined by the pusillanimity of their board of directors, found themselves 3-1 down at Morton. The fact the Ibrox team rallied and claimed a draw was scant consolation as Celtic, with a significantly superior goal average, had regained the box seat in terms of winning the league for the third time under Stein.

In the penultimate fixtures on Saturday, 20 April, Rangers beat Kilmarnock in Ayrshire and Celtic faced Morton at Paradise.

On 14 minutes Wallace headed Celtic into a deserved lead and all was well with the 51,000 inside Paradise. Shocks, though, were to come. Morton had not travelled from Greenock merely to make up the numbers. Allan hit the Celtic crossbar from 35 yards, Gemmell cleared a Taylor shot off the line and, on the stroke of half-time, Mason equalised with a 30-yard drive straight and true to the back of the Celtic net.

The second half was huff and puff from Celtic, more effort than sophistication, grunt and groan from Morton defenders, but no goals for 45 minutes.

Celtic players were hungry ghosts and Stein was apoplectic on the bench. Transistor radios among the crowd told the tale of Rangers' impending victory. There were maybe just ten seconds left.

If the second half had been a boxing match the referee would have stopped the fight to avoid further punishment to the visitors but this was football in which knock-downs without knockouts counted for nothing.

The match against Partick Thistle at Firhill was a 0-0 draw but Celtic's class of 79 swarmed and swirled about the Jags' goalmouth just as the Lisbon Lions had done against Inter Milan in 67

The author attended his first Celtic match at Firhill in October 1979

Centre Stand

(Section **D** Reserved)

PARTICK THISTLE
FOOTBALL CLUB LTD.

Premier League

PARTICK THISTLE
v.
CELTIC

FIRHILL PARK, GLASGOW

SATURDAY, 6th OCTOBER, 1979

Kick-off 3 p.m.

Ticket Holders are requested to be in their Seats
not later than 2.45 p.m.

Row **I**   Seat No. 23

Enter by Gates No. 21 & 22

This Portion to be RETAINED during the Match

Price £2.20

J. C. MONACHAN, SECRETARY

In the event of the game to which this ticket admits being postponed for any reason, the ticket will be available on the postponed date. **On no account will money be refunded.**

No respectful history of the immortals of Celtic Football Club should begin without contemplation of the horrors of the Irish Holocaust of 1845 to 1850

George Frederick Watts, The Famine, oil on canvas, 1850

Detail from bronze sculpture, 1997, John Behan, National Famine Memorial, Co Mayo

John Glass is the man to whom the club owes its existence.

Brother Walfrid planned to utilise a new football club to provide penny meals through the auspices of the Glasgow St Vincent de Paul Society

The statue of Brother Walfrid stands outside Celtic Park

Jock Stein, October 1953

He joined Celtic because the club had offered him and his beloved wife, Jeanie, a way out of misery in Llanelli, and a way forwards without descending deep into the Lanarkshire pits once more

Jock Stein, August 1969

The manager's mental states, his sometimes violent mood swings, his sleeplessness, were all well hidden from the public. Stein was a man stressed to stretching point throughout his managerial career

Sean Fallon and Neilly Mochan at the final whistle of the 1965 Cup Final victory over Dunfermline Athletic

Fallon was the soul of Celtic Football Club, something that never went missing whilst he was employed within the gates of Paradise.
Mochan was the third man – with Stein and Fallon – in this influential triumvirate of power

Together again: the Lisbon Lions in May. 1987 Back row: Craig, Gemmell, McNeill, Simpson, Murdoch, Clark. Front row: Johnstone, Wallace, Chalmers, Auld, Lennox

According to a BBC poll published in May 2022, the Lisbon Lions are the greatest club side in the history of football

Billy McNeill and Bobby Charlton prior to the Manchester United man's testimonial match, September 1972

Stein was blessed with both able lieutenants and with invaluable conduits between his office and the dressing room but without his captain, Billy McNeill, he might still have been lost

Billy McNeill and Jimmy Greaves of Spurs during the August 1967 friendly at Hampden to celebrate the centenary of Queen's Park

Charlie Tully prior to Celtic's defeat at Dundee, October 1949

Jimmy Johnstone's statue outside Celtic Park

George Connelly celebrates (fourth left) scoring the winning goal against Leeds United at Elland Road in the European Cup semi-final, April 1970

Kenny Dalglish during the Ronnie Moran testimonial match at Anfield: Liverpool v Celtic, May 2000

Every Celtic outfield player had at least one attempt on goal. Many supporters were wishing that Celtic had saved some of the goals scored in the Glasgow Cup Final on the Wednesday evening for today's showdown.

The referee's whistle was only moments away when Johnstone jinked once more past a tired defender, crossed the ball, and Lennox turned and shinned the ball over the Morton line. It was the final kick of the game.

Lennox was chased around the playing field by his team-mates, all except Gemmell who was too busy turning celebratory cartwheels, his legs and arms whirling like sparks from a revolving firework. Stein was pushing past a burly policeman to join his players.

Since the draw with Rangers in January Celtic had completed 15 consecutive league victories.

With one match to play, the Bhoys from Paradise were still ahead of their great rivals on goal average.

Rangers were at home to Aberdeen who had nothing to play for other than pride, win bonuses, and a battle for fifth place with Morton. Celtic had to visit old rivals Dunfermline Athletic who were firmly ensconced in fourth place in the league, just behind Hibernian in third. Neither match was a shoo-in.

There was, however, a matter of a Scottish Cup Final at Hampden on the following Saturday between Dunfermline and Hearts and it was suggested to the Rangers board that it might be nice if they permitted the two teams from the east of Scotland sole use of Glasgow on the day of the final. Would Rangers mind playing either on the Friday or share the stage in a thrilling climax to the league championship on the subsequent Wednesday evening? Lawrence and his fellow directors did mind.

It was another own goal in the net of public opinion and Stein exploited the situation in a way that only this Protestant hater of all things Protestant could do.

Stein suggested he at least understood the importance of the Scottish Cup to the nation as well as to football fans who valued the traditions of the ancient and venerable competition. He announced he would be taking all his players in a bus to Hampden to watch the final and encouraged all Celtic fans to do the same.

Thus it was that Celtic won its three-in-a-row league championship while watching from the Hampden stands as Stein's former team beat Hearts 3-1.

As the Pars fans were beginning to celebrate, across at Ibrox Park, the Dons scored a late winner. Celtic would now have to lose 16-0 to the cup winners on the following Wednesday if they were to finish the season behind Rangers. They did not do so.

For the record, Celtic won 2-1 at East End Park with second-half goals from Lennox in response to Pat Gardner's first-half opener.

An estimated 50,000 Celtic fans had travelled from Glasgow, around half of whom were locked out of the stadium and missed the game as the turnstiles were closed 15 minutes before the kick-off. Amid chaotic scenes, in which both sets of fans had cause to celebrate, fans climbed floodlight pylons and watched and cheered from rooftops.

Lennox's brace of goals were his 19th and 20th in the previous dozen matches. In the 1967/68 season the man from Saltcoats scored an astonishing 44 goals in 44 matches.

Before Stein's arrival, Lennox had been someone the Celtic board were willing to sell to Falkirk for a peppercorn fee.

Since the draw with Rangers in the New Year's Day fixture, Celtic had won 16 league games in a row and the man most responsible was the immortal Lennox.

* * *

4. DOUBLES, PREJUDICE, AND FOUR-IN-A-ROW
1968/69

It started so well.

Celtic defeated Rangers home and away in August in the League Cup and progressed to the semi-final with a 10-0 demolition of Hamilton Academical in which both Chalmers and Lennox scored five goals apiece.

In the league, too, Clyde were brushed aside at Shawfield with three unanswered goals by Brogan, Lennox and Gemmell.

The first intimation of mortality came on 14 September at Parkhead against the old enemy from across the Clyde in front of 75,000 souls crammed into Paradise, joyous and expectant of victory.

Celtic's confidence, however, received its first jolt in the 15th minute when Rangers' Swedish import, Örjan Persson, headed past a stranded Simpson.

One minute later, Lennox, of all people, missed a glorious chance to level the scores. The striker's speed was legendary but this time he was too fast for his own good, arriving in the back of the Rangers net before the cross from Wallace arrived from the wing. Another minute passed and the Ibrox men were two goals to the good when Johnston's shot from Penman's pass fizzed past Simpson.

Celtic did not play badly and luck, perhaps, was not on their side in this 4-2 loss. There was a disallowed goal from Lennox when the score was 3-1 and a penalty claim late on when Hughes was brought down in the box but Rangers, in the end, inflicted on Celtic their first defeat in 34 league games, a run that stretched back to September 1967. The *Glasgow Herald* suggested 'Rangers victory gives Scottish football new life'.

The poor result was compounded by a defeat by Saint-Étienne in the European Cup and a draw at Dunfermline in the league. Notions of infallibility were replaced by doubts, by a loss of faith.

The old year ended with three consecutive draws all played out on ice-bound surfaces unfit to most eyes for football.

A 0-0 at Falkirk was followed by 1-1 at home to Kilmarnock and another goalless debacle at Airdrie.

By the end of 1968 Celtic had dropped seven points, two more than during the entire previous season. Something had been lost or misplaced, something which even the appalling weather in December failed to excuse completely.

Stein and Fallon struggled to put a name to a problem. Even Kelly's suggestions of promotion of more of his fabled Kids was listened to with respect. In the Celtic reserve team that beat Rangers' reserves on the same day the first-teamers were defeated at Parkhead were Danny McGrain, Kenny Dalglish and Lou Macari. Of the Celtic 11 facing Airdrie at the fag end of the year, only three of the Lisbon Lions were missing, Simpson, Clark and Auld. Perhaps it was because the advice came from the Celtic chairman that it was ignored.

There was an intensity that had been replaced by complacency, a competitiveness that had been diluted by an acceptance of the fickleness of fate. Even Lennox was misfiring with a miserable return of four league goals by the end of December.

In spite of it all, however, at the turn of the year, Celtic were still five points clear of a Rangers side in fifth place and who were behind Dundee United, Kilmarnock, and Dunfermline.

When the Ibrox club defeated Celtic again on 2 January 1969, Stein was apoplectic. It mattered to him not one jot that the solitary goal in the Old Firm battle was a debatable penalty when McNeill's arm was struck by a close-range shot by Willie Henderson.

The manager's mood was not improved when he was told that BBC Scotland had prefaced a report on the match with the comment, 'Here is the news all Scotland has been waiting for.'

That Celtic had always been the enemy within, at least to the pillars of the Scottish establishment, the guardians of the Protestant ascendancy, had been clear from historical shenanigans.

Sometimes, to Celtic fans, it seemed as if their club had not only to battle against Rangers, who had become since the early years of the 20th century the sporting arm of the ruling classes in Scotland, but also a host of biased referees and newspapers together with a Scottish Football Association that would down Celtic at every opportunity.

If there were signs in tenement windows pronouncing 'No blacks, no dogs, no Irish', there might just as well have been notices headed 'Stop the Catholics' outside the offices of the SFA.

The prejudice and the persecution probably began in 1896 when the *Scottish Sport* labelled Rangers 'Scotia's darling club,' and issued a rallying cry to Protestant clubs to restore the natural order of footballing sovereignty recently usurped by Celtic and a reborn Hibernian.

The nativist Scottish counter-revolution continued with the arrival of Harland and Wolff in Glasgow and with the overtly racist 1923 Church of Scotland report on the evils of Irish immigration.

With a prolonged period of Rangers footballing superiority between the two world wars and the overt assertion of the Ibrox club's policy of signing only Protestant footballers, the bigotry merely simmered.

The culture war in Scotland had apparently been won. In both football and in society the Protestants appeared firmly in charge. In August 1949, however, there was confirmation that the SFA would not suffer any reassertion of minority rights.

The League Cup campaign for that season opened with a group game success against Rangers at Celtic Park in which John McPhail scored twice and Mike Haughney netted the third and decisive goal.

The return game at Ibrox was played in front of 95,000 baying and baiting fans. On the half hour, Charlie Tully, the maverick Celtic winger, engaged in a forlorn chase of an over-hit pass that was easily gathered by Bobby Brown in the Rangers goal. Sammy Cox, a stalwart of Rangers' Iron Curtain defence, without rhyme or reason, then booted Tully in the stomach. Tully collapsed in the middle of the penalty area and the Celtic supporters waited for the inevitable penalty and dismissal of Cox.

When neither was forthcoming, they protested by throwing bottles on to the pitch and the game was temporarily halted.

Rangers won the game 2-0, and Celtic appealed to the SFA for an investigation into the causes of the chaos on the terraces. The report reprimanded both Cox and Tully for 'provoking violent disorder'. Kelly seethed and demanded an explanation. The SFA claimed Tully had 'exaggerated any slight injury he may have received', while the referee claimed to have 'not seen the incident'.

Decades of questionable refereeing decisions followed the Cox-Tully affair. Prejudice and the political culture of Scottish football have been constant thorns in Celtic flesh throughout the club's history.

It was a relief to return to the football, even though the turning of the year to 1969 brought defeat at Ibrox.

* * *

After the New Year's Day derby, Celtic's lead over their Glasgow rivals was reduced to three points and a revitalised challenge to the East End club's recent supremacy seemed inevitable.

If Stein was incandescent at a double defeat by Rangers, Kelly was in a different kind of bewilderment.

The Celtic chairman was knighted for 'services to football' in the New Year's Honours list. More probably, however, it was awarded by Harold Wilson's Labour government as a result of his principled stand against playing European Cup football in eastern Europe after the Soviet invasion of Czechoslovakia in 1968.

In threatening his club's withdrawal from the competition, there were no nit-picking rulebook consultations this time.

Kelly was a proud man but not arrogant. His was a warm glow felt throughout the club. When he said the award was for his club and his country in general he meant it. Above all, he was pleased for his wife, now Lady Kelly, who had been at his side throughout the years when his every appearance in the directors' box had been greeted with derision and disapproval.

Stein inquired politely whether or not he would now have to call his chairman Sir Robert but his question was accompanied with a wry smile.

The manager's mind, though, was elsewhere, plotting a return to winning ways against Dunfermline on the following Saturday.

* * *

The truth was, however, that Rangers under David White in 1969 were not up to the task. Immediately after beating Celtic at Ibrox, the Govan men were pegged back three times in a draw at Kilmarnock that was notable both for its excitement and for the violence of the tackling on both sides. Celtic, meanwhile, beat Dunfermline 3-1 but 'lacked conviction' according to Glyn Edwards in the *Evening News*.

Rangers then embarked upon a seven-game winning streak matched by their rivals. Pressure, however, was building on White and his men.

As February turned to March and the mad month itself was nearing its close, Rangers failed to find the means to victory in three consecutive away matches. A 3-2 defeat at Airdrie was followed by a 2-1 loss at Dundee United and a 0-0 draw at Aberdeen.

A 3-0 home win by Rangers over Morton on 19 April prolonged the agony but now Celtic needed just a solitary point at Kilmarnock on the following Monday.

It was an evening of portentous gale force winds in Ayrshire. Celtic kicked off into the maw of the storm and by half-time found themselves two goals down. Harsh words were spoken in the dressing room by Stein, so much so that the players would not have dared to return there at the end of the match without at least a share of the spoils.

On 63 minutes, Murdoch, named before the game as the Scottish Footballer of the Year, clipped a high ball into the Killie goalmouth where Frank Beattie turned it past his own stranded goalkeeper.

At 2-1, Tommy McLean, the Ayrshire club's tricky winger, squandered two glorious chances with the goal at his mercy on both occasions.

Celtic were pressing for an equaliser but, as the correspondent for the *Evening Times* admitted, their play was made of 'more weight than wisdom'.

Injury time commenced; maybe a minute or slightly more remained for the Celts to make amends. The ball danced and bounced in the wind that swirled about the Kilmarnock penalty area. Shots cannoned off defenders' legs. But then Gemmell pounced with mere seconds before the final whistle, stabbing the ball into the back of the Killie net.

The league championship was returning to Celtic Park unless Stein's men lost their remaining two games at home to Morton and away at Dundee by cricket scores while Rangers won their remaining matches.

On the following evening, the Ibrox club lost 3-2 at Dundee.

Four-in-a-row.

On Saturday, 26 April, at Hampden, Celtic claimed the Scottish Cup by thrashing a demoralised Rangers 4-0.

Two days later they paraded three trophies before their adoring fans at Paradise: league championship, Scottish Cup, and League Cup.

There was a frisson of disappointment in the game against the Greenock side as Morton's Danish forward Per Bartram scored a hat-trick inside the first ten minutes and the game finished 4-2 to the visitors, but the championship was secure.

At Ibrox, meanwhile, Rangers, in front of a crowd of only 6,400 supporters, managed only a last-minute equaliser against Dundee.

Rangers finished five points behind Celtic and a sense of crisis and a gathering of dark days ahead enveloped and dispirited the denizens of Ibrox Park.

Someone on the terraces of Paradise suggested Stein's team might break their own record of six consecutive league titles. Someone else said, 'Nah, this team could go on winning forever.'

The only danger, surely, was hubris.

* * *

5. TRANSITION AND TRIUMPH, PRIDE AND FALL 1969/70

This time it did not begin well, did not augur well for the future.

On 13 August, there was a 2-1 defeat in Group 8 of the League Cup at Ibrox. Harry Hood, signed from Clyde in March 1969 for £40,000 and playing in place of Chalmers, opened the scoring in the eighth minute. It was a sign of the times. Only six of the Lisbon Lions made the starting line-up at Ibrox – Gemmell, Murdoch, McNeill, Clark, Wallace and Lennox – although Auld made a belated appearance as substitute.

Of all the Lions, 'Jinky' Johnstone was the most notable absentee. He had suffered a groin strain in an earlier friendly at Carlisle but was fit enough to play for Celtic's reserves in a 5-0 victory over Rangers in which Lou Macari scored a brace. Stein's relationship with Johnstone was one of occasional unbounded love, and blind exasperation, tending to hatred. He was a father figure to the still young and still wayward talent but his dealings with Johnstone were too often akin to those of his own father and his apostate and celebrated son. The winger had seriously contemplated asking for a transfer when Stein arrived, only persuaded by Sean Fallon to stay with the club of his heart for whom he had been a ball boy as a young teenager.

In October 1968, the four-in-a-row season, in a game at Celtic Park against Dundee United, Stein, arms whirling with frustration at Johnstone's ineptitude on the afternoon, and with Celtic only one goal to the good, decided to replace the wee man with George Connelly. As Johnstone left the field, he took off his jersey and threw it in disgust at the dugout where Stein and Fallon were sitting. To Johnstone's horror, he watched as his jersey landed smack on his manager's face. The winger set off down the tunnel, running as fast as he had done in any part of the match. There was a sharp collective intake of breath by all those present. Johnstone heard his manager hurrying down the tunnel after him. Even with Stein's hampering limp, escape seemed impossible. Celtic's greatest ever player, as voted by fans in 2002, later told his story to Archie Macpherson of the BBC who reproduced it in his wonderful biography of Stein:

'As soon as I did it I thought, "My God, what have I done?" and I belted up the tunnel as fast as I could, but I knew he would be right behind me. My first notion was to run straight out of the front door without changing and head down London Road and disappear for ever. But I got into the dressing room, slammed the door shut, then locked it. I was about to dive into where the big bath was and shut that door when I heard him kicking the door, then battering it with his fist. I knew then I was in deep shit.'

Even in his rage, however, Stein was calculating.

Johnstone was infuriating in his inability to perform with consistency but, on his day, he would take on the best defenders in the world and leave them with their brains and their feet equally befuddled.

Johnstone, in his turn, knew there were consequences that had to be faced.

'I shouted out, "I'll let you in if you promise not to hit me!" The battering suddenly stopped and there was a kind of silence and, would you believe, he burst out laughing at what I had said? He just laughed and I heard him walk away.'

Johnstone was suspended for seven days.

In truth, Stein was plotting something between evolution and revolution at Celtic Park. The odd defeat might even help this process on its way, would clarify his thinking. Loyalty to players, even Lisbon Lions, would stretch only so far.

The early defeat to Rangers was not terminal to their hopes of claiming a fifth successive League Cup. A win in the return match at Paradise saw Celtic qualify for the quarter-finals and at Hampden in October an Auld goal was sufficient to create a record that still stands today.

Celtic's league form, however, was a matter of concern. After four games Stein's side had acquired a meagre four points, losing at Dunfermline and at home to Hibernian.

Rangers, however, were possessed of their own demons, losing at Ayr and drawing 0-0 at Dundee United. Nevertheless, the Ibrox side held a two-point lead over Celtic when the first Old Firm battle for league points occurred on 20 September.

Lose at Ibrox and Celtic's prospects for five-in-a-row league titles to match their League Cup successes would be as slim as a new moon setting over Paradise.

The omens were not encouraging. Celtic had not won at Ibrox for 12 long years and injuries and illnesses were rife among Stein's squad. Murdoch and Connelly were both flu victims and Callaghan suffered from a painful boil. Hughes and Auld were possessors of unspecified leg injuries.

The match itself overflowed with bickering and battering. Jim Craig was sent off for what the *Herald*'s correspondent, Glyn Edwards, described as 'wilful barbarism', violence against Rangers winger Willie Johnston, which was completely alien to the defender's normally placid and unruffled demeanour.

By that time, however, Celtic were a goal in front when Hood picked up on a long McNeill clearance and shot past Gerry Neef, Rangers' German goalkeeper.

Just before the commencement of the 1969/70 season, Stein had said on television, 'Rangers' time will come again.' It would not do so yet, however.

By the end of December, Celtic had completed a run of eight consecutive league victories including spectacular scorelines of 4-1 at St Johnstone, 7-2 at home to Dundee United, and 8-1 at home against Partick Thistle.

Celtic were two points clear at the top of the table as well as claiming the League Cup and Glasgow Cup and were in the quarter-finals of the European Cup in which Stein's team were drawn to play the Italian champions, Fiorentina.

Loose talk was of another *annus mirabilis*, of winning it all once again, and a goalless draw at Parkhead in the New Year derby with Rangers did nothing to dampen the excitement.

Evan Williams, a goalkeeper signed recently from Wolverhampton Wanderers, made his Old Firm debut and was another sign of Stein's rebuilding work.

The game was as dreary as the day was bright but the problem was the frozen ground which put fear of broken bones in the heads of professional footballers whose careers might be ended by one slip, one slide, one twist or turn or mistimed tackle.

The match turned, however, not on the weather, but on one refereeing decision. As usual these days, McNeill trundled forward into the opposition box as a corner swung in towards his head. The football flashed into Neef's net. John Paterson, the referee, had ideas other than signalling for a goal. Apparently, he had spotted a 'prior infringement'.

It was not the first and would not be the last occasion during this season Celtic had suffered from incomprehensible officialdom.

In the League Cup Old Firm game at Celtic Park in August 1969 the referee, Jim Callaghan, possibly as well versed in matters football as his namesake, the UK Home Secretary, failed to send off Celtic's John Hughes for a potential second booking. After the game Rangers lodged a formal complaint and Callaghan was suspended for two months.

Had the Labour Party politician been moonlighting in Glasgow? Even if that had been the case, the decision of the SFA could not have been more bizarre or more biased. As Brian Wilson, the former Celtic director and author of *Celtic: the Official History*, said, 'It was difficult to imagine that a complaint on similar grounds from any other source would have met with the same outcome.'

In April 1970, too, with Celtic still on target for a second clean sweep of trophies under Stein, the Scottish Cup Final was ruined by the performance of the referee, R.H. Davidson, who, as Wilson delicately put it, 'was not highly regarded in Celtic circles'.

First of all a penalty was awarded to Aberdeen when a Derek McKay cross hit Murdoch's hand when it was clearly beyond his competence to avoid the ball. To add insult to injury, Gemmell was booked for throwing the ball at the referee in disgust at the decision. Just after the half hour, with Celtic one down, Dons goalkeeper Bobby Clark dropped the ball at the feet of Lennox who put it in the back of the net only for the goal to be disallowed.

Johnstone was booked for his protests. Finally, on 38 minutes, Lennox flew towards the Aberdeen goal and was hacked down by Martin Buchan, the Dons' captain, and no penalty was awarded. Stein on the touchline was incandescent.

At half-time in the dressing room the talk was of a fix, of how the SFA would never permit Celtic to keep on winning all the domestic trophies.

League titles won over a spread of 34 games were impossible to control but a one-off cup final, well, here it would be much easier to influence a result.

When the number of Scotland international caps awarded to each of Celtic's Lisbon Lions is considered it is impossible to discount both bias and bile at the heart of the SFA.

Simpson	5
Craig	1
Gemmell	18
McNeill	29
Clark	4
Johnstone	23
Wallace	7
Chalmers	5
Auld	3
Lennox	10

How could such reluctance to recognise and honour the genius of these immortals be a result of anything other than prejudice against the institution that was Celtic and the culture the football club represented?

The men from Paradise were tolerated when unsuccessful under McGrory but something had to be done when Stein looked as if his team would sweep all before them once again in 1970.

After the Old Firm game in January there were 13 league games left to play and Celtic remained two points clear of their bitter rivals.

If transition and evolution were the names for Stein's game, revolution was once more the word for Rangers.

In December 1969, Rangers had dispensed with the services of Dave White, whose two-year term of office had yielded no major trophies. The man from Clyde was the only Ibrox custodian to fail to add to the Govan club's trophy cabinet.

The new man in the hotseat was Willie Waddell, a former Ibrox legend who made 558 appearances for the Gers, scoring 143 goals from his wide position. More pertinently for his new role, Waddell had led Kilmarnock to the league championship in 1965. Appointed as his assistant was Jock Wallace from Hearts, whose talents included the public singing of sectarian songs like 'The Sash' which commemorated victories by William of Orange over Catholicism and its Irish adherents in 1690 and 1691.

It was worn at Derry, Aughrim, Enniskillen and the Boyne,
It's a terror to them Papish boys, the Sash My Father Wore,
And on the Twelfth, I love to wear the Sash My Father Wore.

Rangers' managerial appointments caused celebrations in the Protestant press and Stein was moved to public comment. 'Are you all forgetting us now?' he teased, before adding that larger-than-usual crowds at Ibrox would be to do with 'factors other than football'.

In fact, Waddell had not been the first choice of the Ibrox board. That had been Stein himself.

There was a feeling among the Rangers board that the Celtic boss would be unable to resist the lure of his father's team and that he remained 'one of us'.

So, while Waddell was campaigning against White in his *Daily Express* column, referring constantly to 'the Boy David', secretive and tentative approaches were made to Stein.

It showed, however, just how little John Lawrence and his fellow directors understood the complexities of Stein's psyche, the bitterness and the disconnect between him and his Orange father, the hatred Stein had stored up in his heart for the bigotry that still held sway at Ibrox Park. Stein might have sung 'The Sash' as a boy but now he was a man.

The Celtic manager might even have played Lawrence like an angler plays a fish, delighting in his sport, striking, reeling in, and landing his victims on the Rangers board, before walking away with bitter laughter in his heart.

* * *

March 1970 was a bad month for the new duo in charge of team affairs at Ibrox. Three consecutive away games were lost, all by 2-1 scorelines, at Raith Rovers, Dunfermline and Dundee, and the title was lost too.

On Saturday, 28 March, Celtic travelled to Edinburgh needing only to equal Rangers' result at Airdrieonians to clinch the championship.

A 1-1 draw for Rangers at Broomfield Park was matched by a goalless draw for Celtic at Hearts.

Stein had one eye on securing the title and one eye on the impending European Cup semi-final tie against the English champions, Leeds United. McNeill, Auld and Johnstone were rested, but it made no difference to a dominant performance that lacked only goals. The man of the match at Tynecastle was Hearts' goalkeeper, Jim Cruickshank.

Jim Parkinson of the *Herald* described Celtic as 'the undisputed masters of the Scottish League'.

Five-in-a-row.

By the time the whistle sounded at the end of the final league game of the season, a 3-2 win at St Mirren, Celtic were 12 points clear of Rangers in second place.

They also had one foot in a second European Cup Final courtesy of a Connelly goal after 40 seconds of the away leg of the semi-final against Leeds.

* * *

It is difficult to ascertain the high tide mark of this 1969/70 Celtic team.

Although the solitary goal at Elland Road had been a scruffy one with Paul Madeley, the English defender, misjudging a high, bouncing ball latched on to by Connelly whose shot ricocheted off an opposition player and squeezed over the line as reluctantly as a drunk leaving a pub at closing time, Celtic were superb.

The Glasgow team forced 12 corners to Leeds's one, and took 16 shots to the Yorkshire side's six.

Tony Queen, the Glasgow turf accountant and best of friends with Stein, had laid heavy bets on the Scottish champions at odds of 4-1. It would be surprising if Stein had not asked for 5-1 and been given 9-2 together with a tip for top weight Gay Trip to win the Grand National on the following Saturday and an admonition to find another bookie to bet with next time.

By the time Celtic had won the second leg 2-1 against Leeds, played at Hampden before a European Cup record attendance of 136,505, Stein's team had lost the Scottish Cup Final 3-1 against Aberdeen. It was the first of two bitter blows from which the Celtic manager never truly recovered.

At full time, in the sour aftermath of the ending of dreams of another clean sweep of trophies, Stein unleashed a foul-mouthed tirade against Bobby Davidson, the referee, for his sequence of decisions that cost Celtic the cup. The manager was fined £10 by the SFA.

The refereeing had been so shocking that the triumphant Aberdeen manager Eddie Turnbull, when asked about Stein's punishment, said, 'If I'd been in Big Jock's shoes, I'd have had 20 quid's worth.'

The second, and greater, hammer blow to Stein's pride arrived on 6 May 1970 at the San Siro Stadium in Milan where Celtic lost to Dutch champions Feyenoord in the club's second European Cup Final.

There is no doubt that Stein, along with his players, underestimated the opponents, but there is no doubt, too, that the original misjudgement and its confirmation to his staff and football team came from the manager himself.

It was a miscalculation of colossal proportions that changed the course of Celtic's history, replacing the prospect of grand European dreams and adventures with a narrow parochialism that still haunted the club deep into the 21st century.

The meticulous preparation and attention to minute but important details, which characterised Stein's work prior to the 1967 final in Lisbon, was nowhere to be seen. Admittedly, Stein had travelled to watch Feyenoord play, but he returned with reports so inaccurate it beggared belief. He told his players the Dutch champions were 'lacking pace, lacking mental toughness, lacking hope'.

Wim van Hanagem, Stein told Auld, had 'a right foot just for standing on', and Wim Jansen – a future Celtic immortal – would 'last no more than 20 minutes before disappearing'. In fact, as Auld admitted, Jansen 'got faster as we got slower' and was 'just too good for me'. Tommy Gemmell confessed, too, that Van Hanegem 'was still running stronger than anybody in extra time and pinging beautiful passes all over the field'.

There was talk of the impossibility of a team from the Dutch league that had only been fully professional for 13 years challenging the Scottish champions whose league had been stuffed with legal mercenaries since 1893.

Tony Queen in Glasgow was offering odds of 6-1 against Feyenoord. 'These Dutch players will be shitting themselves,' Stein told his charges in the dressing room before the game. The problem was that the players believed every word Stein said as if it were the word of God.

There had been ill discipline, too, in the run-up to the final. Players were mingling with journalists, some of whom were trying to arrange cash deals and sponsorship for them, and some were drinking and lounging in the sun. They might have been at a holiday camp in between seasons.

All this was in complete and, in retrospect, bewildering contrast to Lisbon.

Stein had based his assumptions after watching one Dutch league match. Had he been hoodwinked by his Feyenoord counterpart Ernst Happel, the master and founder of the concept of Total Football?

Everyone seemed to have forgotten that Feyenoord had reached the European Cup Final by beating the champions of Iceland, Italy, Germany and Poland.

In the event, Celtic, strung out on the rack of wave upon wave of Dutch torture, almost held out for a replay in which there would have been urgency as opposed to complacency.

Feyenoord's winner came deep into extra time from their talismanic Swedish striker Ove Kindvall, who had run McNeill ragged throughout the match.

Five-in-a-row was of little consolation.

* * *

If the shenanigans surrounding Celtic's preparations for the European Cup Final represented high tragedy, what followed was low farce.

If the US tour at the close of the 1966 season had forged a team spirit so strong it could break Inter Milan in Lisbon a year later, the 1970 tour confirmed the disintegration of that same spirit.

At half-time in a supposedly friendly match against Bari in which fists and boots flew, Stein lost his cool and dived into the Italian team's dugout where he proceeded to lay into the Bari coach as if he had been on the street corner of Burnbank and some drunk had called his mother a whore. Stein then picked himself up, dusted himself down, limped down the tunnel and was not seen again by his players until the preparations began again for another season of football in July.

The game with Bari was abandoned and it was later announced Stein had left to see a specialist about his damaged ankle that had plagued him since May 1956 when he had landed awkwardly during a Celtic friendly against Coleraine. It was a lie, of course.

After the Feyenoord debacle, after the guilt over his woeful lack of preparation for the match against the Dutch champions, his mental health was the real issue. Stein had simply lost the plot.

Sean Fallon took charge of the squad and Desmond White flew from Glasgow to assume overall command. Some players, with the headmaster absent without leave, decided to act like schoolboys with a supply teacher. It was impossible to cover up the booze and sex exploits of Celtic's players in New Jersey and Fallon felt he had no alternative but to attempt to re-impose a semblance of discipline.

Auld and Gemmell were deemed the ringleaders of the rebellion and sent home on the next available flight.

There had never been such dissension and division within the football club that followed Stein's desertion of his players.

European Cups and league titles all seemed like dreams now amid the nightmares that engulfed Celtic in the final days of the 1969/70 season.

Light and dark played out their humbling games in Stein's heart and head. In his sleepless nights, he replayed the joyous film of the American tour of the summer of 1966, the film noir of its ugly 1970 reprise. To become an immortal in 1967 was to live too long, to see the humiliation of defeat, the ignominy of footballers beyond his control, the shame of his attack on the Bari coach and of his flight from reality.

* * *

6. DECONSTRUCTION, RECONSTRUCTION
1970/71

A febrile atmosphere persisted through the summer of 1970. There was doubt, despair, disillusionment, all casting their destructive spells of disunity at Celtic Park. Would Stein emerge from his depression and destructive behaviour and resume his former dictatorial role within the footballing arena of the club?

Big Jock had built one great side but would he now be able to rouse himself from his slough of despond to create a new team? The remnants of the Lisbon Lions had enjoyed and endured their days in the sun but were now in urgent need of replacement. There was a new generation of Kelly's Kids – more properly now called Fallon's Kids – waiting in the wings.

Greatness required that the Celtic manager deconstruct and reconstruct. Busby at Manchester United had built and rebuilt, beginning with the great postwar side that won the English First Division in 1951/52, continuing with successive championships in 1955/56 and 1956/57 which saw the gradual integration of the Busby Babes. His immortality, however, was sealed by the creation of his third great side of the late 1960s – resplendent with George Best, Bobby Charlton and Denis Law – that won the league title in 1966/67 and the European Cup in 1968. Stein's great friend Bill Shankly built two great sides, the early 1960s iteration that won promotion from the Second Division and league titles in 1963/64 and 1965/66. Before his premature retirement, however, in 1974, Shanks had created a second great side that won the championship in 1972/73 and which he bequeathed to his successor, Bob Paisley. Brian Clough created three great teams at two different clubs, Derby County and Nottingham Forest.

These were the standards by which Stein would later be judged and found to be lacking nothing by way of comparison.

Season 1970/71 would find unity from brokenness. First, though, Stein had to convince the board of directors that he was fit, in all senses of the word, to continue as manager.

The boardroom triumvirate of White, Devlin and Farrell were unnerved both by Stein's summertime breakdown and by news of their chairman's illness. By this summer of discontent, Kelly knew he was dying, knew his hold over the club was weakening, and understood he had to make one last effort to save Stein, his friend, from self-destruction.

While Stein prowled about his house in sleepless early hours of the night and the corridors of Celtic Park before the arrival of players, coaches or office staff, Kelly lay abed. The chairman pondered past and future, unable to lie easy with the present moment in which his body was betraying him.

Players lounged by pools, and by seas and sandcastles, most travelling no further than the west coast of Scotland, all dreading the return to fierce training regimes and to fierce managerial tantrums from Stein. Many were worried sick about their futures now that their aura of invincibility in Europe had been blown away in the storm of Feyenoord's perfect football at the San Siro, now that their bodies were showing signs of irreversible decline.

Stein, though, was back in his office poring over details of the players at his disposal for the new season, ages, strengths, weaknesses, lifestyles, working, niggling away at plans for transfers in and out of the club, possible promotions for Fallon's Kids from the reserves, but pondering, too, his own future.

* * *

The league championship campaign, however, began well with two wins and two clean sheets against Morton and Clyde.

Stein's teams were amalgams of new and old. The new guard was prominent: Evan Williams, Danny McGrain, George Connelly, Jim Brogan, Vic Davidson, Davie Hay, Harry Hood and Lou Macari, but the old guard still stood its ground, with Lennox scoring both goals in the opening-day victory, and McNeill still prominent and powerful at the back.

The test of the team's resolve, however, would come with the visit of Rangers in the third league fixture of the campaign.

In August, the Bhoys had already airily dismissed the Ibrox club's challenge in the held-over Glasgow Cup Final with a 3-1 win in which McNeill, Clark, Johnstone, Lennox, Chalmers and Auld were all omitted from the Celtic team. It was an early marker of Stein's determination to rebuild his ageing side.

In front of over 70,000 fans, Celtic simply outclassed their great rivals, demonstrating composure and a swirling movement off the ball that contrasted favourably with Rangers' dour and sweaty determination and hard running. Only four Lions graced Paradise that afternoon: Murdoch, McNeill, Johnstone and Lennox.

By the evening of 12 September, dark forebodings had dissipated as surely as the morning mists over the Clyde.

* * *

The evolution of the team, which had begun in the previous season, continued apace. When push came to shove, Stein was utterly ruthless, making enemies at every turn. There was not a single member of the Lions who did not harbour some degree of anger and resentment at the way the Celtic manager handled the twilights of his charges' careers. Man management was not Stein's greatest strength. He was a man of bluster and brutality in his dealings with players who were treated mostly as if they were members of some lesser species and whose behaviours he regarded as erratic at best and potentially damaging to his work at worst.

He was fortunate indeed in having Sean Fallon as his assistant who would do his utmost to mitigate the worst effects of Stein's blasts of intemperate behaviour.

Having Fallon as friend and as both moderator and mentor as well as a recruiter and a developer of young talent was akin to possessing a double-headed penny when gambling for your life on the toss of a coin.

* * *

Fallon's extraordinary genius – and gift to Stein – was his ability to recognise footballing talent and to use his persuasive tongue, his blarney, to convince both boys and their parents that Celtic was the only football club worth joining.

Stein's gift in return to Fallon was his absolute trust in his assistant's judgement of players. For a man like Stein, for whom control was all, this was remarkable.

Without Fallon, Celtic's manager's legacy would have been halved at best and maybe less than that. Remember, it was Fallon who signed both Ronnie Simpson and Bertie Auld back in 1965 before Stein arrived. In fact, when Fallon mentioned to Stein that Auld was returning to Parkhead, the manager of Hibernian told him, 'You're signing trouble there.'

It was Fallon who signed and nurtured the Quality Street Gang of young Celtic talent that lifted Celtic to the club's first nine-in-a-row. They were all Sean's Bhoys.

The first to arrive at Paradise, in July 1964, was George Connelly. Following up on a report from one of his unofficial scouts, Fallon watched the 15-year-old Connelly playing for Tulliallan in a Junior Cup tie in Kincardine, Fife. Fallon said he was 'magnificent'. McGrory's assistant was astonished to find there was limited competition for the youngster's signature. 'There should have been a queue half a mile long to sign him,' Fallon admitted to his biographer, Stephen Sullivan.

The sole rival club vying with Celtic for Connelly's future was Dunfermline Athletic, managed by a certain Jock Stein.

When Stein arrived at Celtic he was still excited by Connelly so invited him in December 1966 to demonstrate his skills at keepy-uppy in front of a crowd of 64,000 prior to the European Cup Winners' Cup quarter-final, and paid him £5 to do so. Some Celts still refer to the occasion as Connelly's debut but his official maiden appearance for the first team had to wait until he appeared as a substitute in April 1968 against Dunfermline.

Connelly went on to score and play memorable parts in the 4-0 Celtic victory over Rangers in the 1969 Scottish Cup Final, including walking the ball into the net for his goal, and performing more keepy-uppy antics, this time mid-match, to infuriate the Rangers supporters. He scored, too, in the first-leg victory over Leeds United in the European Cup semi-final.

Bob Rooney, the Celtic physiotherapist, who doubled as a coach in his spare time, said Connelly was 'the best young player I ever saw at Celtic Park'.

Of all the harsh words Stein doled out to his players, especially from 6 May 1970 onwards, not one was spat in Connelly's direction.

* * *

Connelly was merely the first fruit of Fallon's extensive network of spies that might best be compared with Sherlock Holmes's Baker Street Irregulars.

A bookmaker tipped off Fallon about Lou Macari. Danny McGrain was recommended by a publican; Davie Hay by a priest; and, later, Tommy

Burns by a car dealer. These players, together with Kenny Dalglish, might have formed the beating heart of Stein's second great side.

That this never quite happened, that these players never quite fulfilled their potential as a team was primarily because of the lure of greater wealth to be found south of the border and, secondarily, because of the parsimony of the Celtic board under Kelly's successor, Desmond White.

They were, though, all Fallon's men. McGrain later admitted, 'I owe Sean everything. If he hadn't signed me, I don't know where I would be today. He was the one who saw me, believed in me and took the bull by the horns. Before then, I'd never seen myself becoming a footballer. I didn't believe that people like me, boys from Drumchapel, could become stars like the ones I saw on telly on a Saturday night.'

Dalglish, too, was a Fallon signing, whisked from beneath the noses of Rangers. The young man's bedroom overlooked the Ibrox training ground and its walls were adorned with posters of Rangers legends.

This time, however, Fallon's signing was not a result of a report from one of his Irregulars. It happened by accident and as a result of a letter from a Mrs Davidson. The woman in question was the mother of a 15-year-old midfielder playing for Glasgow United. Dutifully, Fallon went to watch Vic Davidson playing on a red ash pitch in Cambuslang and saw immediately that the mother was a fine judge of a footballer. Davidson went on to play 55 times for Celtic and scored 21 goals but Fallon's eyes were taken most of all by one of his team-mates by the name of Dalglish. There was something about his composure on the ball, his balance, his grace under pressure, as well as his surliness when approached by Fallon at the end of the match. Later, when he realised Dalglish was desperate for an approach from Rangers, he understood and forgave the ungracious response to a Celtic representative.

Still, though, the signing of Dalglish would never have progressed to completion without the persistence of Fallon and two whole hours of persuasion in the Dalglish family flat while his wife and children waited outside – all on his wedding anniversary.

Stein was initially unconvinced, thought that Dalglish was too slow and might not make the grade, but by May 1967 he had come to trust more in his assistant's judgement than he had ever trusted anything in his life, and agreed to the deal.

Dalglish went on to play for Celtic 322 times and score 167 goals.

* * *

By the close of November 1970, there were more changes afoot.

For a start, Rangers had been overtaken by Eddie Turnbull's Aberdeen as the principal rivals for Celtic's crown as league champions.

On Saturday, 12 December, Aberdeen were the visitors having won their previous nine games, and having closed to within one point of Celtic at the top of the league. Curiously, both teams boasted identical goal differences – the Scottish Football League had just switched from goal averages – of 37 for and seven against.

Aberdeen were aiming for a third consecutive victory over the Celts having won both their previous encounters in 1970 including their controversial cup final win the previous spring.

In the week prior to the match, Glasgow had been in a ferment, with demonstrations in protest at the Conservative government's attempts to curb trade union powers through their Industrial Relations Bill. There had been a rally at Govan Town Hall organised by the Liaison Committee for the Defence of Trade Unionism and a march the following day from North Frederick Street to the Church Institute in Bothwell Street. The Citizens Theatre had offered free tickets for trade unionists. In addition, like the rest of the UK, Glasgow had suffered from intermittent power cuts as the nation's electricity supply was interrupted by the power workers' overtime ban and work-to-rule in pursuit of increased wages.

Stein, mindful of his own earlier life as a miner who produced coal for the power stations, was telling all and sundry of his support for the trade union movement.

On the day of the game, a magnificent 63,000 found their way to Celtic Park in spite of the difficulties with public transport. The match kicked off ten minutes earlier than the traditional 3pm and the half-time interval was cut to five minutes in order to avoid dependence on floodlights during a potential power cut.

In the event, Aberdeen's defence throughout the 90 minutes was as tight as the bargaining between the Electricity Council and Frank Chapple's trade unionists, and the tackling was as feisty as the exchanges in the House of Commons between Harold Wilson, the leader of the opposition, and Ted Heath's employment minister, Robert Carr.

Time and time again, Celtic fell victim to a well-drilled Aberdeen offside trap and, in the 53rd minute, Joe Harper headed home a long throw, making contact with the ball as it appeared to be inches from John Fallon's gloves. There was no way back for an uninspired Celtic team, even one that contained Connelly, Macari and Hay from among Sean's Bhoys.

Aberdeen were immediately installed as favourites to halt Celtic's attempt to equal their own record of six-in-a-row.

A note in the Celtic programme, however, recalled that when the Dons won their one and only league title in 1954/55 they were beaten home and away by the previous champions, Celtic. The point was well made.

If Aberdeen were to win the current edition of the league championship, beating Celtic was only worth the same two points as beating Cowdenbeath.

Title winners do sometimes lose to their close rivals but champions rarely slip up against the supposedly lesser teams.

This reminder was of some consolation to Celtic fans though not to Stein, who continued to rumble and grumble inside and outside of the dressing room and continued to ponder the transition from wizened Lions to baby-faced Bhoys.

* * *

By the end of March 1971, Aberdeen had indeed dropped points against a clutch of mere mortals residing in the middle and lower reaches of the league.

Their winning run of 15 league matches ended at Hibernian (12th of 18 in the final league table) with a 2-1 defeat in mid-January and was followed, in a frightful February, by a 1-0 defeat at Dunfermline (16th), a goalless home draw with Rangers (fourth), and a 1-1 home draw with St Mirren (17th and relegated).

Still, though, Aberdeen were within striking distance of the top, as their form had recovered throughout March with four wins from four games, while Celtic were preoccupied with European exertions and diminutions.

In Ajax, Celtic discovered another Dutch nemesis. In the quarter-final of the European Cup, the Glasgow side were treated to another masterclass of modern football by Johan Cruyff and his compatriots in

Amsterdam. The away leg was lost 3-0 and the 1-0 victory in the return leg at Celtic Park counted for nothing but pride.

Stein was depressed, disconsolate. He had trusted the remnants of the Lions in both legs in the hope of a last hurrah from Craig, Gemmell, McNeill, Johnstone, Wallace, Auld and Lennox.

In his heart and in his soul, Stein knew this team would never again take Europe by storm. There was misery and regret, too, in the fact that only one European Cup had been plundered.

Rumours, too, swirled like autumn rains, settled like winter snows, and froze like ice in the hearts of Celtic fans, and opened cracks in the boardroom at Paradise.

Stein was distracted, disillusioned, discontented and disconnected from the team, the club. Fans and directors alike recalled the manager's abandonment of the American tour. Official explanations – returning for treatment on his troublesome ankle, returning to catch up on a mountain of paperwork – were mulled over and suspected. Later, Stein's wife, Jean, told the truth: 'He just didn't have his heart in it.'

On that ill-fated foreign escapade, too, Stein held secret talks in Canada with representatives of Manchester United who were tasked with finding a replacement for Matt Busby's replacement, Wilf McGuinness.

By the time of the Ajax ties, Busby was back in the Old Trafford hotseat and desperate for retirement and deeply involved in the recruitment of his own successor. He met Stein at a motorway service station near Haydock and terms were agreed.

Jean, however, was having none of this moving south business. She had done that once before, leaving all behind her to join her husband in Wales in the days when he was a journeyman professional footballer. Stein ended his dalliance but with regrets.

The consensus among players and directors – and many fans too even though they were much more willing to believe only the best of Stein – was that he was never the same after the European Cup defeat by Feyenoord, that he was in some senses already a broken man.

The club, too, listed like a slowly sinking ship. League titles were not enough, not once the delights of European conquests had been tasted.

Kelly, too, was still dying. He resigned his chairmanship to become the club's president and White replaced him at the head of the board of directors.

Kelly's life ended in September 1971 and the man whose life was Celtic was missed in so many ways. Sean Fallon, for one, reckoned the day of the chairman's passing as the day when the club's hopes of climbing new peaks of achievement also passed away.

Stein was desolate, inconsolable. Although the manager had dismissed his chairman's idealism and passion for fair play above all else in front of his players, Kelly had been his mentor since the day Stein had first arrived at the club from Llanelli. Another light, another inspiration, another friend, had been extinguished.

Celtic, too, were never a selling club under Kelly. No pressure to sell footballers was ever brought to bear on Stein by his first chairman.

* * *

On Saturday, 17 April a match billed as a league title decider took place in Aberdeen.

The bleak north-east coastline with its offshore oil rigs, platforms and pipelines was buried overnight in a blanket of heavy snow, as was the playing surface at Pittodrie, and a postponement looked possible. A thaw, however, arrived in the nick of time, permitting the game to take place without the need for an inspection, and allowed, too, the 15,000 Celtic fans to complete their pilgrimages by car, bus and train in time for the 3pm kick-off.

The pitch might have been playable but was devoid of grass and a spirit level placed on the mud of the penalty areas might have seen its bubble swing wildly between extremes of imbalance. Good football was impossible but exciting football was still guaranteed as a cold wind from the North Sea huffed and puffed in energetic gusts.

Harry Hood opened the scoring to cap a frenzied squall of early Celtic pressure. On 38 minutes, however, Evan Williams in the visitors' goal fumbled a cross to the feet of Steve Murray. He passed to Alex Willoughby, who had the simple task of netting the Dons' equaliser.

The turning point of this evenly poised match arrived after 56 minutes. Arthur Graham, Aberdeen's teenage left-winger, advanced forward at great pace and in splendid isolation. As he swerved around Williams, the Celtic goalkeeper managed the faintest of touches on the ball, buying just enough time for McNeill to reach the goal line and stick out a leg to block Graham's belated shot.

It was not the first last gasp clearance by the Celtic skipper and nor would it be his last. McNeill's appearances have been counted and constitute a record number of 822 games for his only professional club but the number of times his legs, his body, his head saved Celtic from conceding crucial goals remains countless.

From that moment, the Celtic players knew the title was theirs. Stein's transitional side had discovered a resolution to accompany their talent, a determination to continue winning whatever was possible in spite of the recent and damning defeat by Ajax in the European Cup.

The first 11 that took a deserved point from Pittodrie still contained five Lions in Craig, McNeill, Johnstone, Lennox and Wallace, but the reserve 11 that played the mirror fixture with Aberdeen at Celtic Park that afternoon was overflowing with talent. The line-up in that match was Lally, McCluskey, McGrain, Dalglish, Gemmell, Cattanach, Wilson, Davidson, Macari, Murdoch and Hughes. Unsurprisingly, with such a stellar team, Celtic won 3-2, with Vic Davidson scoring a hat-trick.

There was a future and a present to be grasped. If only Celtic could steady the ship, bereft and rudderless without Kelly's constant beavering presence, without the former chairman's abiding principles, without his lifelong love for his father's club, his own dearly beloved club.

Kelly had informed his fellow directors of his decision to retire at a meeting of the board on 22 March, two days before Celtic were eliminated from the European Cup by Ajax.

Curiously, Stein had informed the board of his decision to stay at Celtic, in spite of the blandishments of Manchester United, at the very same meeting as Kelly revealed his decision to go and prepare for his death at his home in Burnside.

Would the manager be the same, though, without Kelly? Would Stein find it possible to rouse himself to the same heights of motivation without Kelly's constant optimism, his faithful enthusiasm, his selfless devotion? 'No man,' Stein said, 'has ever done more for the club in every way.'

Kelly was an original – in spite of his father's domineering influence – a maverick idealist in an age of cynicism, a moralist in an age of relativism, a true immortal.

The manager, meanwhile, had been walking a dark path since the disaster of Feyenoord. The footballing talent at Celtic's disposal was unquestionable but to reach its fulfilment would require leadership both from the diminished board of directors and from an apparently diminished boss.

* * *

Still, after the draw at Pittodrie, the sixth title under Stein was Celtic's to lose.

Aberdeen, with one match remaining, were now three points clear of Celtic, but the latter enjoyed the advantage of three games to play and the possession of a far superior goal difference. One week later, Aberdeen lost their final match 1-0 at home to Falkirk.

Celtic, now needing just three points to clinch the title, also faltered, drawing 2-2 at home to relegation-haunted St Mirren. The team from Paisley were twice ahead but were pegged back and sent down to the second tier by goals from Hood and Lennox.

The six-in-a-row was won eventually on a Thursday evening at Hampden due to renovation work on the main stand at Celtic Park.

The opponents were Ayr United and just over 20,000 Celts travelled and turned up for the coronation of the champions.

It was a nervy night, made worse in the very first minute when a shot from Alex Ingram rattled the Celtic crossbar. Two more chances came and went for Ayr before Lennox settled churning stomachs on the terraces with an 18th-minute goal, to which Wallace added a second just before the hour.

It was a low-key success, celebrated in the shadows of Hampden's floodlights. To some Celts, success had become routine.

There was more interest in Stein's announcement that the Lisbon Lions would play together in one last grand hurrah in the final fixture of the league campaign against Clyde, and that the match would be at Paradise too.

* * *

Yet there was something enduring to commemorate and honour with this title with which Celtic had equalled their own record of consecutive championships.

Between 1904 and 1910, Celtic's first truly great side and winner of the first six-in-a-row, flourished under the management of Willie Maley.

If ever a man was immortal it was Maley. He played at half-back in Celtic's first fixture, a friendly victory over Rangers to the tune of 5-2, on 28 May 1888.

He was appointed player-secretary in May 1894 and as secretary-manager in April 1897 and remained as manager for a record 43 years until his retirement in February 1940.

As important as his longevity as a legend were the man's principles. 'It's not the creed nor his nationality that counts. It's the man himself.'

The team that represented Celtic in those years was Maley's creation. In the club's earliest seasons, Celtic bought their success with a ruthless programme of investment in seasoned professionals from rival teams. Maley's was a different way of spotting and developing and moulding of young footballers.

By the beginning of season 1904/05, Maley's fledglings were ready to take on the teams that ruled the Scottish roost in the early years of the 20th century.

Rangers had won four titles in a row between 1899 and 1902 – a record as no one bar Dumbarton had successfully retained the Scottish league title in the 19th century – but had since declined. Since then, Hibernian and Third Lanark had garnered championships.

In 1903/04 Celtic and Rangers finished joint third in an era before goal average was introduced to separate teams finishing level on points.

Celtic's first league title of the 20th century and fifth overall was a tight affair; so close, in fact, that Rangers would have been declared champions if either goal average or goal difference had been in play. The Ibrox team's goals for and against were 83 and 28 compared to Celtic's 68 and 31. A play-off match was required at Hampden Park on 6 May.

Testament to Maley's rebuilding of Celtic was the fact that of the previous championship-winning side of 1897/98 only Willie Orr, a wily and experienced left-back, remained.

Celtic's short passing in the second half in the face of a strong wind was in marked contrast to Rangers' long balls and shots from distance. Around three-quarters of the way through the match Jimmy McMenemy and Davie Hamilton scored two goals in quick succession which allowed Maley's men to see out the win with only one goal lost to Rangers in the closing minutes.

An inside-forward, McMenemy was known as Napoleon for his inspirational leadership qualities and retained his place into the next decade as Maley built his second great side that played and won four consecutive titles from 1914 to 1917 during World War One, eventually making 453 appearances for Celtic. In the New Year's Day match of 1914 McMenemy dribbled around what seemed like an entire team of Rangers players before unleashing a shot that nestled high in the Ibrox net. His intelligent and probing passing, too, was a prominent feature of the Maley – and the Celtic – way of playing football.

In the following five seasons of total Celtic dominance Rangers failed to claim a single runners-up position. Second places were recorded by Hearts and twice each by Dundee and Falkirk.

Alongside Maley and McMenemy, there was a host of other candidates for Celtic immortality, but two stand heads and shoulders above their colleagues.

Surpassing even Napoleon's appearances for Celtic was long-serving legend Alec McNair, who played 640 league and cup games between 1904 and 1925.

McNair was the 'Icicle' whose calm presence at right-back as part of Maley's second great side and as part of the Holy Trinity of Celtic's defence – which also included goalkeeper Charlie Shaw and left-back Joe Dodds – earned him 12 league championships and six Scottish Cups.

McNair, too, was the first in a long line of Celtic immortals who began their lives as outwardly diehard Rangers fans. Stein, of course, was to follow in those footsteps, as were Dalglish, McGrain and, later, Paul Lambert.

The signing of McNair, a Protestant Scot, from Stenhousemuir in May 1904, was a public declaration of Maley's creed that it was the man that mattered.

The manager, too, was far from a stereotypical Celt. Although Maley was born in Ireland in 1868, and was not unsympathetic to the cause of Irish nationalism, he was also a royalist and a militarist, putting his personal beliefs at odds with the majority of the Celtic support in Glasgow and beyond. His beliefs were his own as were his players'. In addition to McNair, Maley also signed Jimmy Hay, Willie Buchan, Willie Cringan, George Paterson, and John and Robert Thompson, Protestants all. As the great man proclaimed, 'For 48 years we have played a mixed team.'

McNair, though, could not have been more dedicated to the cause. During the war years, after the death of his beloved wife of cardiac valve disease at the age of 28, the defender raised five children while working 12-hour shifts in a Bo'ness munitions factory, and still finding time to play for Celtic.

If McNair was the mainstay of the defence in the wartime team, up front and providing the goals was Jimmy Quinn.

Spotted by Maley playing junior football for Smithston Albion, and signed after full use of the manager's persuasive powers in January 1901, Quinn soon became the most feared forward in Scottish football. According to Maley, he was 'the keystone in the greatest team Celtic ever had'.

In those six-in-a-row years, Quinn scored 19, 20, 28, 19, 22 and 24 goals. In total, he played 331 games for Celtic and netted 216 times.

* * *

For the Lisbon Lions, the 1970/71 season concluded with an emotional reunion in the 6-1 victory over Clyde before an exultant but limited – because of the reconstruction of the main stand – crowd of 35,000.

Ronnie Simpson, injured and unavailable, led out the team but was replaced for the 90 minutes by Evan Williams. He was the only Lion to miss out on the day. John Clark, Bertie Auld and Steve Chalmers all played their last senior game for Celtic.

It is interesting to compare Chalmers with Quinn, both immortals. Quinn scored on average in 65 per cent of games whereas Chalmers's equivalent percentage was 56. The Lisbon Lion, though, scored the most important goal in Celtic's history and, overall, sits in fourth place behind McGrory, Lennox and Henrik Larsson in the all-time list in Paradise.

He also scored the sixth goal against Clyde, the final goal for the Lions. If ever an immortal was underrated it was Chalmers.

* * *

From now on, though, Stein would rely on Fallon's Bhoys. Dalglish, McGrain, Davidson and Paul Wilson would join Connelly, Hay and Macari in the first 11 for 1971/72 in an attempt to raise the bar of accomplishment to seven league titles in a row.

* * *

7. THE EXCEPTION THAT PROVES THE RULE
1971/72

It was a gamble of immense proportions, far greater than any hefty wager with Tony Queen or on the racetrack at Ayr.

Five days after being carried shoulder high from the field of play at Paradise at the conclusion of the 6-1 victory over Clyde that marked the last roar of the Lions, Bertie Auld left Celtic on a free transfer to Hibernian. The registrations of John Clark and Stevie Chalmers were then transferred to Morton, before in October 1971, John Hughes and Willie Wallace left for Crystal Palace and, before Christmas, Tommy Gemmell left for Nottingham Forest. In February 1972, John Fallon was transferred to Motherwell. Jim Craig left the club at the end of the season for South Africa.

None of these players wanted to leave Celtic and most were lost souls after leaving.

Stein was ruthless and rude in their dismissals. It was the only way he knew how to recover his command of the club, his command of himself. He had to purge himself of the old guard, the players who had let him down against Feyenoord, even those who had not played in that disastrous game, memories of which still burned.

John Fallon, for example, returned home one day to find Stein waiting for him in his living room. Stein then proceeded to tell his second-choice goalkeeper, who had been an unused substitute in Lisbon, that he had arranged a transfer on his behalf and that there would be no further discussion on the matter.

Many of these players endured icy relations with the manager before leaving. Craig provides a case in point. The full-back was married to the daughter of one of the Celtic directors, James Farrell, with whom Stein also endured a cold and distant relationship.

'He fell out with me,' Craig explained. 'He just snubbed me, didn't talk to me, didn't look in my direction ... I spoke up ... Jock demanded a master–servant relationship.'

The Stein–Craig quarrel was indicative, too, of a second and parallel gamble undertaken by the manager.

After the death of Kelly, Stein had no more empathetic relations with any of the remaining directors, and he was not minded to cultivate new pathways of tolerance and mutual respect and approval between the manager's and the chairman's offices.

Desmond White was not Stein's cup of tea. Whereas Kelly would chew the fat with his manager about football, life and possible winners in that afternoon's racing programme, White was an accountant with no time for turf accountants.

Stein, too, suspected White of cheating the taxman of revenue that might have been used to subsidise mining communities running out of coal and political capital under a Conservative government. Or to improve the NHS.

Of course, it was a common strategy within the football industry, whose income in the 1970s came primarily cash-in-hand through the turnstiles, to downplay attendances and income and thus reduce tax liabilities.

Still, Stein knew what a 50,000 crowd looked like at Paradise and would turn away in disgust when being told the attendance was 40,000.

It was a dangerous game the manager was playing. With no pretence of cooperation with the chairman or his directors, with no allies in the boardroom, and with cliques in the dressing room – until the clearout was complete – Stein was utterly dependent on results.

And on Sean's Bhoys, aka the Quality Street Gang.

If these kids, though, were as good as he and Fallon knew they were, the manager reckoned he was only a shade of odds against to produce another season in which Celtic indulged in a second clean sweep of four major trophies. Only four this time around, in contrast to 1966/67, as the Glasgow Cup was now in abeyance.

* * *

By the time of the League Cup Final at Hampden on 23 October 1971, in which Celtic were due to play Partick Thistle, the team from Paradise was sitting comfortably in second place in the league, just one point behind Aberdeen.

Rangers, under Willie Wallace, had lost four of their first five league games. Celtic had defeated them 2-0 and 3-0 in the League Cup and 3-2 in the league championship.

Aberdeen, under the dynamic leadership of chairman Dick Donald and the new management of Jimmy Bonthrone, a prolific striker in his day with East Fife, were the new kids on the block in terms of challenging Celtic's title credentials. They were to remain unbeaten in the league until a surprise 3-2 home defeat to Heart of Midlothian in late November.

Celtic's kids were playing scintillating stuff and scoring goals for fun, including a 9-1 win over Clyde and a 5-0 thrashing of Airdreionians.

Stein was sighted smiling benignly at his players. He would never fully recover from the loss of Bob Kelly on 21 September but football could be a great healer and a healthy distraction from the process of grieving. It could also destroy and damage, especially in the midst of delights.

The opening half hour or so of the League Cup Final were perhaps the most astonishing minutes of football ever played at Hampden. After 36 minutes, the score was Celtic 0 Partick Thistle 4.

Tony Queen might have offered odds of thousands to one against that happening. In fact, he hadn't bothered pricing for such impossibilities. Prior to kick-off, Thistle had been 8-1 to win the cup, stingy odds for which there were few takers even among their supporters.

On the BBC's *Football Focus*, Sam Leitch's closing words were, 'In Scotland it's League Cup Final day at Hampden Park where Celtic play Partick Thistle, who have no chance.'

In spite of McNeill's unavailability through injury, and Johnstone's injury during the match, there were no excuses for the 4-1 defeat, and Celtic fans stayed on after the final whistle to applaud the Jags' youngsters off the pitch.

Thistle were newly promoted to the top echelon of Scottish football and the average age of their team was 22.

Alan Hansen, later to find fame in the red shirt of Liverpool, was a 16-year-old Thistle apprentice and was sitting in the stands that day, primarily to support his older brother, whose unenviable task was to mark 'Jinky' Johnstone. John Hansen later recalled, 'It was surreal ... This was Celtic, the best team in Britain.'

Many of the Thistle players were part-timers. Alan Rough, who would play in goal 53 times for Scotland and make 410 league appearances for Thistle, was a Celtic fan and a recently qualified electrician; centre-half Jackie Campbell was a draughtsman; centre-forward Frank Coulston was a PE teacher; and teenage winger Denis McQuade was studying classics at Glasgow University.

Most of the League Cup winners were playing in Thistle's reserves the previous season watched by one man and his dog against Glasgow Police and Glasgow Transport.

Before the match kicked off, Lou Macari said to Hansen, 'At least you'll be going home with a runners-up medal.'

After the match, the Celtic dressing room leaked that Stein went 'loopy'. The Celtic manager later described the 4-1 League Cup defeat as 'the biggest blow we ever had as a club'. There was undoubtedly over-confidence among the players, as there had been in both playing staff and management in the defeat by Feyenoord in the previous season.

'We needed players who were hungry,' Stein lamented.

* * *

Still, the League Cup was the least of Stein's four targets.

In the race for the league title, there was an upcoming match the following month at home to Aberdeen.

An official attendance of 64,000 was recorded at Celtic Park for this top-of-the-table clash. Some critics thought the ground looked almost full. Still, it was the highest gate that season in the UK bar the Old Firm matches.

The crowd witnessed constant Celtic pressure, so much so that Aberdeen's centre-forward Joe Harper hardly touched the ball outside of his own team's penalty area. Alan Herron of the *Sunday Mail* exclaimed, 'Never have Celtic given so much over 90 minutes for so little.'

Eventually, in the 60th minute, a swirl of passes involving Connelly, Dalglish and Johnstone ended up with a fine pass threaded through the Dons' defence for Hood to score.

Johnstone, one of only three Lions in the first 11, roved tirelessly from left to right and left again.

Celtic continued to press forwards but, in a rare Aberdeen breakaway, Harper's cross was sent like a bullet from McNeill's head past Connaghan. At the end of the 1-1 draw the skipper hoofed the ball high into the grandstand, distraught and downbeat after his own goal.

Raymond Jacobs, the doyen of the Glasgow press, was less inclined to bemoan Celtic's luck than Herron. His pertinent contribution to the post-match debate was that Celtic were in a 'period of transition' and had 'not yet finished shedding the old skin'.

In his rebuilding work, Stein did not rely entirely on promotion from within. At the end of October he signed Dixie Deans, a prolific goalscorer from Motherwell, for approaching £20,000.

Deans scored on his debut against Partick Thistle in a 5-1 win at Firhill on 27 November that seemed as if it had come one month too late.

Nevertheless, it was a crucial two points and a boost to Celtic's goal difference on a weekend when Aberdeen suffered their first defeat, to Hearts. Celtic were top of the league for the first time since the end of September.

On 3 January 1972, the Bhoys played host to Rangers. Any dropping of points might hand the initiative back, not to Celtic's Old Firm rivals, but to Aberdeen, who had responded to that first loss with a series of storming performances and results: 5-1 at Ayr, 4-1 at home to Clyde, 3-0 at Pittodrie against Dundee United, and 3-0 at Falkirk, with a 1-1 draw at Dundee on New Year's Day the sole blemish.

On 3 January, the Dons welcomed St Johnstone, a match they won comfortably by four goals to two. Celtic faced a revitalised Rangers, fully recovered from their disastrous start to the season, and having won their previous seven league encounters.

After 35 minutes, a lofted ball into the Rangers penalty area from Hood found Johnstone in splendid isolation and the winger stooped to head home past Peter McCloy. This, though, was not going to be another Celtic canter to victory, and Rangers' pressing and harrying was rewarded in the 81st minute as Colin Stein's shot deflected into the Celtic net off Denis Connaghan's outstretched glove.

A draw seemed inevitable and there were mutterings of discontent among the Celtic faithful as news of Aberdeen's impending victory at Pittodrie leaked from transistor radios.

With mere seconds before the sounding of the referee's whistle, however, McNeill, all pretence at sophistication abandoned, launched the ball deep into enemy territory. Hood controlled and lobbed a cross towards the far post where Jim Brogan, ghosting from nowhere like Mill Reef in that summer's Epsom Derby, headed the ball past a desperate McCloy.

It was Brogan's finest moment in a Celtic shirt and his father, who had left the main stand five minutes earlier to avoid the roiling crowds, had missed it.

It was Celtic's first league double over Rangers since 1912 and that last-gasp goal deflated Aberdeen every bit as much as it burst the Ibrox team's recent bubble.

Before January was out the Dons had drawn at home against Rangers and lost at relegation-bound Dunfermline and any realistic chance of catching the league leaders was as remote as a Glasgow winter without snow.

In March 1972, the title was effectively confirmed when Celtic held Aberdeen to a 1-1 draw at Pittodrie. In a closely contested tussle, Lennox put Celtic ahead with 17 minutes remaining but the Dons gained a deserved equaliser through Harper with nine minutes left. Stein declared: 'It's our title.'

In fact, the seventh championship in a row was formally won on a mid-April weekend with a 3-0 victory at East Fife just prior to Celtic's crucial European Cup semi-final second leg at home to Inter Milan.

The first leg at the San Siro had ended 0-0 and optimism was unbounded in the East End that Celtic would progress to the final and make amends for the shambolic performance against Feyenoord in 1970.

Four days after the celebrations of another title, a huge football jamboree took place in Glasgow with 75,000 jammed into Celtic Park for the second leg against Inter, and 80,000 at Ibrox to see Rangers reach the final of the European Cup Winners' Cup by beating Bayern Munich 2-0.

At Celtic Park, Stein's team started as they meant to go on, attacking with relentless ambition, going close on occasions but with no end product. The Italians man-marked their opponents with precision and occasionally brutality. Gabriele Oriali followed Johnstone all over the pitch, while Giacinto Facchetti stayed so close to Lennox he might have worn the same jersey. Tarcisio Burgnich was the spare man in the system, detailed to clear up loose ends, sweep up any mess or mistakes. The war of attrition worked for 120 minutes, including extra time, just as it had worked for 90 minutes in Milan. Murdoch was in inspired form, probing, prompting, but all to no avail. On the hour Dalglish was replaced by Deans, but still it made no difference.

In fact, as Malcolm Munro of the *Evening Times* reported, the longer the game progressed the Inter team came on stronger and stronger.

Stein looked on with increasing frustration, with increasing gesticulation at players, referee and linesmen, the gods of football, anyone who thwarted his will. It was too late to compensate now for the level of over-confidence that had been spawned by the away draw in Italy.

Penalty shoot-outs were a new game in town for UEFA. No one could dispute that this new method of settling drawn games was an improvement on the coin tosses of the past that had benefitted Celtic in the European Cup quarter-final against Benfica in 1970.

The first UEFA tie settled in this dramatic fashion was in the Cup Winners' Cup on 30 September 1970 when Honvéd of Hungary knocked out Aberdeen 5-4 on penalties. The initial shoot-out in a European Cup match was on 4 November in the same year when Everton won their duel with Borussia Mönchengladbach by four penalties to three.

Now it was the turn of Celtic and Inter. Up first was Sandro Mazzola, veteran of four Serie A titles, two European Cups and two Intercontinental Cups. His penalty was stroked along the ground and past Williams's outstretched right hand.

The contrast with Celtic's first penalty taker could not have been more stark. Deans was a veteran of one appearance for Albion Rovers as a trialist and 191 domestic games for Motherwell. As he struck the ball he committed the cardinal sin of leaning backwards and the side-footed shot sailed over the crossbar.

The third penalty was taken by Faccetti whose experience incorporated a footballing lifetime with Inter since his debut in the 1960/61 season, including a European Cup Final appearance against Celtic in 1967. Even seasoned professionals, however, make mistakes. The Italian left-back hit the ball with zip and zest but his placement was awry and the ball headed for the middle of the goal. Williams, though, was already diving in anticipation of a better-placed spot-kick. The ball struck the Celtic goalkeeper and continued past him into the roof of the net.

The rest of the penalties were dispatched with aplomb and no one was to blame, especially Deans, whose selection as the opening taker was perhaps unwise, but Celtic had missed their one remaining realistic chance of adding to their European Cup glory.

Raymond Jacobs in the *Glasgow Herald* wrote that, after a war of attrition, 'Sadly, undeservedly, and by the most bitter of means, Celtic are out of the European Cup.'

Malcolm Munro of the *Evening Times*, however, was perhaps more realistic, as he insisted 'this was not vintage Celtic' and that 'there were too many bad players'. Macari 'lacked support' and there were too many long and high and hopeful balls played to forwards who lacked height. All could agree, however, on the sadness of the occasion.

Celtic's seventh successive title and the club's progress through to the penultimate stage of the grandest stage of European football suggested all was well.

There were, however, dark and destructive agencies already at work. All dreams are born, live, and die, and the forces of entropy and of chaos, iron laws of the universe, were readying themselves to take centre stage.

Celtic now lived in a land of limbo, stranded between routine domestic success and ongoing failures abroad.

It was a foreign country in which the steadying hand of Kelly was absent and in which Stein was a rambling malcontent and in which the players were pawns in a game which passed them by as wickedly as a winter wind.

Fans, too, were sated with success, grumbling like an angry appendix, as the conquest of Europe in 1967 receded further into the past.

Celtic were on a downcast path and their relative success was an exception that only proved to illustrate the general rule of stasis and of consequent descent.

* * *

8. CHAMPIONS IN DECLINE
1972/73

Some supporters, however, posed legitimate questions to the soothsayers of doom. Where are all these dark clouds? What is your problem, pal?

After all, Celtic commenced the new season with an unbeaten cruise through to the quarter-finals of the League Cup, compiled four wins out of five in the early league fixtures, including a comprehensive 3-1 beating of Rangers at Paradise.

The one dark cloud here was the inexplicable 2-0 loss at Dundee on 23 September; inexplicable, that is, until match reports are revisited and it became clear that Dundee were simply and clearly the better side on the day, who might have won 5-0 and not been flattered because, according to the *Sunday Mail*, 'so far ahead were clever Dundee'.

Meanwhile, in those same opening salvos of the campaign, Aberdeen dropped points in goalless draws at Dundee and at home to St Johnstone and, in their sixth match, lost 2-1 at Hearts.

Rangers, too, endured a blighted start to the new season. After five league rounds had been played the Ibrox team were in the bottom half of Division One having lost three away games at Ayr, Celtic and Kilmarnock.

What was there not to like? The answer, of course, comes from another foreign land called hindsight. From inside information, too, revelations in books about Stein, about Fallon, from players ghosted autobiographies, unavailable at the time.

Stein now had two so-near-yet-so-far European Cup defeats – against Feyenoord in 1970 and Inter Milan in 1972 – that crushed his soul. He had bolshy players, teenagers in the rebellious 1960s, to deal with, and never had he felt so old and so powerless and alone as in dealings with Macari who did not fear his manager as the Lions had done, who absented himself from training, apparently without a care in the world for Stein.

It was difficult to escape the feeling Scottish society had moved on and left a desolate Stein scrambling for anchors in a turbulent world.

Fallon, too, was mourning the death of Kelly, at the same time as his concerns for the wellbeing of his boss were mounting.

* * *

The victory over Rangers, though, on 16 September, was one for the ages. The main stand at Celtic Park was closed for renovation after a fire and after the discovery of safety issues with the press box. The Old Firm match was switched to a midday kick-off at Hampden, high noon because Queen's Park, the owners of Hampden, had a home match later in the day.

The match was so one-sided that John Downie of *The Times* asserted that the Celts could and should have numbered their goals in double figures. The Bhoys were 3-0 up after 49 minutes and thereafter concentrated upon teasing their opponents rather than hurting them with further strikes. Rangers fans had long since poured out through the open Hampden gates like a crowd in a Lowry painting when John Greig netted a last-minute consolation for the Ibrox club. Celtic fans stood and laughed and cheered the Gers' captain; whether in high irony or out of genuine appreciation of Greig's inability to surrender is a moot point.

Rangers, under the new management of Jock Wallace, were in crisis. Unlike Celtic, whose scouting system under the tutelage of Sean Fallon had unearthed local gems like Dalglish, who scored the day's opening goal, Rangers seemed incapable of unearthing footballing talents from within the Glasgow area.

All depended on the relative qualities of the scouting setups. Within Glasgow the best players and their parents were convinced by Fallon's blarney and by Celtic's ongoing success.

Rangers, naturally enough, were hindered by their sectarian recruitment policy. Stein exploited this sickness by claiming that, if he had the choice of two players of equal ability and one was a Protestant and one was a Catholic, he would always sign the Protestant in the sure knowledge that Rangers would never sign the Catholic.

Even Partick Thistle were beating Rangers in the race to sign stellar youngsters. Where were the Rangers scouts when the Jags signed Alex Forsyth, Ronnie Glavin, Denis McQuade, and Alan Rough? Where were Celtic's come to that?

Thistle's success, like Celtic's, was down to one genius. If Celtic possessed the talents of Sean Fallon, the Jags had the unheralded but indispensable Jimmy Dickie whose wit and wisdom lay in the recognition of footballing talent.

* * *

On 28 October, when Celtic visited Aberdeen, their sole rivals for the league title in the previous two seasons, it was tight at the top, involving not just the day's two protagonists but also Dundee, Dundee United, Hibernian and Hearts.

Queen Street Station was awash with fans as the Celtic players and management team arrived in good time for their train to the Granite City. Banter was exchanged, autographs signed. Stein was in a mellow mood, breakfasted on British Rail Dover sole, conversed with Ian Archer of the *Herald*. 'This is what it should be all about,' Stein said, 'big matches, big occasions.'

The gates of Pittodrie were closed long before kick off with 36,000 spectators sardined into the compact stadium.

Celtic had every excuse to be too tired to lay siege to the Aberdeen goal after their relentless display of attacking prowess against Ujpesti

Dozsa in a 2-1 midweek European Cup victory. Nevertheless, the Bhoys scored twice inside the first 20 minutes, Deans and Macari the goal scorers, with Lennox and Callaghan the provideers.

Aberdeen's resident wizard, the Hungarian Zoltán Varga, pulled one back after 25 minutes. The game was not yet done and surely Celtic had to tire as it progressed.

On 66 minutes, Deans passed to Connelly, and his cross to Dalglish was exquisite. The forward hung in mid air, his body forming an arc as perfect as a rainbow, and headed home the Bhoys' third goal.

With less than ten minutes remaining, Varga chased a long ball and lofted the ball over Williams's head and into the back of the Celtic net.

Celtic, with fisticuffs and a touch of time wasting, clung to the two points like a drowning man holds fast to his rescuer. Allan Heron of the *Sunday Mail* called the match a 'tremendous collision of talent and strength'.

Varga, arriving at Aberdeen for one season only, via Ferencváros, Standard Liège, and Hertha Berlin, provided a wonderful example of how it was not necessary to rely solely on local talent. His goals were exquisite; his will o' the wisp talents graced the Scottish game for all too short a time.

After the match, Celtic were one point clear of Dundee United, themselves one ahead of Hibernian, who were two in front of Aberdeen, Rangers, Hearts and Dundee.

* * *

Stein always knew, though, that darkness and light are bedfellows of the same universe. He was perhaps more aware of the dark than his colleagues and his charges, having no gifts of sleep that brought balm to most nights for most men.

After the stirring victory over Aberdeen, and a further league win at home to Dundee United, came the crushing defeat in the European Cup in Hungary, 3-0 to Újpesti Dózsa. It was not even close, the gulf in class there for all to see, and Stein was devastated, with no Kelly to share his heavy burden.

On 9 December, Stein lost the League Cup Final for the third consecutive time at Hampden and, to the manager, it was indeed his loss, a bereavement of sorts. Again, there was no misfortune about the defeat on the day, although Celtic, it is true, were missing Deans and Murdoch with injuries.

The pressure on Stein was unremitting and cruel, as it is on all managers, but more so on the boss of Celtic whose early and significant successes had made rods for his back that were impossible to evade. All revolutions occur, not when the yoke of oppression is at its most harsh, but when the disparity between raised expectations and failure to provide for those raised presumptions becomes unbearable.

When Celtic won the European Cup in 1967, expectations among the support raced high into the skies and beyond. Every failure to replicate and enlarge upon that success with an Intercontinental Cup or two was a nail in Stein's coffin, and a hammer blow to his psyche.

Now, too, there were presumptions of winning the league every year from now unto eternity, and it was never that easy.

By Christmas, Celtic had dropped another point in a home draw with Hibernian.

Around this time, Stein, who was normally resolutely private, opening up solely to Kelly in occasional unguarded moments of shared intimacy, confessed something strange to John Clark, his Lisbon Lions sweeper.

'I have to be careful about myself, John, you know?' Clark, now playing for Morton, asked his former boss what he meant. 'Every night,' Stein said, 'when I get home, I place six pebbles on the bonnet of my car.' There was a pause, Stein gauging just how much he could trust his erstwhile defender. 'If I come out in the morning and I see any of those pebbles have been moved I'll know someone's after me.'

Clark was stunned. Eventually, Stein confessed to receiving an anonymous phone call the day after changing his route home for the first time in years. 'Why did you go home a different way? I'm watching you, don't forget that.'

Mentally, emotionally, physically, Stein was driving at night with one headlight smashed and the other flickering spasmodically as its bulb burned out.

Just after Christmas, leaving Celtic Park in his Mercedes, Stein began to cough uncontrollably, his breath coming in ragged bursts. He spent the next 12 days in Glasgow's Victoria Infirmary's intensive care unit. Still, he insisted on listening to the radio commentary of the New Year's Day fixture against Rangers for which match Fallon was asked by White to take charge of team affairs.

* * *

Prior to the derby game at Ibrox on 6 January, Rangers had won their previous three matches, putting their early season disasters behind them and, after the postponement of Celtic's games against Kilmarnock and Morton due to an influenza epidemic, had climbed to third place in Division One, just a single point behind their great rivals. Hibernian had displaced Celtic at the head of league affairs.

Fallon was beside himself with worry over his friend's hospitalisation, did his best to exude an aura of calm, and picked a team that was barely recovered from the flu.

Unsurprisingly, Rangers controlled most of the game, taking the lead midway through the first half through Derek Parlane. This Ibrox team was a reflection of their workaholic manager, Jock Wallace, and stifled all attempts by the Celts to equalise. In truth, Fallon's team never looked like scoring until a solitary goal came courtesy of a wicked deflection of a Deans shot by Dave Smith. It looked as if a draw would be an unsatisfactory result for the Ibrox club until the very last minute when a floated cross from Quintin Young found the head of Alfie Conn who placed the ball perfectly past Williams in the Celtic goal.

With Stein absent, and Fallon not one for the limelight, Wallace took centre stage after the match. 'Don't write about me,' he told the assembled journalists, 'just tell them I'm a good-looking chap.' Rangers were now serious contenders for the title.

The race was still led by Hibernian under the astute management of Eddie Turnbull. Rangers were one point behind having played one game more than the Hibees and Celtic were now one point further in arrears.

The saving grace for Fallon and White – and Stein in his hospital bed with radio headphones now discarded in disgust – was that the Bhoys had two games in hand over Hibs and three over Rangers. Those matches, though, still had to be won.

* * *

Stein was diagnosed with an irregularity of his heartbeat which caused an accumulation of fluid in his lungs, and he was told he must take diuretics for the rest of his life. The alternative was drowning as a result of his pulmonary oedema.

When he was discharged from hospital, he was warned, too, that his lifestyle, his obsession with work, was dangerous.

Stein was instructed to take things easy, a thankless and useless task for doctors and friends alike. Telling Stein to do anything was more than likely to result in him taking a diametrically opposite course.

Neither his mood nor his workload was improved by Macari's request for a transfer shortly after the conclusion of the match against Rangers.

Accepting the reality of his player's determination, Stein attempted to engineer a move to Liverpool, where his close friend Bill Shankly was in charge. Fallon even drove Macari to Anfield to put his signature to the contract. The deal, however, was hijacked by Tommy Docherty, recently installed at Manchester United.

Stein was incandescent, insisting by way of revenge that the Old Trafford club must pay £200,000 instead of the fee of £180,000 agreed with Liverpool.

In truth, the sorry saga revolved about money from beginning to end. Macari had not wanted to leave Celtic until he discovered the club's offer of a new contract centred upon an increase of a mere £5 per week.

Neither White nor Stein seemed keen to retain Macari and, in this instance, Fallon's powers of persuasion carried no weight.

Celtic's parsimony and the way the players' wages were structured with an emphasis on bonuses rather than basics was to prove fatal to the club's hopes of retaining the core of Fallon's Quality Street Gang, and to Celtic's hankering for further successes on the European stage. Ambitions in this direction were rapidly becoming pipe dreams.

Macari quadrupled his wages overnight by moving to Old Trafford. The player tried to emphasise aspects other than personal finances when he spoke to the press about his transfer. 'I feel the game in Scotland is dying,' he said. 'I need to protect my future.' What Macari said next, however, was something that might have resonated with Stein, 'It's not easy being a Celtic player. I don't go out much socially because you can run into stupid people.'

Someone was watching Stein. In fact, there was always someone watching all the players in the Celtic melodrama all of the time. In later days, Neil Lennon, too, understood the danger of nutters wandering the streets of Glasgow. Stein might have shifted his pebbles more assiduously from pocket to car bonnet.

Macari's transfer was the beginning of some kind of end for Celtic. It was a demonstration by one player that Celtic players could now avail themselves of alternative sources of employment.

Bobby Lennox later described contract negotiations with Stein. 'It would just be shoved in front of you. "There it is, sign!"' It was the old way of doing things and it was passing. 'You didn't dare to try to question things,' Lennox added.

McNeill, Stein's lieutenant on the field and occasional confidant, was angry in retrospect, 'When we learned what players were earning in England we were staggered. We were paupers by comparison, yet we had won the European Cup.'

The manager was the problem and his unfailing bad grace in any wage negotiations was a major reason for discontent among his staff.

If Stein thought he had solved Celtic's difficulties with players' wages by showing Macari the exit door, he was sadly mistaken.

By 1973, the innovator of 1965 had become an out-of-touch reactionary doing down footballers for a board of directors who lacked both Kelly's passion and the former chairman's undying commitment to the Celtic cause.

* * *

After Rangers' January victory at Ibrox, Wallace's team continued their winning run for a further 12 matches.

Celtic faltered twice in February, drawing at home to Partick Thistle and away at East Fife in consecutive matches.

A desperate performance against the Jags saw Bobby Murdoch eventually score Celtic's equaliser and the club's historical 6,000th goal 20 minutes from time. Stein left his seat in the stands to prowl the dugout area as early as the 11th minute. The referee, Ian Foote, attracted both ire and irony from Celtic's manager as he denied five halfway decent penalty claims from the home players.

Stevie Chalmers excelled for Thistle.

Against East Fife, after the postponement of Rangers' home game, Celtic had the opportunity to reclaim top spot.

Three penalties, however, were missed by the team in hoops; the guilty were arraigned and named and shamed as Murdoch, Hood and Dalglish. The 2-2 draw left Celtic one point behind Rangers with one game in hand.

Hibernian had dropped away in the new year with a defeat at Dundee United and a home draw against Dundee.

Tony Queen offered even money on Celtic to claim an eighth title in a row but, as anyone who has ever tossed a coin or bet on red at roulette knows, even money shots are far from home and hosed. Stein himself would rarely take the odds at Ayr on a short-priced favourite.

By 21 April, with games in hand all played out and with two matches left for both Glasgow rivals, Celtic hosted Arbroath and Rangers headed north-east to Pittodrie.

On the previous Wednesday evening Celtic had used up their remaining spare game and coasted to a 5-0 victory over Dumbarton and reclaimed top spot on goal difference, with a Deans hat-trick supplemented by goals from Dalglish and Callaghan.

On a sunny afternoon at Paradise, Celtic romped to a 4-0 victory over Arbroath, with four second-half goals from Hood, Hay, Deans and Dalglish.

At last, too, after 15 consecutive victories, Rangers blinked in the game of brinkmanship with Celtic and were held to a 2-2 draw, only a late goal by Conn preventing defeat, and forcing the title race into a last-day, winner-takes-all scenario.

In effect, Celtic now needed a solitary point at Easter Road, home of Hibernian, on the following Saturday.

At half-time on the final day of the season, Rangers were 2-0 up at Ibrox against East Fife and a dejected crowd digested the news that Celtic were also winning at Easter Road, courtesy of a Deans goal just after the 20-minute mark.

Celtic, though, were made to fight long and hard by a spirited Hibs side and it was not until Dalglish added a second goal on 71 minutes and Deans a third after 80 that the 40,000 Celtic fans inside the ground could relax and celebrate.

As the final whistle sounded, inside the Celtic penalty area, McNeill, McGrain and goalkeeper Ally Hunter embraced and then danced, as Celtic fans sang, 'Eight-in-a-row, eight-in-a-row, hello, hello!'

Stein shrugged his shoulders and limped away. The Big Man had seen it all before. Surely, all was now sweetness and light inside Celtic Park.

* * *

9. HANGOVER AND NINE-IN-A-ROW
1973/74

The previous season, though, did not end well. On 5 May at Hampden Park, to conclude proceedings, there remained the small matter of a Scottish Cup Final against the old enemy.

It was a westerly wind-and-rain day in Glasgow with louring clouds and a feeling that dusk had arrived at the same time as the dawn. Over 11,000 fans with tickets failed to turn out of their beds and turn up at the match, reducing the attendance to a mere 122,714; the last occasion, incidentally, when an attendance at a Scottish Cup Final broke 100,000.

With a half-time score of 1-1, Rangers' Parlane having equalised a Dalglish opener, the turning point of the match occurred just 30 seconds into the second period. Stein's blandishments and sweet nothings were still ringing in his players' ears when Conn raced, unchecked, through the centre of Celtic's defence and slotted the ball past an aggrieved Hunter.

Six minutes later, John Greig dived across the Rangers goal line to punch away a shot from Deans and Connelly equalised from the spot. On the hour, however, Celtic left-back Jim Brogan limped from the field to be replaced by Lennox. While the Hoops dallied and dithered with their reorganisation, Rangers went about their business and a cross from Tommy McLean was headed by Derek Johnstone on to one Celtic post and then the other. Time paused but Tom Forsyth did not as he waited in the gap left by Brogan's absence and tapped the ball home to win the Gers' 20th Scottish Cup and in their centenary year too.

At the final whistle, Stein walked, head slightly bowed, towards his Rangers counterpart Jock Wallace and muttered a muted, 'Well done, you deserved it.'

Ian Archer in the *Herald* thought the result portentous, perhaps a turning of the tide in a resurgent Rangers' favour.

* * *

As the 1973/74 season began, Celtic were like a man who could not quite shake off a hangover from a night on the town..

175

The opening round of fixtures in Division One on 1 September pitted the Celts against newly promoted Dunfermline Athletic at a blustery, autumnal East End Park.

Both sides were committed to all-out attack, leaving wide-open spaces at the back for speedy forwards to exploit. McNeill and Connelly were unsure and insecure partners in central defence for Celtic. It was a surprise, therefore, that no goals were scored after Hood's 20th-minute opener until ten minutes before the final whistle.

The game roiled and raged in concert with the wind and its doughty protagonists, and Dunfermline's equaliser arrived deservedly when Alex Kinninmonth touched in a goal-bound Ken Mackie header.

Within a minute, however, Celtic regained the lead through Paul Wilson, whose very first touch as a substitute for Brian McLoughlin delivered a goal from a Harry Hood centre.

Twice Brogan cleared shots from off the Celtic goal line before Jim Leishman turned a Steve Murray cross past his own goalkeeper.

The game was safe for Celtic in spite of the latest of late consolation goals for the Pars; so late, in fact, that the referee blew for the end of the match without allowing Celtic to kick off from the centre spot; so late that most fans left the stadium thinking the score was 3-1 and not 3-2.

Two points on a potentially tricky away day when rivals Hibs won 2-1 at home to Partick Thistle and Rangers could only eke out a goalless draw at home to Ayr United was not a bad haul.

Every silver lining, however, has its cloud, and so it was with Celtic. Davie Hay, who played against Dunfermline in the manner of a man not expecting his name to be mentioned in despatches, had been placed on the transfer list at his own request following a series of failed pay negotiations with Stein.

Hay's was a brilliant talent. Of the Quality Street Gang members who lined up against Dunfermline, only Connelly and Dalglish could hold a candle to Hay's sublime creative gifts. He was known as the 'Quiet Assassin' not only for his ability to pick a pass but also for his knack of picking the pockets of opposing attackers. He was the beating heart of Stein's early 1970s side and quite simply indispensable.

The young midfielder played in all six of Scotland's internationals in the spring and summer of 1973. Macari, too, played in the British Home Championship match against England and was a substitute for the games against Wales and Northern Ireland. The former colleagues talked money and Hay learned his Celtic wages were dwarfed many times over by those paid at Old Trafford. He resented, too, the way the financial rewards at Celtic were leveraged around bonuses for winning matches rather than basic pay. Hay had been injured enough himself to understand that life without bonus payments made it impossible to manage and maintain regular financial outgoings. Hay's colleague, John Hughes, provided an acerbic assessment that, without bonuses, players were left with buttons.

Hay had been injured throughout the run-in of the 1971/72 season, missing not only all remaining league matches after his leg muscle injury in the Scottish Cup quarter-final replay against Hearts in March, but also the 6-1 cup final victory over Hibernian and the crucial European Cup semi-final matches against Inter Milan. It had been hard to watch from the stands and even harder to budget.

In the autumn of 1973, Hay approached Stein about a pay rise. His basic money was £65 a week and he wanted £100. It had been 12 years since Johnny Haynes of Fulham became the first footballer to earn a ton. Hay was rebuffed by Stein in the brusque, discourteous and disrespectful manner that had become the manager's stock-in-trade when dealing with players' requests.

Hay went straight to the top and saw White, who was non-committal though more polite than Stein. On 1 September, Hay was placed on the transfer list.

In November he went on strike and refused to play for five matches, but still neither Stein nor White would deal with the recalcitrant player. At first his action was disguised in official announcements of small injuries, a thigh strain being the most popular explanation. By 21 November, however, there was an admission that Hay was refusing to train and that he had been suspended for breach of contract.

Rumours abounded that Hay was in talks with Tottenham Hotspur, Leeds United and Manchester United. He was joined on strike for one match by George Connelly but the action never spread beyond those two supremely talented members of the Quality Street Gang. In desperation, Hay and Connelly agreed to re-sign for Celtic with no additional wages on condition that the players were loaned £30,000 to purchase some flats they had been offered in London near the BBC studios. The system of offering players loans was a commonplace practice at the time at Celtic and in other football clubs. It was a means of compensation for low basic wages and, importantly, a way of tying players closely to their clubs. Colleagues of Hay and Connelly were offered and accepted loans to purchase pubs in Glasgow and beyond but the contract rebels were refused point blank. White began to plot a profitable resolution to the drama.

Hay was back in the Celtic team, though, for the winning League Cup semi-final against Rangers, and would play an important role for the club throughout the rest of the season, but while giving his all for the cause he was plotting an exit route.

Stein, meanwhile, was busy fighting sustained and apoplectic guerrilla warfare with both Connelly and Johnstone. Neither player comprehended Stein's concepts of increasingly anachronistic discipline and loyalty.

Connelly was the very paradigm of a wayward genius whose problems were complex and ultimately unresolvable. The young man who was earmarked for stardom by Stein when he made his debut in 1968 at the age of 19 suffered from depression, alcoholism and an unhappy marriage. He walked out of Celtic five times and returned only on the first four of those occasions.

As for Johnstone, Stein had wanted to offload the wayward genius on his own arrival at Celtic Park in 1965. Many times over the ensuing years he wished he had succeeded, cursing the fact that he had been persuaded to keep the errant winger by Fallon's blarney.

Stein, the teetotaller, tried his damnedest to save Johnstone from the demon drink. There was a continuous trade-off between the winger's toxic behaviour off the pitch and his genius on it. Sometimes Stein played bad cop and sometimes good. He probably kept Johnstone's career on some kind of track for longer than anyone else might have done. Stein, the ranter, the raver, perversely loved Johnstone with a tenderness, and occasional over-indulgent kindness, usually reserved for only sons.

In season 1973/74, though, Stein's patience was sorely tried. There was a sending off against Rangers in a League Cup defeat and a winning goal against the Ibrox men in the first league encounter that followed. There were droppings and reinstatements. There was an absence against the Danes of Vejle in the second round of the European Cup due to Johnstone 'feeling unwell'.

Right to the end of his Celtic career there were hallelujahs and damnations, disbelief and tears when it ended in White's office in June 1975.

* * *

It was a wonder Celtic were still – mostly – winning football matches.

On 15 September, Johnstone's stooped header from a low Hay cross won the day in Govan and the Hoops cantered into a three-point lead over their rivals. The visiting contingent at the Celtic end of Ibrox Park were already singing about nine-in-a-row.

On 17 November, Deans scored six times in a seven-goal rout of Glasgow's third team, Partick Thistle.

On 5 January 1974, Celtic completed the league double over their big rivals in a 1-0 victory at Celtic Park and the Bhoys climbed seven points ahead of Hibernian and nine clear of Rangers. Lennox scored the solitary goal after 27 minutes but the win was comfortable and Deans, in particular, was guilty of spurning chances in the second half that would have put a further gloss on the result. Lennox, too, rounded Rangers goalkeeper Peter McCloy and then allowed him to recover and save. Bad boys Johnstone and Connelly were on the substitutes' bench, but Hay was a dominant figure in midfield.

The league was as good as won with only two games played in the new year and 15,000 unsold tickets at Paradise told an unwelcome story of acceptance of entitlement at Celtic and acceptance of inferiority at Rangers.

In his small office at Celtic Park, Stein fretted about people who watched him, about footballers who didn't know they were born, and who had never lived in mining communities being threatened by a Conservative government in remote London, about his own meagre remuneration as manager of Celtic, about missing Bob Kelly, and eventually turned his attention to Europe and a forthcoming quarter-final against Basel of Switzerland.

In his small office at upmarket Bath Street, White fretted about finances, about his dislike of Stein, about footballers who didn't know they were born and about the good old days when footballers did as they were told, about how absolute power had fallen into his lap after Kelly's death, and about selling Hay, and Connelly too, if possible, about realising marketable assets while keeping lids on wages and other inessential expenditures at Celtic Park.

In truth, Celtic, in this nine-in-a-row season, were fortunate that their domestic opposition was so relatively weak. The world was moving on and Celtic were standing still. There was, however, the excitement of nine-in-a-row to look forward to as well as the apparent inevitability ten in the following year.

* * *

In the event, it was almost too exciting.

On Saturday 27 April, the exodus from Glasgow began early. From terraces and tenements on London Road, from sky-rise flats on the far horizons of Bishopbriggs, Balornock and Barmulloch, from former villages now swallowed by the greed and need of urban sprawl, from the birthplaces of the Lisbon Lions, from Bellshill, Bothwell, Govan, Kings Park, Kirkintilloch, Maryhill, Motherwell, Roystonhill, Saltcoats, and from Viewpark, the supporters of the Bhoys rose early for the pilgrimage to Falkirk.

There were sandwiches to pack, masses to be said, beers to be bought, wives and sweethearts to kiss goodbye, form to be studied and bets to be placed, green-and-white-hooped scarves to wrap around necks, pound notes and 50p pieces to be found with the crumbs in between settee cushions, and change for the telephone box to call home with the score from Brockville. Battered VW Beetles and ageing Ford Anglias jump-started into life, bodies crammed inside, suspensions and tyres sinking kerbside with the heavy loads.

Those without private means of transport boarded buses to Queen Street Station, bought morning papers from Flax Flaherty from his pitch by the North British Hotel, the place where Jock Stein had been offered the manager's job by chairman Bob Kelly back in 1965.

The day was fine and it was good to be alive and to be a Celtic fan in search of a ninth league championship in nine years.

Cars from the northern and eastern outskirts of Glasgow headed for the A803 with its twists and turns towards Falkirk. Cans of Younger's Tartan sprung open and splashed on passengers' faces. Someone mentioned Atlético Madrid and someone else spat out the open Mini window. The events of the previous Wednesday evening at the Vicente

Calderón Stadium when Celtic exited the European Cup were still raw wounds on the soul.

Trains emptied, cars emptied, and turnstiles clicked. Celtic fans took their places inside Brockville. 'Hello, hello, it's nine-in-a-row!'

By three minutes past three, however, a nightmare scenario was looming all too large for Celtic in the Forth Valley.

From the first minute of this last-chance-saloon-to-avoid-relegation match, the Falkirk forwards swarmed towards their opponent's goal in a five-pronged attack and the Celtic defence stuttered and swayed, with skipper McNeill and his fellow denizens of the back line looking like seasick sailors adapting to dry land. In this opening foray, Kirkie Lawson, a striker combining bustling elegance and sharp shooting, had already come all too close to bulging Denis Connaghan's net.

Lawson, however, was not about to look a second gift horse in the mouth. As the ball was gathered in midfield by Wilson Hogan, a Bairns stalwart since 1968, and punted forwards once more, both Celtic goalkeeper and captain stood transfixed as Lawson slipped between them, his long hair waving its disdain for the shorter backs and sides of the defence, and finessed the ball unerringly into the visitors' goal. This was a man, after all, who had scored a quarter century of goals for Motherwell before joining Falkirk in their doomed fight against demotion from Division One.

The visiting supporters standing on the Watson Street terracing were stunned momentarily into silence.

It was true that this match was merely the first of three available to Celtic to claim the one point necessary to ensure a ninth successive title. It had, though, been such a bad week so far for Hoops supporters that there were those of a glass-half-empty persuasion who considered that things might still get worse.

Celtic had been eliminated from the European Cup after a bitter 2-0 defeat away to Atlético Madrid. Such was the ill feeling consequent upon the goalless draw in the first leg at Celtic Park a fortnight earlier that fans had been advised not to travel to Spain. Both Jimmy Johnstone and Jock Stein had received death threats on the eve of the game in Madrid, and the Celts were escorted everywhere by intimidating armed police. In the opening leg of the tie, Atlético had kicked and punched their way to a result with three of their players sent off and a further seven booked. The fanzine *Not The View* pilloried the Spanish line-up as, 'Thug; Psycho, Punch; Spit, Hatchet, Bludgeon; Hammer, Thump, Wallop, Gouge, Axe-Murderer.'

So Celtic supporters now crammed into the away end at Brockville were entitled to their sense of impending doom. How could they expect their team to play to form after such crushing disappointment and such unambiguous injustice?

While the denizens of the away end at Brockville were pondering the fickleness of fate, the Bairns almost scored a second goal. In the 18th minute of the match, Jim Shirra, another devotee of flowing locks, another proven goalscorer, carved his way through a dozing Celtic defence, sliced his way towards Connaghan, and shunted his shot inches wide of the post. Fans decked in green and white sucked desperately at passing oxygen to calm their shattered nerves.

It was not supposed to be like this.

Older fans tended to blame the youngsters for singing 'Hello, hello, it's nine-in-a-row!' prior to kick-off on the basis that presumption was never a good thing. Some thoughts drifted way back to 1957 and the 7-1 victory over Rangers in the League Cup Final. Young boys then dreamed of years of supremacy over their rivals and wiser men now recalled that the Hampden triumph was followed by seven barren years without a further trophy.

Understandable as it undoubtedly was that the Bhoys would be hungover from their Spanish disaster, there was a Scottish Cup Final against Dundee United to follow at the weekend, and it was imperative that form should be reclaimed sooner rather than later, and ideal that the championship be done and dusted before the end of the day.

Disagreements and debates in the Celtic end of Brockville Park were still raging like misplaced passes in the away team's midfield when attention was wrenched away from futile discussion and back to the events on the field of play. Someone shouted, 'It's Kenny!'

Dalglish had the ball at his feet some 30 yards from the Falkirk goal. This time, it was a Bairns defender who had lost control of the ball. The young forward was a will-o'-the-wisp talent, a light for Celtic souls, a ghost of a footballer, appearing and disappearing at the whim of his muse, always one step ahead of pursuers, a kinsman of Macavity the Mystery Cat in T.S. Eliot's poem.

Dalglish approached one Falkirk defender who scythed at thin air, beat a second, dragging the Falkirk defence one way and then another. In the 20th minute his left foot made sweet connection with the ball and sent it streaking low past Ally Donaldson's outstretched hand. The equaliser seemed to drain the hope from Falkirk's players, appeared to accommodate them to the inevitability of relegation, and Celtic's professionalism, in spite of the weary legs and heavy heads and hearts of their players, held the key to the momentum of the match. Play meandered now like the slow-moving waters of a summer stream.

At half-time, though, John Prentice, a member of the Bairns' legendary Scottish Cup-winning side of 1957 and now their manager, rallied his troops in the home dressing room and they came out for the second half fighting for their lives like boxers behind on points and swinging haymakers in the hope of a knockout blow.

Five minutes after the restart, Will Hoggan, a defender or reluctant midfielder and out of his comfort zone inside the opposition's half, found himself in possession of the ball and homing in on the Celtic goal. There was a collective in-drawing of breath among the support. Hoggan's shot fizzed low and hard and inches past Connaghan's left-hand post. Breath held was now exhaled.

After Hoggan's missed chance, the rest of the second half at Brockville was an exercise in patience, with neither side capable of raising sufficient spirits of adventure to claim both points.

Celtic survived and controlled the rest of the match in relative comfort. In boxing terms, here was the old pro, the champ of many years, holding and holding on, weary, muscled arms squeezing the life out of both opponent and contest. Sometimes, that is how titles are won and retained.

When the final whistle shrilled, both sets of players sank to their knees as if in prayer, Falkirk's men in sorrow and shame at the admission of relegation, Celtic's Bhoys in gratitude and in exhaustion.

From among the 14,000-strong crowd, the younger element of the Celtic support resumed their chanting of the reworked Gary Glitter anthem. 'Hello, hello, it's nine-in-a row, hello, hello.'

Afterwards, some climbed and leapt over barriers and partied on the pitch. Someone jumped high, caught hold of the crossbar of the goal at the Celtic end, hung there one-handed, beckoned friends to join him with his free hand, and the bar bent under their weight like a boomerang.

Fathers and grandfathers looked on with jealousy and disapproval. Or perhaps their faces were still soured by the misery of the defeat to Atlético in midweek. Either way, it had almost been another bad day at the office for Celtic.

Jock Stein admitted it had not been one of Celtic's better displays. He reminded journalists, however, that the league title had, in effect, been won the previous Saturday at Parkhead with the 2-0 defeat of Aberdeen, goals by Dixie Deans and Bobby Lennox virtually sealing the deal.

It had been a long day. On the journey home, there were many assumptions that this nice ninth title was merely a staging post on the way to a terrific ten, a tremendous 12, and ever onwards, amen, and thanks be to God the Father and Mary the Mother, world without end.

HALF-TIME ENTERTAINMENT

Stopping the Ten: 1998

IN CELTIC'S previous 110 years of history there may never have been such a frantic and febrile atmosphere at Celtic Park as the one that prevailed on the Saturday afternoon of 9 May 1998.

Henrik Larsson, signed from Feyenoord at the beginning of the season and later to play for Barcelona and Manchester United, reviewing his career from the perspective of retirement, said it was the most pressurised game he had ever played in.

The sun shone, as it had done all week, and inside Paradise it burned. Bodies sweated and sweltered and minds frazzled with the multitude of permutations and possibilities to be played out on the closing day of the season. At Tannadice, where Rangers were the visitors, those of an Ibrox persuasion were wishing and hoping for a Celtic slip-up at home to St Johnstone at Parkhead.

If Rangers defeated Dundee United then only a win would do for Celtic to stop the ten as Rangers had overtaken the green and whites' earlier lead on goal difference but still trailed by two points going into the last day. A Rangers win and a Celtic draw would hand the title to the Ibrox club for a tenth successive season. A repeat of nervous and distracted performances by Celtic – as in the recent drawn games, 1-1 at Dunfermline and 0-0 at home to Hibernian – would surely deliver the championship to Rangers.

Young fans trooping down London Road, the ones who had never tasted the sweet fruits of success, superiority over Rangers, joshed and jostled each other, settled nerves with swigs from cans of Tennent's or bottles of Irn-Bru, sang Irish rebel songs to make them brave before the battle. Older fans tutted at the bairns' behaviour, talked of perspective, reflected on life's cycles of success, how things would turn in Celtic's favour soon, if not this very afternoon; they recalled how Robert Tennent began brewing in Glasgow in 1556, and some smart arse said that made it the oldest continuous commercial concern in the city; they reminded each other of the charitable foundations of Brother Walfrid and how God was a good Catholic and would bestow his blessings on Celtic Park this very afternoon. The know-all said Tennent was a Catholic too as his brewery opened before the Reformation. 'So let the kids enjoy their bevvies.'

'What about Irn-Bru then?' someone else said. 'Were the Barrs Catholics too?' No one knew the answer.

The talk was of anything but the match ahead, anything to avoid thinking of the dread possibility of Rangers' record-breaking ten.

Fans already inside Paradise sweated and sung their songs. Right up until kick-off, the youngsters, in particular, were celebratory, jubilant as if the title was already won, but there was an undercurrent of something akin to terror in the hearts of all, and nausea in the pits of stomachs that swirled and swilled with lager and with Robert Barr's sickly fizz.

The tension was so thick it could never have been cut with any knife. A win, a win, a win, any kind of win would do, but it had to be a win.

* * *

At the beginning of season 1997/98, such a showdown with the city rivals had seemed unlikely in the extreme.

Rangers by the summer of 1997 were at the peak of their spending powers. The *Daily Record*, prior to the commencement of the new season, confidently predicted a continuation of the Ibrox club's domination of Scottish football, even setting out three teams from among their swollen playing rota that would be good enough to defeat Celtic and win the league for the tenth time in succession.

The Parkhead club, by contrast, had offloaded three of their star forwards, Jorge Cadete, Paolo Di Canio and Pierre van Hooijdonk, all three scouted by Davie Hay and signed by Tommy Burns, manager since replacing Lou Macari in July 1994. The trio had been purchased with the approval of Fergus McCann in order to break the back of Rangers' domestic dominance, but when Celtic finished second in the league once again at the conclusion of the 1996/97 season the chairman decided enough was enough, Burns was sacked and his triumvirate of celebrity strikers were sold.

Replacing them was a solitary frontman, Henrik Larsson, a relative unknown whose strike rate in Dutch league football was an inauspicious 26 goals from 101 appearances. The fee was a mere £650,000 which only served to emphasise the financial chasm between McCann's frugal Celtic and profligate Rangers under David Murray.

Worse was to follow on the opening day of the season at Hibernian's Easter Road. On his debut as a substitute, and with his very first touch, Larsson misplaced the ball into the path of Chic Charnley who scored the Edinburgh side's winning goal.

Celtic's second match, too, was lost, 2-1 at home to Dunfermline. By contrast, Rangers had won their opening games, 3-1 against Hearts and 5-1 against Dundee United. The team from Paradise were in hell at the bottom of the league.

If Stein had been around to ask his friend Tony Queen for odds on a Celtic championship, he might have been offered 100-1 and asked for 1,000-1.

Neither was it just Larsson struggling to come to terms with a new club, a new league and a new culture.

Wim Jansen had been headhunted as Burns's replacement, a search headed by McCann and his new general manager Jock Brown, an abrasive Glasgow lawyer who had been placed in charge of player transfers and administration so that the new manager could concentrate upon events on the training pitch and on matchday matters.

Jansen had been managing in Hiroshima, Japan, but remembered Larsson from his contacts at Feyenoord and had faith in his talent.

The coach, though, had to win over the Scots in his new team. There were sniggers at Jansen's 'wee perm' and his shellsuit but the players were soon taken by imaginative training sessions.

And by winning football matches. Following the upset at home to the Pars, Celtic went on a run of eight victories and, after a 2-0 revenge win over Dunfermline on 1 November they were ensconced at the top of the Premier League, having returned there after their previous win over St Johnstone at the end of October.

Jansen's approval ratings increased again after elimination from the UEFA Cup by Liverpool, drawing both at home and at Anfield and losing out only on the away goals rule. As Simon Donnelly said, the games against the four-time European Cup winners 'made us realise we weren't a bad side and that we could compete with the best including Rangers'.

By the beginning of November, too, Jansen had won consecutive Manager of the Month awards and had signed Marc Rieper from West Ham to strengthen the defensive ramparts.

On 8 November there was a setback as a Richard Gough goal for Rangers at Ibrox bloodied Celtic's nose and Hearts claimed top spot in the race for the title. There was compensation, however, in the debut of Paul Lambert, a European Cup winner signed from Borussia Dortmund for £1.9m.

Lambert, a combative and talented midfielder, was the final piece in the Jansen jigsaw puzzle that had been pieced together in four short months of intense efforts by the new manager and by McCann and Brown. In the New Year's Day Derby in January 1998 Lambert scored the crucial second goal for Celtic, ensuring a win that prevented Rangers and Hearts from disappearing over the horizon at the top of the Premier League.

Prior to the game, Rangers were four points clear of Celtic and a second league victory over the team from Paradise might well have imposed an insurmountable physical and psychological barrier between themselves and their pursuers, between the hunted and the hunter.

The game was fast and furious, and thoughtful football was as rare as a teetotaller in a crowded Glasgow bar. Celtic provided most of the pressure but their attacking waves broke upon the rocks of a Rangers back line marshalled by Andy Goram in goal and by Gough in central defence. Goram, in particular, looked unbeatable. On one occasion, he tipped a Harald Brattbakk shot around the post while simultaneously waving his free arm in the air appealing for offside.

It was in Lisbon time, the 67th minute, when the deadlock was broken by a long ball from Lambert which found Jackie McNamara who flicked it on for Craig Burley to beat Goram from ten yards.

The three points, putting Celtic back within touching distance of their rivals, were made secure with just five nervous minutes to spare when Lambert placed a piledriver of a shot into the back of the net from 20 yards.

Celtic fans bounced out of their temporary seats – the rebuilding of Celtic Park was still incomplete – and began to sing:

'Jingle bells, jingle bells, jingle all the way. Oh, what fun it is to see Celtic beat the Gers on New Year's Day!'

Fast forward to the evening of 12 April, however, and the final Old Firm fixture of the season saw Celtic returned to second place after a numbing 2-0 defeat at Ibrox. Prior to the game, the Hoops had battled their way to a three-point lead in the race to stop the ten. One week earlier, however, Rangers had seemed to confirm their Glasgow supremacy in a Scottish Cup semi-final victory over the Celts. The sole Old Firm victory for Celtic had been in the new year fixture.

When Brattbakk replaced Darren Jackson, one of Jansen's first signings from Hibs, after 15 minutes with the latter suffering from stomach pains, it seemed as if the Celtic manager was making a cardinal tactical error. The Norwegian was stuck up front like a coconut in a fairground shy when his best form for Rosenborg had been as a link man. At the same time, Larsson, a supreme striker, was asked to provide service for Brattbakk.

Goals, admittedly against the run of play, by Jonas Thern after 25 minutes and Jorg Albertz midway through the second half, did for Celtic.

In a report for *The Scotsman*, Glenn Gibbons suggested that Rangers had 'taken out a freehold on the Scottish league championship, still capable of making the payments that preclude the possibility of dispossession'.

There were four games to go, and Celtic were not only struggling to come to terms with opponents on the pitch but, behind the scenes, a power struggle between Jansen and his superiors, McCann and Brown, was threatening to derail a title challenge in this season of all seasons.

In the preceding month of March, after the hard-fought victory over Aberdeen that was akin to two heavyweight boxers slugging it out mid-ring, Jansen asked if he could provide an interview with the Celtic Hotline, a premium rate telephone service, through which those fans with more money than sense could access usually bland news from inside the club without waiting for the same information from the evening papers.

Strangely, Jansen laid down one condition, that his words would not be cut or edited in any way. His request should have sent alarm bells ringing that this statement would not be the usual fodder for fools.

The Dutchman's revelation was that his contract, a three-year deal, contained a get-out clause allowing both him and his assistant, Murdo

MacLeod, to walk away from their positions without penalties at the end of their first season.

Was Jansen unhappy? Surely not? After all, Celtic were top of the Premier League at the time.

Yes, Jansen said, he was not impressed by the fact that, in spite of the clear progress made at the club since his arrival at Parkhead, there had been no approach by the hierarchy to discuss plans for the following season.

Clearly, what Jansen meant was that there had been no offer from McCann or Brown to renegotiate an improved contract.

Clearly, too, McCann and his oppo had reservations about Jansen. There were rumours the Celtic manager was a divisive figure among his coaching staff, that there were splits and cliques, ins and outs, and an unhappy atmosphere fuelled by favouritism and resulting in resentments. Jansen made it clear his sole interest was working with the first team and coaches and players within the reserves and the youth setup felt the cold draught of exclusion. McCann could detect no long-term planning, no durable or discernible commitment to the future.

The press were as happy as pigs in shit and as prolific as pigs at shitting on Celtic.

Brown moved to calm the storm. Neither Jansen nor MacLeod had ever expressed dissatisfaction at any time with any aspects of their contracts.

McCann consoled himself with the thought that the get-out clause revealed by Jansen was a two-way highway and that the club, too, might dispense with him without need for compensation, after just one year of the planned three-year project.

Meanwhile, there was a league championship to be won or lost, ten-in-a-row to be stopped or conceded. Nerves were top of the bill early on against Motherwell on Saturday, 18 April.

In these teams' three prior meetings in the current term, Celtic had failed to establish genuine superiority over Motherwell, winning only once, and losing once too.

After 12 minutes the Well took the lead through Stephen McMillan and alarm bells were not just ringing but clanging, clanking and crashing too in a cacophony of Celtic discordance.

After 25 minutes, however, sweet tunes were restored to Celtic's play when Craig Burley equalised and, from that point onwards, Paradise was treated to accomplished play and an easy 4-1 victory, giving the league leaders a three-point cushion before Rangers' fixture on the Sunday against Aberdeen.

Prayers were said at Glasgow Masses for dropped points by Rangers in the afternoon and, glory be, a Stephen Glass header for the home side was the sole goal at Pittodrie. Surely, now, one-in-a-row and cheerio to ten-in-a-row was a formality.

With three games outstanding, Celtic faced two at home, against an already-relegated Hibernian and a mid-table St Johnstone, and an away visit to lower-end Dunfermline. Rangers had two matches away from Ibrox, against a Hearts team only recently dislocated from the title race and at Dundee United from the nether regions of the league table, and, in between these two, a home tilt against fourth-placed Kilmarnock.

God, though, moves in more mysterious ways than perceived by some Celtic fans.

On 25 April, Rangers destroyed Hearts 3-0 at Tynecastle with two goals from the highly paid Rino Gattuso and one from Albertz.

Celtic, meanwhile, were shades and shadows, played like hungry ghosts from the regions of hell, distributing passes to places where no passes should be passed. A goalless draw with Hibernian at Parkhead sent grey-faced fans into a dreary London Road and down side streets and into homes not lightened by their return.

Two games left and a precious lead of one point. Once heads were cleared and reason returned, ready reckoners were consulted and revisited for confirmations that Celtic needed just two more wins and then it could not matter what results Rangers achieved.

Just to be sure, though, eyes would be kept on TV teletext scores from Ibrox on 2 May and ears would be kept tuned to transistor radios for news either good or bad.

Rangers' final home game of the season against Kilmarnock had been earmarked early as a day of celebration. Ten-in-a-row would be long since wrapped up and ribboned. Plans, too, for emotional farewells to Walter Smith and to Ally McCoist and Brian Laudrup, were signed, sealed, and almost delivered, and had to take place in spite of the precarious nature of ten-in-a-row. Both manager, heading south to take charge of Everton, and star players – McCoist Kilmarnock-bound after 581 games and 355 goals, and Laudrup heading to the bright blue lights of Chelsea –

paraded with their families before adoring fans and before kick-off. The atmosphere inside Ibrox, though, had something of last night's re-fried fish and chips about it, and the fare served up by the Rangers players was stale and tasteless.

Curiously, too, it was the last game in the refereeing career of Bobby Tait, the author of a plethora of dubious decisions that appeared to favour the team from Ibrox. Hugh Keevins, doyen of *Daily Record* journalists, had already outed Tait as an ardent Rangers supporter and now there were rumours swirling around Glasgow that compliant authorities had acceded to Tait's request for a swansong performance at Ibrox.

Throughout the 90 minutes Rangers huffed and puffed and failed to blow the Killie house down. In truth, the Ibrox team misfired as badly as Celtic had done against Hibernian.

What happened next, however, was almost beyond belief. For over five additional minutes, Tait did not blow the final whistle. Where the added time came from only the retiring referee could say. It was as if he intended to play on until Rangers scored, but things played out differently. In the 95th minute, Killie's McGowan swung in an awkwardly bouncing cross from the right wing. Gattuso, at the back post, dreaming of return flights to Italy, was fast asleep and allowed substitute Ally Mitchell to steer the ball past goalkeeper Antti Niemi.

Still the match continued, Tait presumably thinking just one more minute might turn the trick, but eventually even a referee in the pocket of his prejudices has to admit defeat and blow one final dreadful whistle.

To add balance to the proceedings at Ibrox, and for the sake of completeness, Tait had added a similar amount of supposed injury time at the end of the first half. Still, as Richard Gough admitted, 'We could have played forever without being able to get a goal.'

Instead of wild celebrations and a jubilant send-off for departing heroes, the Rangers players were booed from the field of play.

One win more for Celtic, a Sunday jaunt at East End Park the following day, would seal the deal.

* * *

Just in case everyone thought it might be all sweetness and light in Celtic Park, however, Jansen spoke out once more on his contract situation. All would be resolved one way or another at the end of the season.

McCann talked publicly about the backstage dramas for the first time. Celtic was bigger than one man, he said, without saying whether he was referring to himself or to Jansen.

* * *

Sunday rose from its sleep and opened windows to brilliant sunshine in Glasgow and in Fife. If the weather was an omen, the day might yet witness the coronation of a new king of Scottish football.

Banks of green-and-white hoops filled the stadium in Dunfermline. Of course, Celtic were nervous, their passes ragged, their movement stillborn, their confidence drowned in a sea of fear, their shots wild and fanciful. Until Simon Donnelly scored in the 35th minute.

In the second half, the paranoia, the quality of being frozen while oozing sweat, the ability to stand still while apparently running hard, all returned to Celtic's play. In spite of Jansen's urgings from the touchline, the men in hoops retreated, passive to the touch. With seven minutes remaining, Dunfermline's gangly beanpole substitute Craig Faulconbridge headed a deserved equaliser for the home side.

It had all mattered just too much.

* * *

On the final day of the 1997/98 season it had come to this. Still, Celtic were one win away from stopping the ten. Rangers were one win away – if Celtic failed to beat St Johnstone – from an unprecedented tenth title in a row.

* * *

Inside Ibrox a big screen relayed the events at Dundee United's Tannadice to a fearful audience of 30,000.

Red necks craned and sweated in the sun and swivelled eyes hardly dared to watch the flickering movements of players on the screen. Three minutes only had passed before an Ibrox announcer passed on the news that St Johnstone had scored at Celtic Park and the tension that crackled and spat between fans was transformed into ecstatic roars of approval that drowned out commentary on the match at Tannadice.

Inside Paradise, an equal electricity danced, charging fans and players alike. Celtic had started the game as brightly as the sun had dawned, as hot as the sun still warmed. In the third minute, Lambert intercepted a Saints clearance and played the ball deftly to his left across 35 yards to a perfect place where Larsson waited. The Swedish maestro, on whose muse Celtic increasingly depended, cut inside, feigned to shoot, feigned not to shoot, and shot. His right foot curled the ball and fizzed it past goalkeeper Alan Main.

Inside Ibrox, radios crackled with the news and it dawned on Rangers fans and players alike that the earlier news was fake news, a sick joke, an horrendous error, and that Celtic were ahead and not behind.

At Celtic Park, Larsson missed a further opportunity to make the title safe for the side from Paradise, and a great dawning dawned on the Celtic players. The championship might still be lost.

At 11 minutes past three, news reached Celtic Park that darkened brows and tightened hearts. Laudrup had scored, and Rangers, too, were a goal to the good.

The majority of the crowds at both games were unable to watch with any degree of concentration. Radios were glued to ears. What happened away from the match attended mattered as much, if not sometimes more, than the feast spread before the spectators.

At half-time, Smith and Jansen cavilled and cajoled, and calmed their players. At Paradise, Celtic restarted as brightly as in the first half until Donnelly shot straight at the Saints' goalkeeper with the goal and the title at his mercy. At Tannadice, an Albertz penalty put Rangers 2-0 ahead, but it would not matter unless St Johnstone scored at Celtic Park.

At Paradise, Jansen abandoned his cool and his seat on the bench, patrolled and prowled the touchline. With an hour to go the manager introduced the enigmatic Brattbakk.

After 65 minutes, Lars Zetterlund pulled one goal back for the home side at Tannadice. Could Rangers be bottling it too? Could St Johnstone equalise and could Dundee United equalise too – and hand the title to Celtic by default? Nerves jangled and tangled and hearts tick-tocked and some must have stopped.

At Celtic Park, St Johnstone pressed and pressed again. With a mere 18 minutes to go, however, Tom Boyd sent a long and lofted ball to the right wing where it was trapped by Jackie McNamara. In truth, the pass was a message in a bottle from a stranded castaway in the Celtic defence. The midfielder sent the message on to an inrushing Brattbakk who slotted the ball beneath the body of the diving Main and into the back of the net. It was as if the Norwegian had never missed a chance in his life.

At Ibrox the game was up, and crowds drifted away from the big screen showing ghosts of players going through some motions demanded of them by their professional status. At Paradise, the remaining minutes passed in a haze of delirium, with St Johnstone a spent force.

Just before the final whistle, McCann appeared at the entrance to the tunnel. Afterwards, Brown issued a statement apparently with regard to Jansen's future. 'Wim,' he said, 'is calling the shots in the matter.'

Jansen himself admitted, 'I have made up my mind about what I will be doing next season but I will not be explaining it here. The first person to know will be Fergus McCann and the only other person to know will be my wife.'

Only Celtic could win such a crucial one-in-a-row amid so much confusion.

THE SECOND HALF

The Second Nine-in-a-Row: 2011–2020

Foundations

FERGUS McCANN AND THE FINANCIAL REVOLUTION

1. THE DAY THE WORLD WAS SAVED: HIGH NOON, 4 MARCH 1994

As day dawned on the East End of Glasgow only one thing was certain. If £1m was not deposited with the St Vincent Street office of Celtic's bankers by midday, Dr Rowland Mitchell, general manager of the Glasgow division of the Bank of Scotland, would call in administrators to run the club, and the football institution that was Celtic, and Paradise to its fans, would be no more.

In the skies above the city, dark and lowering clouds presaged incoming weather typical of the west of Scotland.

Above, too, a plane circled prior to its descent. Aboard this flight from Phoenix, Arizona, was an unprepossessing Scots Canadian, a man with gold-rimmed spectacles, an undistinguished moustache, and a hairline long since receded beyond the possibilities of disguise. He might have been mistaken for a bank clerk or a minor official from the ministry, a man deputed to bear bad news to grieving widows that their pensions had been lost or misplaced in some disastrous financial scandal.

In fact, he was a man of single-minded and ruthless intent, a man apparently at war with the world but determined to bend both time and tides to his will. His current resolution was to save from extinction the football team he had supported as a boy. He would be easy neither as friend nor foe and his name was Fergus McCann.

Worries, though, buzzed about his head like wasps at a picnic. Most pressing was the fear that the money he had wired from the US in accordance with the Bank of Scotland's instructions might not arrive in Glasgow before the expiry of the bank's deadline.

It had come to this last chance saloon, this brinkmanship, largely as a result of the failure by the 'ancient regime' at Celtic Park to recognise the necessity for change, for new blood, new investment. McCann had been consistently rebuffed, both offers of money and new ideas for commercial development rejected out of hand. Only when pressure from the Bank of Scotland became intolerable in the final few days of the crisis and when McCann's proposals were accepted by the bank did some of the entrenched members of Celtic's boardroom consider the possibility of selling their shares.

Even though McCann and his team now enjoyed preferred bidder status, nothing was yet settled. Even though his allies, led by David Low, an investment adviser and financial fixer known to McCann since 1992, had been busy buying Celtic shares from smaller investors in Scotland and Ireland, the strategy for revolution was still a risky one. There was still no agreement with members of the old board and time for completion of the deal was woefully short.

As McCann's plane landed, nothing was signed, nor sealed, nor delivered.

* * *

McCann was met off the plane by Low and driven fast to the Glasgow offices of property developer and Celtic fan Brian Dempsey.

It was 9.30am.

Low had already done half a day's work, meeting with Dempsey at eight to discuss strategies. It was agreed that John Keane, who had made his fortune from construction and civil engineering projects managed for BT and British Gas, would provide the required £1m guarantee to grant Celtic's stay of execution. If McCann's money arrived in time, all well and good, but Keane's involvement would guarantee survival for Glasgow's East End football club.

Low phoned Keane in Edinburgh. Keane phoned his branch of the Bank of Ireland in Glasgow. The bank was sorry but the paperwork involved in a legal guarantee was more complex than a cash deposit and, sorry again, the processing could not be completed before midday.

Just as one saving grace appeared on the horizon, it was obliterated by darkening clouds. It was not just the possibility of failing to meet the bank's deadline that troubled McCann. He was concerned, too, that the Glasgow businessman Gerald Weisfeld, millionaire founder of the shopping empire What Every Woman Wants and recently arrived from Australia, might hijack his deal. Weisfeld was increasing his portfolio of Celtic shares by the minute, might beat McCann to the punch with his offer to the Celtic board of £3m in personal guarantees, and might deliver a knockout blow to McCann's putative role as saviour of the beleaguered football club so close to his heart.

* * *

At ten sharp, within the walls of Celtic Park, an extraordinary meeting of the Celtic board of directors was convened and the chairman, Kevin Kelly, descendant of James Kelly, opened proceedings amid an acrid and acrimonious atmosphere of mistrust and mutual hatred.

Present were all seven directors of the old Biscuit Tin Board, so named after its members' parsimony and for its small-minded and old-fashioned and curmudgeonly ways.

White shirts were stained with sweat born of fear. Not only was Celtic Football Club on the verge of bankruptcy but its custodians, the directors, were riven with dissension, with plots and counter-plots, most revolving around matters of self-preservation, though some including plans for self-enrichment.

By the time of the meeting, the board had split into two cliques. One, led by chairman Kevin Kelly, had entered into negotiations with the Bank of Scotland and the bank's favoured saviour, McCann. It was the chairman's bumbling stewardship, however, that had led the football club to the edge of oblivion. His colleagues who were belatedly willing to countenance change were Jack McGinn, whose shareholding was minimal, James Farrell, an outsider on each and every day inside the boardroom since his appointment in 1964, and Tom Grant, a previous member of the Families' Pact, an agreement never to sell shares independently, who had jumped from the reactionaries' sinking ship.

It was hardly a prepossessing alliance, with marriages of convenience bolstered by short-term collusions of interests, all among the cracks and fissures between these men, and clearly visible to the outside world. It was a grouping upon which change had been forced and foisted. Farrell, alone, perhaps, truly understood the need for change within the club, even wanted change for the good of the club. He was the longest-serving member of the Biscuit Tin Board but had no power or real influence over proceedings. The true feelings of the majority of this coterie may perhaps best be summed up in Kevin Kelly's words on Celtic fans demanding change. 'Most decent Celtic fans,' he said, 'will be embarrassed by what Celts for Change are doing.' It was a patrician's response to the ungrateful and rebellious behaviour of the plebeians who were marching, publishing, meeting, and demanding an overthrow of the old regime.

Opposing the reluctant reformers was a trio of reactionaries led by Kevin Kelly's cousin, Michael. Chris White, grandson of Tom White, chairman from 1914 to 1947 and son of Desmond White, chairman from 1971 to 1985, an accountant and major shareholder in 1994, was Michael Kelly's major cheerleader and upholder of the familial faith.

As for the connections and disconnections of the dynasties of families that had ruled Celtic since the foundation of the club, you really could not make it up. These were the last, dissolute knockings of nepotism, the original entrepreneurial and custodial vigour of the Kelly, White, and Grant clans long replaced by pale shadows, imbecilic imitations of the Founding Fathers.

The third member of the group clinging to power and status was David Smith, the vice-chairman, yet both a newcomer and outsider. He had become a non-executive director, brought on to the board by Kevin Kelly in 1992, as a supposed financial guru who would revolutionise the club's finances. His failure may be measured by the emergency meeting held at Celtic Park on the morning of the arrival of McCann to Glasgow.

Michael Kelly, former Lord Provost of Glasgow and former Lord Rector of Glasgow University, now spokesman of the gang of counter revolutionaries within the board, was hot with anger and indignation.

The day previously, he and his fellow diehards, Chris White and David Smith, had been excluded from an unofficial and secretive meeting of the other four members of the board with Rowland Mitchell and Dominic Keane, a banking ally of McCann.

This was the meeting which concluded with Mitchell agreeing not to pull the plug on Celtic's continued existence on condition that £1m be deposited with the Bank of Scotland 'to support the bank's overdraft' and that this deposit would be 'superseded by a £5m guarantee' once 'Mr Fergus McCann has reached the UK and has had a chance to apprise himself of the situation, latest the middle of next week'.

Mitchell then wrote to Kevin Kelly saying, 'I am delighted that we seem to have identified an acceptable way forward.'

Michael Kelly, however, was far from delighted and raged against his colleagues' participation in a meeting that was 'precipitate and wrong'.

By way of reply, Kevin Kelly called on his cousin and on White and Smith to resign.

* * *

McCann, meanwhile, was horrified to find he had arrived in Glasgow in advance of the funds required to save Celtic.

After the disappointment of the failure of John Keane's guarantee, disaster loomed.

Frantic faxes and furious phone calls were expedited from Dempsey's office. Mitchell confirmed that the deadline would not be extended.

* * *

Celtic's descent from the frugal parsimony of the Kelly–Stein axis was steep and alarming. At the beginning of 1994, Celtic's overdraft with the Bank of Scotland stood at an unsustainable £4.7m. Total debts stood at £7.2m, costing the club £30,000 in annual interest payments.

In addition, the club was dangerously undercapitalised with a risible share value of a mere £20,000. One shareholder, at the EGM of November 1993, explained, 'I have never come across a company that has survived when its liabilities were 360 times its share capital.'

With a wage bill accepted by manager Lou Macari as 'very high', and with expenditure on transfer fees in the early 1990s rising to unprecedented levels – Gary Gillespie from Liverpool for £1.67m, Tony Cascarino from Aston Villa for £1.58m, Tony Mowbray from Middlesbrough for £1.04m, Tom Boyd from Motherwell for £1.01m, Phil O'Donnell from Motherwell for £2.39m, Pierre van Hooijdonk from Breda for £1.53m – Celtic were facing a perfect storm of financial irresponsibility.

As expenditure soared, income plummeted. Apart from the Old Firm game that heralded the new year when an apparently full house was recorded, attendances at other home matches in January 1994 were a paltry 19,083 for the 2-2 draw with Aberdeen and an even worse 17,235 for the dismal 0-0 against Dundee United. In days when gate revenues made up more than 90 per cent of Celtic's income, when TV payments were negligible, when revenue streams from merchandising were risible, and when season ticket holders were despised as 'nothing but trouble' by the board, these matchday statistics were damning indictments of the Biscuit Tin Board.

A fans' boycott organised for the match against Kilmarnock on 1 March further reduced the attendance to 10,882, a figure disputed by Celts for Change who counted a mere 8,225.

After that, there remained only six more home games; only six more opportunities to improve Celtic's dire liquidity. Out of Motherwell, Raith Rovers, Dundee, Hearts, St Johnstone and Partick Thistle, only the Edinburgh club might bring any substantial travelling support to swell Celtic's coffers.

In a summer without income, and with an overdraft at breaking point, the East End club would have to find a £350,000 transfer fee for Willie Falconer from Sheffield United, and the Bank of Scotland had already blocked the first instalment of cash needed to complete that deal. There was, too, another £350,000 to go to Manchester United for Lee Martin, a disputed figure eventually settled by tribunal. Former player Charlie Nicholas was still owed £100,000, and former chief executive Terry Cassidy was suing the club for wrongful dismissal in a case that might cost Celtic as much as £200,000. Realistic cash flow projections suggested none of these liabilities could be met.

The numbers were duly noted by Rowland Mitchell, whose concern for the viability of his bank's lending had turned to alarm.

* * *

Celtic's overspending was a response to the extraordinary spending of Rangers under manager Graeme Souness and chairman David Murray.

The revolution at Ibrox began with the appointment of David Holmes to the board of directors in November 1985. Holmes, a joiner by trade, was the frontman for his boss at the Lawrence Building Group, Lawrence

Marlborough, the grandson of the former Rangers chairman John Lawrence, who had made his fortune through opportunistic exploitation of Glasgow's slum clearance programmes.

It is interesting to note, in passing, that Celtic were not alone in their speciality of dynastic succession.

Marlborough, a tax exile in Nevada, began his bid to acquire full control of Rangers in 1985 through a campaign of aggressive share purchases, culminating in January 1986 with the buying of a significant block of shares owned by the vice-chairman, Jack Gillespie. Marlborough now owned 52 per cent of the Ibrox club's shares and possessed effective control of Rangers.

On 14 February 1986, Holmes was appointed chief executive officer and what followed was a St Valentine's Day Massacre of the old directors of the football club. 'I did what I had to do,' said Holmes, 'and I didn't flinch from it.' Stooge and surrogate for Marlborough he might have been, but Holmes was ruthless in the execution of the absentee landlord's plans.

Displaced members of the Rangers board retreated to the darkness and secrecy of their Masonic lodges.

Later in February, Holmes flew to Italy to negotiate a deal to bring in Souness from Sampdoria, and the former Liverpool midfielder, only 32 years old, was unveiled as Jock Wallace's replacement as manager two months later.

When the old warrior Wallace was sacked, it is reputed he was carried out of Ibrox on his shield, still singing a rousing chorus of 'The Sash My Father Wore'.

At the end of the 1985/86 season Celtic, managed by Davie Hay, regained the Premier Division championship after a period of dominance by the 'New Firm' of Dundee United and Aberdeen. A fragile Celtic won the title only on goal difference from an even more brittle Heart of Midlothian – the Edinburgh club needed only to draw against Dundee but lost 2-0, but were 15 points clear of Rangers in fifth place.

The response of the Marlborough–Holmes–Souness axis was to drive deeper into debt, to buy the next league title in an era of Celtic frugality.

By the end of Souness's first season in charge, in which the championship was regained after overhauling an apparently insurmountable Celtic lead of nine points, the player-manager had spent more than £2m of Marlborough's money. Eye-catching signings arrived from English football including Chris Woods from Norwich City for £600,000, Terry Butcher from Ipswich Town for £750,000, and Graham Roberts from Spurs for £500,000. By contrast, Celtic, in the same period, signed Allen McKnight from Lisburn and Dougie McGuire from Dumbarton, for undisclosed, but inevitably paltry, fees.

In November 1988, after Celtic under Billy McNeill had won a centenary year league and cup double, Marlborough, tired of the expense and relative lack of success, sold his majority shareholding to Souness's friend, the businessman David Murray.

At this point, the second and darker phase of the Rangers revolution began.

If Marlborough was desperate to escape the vortex of spiralling debt and expenditure, he might at least have performed due diligence upon the man who bought his shares for a bargain £6m.

At the time of the sale, Murray's business and Rangers' new parent company, Murray International, a steel trading company, was already burdened with around £40m of bank debt.

For the following 20 years, in an era of deregulated financial markets, of easy money and greed, and of capital's dominance over labour, Rangers under Murray embarked upon an orgy of debt-fuelled spending leveraged upwards by the use and abuse of tax avoidance schemes. In July 2017, the five judges of the UK Supreme Court unanimously ruled the use of employee benefit trusts by Rangers to be 'invalid' and 'contrived arrangements that try to deliver tax advantages never intended by parliament'. EBTs were further described as 'disguised remuneration tax avoidance systems'.

During this era, Rangers won 16 league titles including their much vaunted nine-in-a-row between 1988/89 and 1996/97.

In view of what is now known concerning Rangers' immoral use of an employee benefit trust and discounted options schemes, and in view of the seemingly limitless streams of cash provided to the football club by the Bank of Scotland, an asterisk ought to be placed against all of these 16 championships.

Murray resigned as chairman in July 2002, leaving his toxic legacy of implacable debt and criminality to his successor, John McClelland.

Souness's own lasting legacy, aside from three tainted titles and four tainted League Cups, was Murray himself.

With the global financial crash of 2008 and the end of easy finance the writing was on all of Rangers' walls.

In May 2011 Murray sold his controlling interest in Rangers to Craig Whyte, a man with a string of business failures and criminality resulting in a seven-year ban from company directorships included in his curriculum vitae.

In 2012, The Rangers Football Club plc entered into administration in February after demands of unpaid tax by HMRC and the company was liquidated on 31 October.

* * *

'Keep trying, Fergus.'

Brian Dempsey was sweating, the central heating in his office overpowering. McCann tugged nervously at his bunnet, smoothed escaped hair at the nape of his neck back into place.

'Phone them again now, Fergus.' Dempsey's voice was a cry for help.

'I arranged everything yesterday, dammit, clear instructions for £1m in dollars to be wired from New York to London.' McCann was shouting down the telephone line from Dempsey's office to the Clydesdale Bank in St Vincent Street.

Outside, a cold and unpleasant wind blew litter through the Glasgow streets, presaging a storm.

'I'm sorry sir, but these things take time.'

'Which we have too little of.'

'Mr McCann, we're doing all we can. The money has to be converted into sterling and it has to get from London to Glasgow.'

It was one minute shy of 10am and the deadline for Celtic's extinction was only two hours away.

* * *

At Celtic Park, crowds began to gather, mostly silent and brooding, but with occasional outbursts of 'sack the board' and 'fuck the board'.

Had it not been for the industrial language, it might have been a crowd in St Peter's Square waiting for the puffs of white smoke to indicate a change of regime.

Inside the boardroom, the seven directors were locked in an antagonistic embrace.

* * *

McCann had always been interested in Celtic, passionately so as a boy and as a young man. He was brought up in the frenzied atmosphere of Kilsyth, notorious for its history of religious revivalism, and for its discrimination against the town's Catholic population by its majority Protestant community. McCann, however, spent much of his time in the nearby mining village of Croy, part of the Celtic heartland of North Lanarkshire. There he worked as treasurer and bus convenor for the Croy branch of the Celtic Supporters' Club. Always the revolutionary, always a man at war and at battle stations, he argued for full membership of the Croy CSC for women.

After emigrating to Canada, McCann's initial business venture involved reaching out to Celtic by way of broadcasting 'as live' delayed pictures of the club's 1972 European Cup semi-final against Inter Milan in the Maple Leaf Gardens in Toronto. He bought the rights from Desmond White for £300 after reminding the chairman of their meeting at a European Cup Winners' Cup tie in Basel in 1963.

He was almost bankrupted by the reluctance of the Italian community in Toronto to turn out for a match they wrongly believed they were certain to lose. It took McCann ten years to wipe out the debts incurred through this venture.

By 1988, however, the Scots Canadian had built a thriving golf tourism business and enjoyed sufficient surplus cash to approach Celtic's chairman, Jack McGinn, with some imaginative investment proposals.

Already, McCann understood the club's lack of capital and lack of understanding of basic principles of marketing.

'Repeat business,' he told McGinn, 'it's crucial.'

He suggested expanding the club's season ticket sales but it was too 'complex' to do so. He offered a £6m loan at half the bank rate of interest. Redevelopment of Celtic Park would have provided capacity for 72,000 fans with increased seating together with executive boxes. In addition, he would market season tickets in return for a commission on his sales.

McCann was turned away. 'I realised,' he said, 'there was no way to work with these people.'

A plan was hatched to acquire control of the club, to save it from itself.

* * *

At 10am Low asked McCann to try once more. Charles Barnett from accountants Pannell Kerr Forster, recently arrived in Dempsey's headquarters, muttered supportive encouragement.

Tempers were as taut as wire in a garrotte. The disembodied voice from somewhere inside McCann's Glasgow bank said, 'The money's just arrived.'

Four grown men danced and hugged each other, relaxing momentarily before hurrying to the Clydesdale Bank. From there, McCann phoned the Bank of Scotland and asked in what form the promised money was required. They walked the short distance between the two banks. The threatened rain was holding off. They shook hands with Rowland Mitchell and with Douglas Henderson, the Bank of Scotland's divisional manager of UK banking.

At 11.52am on 4 March 1994, Low added his signature as witness to the paperwork, and serene smiles were shared while hearts were still beating crazily. One act of the day's high drama was concluded but the revolution was not yet complete.

* * *

Inside the locked gates of Paradise, news reached the seven directors of the Biscuit Tin Board.

Attentions turned to haggling. How much might each receive for his shares?

White, Smith and Michael Kelly might still sell their shares to Gerald Weisfeld and they might extract £300 per share from the deal.

* * *

In negotiations with the board, Low had abandoned his original position of offering nothing to the current shareholders and had authorised Dominic Keane, on behalf of McCann, to offer a maximum of £1.4m for all shares, a more than fair pay-off but significantly less than Weisfeld's offer.

When McCann arrived at Parkhead at 2pm, however, his verdict was chilling and straightforward. 'Not one thin dime,' he said. To buy shares from the Biscuit Tin Board was to reward failure.

This was brinkmanship of the highest order. McCann's allies were dismayed and distraught. Low was forced to backtrack on the earlier offer. 'They're getting nothing,' he said.

For McCann, this was personal, this was principle, although it was true he was emboldened in this approach by the deposit of his cheque with the Bank of Scotland and by Mitchell and Henderson's backing of his coup.

Still, though, the three recalcitrant members of the Celtic board, White, Smith and Kelly, might sell elsewhere.

Dempsey was worried. 'After all this,' he muttered to Low. He did not need to finish his sentence.

How did McCann expect to enjoy workable control at Celtic Park without purchasing the shares of White, Smith and Michael Kelly, the hardliners on the old board?

'Speak to him, David, please.'

After seconds that seemed to stretch into eternity, McCann's voice broke the strain of the silence.

'Go for it,' he said.

It was the only occasion on which McCann had ever been known to change his mind.

* * *

At 7pm two antagonistic groups dined in Brother Walfrid's Restaurant inside Celtic Park. One group was celebratory, the other drowning sorrows. With David Smith and Michael Kelly was a consolation of lawyers from Dickson Minto. Chris White had already made his excuses.

A larger group, occasionally raucous and separated from the representatives of the 'ancient regime' by surprisingly few tables, were eating fish and chips and drinking champagne. The irony of eating in luxury in a place named after Celtic's Founding Father who wanted to put meals on the tables of Glasgow's East End poor may have been lost on them as they ordered more champagne and fat cigars.

Around this table were McCann, Dempsey, Low, John and Dominic Keane, the latter's business partner, Jack Flanagan, and accountant Barnett, together with a rump of surviving directors in Kevin Kelly, Tom Grant and Jimmy Farrell, mostly heroes, sometime villains, but all immortals in the day the world was made safe for Celtic.

As midnight neared, McCann approached the table of the vanquished. 'Goodbye, Mr Smith,' he said, having never once spoken to Smith before. He turned on his heels, thought better of an immediate retreat. 'We're all glad you're going, Michael,' he said. 'You've been a disaster for Celtic.'

* * *

Outside, in the drenching and irrepressible rain, thousands of fans were still waiting for news. Someone remembered them just in time.

McCann felt he could not speak. 'I'll go then,' said Dempsey, never shy of public speaking. He braced himself for the wind and the rain and did not care one jot for the soaking. 'The game is over,' he announced. 'The rebels have won.'

* * *

2. RANGERS IN THEIR PLACE

When Bob Kelly died on 21 September 1971, his leadership of the club, both financial and moral, was under-appreciated. So was the indispensable nature of his friendship with Jock Stein an undervalued aspect of the legendary manager's success at Paradise.

It took almost a quarter of a century of both moral and financial bankruptcy and a defining lack of leadership by the chairmen and directors who followed in his wake for an understanding of Sir Robert's true worth to the football club he cherished more than life itself.

It was not until Fergus McCann became chief executive in 1994 that Celtic once again enjoyed leadership worthy of the club's traditions.

Naturally enough, both Kelly and McCann had their faults. Kelly interfered with team selection, sometimes ludicrously so, a practice that continued under Jock Stein's management for longer than is generally supposed but Celtic's great chairman loved his football and Stein loved chewing the football fat with his boss.

McCann courted unpopularity, transformed stubbornness into an art form, and was misjudged as a result.

His five-year tenure was undoubtedly a torrid time for fans, so much so that when McCann unfurled the championship flag on 1 August 1998 – after Celtic had stopped Rangers' run for a tenth successive league title – he was roundly booed for his pains.

McCann ran a tight ship financially but what else was he supposed to do after Celtic's near death experience in 1994? There were dark mutterings about his obsession with protecting his investment and it is true that McCann turned his £9.5m purchase of Celtic into a £40m sale five years later. Brian Dempsey, a staunch ally in the revolutionary days, who did not invest in the share issue launched by McCann in 1995 in the process of converting the football club into a public limited company, and became a caustic critic. Dempsey, though, was a man twice disappointed, thwarted in his ambition to become chairman and frustrated in the rejection of his schemes to relocate the club to Robroyston.

The taunting of McCann in 1998, in front of his wife who rarely visited Celtic Park, was a shameful, if understandable, reaction on the part of fans who had hoped the club would retain the services of Wim Jansen and would build on the title success with major signings.

It is easy to forget, though, that under McCann's ownership Celtic brought in a plethora of high-calibre players for fees often running into millions of pounds. The relative lack of on-field success was not owing to a lack of effort or a lack of backing for McCann's managers.

The sad truth, however, is that after Stein's departure on 28 May 1978, Celtic had struggled to find a worthy successor.

Billy McNeill, captain of the Lisbon Lions, came nearest to succeeding Stein's success. In his first spell from August 1978 to May 1983, Big Billy won three league titles, including the miraculous Ten Men Won the League team of 1978/79 when the Bhoys beat Rangers 4-2 in the last game of the season after Johnny Doyle was sent off with his team a goal down and 40 minutes still to play.

Like Stein, McNeill earned a reputation for developing young players. On his inaugural watch, Paul McStay and Charlie Nicholas both made their debuts.

Life for the tyro manager, however, was not easy under Bob Kelly's successor, Desmond White. McNeill felt underpaid and underwhelmed by his chairman's lack of support.

In the close season after his third title success, the only arrivals to strengthen the team were from the Celtic Boys' Club (Peter Grant) and from the club's under-20 side (David Moyes, John Buckley, John McGoldrick and Lex Baillie).

McNeill was furious, too, when discreet enquiries uncovered the fact that he was being paid less than his managerial counterparts at Rangers, Aberdeen, Dundee United and even St Mirren.

The board of directors at this time was made up of two Whites, Desmond and son Christopher, Tom Devlin, Jimmy Farrell and Jack

McGinn. Biscuit tin tendencies were already well ensconced inside Paradise. The nickname for the Celtic directors was coined by fans and fanzines and, unbelievably, was nearer the truth than anyone might have dreamed. In the years prior to the arrival of McCann, Celtic's cash, receipts and invoices were kept in used shoe boxes in the chairman's office and shifted when needed to the club secretary's office.

When Charlie Nicholas, at the end of season 1982/83 in which he scored 48 goals, was sold to Arsenal without the consent of McNeill, the manager plotted his escape to England.

McNeill's second spell, from May 1987 to May 1991, was less successful and undermined his reputation as a coach. Although the club's centenary season of 1987/88 was rich in double glory, the following two seasons were barren of trophies and, in fact, the manager's final three seasons resulted in two third places and one fifth place.

There is something of the victim about McNeill as a manager, a club immortal who was exploited by those in the boardroom in order to balance shoe box books.

When Liam Brady was appointed in McNeill's place in June 1991 his salary was immediately twice that received by his predecessor. As manager, McNeill had won four championships, three Scottish Cups, one League Cup and one Glasgow Cup. On his appointment, Brady had never managed a team in his life.

McNeill's appointment as club ambassador in 2009 and the unveiling of a statue of this immortal Lisbon Lion in front of Celtic Park in 2015 might be seen as overdue apologies to a great man who made a more than halfway decent stab at filling Stein's shoes in the manager's office at Paradise.

* * *

Other managers who followed Stein and McNeill were not fit to tie the bootlaces of their predecessors. Most were callow youths, lacking in experience: Brady, Lou Macari, Tommy Burns and John Barnes. Even when the various Celtic boards turned to those with a track record of work in European leagues, Wim Jansen and Josef Vengloš, the experiences were short-lived.

McCann, in spite of his undoubted success in turning the football club upside down and the right way up again in a business sense, failed – apart from the momentous achievement of stopping the ten – to make a lasting impact on the playing side of Celtic's history.

To be fair, while McCann's Celtic were re-establishing financial probity within the walls of Paradise, at Ibrox, Murray's Rangers were playing fast and loose with money borrowed from banks and eased surreptitiously from the righteous grasp of the taxman.

It was not easy being Lou Macari, Tommy Burns, Wim Jansen or Dr Jozef VenglOš. Nothing was easy with McCann.

After Celtic's saviour returned to North America, the new regime, headed by Frank O'Callaghan, previously boss of MacDonald Hotels, as chairman, and by Allan MacDonald, previously with British Aerospace, as chief executive, appointed John Barnes as head coach. It was another reckless throw of the dice.

Barnes, likeable and erudite, was an unmitigated disaster. He failed even to last one entire season before being sacked after Celtic's embarrassing and humiliating home defeat to Inverness Caledonian Thistle in the Scottish Cup. The famous headline in the *Scottish Sun* ran 'Super Caley go ballistic, Celtic are atrocious'.

If the ramshackle slide towards bankruptcy leading to the Bank of Scotland's deadline call for £1m in surety for their overdraft in 1994 was a nadir off the pitch, Celtic's exit from the cup in February 2000 to a team only five years out of the Highland League was a moment of footballing bankruptcy.

It was not just the defeat, it was its spineless manner, and the reported shenanigans at half-time in the home dressing room. Eric Black raged at slackers, slouchers, shirkers and sluggards. Mark Viduka took exception to the first-team coach's rage and rants, and had to be restrained by team-mates from attacking Barnes's man. As the second half beckoned, Viduka took off his boots, threw them in the dressing room waste bin, and refused to play any more while Black and Barnes were around. According to Ľubomír Moravčík, Celtic's mercurial Czechoslovak midfielder, the head coach merely looked on helplessly while pandemonium prevailed all about him.

In 2002, Barnes commented that the dressing room mayhem and the defeat to Caley Thistle was 'just an accident waiting to happen'.

It was typical of the former Liverpool and England winger's detached approach to his life and times at Paradise. The shocking exit from the Scottish Cup had nothing to do with him.

For the remainder of the season, Kenny Dalglish took on the team. He had been appointed as director of football by his golfing companion, MacDonald, and now he was summoned from a Spanish holiday by his buddy and tasked with rescuing the rump of a failing season. The League Cup was secured in a 2-0 victory at Hampden against Aberdeen but a second-placed finish in the Premier League was no cause for even half-hearted celebration as the Celts finished a humiliating 21 points behind Rangers.

Dalglish cut a desolate and remote figure, light years from the joyous genius of his playing days at Paradise. He was suffering still from the trauma of the Hillsborough disaster of April 1989 when the crush in the Leppings Lane end of the stadium resulted in 97 fatalities. In the aftermath of the tragedy, Dalglish, as manager of the Liverpool team who had faced Nottingham Forest on that fateful day, took upon himself a leading role in comforting and counselling the families of the Merseyside dead.

By the end of the summer of 2000, both O'Callaghan and MacDonald were gone from Celtic Park.

As chairman O'Callaghan had limited power but, as it turned out, MacDonald's theoretical leadership role proved to be chimerical.

After the sacking of Dalglish, MacDonald twice met the legendary Guus Hiddink, former manager of the Netherlands and of Real Madrid. The chief executive was set on the Dutchman but was overruled by the club's leading shareholder, Dermot Desmond, who had been negotiating with Martin O'Neill, whose contract had expired at Leicester City.

In September 2000 MacDonald resigned, although it is indisputable that he was shown the exit door by Desmond who had not liked Hiddink's apparent preoccupation with money during negotiations over the managerial vacancy at Celtic Park.

It was all change and revolving doors. With McCann and his proteges O'Callaghan and MacDonald out of the way, a new power base was taking shape at Celtic Park.

Desmond, the founder and chairman of the Dublin-based International Investment and Underwriting Ltd, had been an ally of McCann in the revolution of 1994, had promised £4m investment and an underwriting of a similar sum, had become a non-executive director of the new public limited company in 1995, and Celtic's largest shareholder in 1999. On his departure, McCann had correctly assessed Celtic was in safe hands.

Like his predecessor as power broker, Desmond preferred a low public profile, but was equally direct and outspoken when occasion demanded. Like McCann, too, his was primarily an emotional investment in a football club he loved. Of the ousting of the old Biscuit Tin Board, Desmond said, 'It was all about saving Celtic.'

Having achieved that aim, Desmond was intent on preserving Celtic's sanity. 'I don't believe,' he said, 'in burning pound notes ... if you start that approach, you go bust pretty quickly.'

It was one of the reasons he wanted rid of MacDonald with the chief executive's dreams of emulating the mad spending of Rangers.

Desmond had been the power behind the scenes, the kingmaker in Paradise, since the end of the last century. His detractors describe him as an 'absentee landlord', a term ripe and rich and rotten with the weight of Irish history. By way of response, in 2008, Desmond said that what matters is not where you live but 'what you do with your time and how I take on my responsibilities as a shareholder and director of this club ... I see every Celtic match. I don't have to wear a hooped jersey, I don't have to spend 365 days in Celtic Park to be a good, faithful devotee of Celtic.'

* * *

From the moment of McCann's departure – and probably before – Desmond had been building his team.

Brian Quinn became a non-executive director and vice-chairman of the plc board in March 1996, recruited by McCann from the Bank of England where he had risen to the position of acting deputy governor. His later alliance with Desmond ensured a period of financial probity and security. 'You can't go on losing money at the rate of £5m to £7m a year indefinitely,' he said after becoming chairman in place of MacDonald.

Peter Lawwell, too, became a key component in Desmond's team. He had been financial controller at Celtic as early as 1990/91 when he learned first hand all about the perils of financial incompetence by his superiors. Afterwards, Lawwell moved from success to success at ICI, Hoffmann La Roche, Scottish Coal, and at Clydeport, from where he was headhunted by Desmond to become the club's chief executive.

From the replacement of Quinn by Dr John Reid as chairman in November 2007, Desmond and Lawwell ran Celtic in tandem, and both deserve the status of immortals for their far-sighted and prudent control of the club's finances.

Desmond it was, though, who was responsible for the appointments of a jewelled string of legendary managers and coaches who brought a return of a level of success on the field to rival – and occasionally surpass – the achievements of Stein and Fallon's nine-in-a-row teams.

Without the contributions of two immortals, Martin O'Neill and Gordon Strachan, the sparkling accomplishments of Celtic's second nine-in-a-row managers and players would have been impossible.

The first of these heroes, a man who reversed the steep footballing decline embraced by the MacDonald–Dalglish–Barnes imbroglio, was O'Neill, a footballing genie and genius, appointed by Desmond in June 2000.

* * *

At this stage of his career, O'Neill was at the peak of his powers. His schooling had come from his time as a player absorbing the wit and wisdom and winning mentality of Brian Clough at Nottingham Forest with whom he won the European Cup twice. The best trick he learned from his mentor, however, was the alchemical transformation of solid, workmanlike players like himself into integral components of championship-winning teams.

At Celtic, Chris Sutton, signed from Chelsea in 2000 for £6m, was an early gamble by O'Neill. Without his Premier League-winning buddy Alan Shearer, from his Blackburn Rovers days, Sutton sank without trace at Stamford Bridge.

O'Neill, though, knew he had the incomparable Henrik Larsson to complement Sutton's talents. It was no gamble after all. Sutton scored 86 goals for Celtic in 199 appearances and helped to bring to Paradise three league titles, three Scottish Cups, and one League Cup.

Without O'Neill, however, Sutton was never the same player, failing to cause more than a ripple of interest at his subsequent clubs, Birmingham City and Aston Villa.

Alan Thompson, too, a hero at Bolton Wanderers, a failure at Villa, was revitalised under O'Neill at Celtic.

Like Clough, O'Neill had his favourites, and perhaps his best signing was the man he bought from his previous club, Leicester City, a certain Neil Lennon, who might not have been the most talented player at Celtic Park but was certainly the most influential.

O'Neill's managerial career had taken him from Grantham Town and Shepshed Charterhouse in the dark penumbra of non-league football, through Wycombe Wanderers and Norwich City to Leicester City, who he led to the English Premier League. At Filbert Street, O'Neill won two League Cups and left Leicester in their highest league placing – eighth – in 24 years.

Arriving at Celtic Park, however, the Irishman inherited a broken and bitterly divided and floundering club, one that had just completed its fourth managerial search in four years. In some ways, the malaise was an echo of the struggles under McGrory prior to the arrival of Stein although in the early 1960s it was inertia that was more of a problem, a sense of not even having tried, rather than Celtic's repeated failures as the millennium drew to a dismal close.

In June 2000, O'Neill was just another in a long line of desperately sought messiahs, even if he did come personally recommended to Desmond by Sir Alex Ferguson, recent winner of the treble of Champions League, Premier League and FA Cup with Manchester United.

The second half of that year, though, proved to be a time of miraculous redemption for Celtic. The 2000/01 Premier League season began with a 2-1 victory over Dundee United at Tannadice, a game in which Sutton made a goalscoring debut.

By the time Rangers were due at Celtic Park on 27 August, O'Neill's team had won four consecutive league games and thumped Jeunesse Esch of Luxembourg in the UEFA Cup to the tune of 11 goals without reply.

It had been a promising start but, as Sutton had said on his unveiling at Paradise, 'The first thing we have to do is put Rangers in their place.'

The Second Nine-in-a-Row: 2011–2020

Turning Points

1. CELTIC V RANGERS
SCOTTISH PREMIER LEAGUE, 27 AUGUST 2000

Of course, it was nice to make a good start to the league campaign, but nothing that happened prior to the final Saturday in August really mattered.

The wins were all expected and, in truth, the two home victories, 1-0 against Motherwell and 2-1 over Kilmarnock, were laboured and occasionally painful to watch. O'Neill's honeymoon with Celtic fans would not outlast the first month of the season unless a result – at least a draw – was achieved against the old enemy.

There was a swagger and a strut about Rangers under the management of Dick Advocaat. The Dutchman had led the Ibrox club to two consecutive league and cup doubles as well as a treble in his initial season in Govan. He had previously taken the Netherlands to the 1994 World Cup quarter-finals where his team lost narrowly, 3-2, to eventual champions Brazil. He had led Feyenoord to both the Eredivisie title and to victory in the KNVB Cup. His Rangers team had also begun the new season with a 100 per cent record and, in the process, had looked more convincing than Celtic, especially away from home with two-goal winning margins at Kilmarnock and St Mirren.

In the previous season, Rangers had beaten Celtic 4-2 at Ibrox in November 1999 and twice in March 2000, 1-0 in Paradise and 4-1 in Govan. The season before that Rangers had clinched the league title at Parkhead with an arrogant 3-0 stroll to victory.

Nevertheless, the day dawned fine and dandy in Glasgow on Sunday 27 August and some old-timer mentioned that it reminded him of

Hampden in the sun in 1957 when Celtic had thrashed Rangers 7-1 in that year's League Cup Final.

Cynics and pessimists, were out in force along the long march to Paradise via London Road. It was too early, too soon, to expect miracles from O'Neill.

After 51 seconds the naysayers were confounded. An early corner to the home team was swung into the penalty area by Bobby Petta, an unheralded free transfer from Ipswich Town, and precisely the sort of apparently ordinary player O'Neill hoped to galvanise to stardom. There was Sutton, a somewhat more expensive import, who challenged for the ball and hit it straight at Stefan Klos, the German former under-21 and under-23 international. The goalkeeper parried and, for all the world, the danger to Rangers seemed minimal, but Sutton reacted first and fast to poke the ball into the back of the away team's net.

Within a further quarter of an hour, all, well almost all, of Celtic's fears were erased from memories. Seven short minutes after the opening goal, and another corner spun mischievously into the box by Moravčík, finding the unmarked head of Stiliyan Petrov, who needed no further encouragement to find the back of the net.

Three more minutes passed without a flicker of resistance to the Celtic waves of attacking, and there were two further glories of trickery from Petta, including another humiliation of Fernando Ricksen. Once more the diminutive winger was the creator, slipping the ball through the eye of a needle to find Moravčík, who shifted it for Paul Lambert to slam side-footed and into the Rangers net.

The contrasts in the home and away dugouts could not have been greater. Advocaat was suited and booted, collar and tied, shirt and lip buttoned tight. O'Neill, like his mentor Clough, made no condescension to either smartness or fashion. His tracksuit bottoms and white polo shirt spoke of a man who cared only for his work and these were his working clothes, and fuck you in the nicest possible way if you thought them inappropriate. Advocaat was a man of military precision who looked for all the world as if he had stepped out from a parade of war veterans but who had forgotten to wear his medals. O'Neill was so skinny he seemed held together by the elastic waistband in his trackies. The Celtic manager was a marionette galvanised by electric currents, as if pieced together by Victor Frankenstein himself.

The totality of O'Neill's energy pitchside was transmitted to his charges on the field of Paradise.

When Claudio Reyna, the Ibrox club's American midfielder, squeezed a header past a guilty Jonathan Gould in the Celtic goal in the 40th minute, the doom-mongers were encouraged once more.

'I told you, we scored too early.'

'Too often, more like.'

'We've provoked them now, that third goal, we should have sat tight on the two.'

One minute later, a Rangers 'goal' was ruled out for offside. 'They'll pull it back, you know, the Proddie bastards, you just know they will.' Half-time could not come soon enough.

There had been too many false dawns, such as the centenary double in 1988, the St Patrick's Day Massacre in 1991, and the Moravčík-inspired 5-1 victory in 1998.

After the double under Billy McNeill, the following season was anti-climactic in the extreme, Celtic falling from the heights to a dismal third-placed finish and ten points behind champions Rangers.

The Massacre, when Peter Grant of Celtic was sent off, followed by Rangers' Mark Walters, Tony Hateley and Terry Hurlock, and when Celtic, with McNeill struggling to rediscover a winning formula, an alchemist's stone to transform dross into gold, knocked their great rivals out of the Scottish Cup in the fifth round, only to fall to Motherwell, 4-2, in a replayed semi-final.

In the sole season allocated to Dr Josef Vengloš, 1998/99, Celtic finished second to Rangers in the league championship, lost 1-0 in the Scottish Cup Final to them, lost in the third round of the League Cup to Airdrie, and exited from the Champions League at the second qualifying round stage to FC Zürich.

And now at half-time, fear of yet another Rangers comeback, one like the appearance of Banquo at Macbeth's feast.

Celtic, however, rather than falling foul of a headless ghost, began the second half in a similar style to that of the first.

O'Neill was nothing if not an expert rabble-rouser. Five minutes in, Henrik Larsson scored what some have called the greatest goal in Old Firm history. It began with an apparently harmless punt downfield by goalkeeper Gould, continued with a possibly fortuitous lay-off by Sutton, and suddenly Larsson was on the ball, just inside the Rangers half. He weaved away from Tugay Kerimoğlu, nutmegged Bert Konterman, and proceeded to loop the ball, scoop the ball, up and over the advancing Klos. It was an instinctive, outrageous and sublime finish, showcasing King Henrik's divine grace and composed genius, a goal no one else could have contemplated let alone executed with such nerveless composure and precision. Larsson's trademark outstretched tongue celebrated once again.

If there was a turning point within the turning point of this demolition derby, this was that moment, but to give due credit to Advocaat's men, they did not give up.

Five minutes later, Stéphane Mahé climbed all over Rod Wallace inside the Celtic box and Billy Dodds calmly sent Gould the wrong way, slotting the penalty home for 4-2.

This time, though, there were fewer Celtic jitters among the faithful. Celtic were simply playing far too well.

On 62 minutes Larsson scored once more, a brilliant glancing header from a Petta free kick. Further and final entertainment was provided by a red mist descending on Rangers' Barry Ferguson and a sixth goal for Celtic, a cross from the left by Mahé met by an inrushing Sutton to complete a 6-2 scoreline.

O'Neill's debut season continued to thrive and culminated in a treble of league, Scottish Cup and League Cup.

* * *

Of course, O'Neill was a lucky man. He inherited Larsson, signed in July 1997 by Wim Jansen from Feyenoord, perhaps the greatest player in modern times to pull on a Celtic jersey, and at the peak of his powers under O'Neill.

Even more importantly, though, O'Neill arrived during a period of renewed spending after the departure of McCann. The financial taps were still turned on when the Irishman moved from Leicester. After the expensive arrivals of Sutton, Lennon, Joos Valgaeren, Alan Thompson and Rab Douglas, in the following close season John Hartson was signed from Coventry City for another £6m fee.

In return for such largesse, O'Neill won four SPL titles, three Scottish Cups and one League Cup – and in May 2003 was a whisker away in Seville from returning Celtic to European glory.

* * *

It was Gordon Strachan, however, who bore the brunt of Celtic's return to a policy of sound money, of balancing books, of McCann's principles.

Still, the flame-haired genius who had made his fame if not his fortune as a player at Dundee and Aberdeen – and was thus not universally appreciated at Celtic Park – won three SPL championships, one Scottish Cup, and three League Cups during his time at Paradise between 2005 and 2009.

It was an astonishing achievement especially as Rangers in the dying days of David Murray's regime were still spending as if they held exclusive rights to print their own money. Between 2001 and 2010 the club paid £48m into an Employee Benefit Trust, clearly designed to relieve the taxman's burden, and with lenient bank managers, they might just as well have been rolling the printing presses.

Strachan, in contrast to Alex McLeish, Paul Le Guen and Walter Smith, had to contend with a period of retrenchment and balanced books.

As early as January 2002, 18 months into the O'Neill era, new chief executive Ian McLeod fired warning shots across the bows of the Celtic ship, suggesting 'a different focus on player trading and acquisition' would be necessary in the future. Even with the financial windfall resulting from the run to the UEFA Cup Final in 2003, the bare truth was that Celtic, as well as Rangers, were living way beyond their means.

McLeod reminded fellow board members in October 2002 that Celtic had travelled this road once before and that 'if no action was taken to address the forecast shortfall [of revenue in comparison to expenditure] the Company would breach covenants on borrowing limits'.

Eleven months later, McLeod returned to retailing and was replaced by Peter Lawwell. With the elevation of Lawwell, the triumvirate of himself, principal shareholder Desmond and chairman Brian Quinn was complete and a plan was put in place to return to a policy of sound money. It became fully operational on the arrival of Strachan and has remained in place ever since.

Without it, there might have been bankruptcies in two Glasgow football clubs in 2012. As Lawwell admitted, 'Over the period from about 2000 to 2005 we lost 50 million quid.' The trick was 'to put in place a sustainable business model while continuing to be successful on the pitch'.

It was almost inevitable, then, that the O'Neill years would end in tears. Heading into 2004/05, the new financial realities at Parkhead were already reflected in two signings: Juninho from Middlesbrough on a free transfer and Henri Camara on loan from Wolverhampton Wanderers.

The league title was lost to Rangers on the final day of the season – the second time in the short space of three years. Going into the match at Fir Park, against a Motherwell side managed by the former Ranger Terry Butcher, Celtic held a two-point lead over their city rivals. Chris Sutton opened the scoring just prior to the half hour but a muddy, cloying pitch made good football difficult. All remained well until the last two minutes when Scott McDonald scored a brace of goals, the last a deflected shot that looped over Rab Douglas in a slow and agonising arc that brought the proceedings of Black Sunday to a dispiriting close.

Rangers won 1-0 at Hibs and took the title, tainted as it was later found to be by their financial shenanigans.

At least the O'Neill era, darkened too with his wife Geraldine's serious illness, ended with the consolation of a Scottish Cup Final win over Dundee United at Hampden.

* * *

For Strachan, though, it would be a time of no easy money. Neither was the new manager graced with an auspicious start.

In March 2005, when the recruitment process for O'Neill's replacement began, Strachan was out of work having resigned from his post at Southampton. He was enjoying a relaxing day out in an executive box at the Cheltenham Festival and in the adjacent box was a gathering of raucous Irishmen that included a more sedate Dermot Desmond.

At the time, Strachan was on a shortlist of three – alongside José Mourinho and Rafa Benítez – for the vacant role at Liverpool. There was also the possibility of a vacancy at Manchester City. Strachan explained his situation to Desmond who, with a smile and a wink, told the former Coventry City boss to keep his options open. 'Well, just make sure,' Desmond said, 'you get a get-out clause in any contract you sign.'

Just days later, the call came, and the big job Strachan craved – he later said that even playing for Manchester United held no candle to managing Celtic – was his for the taking, even though he had been warned that an open chequebook was now a thing of the past.

The inauspicious beginning for the new manager came from nowhere predictable, nowhere logical. The board had broken some of its new rules with summer signings to ease Strachan's rebuilding of O'Neill's ageing team. Shunsuke Nakamura arrived from Reggina for £2.75m and Maciej Żurawski from Wisła Kraków for something similar, but other signings were specifically designed not to break the bank. Loans and free transfers were the name of the game: Artur Boruc from Legia Warsaw, Paul Telfer from Southampton, Mo Camara from Burnley, Jérémie Aliadière from Arsenal, Dion Dublin – in January 2006 – from Leicester City.

Still, four drawn pre-season friendlies with Fulham, Leicester City, Sporting Lisbon and Leeds United had not set too many alarm bells ringing.

A stroll in Slovakia was the first competitive fixture in the shape of a Champions League qualifier. Predictions of a comfortable baptism for Strachan, however, proved way wide of the mark. A 5-0 defeat to Artmedia Bratislava was Celtic's biggest in over three decades and the exit from Europe's premier competition cost the club an estimated £10m in lost revenue.

When this humiliation was followed by the wilful discarding of points, the throwing away of a 3-1 lead, at Motherwell in the first league game of the season, the knives were not just out for Strachan, they were sticking into his back and emerging out the other side of his body.

The new manager was made of stern stuff, however. Celtic won the next three games including a nearly-but-not-quite-good-enough 4-0 victory over Artmedia in the second leg, before a bracing 3-1 defeat at Ibrox, followed by a further six consecutive league wins. The championship was won as early as 5 April, with six games still to play, thanks to a 1-0 victory over Hearts at Paradise. Two further titles followed in smooth succession in seasons 2006/07 and 2007/08.

As Peter Lawwell said, 'History will show he [Strachan] was a great Celtic manager.'

* * *

The O'Neill and Strachan eras at Celtic were blessed times.

Under Fergus McCann, foundations had been laid for financial stability, footings which were built upon during the period of the Desmond–Lawwell–Quinn triumvirate – and from November 2007, when Brian Quinn stepped down to a standing ovation from 1,000 shareholders, replaced by Dr John Reid.

By 2007, Celtic were virtually debt free. By the end of the Strachan period, even though Rangers had regained the league title after three blank years, Celtic had re-established themselves as a serious presence on both national and international stages. O'Neill led Celtic to the UEFA Cup Final and Strachan took the club to two consecutive last-16 ties in the Champions League against AC Milan and Barcelona.

The financial and the footballing revolutions were complete. All that was left was to see those two twin metamorphoses take deeper root and flower in the glorious era of Celtic's second nine-in-a-row league titles which also included the unprecedented and scarcely credible season of the invincibles in 2016/17, and the quadruple treble between 2016 and 2020.

* * *

2. THE APPOINTMENT OF NEIL LENNON

When Neil Lennon was summoned from his work with the club's reserve team players on 25 March 2010, someone, somewhere, surely, must have remembered another occasion when a former second-team coach was appointed to take charge of a floundering Celtic side. Not that Lennon would ever compare himself to the incomparable Jock Stein.

Heaven forbid, but still ghosts from the past had been set free to roam in the imaginations of Celtic people.

* * *

Once Celtic had lost 4-0 to St Mirren on a dismal Wednesday evening in Paisley, the inevitable resignation of Tony Mowbray followed the next day.

His spell as Celtic supremo was an unmitigated disaster, during which the achievements of the O'Neill and Strachan eras threatened to unravel alarmingly.

Mowbray's previous work at Hibernian from 2004 to 2006, when the Edinburgh club claimed successive top-four Premier League finishes, and at West Bromwich Albion from 2006 to 2009, when the Baggies won the Football League Championship and promotion to the Premier League, suggested his possession of genuine coaching talents. Celtic, however, might have been warned as the West Midlands team's stay at the top table of English football was nasty, brutish and short.

In hindsight, of course, it is easy to see and to say that Mowbray's fortunes were already waning when Celtic paid a £2m compensation fee to secure his services.

It is a truism that the fates of managers follow the enduring patterns of the universe of ascension and declension, the fractals of rising and falling.

The great managers of Celtic in the modern era have all been appointed at the peak of their powers. Stein was fresh from unprecedented success at Dunfermline and an uplift of power and prestige at Hibernian; O'Neill enjoyed outstanding success at unfashionable Leicester City; Strachan had worked minor miracles at Coventry and Southampton; Brendan Rodgers had worked apprenticeships with Chelsea's reserves, Watford, Reading and Swansea City, before he was only a Steven Gerrard slip away from winning the English Premier League with Liverpool for the first time in a generation. All served their time at relatively humble clubs.

All, though, declined after leaving Celtic, descended towards disillusionment and sometimes desperate pursuits of former glories. Even Stein could work no magic at Leeds United, could find no formula for lasting success as manager of Scotland. O'Neill never won another trophy in the remains of the days of his career, although there were still signs of his transformative powers at Aston Villa, who enjoyed three successive sixth-placed finishes in the Premier League. He was later sacked by Sunderland and by Nottingham Forest. Strachan's final position in club football was at English Championship club Middlesbrough, and it ended with the Teessiders in disarray and 20th in the table. Like Stein, Strachan too failed in his time as Scotland's national team leader, resigning after missing out on qualification for the 2018 World Cup finals. At Leicester, Rodgers's initial success unravelled in 2021/22 with disappointing exits from four cup competitions, an eighth-placed finish in the Premier League and no place in Europe for the following season.

Celtic, too, may have enjoyed a lucky break in the club's repeated failures to appoint Eddie Howe in succession to Neil Lennon in the spring and summer of 2021, as he fitted the manager-in-decline profile perfectly. Just as Mowbray, prior to his Celtic appointment, saw West Bromwich Albion relegated, so Howe's second spell in charge at Bournemouth, prior to his eventual appointment at Newcastle, ended in relegation from the Premier League in 2020. Howe's relative success in helping stave off the drop from the top flight in 2021/22 may be partly explained by the bottomless pit of money available from the sovereign wealth fund of Saudi Arabia's murderous regime.

Any man willing to shake the hand and take the Saudi money may not, in any case, have been a good fit for Celtic with the club's culture and commitment to radical causes.

Ange Postecoglou, eventually appointed in June 2021, though, possessed a similar curriculum vitae to Celtic's managerial immortals, a man who had paid his dues, and harvested rich and successful experiences in Australia with South Melbourne, Brisbane Roar and the national side, and in Japan with Yokohama Marinos, the club winning its first J.League title in 15 years.

Apart from Billy McNeill, in his first spell, and Lennon, managerial tyros have proved almost unmitigated disasters.

Those in palpable decline were McNeill in his second incarnation, after his Aston Villa side finished at the foot of the First Division table in May 1987; Dr Jozef Vengloš, after the glories of managing his beloved Czechoslovakia, plucked from the obscurity of Oman; Kenny Dalglish, a broken man, a ghost of his former self; and Mowbray.

The spanking of Mowbray's team by St Mirren in March 2010 revealed a club bereft of structure and bereft of ideas. It also left Celtic ten points behind Rangers in the race for the league title with the Ibrox club having two games in hand. After the Saints hit their fourth goal in the 87th minute, their supporters raised the chant, 'We want five, we want five!' It was Celtic's seventh SPL defeat of the season.

The depths of Mowbray's inadequacy for the task was further revealed through his post-match comments. 'Maybe,' he said, 'this isn't a league for trying to force the game and be expansive; maybe it's a league for playing defensive, negative football.'

Even allowing for the fact that his words were barbed digs at Walter Smith's Rangers, such drivel had not been heard by Celtic fans since the days of John Barnes.

'We had six strikers on at the death, but it left some young defenders pretty exposed,' Mowbray said.

* * *

Lennon was tasked by Dermot Desmond and chief executive Peter Lawwell with taking care of the first team until the end of the season.

Two days after his engagement as interim manager, Lennon's new charges faced Kilmarnock at home. The new caretaker manager looked relaxed, as if born to the task, and his players responded as if their dismal performances under Mowbray had been figments of critics' imaginations. Robbie Keane, on loan from Spurs, scored two poacher's goals, and Scott Brown, signed in May 2007 from Hibernian for £4.4m, a record fee between Scottish clubs and a rare breach of the Desmond–Lawwell imposition of parsimony on Strachan, added a third goal in a 3-1 victory.

Lennon's team completed the 2009/10 season by winning a further seven consecutive league games to finish a mere six points behind Rangers.

It was a rare Celtic campaign without a trophy – the sole blemish on Lennon's record was a 2-0 defeat to Ross County in the Scottish Cup semi-final at Hampden – but it was clear to all, spectator and denizen of boardroom alike, that progress had been made, that a semblance of pride had been restored. Lennon was remaking the team in his own image: dogged determination and cussedness together with a new-found inability to lose, to surrender. If play was sometimes scrappy, the fans enjoyed the scrappers who ground out win after win, and never more so than on 4 May at Paradise when the Celts beat Rangers 2-1, with goals from Lee Naylor and Marc-Antoine Fortuné. It was the first time the club had beaten their great rivals in the league since December 2008.

Lennon had earned his permanent contract, which he signed on 9 June 2010. It was not just his Catholic work ethic, however, that earned the respect and admiration of Desmond and Lawwell. After the disastrous defeat to Ross County, only his third match in charge, Lennon spoke out, slating his players, claiming they lacked 'hunger and desire'. He would be recommending to the board a wholesale clearout of failing players at the end of the season.

It was not the first time, nor would it be the last, that Lennon displayed his characteristic bravery and, because of it, he was backed by the men in suits. Excluding the endings of loan spells, during the course of the summer and the following season, a total of 23 players were shipped out of Celtic Park. Some, such as Aiden McGeady's £9.5m transfer to Spartak Moscow, raised significant funds for Lennon to try his hand at wheeler-dealing in the bargain basement jumble sale of footballers. Replacements were signed, including Gary Hooper, a striker from Scunthorpe United, Beram Kayal, a midfielder from Maccabi Haifa, and a loan signing of

Fraser Forster, a giant of a goalkeeper from Newcastle United, and still Lennon dickered a surplus for his masters of almost £8m.

He was left with the not inconsiderable task of melding the newcomers with a few remaining stalwarts into a proper team for the new term.

The opening competitive fixture of the 2010/11 season was a Champions League qualifier against Braga, runners-up in the Portuguese top tier. The extent of the Lennon revolution can be seen by the fact that only two players featured in both the disaster of a 3-0 loss in Europe and the satisfactory ending of the previous season when Celtic defeated Hearts 2-1 in Edinburgh: Łukasz Załuska in goal and Scott Brown in midfield.

In spite of the early exit from Europe, Lennon's New Model Army of Roundheads reduced the gap between themselves and Rangers at the top of the league from six points to just one, won the Scottish Cup, and were runners-up in the League Cup. Honours were almost even with Rangers as Celtic won three out of an unprecedented seven Old Firm derbies while the Ibrox team won only two – one of which, unfortunately, was the League Cup Final.

Sadly, too, Celtic chose an away SPL fixture in Inverness on 4 May 2011 to play their worst half of football since the surrender under Mowbray at St Mirren. Prior to the match, Celtic were one point behind their city rivals but with one game in hand.

At half-time the score was 1-1, and Celtic fans expected Lennon to rouse his troops for a second-half onslaught. Instead, Caley Thistle dominated the remainder of the match and the final score of 3-2 would have been an utter embarrassment were it not for Forster's heroics in goal.

Still, Desmond and Lawwell stood by their man, knowing deep in their guts that Lennon was a winner.

* * *

3. 'THIS ISN'T THE END, THIS IS JUST THE BEGINNING'

In spite of subsequent victories over Kilmarnock and Hearts, the defeat in the Highlands was the effective end of Celtic's pursuit of the league championship in 2011.

On the final day of the SPL campaign Rangers needed a win at Kilmarnock to clinch a 3-0 win and the title, which they did, 5-1, their ninth victory in ten games to conclude the season, and to claim their 54th league championship. By contrast, Celtic's total stood at 42 titles.

On the same afternoon, Celtic beat Motherwell 4-0 and, after the game, in a febrile and strangely celebratory atmosphere inside Paradise, Lennon spoke with authority to the acclaim of the fans, saying, 'This isn't the end, this is just the beginning.'

Clearly, the manager was referring to his club's challenge to Rangers' domination on the field of play, a reaction to their third consecutive title, but he might easily have been thinking of recent events that encompassed the wider problems in Scottish society.

Just the previous weekend, seven juvenile Rangers fans had been caught draping Union flags outside Celtic's training facilities at Lennoxtown and posing for photographs while carrying a gun.

The day before, at Tynecastle, while Celtic were strolling to a 3-0 win in their penultimate league game of the campaign, Hearts fan John Wilson evaded the attentions of stewards and assaulted Lennon in front of 16,681 fans and captured for a wider audience by television cameras.

Little harm was done thanks to the prompt intervention of Alan Thompson, Lennon's first-team coach, but the intent to injure was clear.

Wilson was convicted of a breach of the peace but the charges of assault aggravated by religious prejudice were 'not proven'.

When Lennon made his emotional statement in front of 57,294 fans, what he was really saying was that he would not be driven out of Scottish football, not by broken bottles to the head, not by nail bombs or by bullets in the post, and certainly not by John Wilson.

Before the match against Motherwell began, the stadium MC, David Hamilton, announced, 'Today, we are all Neil Lennon.'

Later, the Celtic manager said, 'I love what I do. It's not being stubborn. If I gave it up, what else would I do? I am very fortunate this job fell into my lap so early in my life. I know I've got to get it right. You don't get much time in Glasgow because it's such an unforgiving environment. If I am here for three or four years, then I know I will have been successful. We're going in the right direction, but ultimately you're gauged on winning championships. All the other stuff should not be part and parcel of living in Glasgow, but it was here long before me. I stand up for what I think is right and fair.'

Lennon's character was forged in this crucible of hate and prejudice. In 2014, when he eventually did leave Glasgow for a further challenge at Bolton Wanderers, an article by Kevin McKenna in *The Observer* hailed the native of Lurgan, County Armagh, as the bravest man in Scotland.

* * *

4. THE 2011 SCOTTISH CUP FINAL

Just as Jock Stein needed a first trophy in the cabinet to jump-start his regime in 1965 with the Scottish Cup win over Dunfermline, so Lennon craved something similar in 2011 against Motherwell at Hampden.

Prior to the match, in a major psychological boost to both manager and players, Dermot Desmond announced a new and improved contract for Lennon. If the temporary coach had thought his team had to win the cup in order to extend his stay in Paradise, the gesture of confidence and support from the club's major power player had at least eased that pressure.

Other stresses, however, seemed to weigh heavy in the opening half an hour. Celtic and Motherwell were equally sluggish, beaten down perhaps by the weight of expectation as much as by the unrelenting rain. In the end, though, Lennon knew that what mattered more than the quality of the football was the quality of the result.

The fans were doing their best to lift the team. On the banks of the Celtic end of Hampden, the Green Brigade, the Celtic Ultras, had organised a magnificent tifo display of green and white hoops that ran around the Hampden bowl. The roars of approval and encouragement echoed from their serried ranks. As usual, a visit to the national stadium sounded like a home game at Paradise.

If the financial foundations of renewed success at Celtic had been laid down in the time of Fergus McCann and the footballing underpinnings of recovery had been set out in the times of O'Neill and Strachan, it is easy to forget the role of Celtic's fans in the process of rebuilding and reconditioning of the football club.

In the process of the ousting of the old Biscuit Tin Board in 1994, David Low, the revolution's financial guru and manic curator of shares on behalf of McCann, once correctly asserted that it would be the shareholders' actions that would be decisive, would bring home the final victory over Michael Kelly, White and Smith.

He was not, however, being dismissive of the fans' role in history, merely realising that, in the final analysis, it is money that talks loudest, always has done and always will, amen.

Whether the rebels would have won, though, without the final input of the fans is debatable. The boycott organised by Celts for Change for the match against Kilmarnock on 1 March 1994 was the decisive event that convinced the Bank of Scotland that continuing support of the old board and their burgeoning overdraft facility was no longer tenable.

Beginning in the 1980s, football fans across the UK were beginning to challenge power structures within the clubs they supported. In most cases, humour became the weapon most readily to hand as fanzines sprang up everywhere, mocking the ingrained hapless and hopeless pillars of society, the butchers, the bakers, the candlestick makers who still ran football clubs in the manner of 19th-century patricians. Celtic was no exception. The Kellys and the Whites might have been descendants of publicans, now turned bourgeois bean counters rather than tradesmen, but they needed overturning nevertheless and they were mercilessly lampooned by the writers of *Not the View*, a witty, scurrilous and revolutionary journal produced by Gerry Dunbar in opposition to the solemn banalities of the club's official magazine, *Celtic View*, which played a role not unlike the Communist Party newspaper, *Pravda*, in the old Soviet Union.

Fans were no longer content to be supine recipients of the condescension of football club owners out of touch with the realities of a modern world from which they shrank in horror with hands over their monkey's eyes claiming they saw no evil. There could be no return to the old ways after the storming of the gates of Paradise in 1994.

At Hampden, the club's authorities were provided with stunning reminders of the loyalty and pride of Celtic's supporters. Both visual displays and the sheer volume of the backing were contributors to the winning of Lennon's first trophy.

Since their formation five years earlier, the Green Brigade have not only provided colour and noise inside stadiums in an era of an increasingly gentrified body of support, but have also acted as the conscience of the football club, particularly in relation to Celtic's Irish heritage.

In 2010, one week before Remembrance Sunday, a banner was unfurled at half-time during the match against Aberdeen, posing a clear message to the English armed forces and to supporters of militarism everywhere, 'Your Deeds Would Shame All the Devils in Hell. Ireland, Iraq, Afghanistan. No Bloodstained Poppy on Our Hoops.'

The Green Brigade, though, are football fans first and foremost and only part-time political commentators. In October 2020, on the eve of a crucial derby match against Rangers – played behind closed doors due to Covid-19 restrictions – a banner was displayed along the green fences of Lennoxtown, reading, 'We're Out Here for You, Be In There For Us.'

So often, though, in that doomed and damned season of 2020/21, the players were not there for the fans. A limp Celtic were outfought by Rangers, who won at Parkhead to the sorry tune of 2-0. Steven Gerrard's team went four points clear at the top of the league, and Celtic's pusillanimity, so uncharacteristic of previous Lennon sides, set the tone for a disastrous attempt at a tenth title in a row.

In the Ange Postecoglou era, too, the Green Brigade have been consistent in their insistence on principles as well as points. In a tricky home fixture against an in-form Motherwell, the Ultras staged a silent protest against the proposed appointment of Police Scotland's assistant chief constable, Bernard Higgins, to the club's staff in a senior security role. The silence, broken in some sections of the crowd, was maintained in the North Curve in spite of the team appearing disconcerted by the absence of the usual vocal support. Earlier in the season, an away match at Dundee was interrupted by the Green Brigade's throwing of hundreds of tennis balls on to the field of play. On each projectile was the face of Higgins. There was, too, a sit-in, a refusal to leave the stadium after the 2-1 home victory over Aberdeen.

In truth, the decision by Celtic's chairman, Ian Bankier, and Michael Nicholson, the club's director of legal and football affairs, to even talk to Higgins was a controversial and confrontational one, almost as if the hierarchy of the football club set out to antagonise fans with political sensibilities and fans with a scrupulous conscience.

Higgins's role within Police Scotland as the head of national policing strategies relating to football had been problematic.

He played a leading part in the preparation and implementation of the 2012 Offensive Behaviour at Football Act, ostensibly designed to eliminate sectarian behaviour at matches, but in practice used by police with enhanced powers to criminalise activities at games based on their own subjective opinions of what constituted sectarian behaviour. The legislation was railroaded through parliament at the behest of Higgins by the Scottish Nationalist Party and without consultations with clubs or fans' organisations. A leader at the time in *The Herald* claimed, 'Scotland cannot arrest its way out of sectarianism.' Yet that was what Higgins attempted to do over the course of the next few years until the failing law was repealed in 2018. The spokesperson for Fans Against Criminalisation, Paul Quigley, said that there had been a deliberate decision taken to implement the legislation in 'as heavy-handed' a way as possible, all of which involved constant filming of fans and a brutal use of kettling.

Higgins's association with this most dismal piece of legislation should have been sufficient to debar the former policeman from Celtic Park, but there was more.

On Sunday, 2 September 2018 an incident of potential enormity and tragedy occurred at Parkhead prior to the midday kick-off against Rangers. As fans queued to enter Paradise via the Janefield Street underpass the gate ahead was closed, causing dangerous congestion and a level of crushing that caused five injuries and one hospitalisation and which might have been so much worse as fans were forced to clamber over high fences to escape the crush. One supporter, Dave Flanagan, said, 'Someone was going to die in there.'

The potential similarities with the Hillsborough disaster in 1989, with crushes both outside and inside the Leppings Lane end of Sheffield Wednesday's ground, were alarming in the extreme. Comparisons continued, however, with what appears to have been a Police Scotland cover-up during the course of a 'multi-agency debrief' into the incident. Higgins's police force claimed that the Janefield gate was not closed until ten minutes before kick-off, a finding disputed by Celtic fans including Flanagan who said it happened 'at 11.25[am], latest'. A later review of football policing, instigated by Higgins and led by fellow top cop Mark Roberts, of Cheshire Police, found that the current model of policing football was 'certainly fit for purpose'. Fans Against Criminalisation described the report as a 'whitewashing' of 'the appalling treatment of football supporters'.

On 19 December 2021, Higgins issued a statement saying he would not be joining Celtic when he retired from the police force at the end of the year.

This time there was no Brian Dempsey claiming a revolutionary victory outside Paradise but there was no doubting that the rebels had won once more, just as in 1994.

On a drowned-rat Scottish Cup Final day at Hampden in May 2011, with the match just over half an hour in, there was more cause for celebration. Celtic eventually turned up and turned the heat on their opponents. They were there for the fans at last.

The ball found its way to the South Korean international Ki Sung-yueng, as impossibly far from goal as a sinner from heaven, but a thunderbolt from his left boot saved the day for Celtic. The midfielder, signed by Lennon in January 2010 from FC Seoul for £2.1m, stood tall to receive the acclaim of the faithful, hands cupped behind his ears and tongue outstretched, tasting and savouring the moment of success.

It might have been different if Daniel Majstorović, Celtic's Swedish international central defender, had been sent off for a leg-breaking lunge on the Well's John Sutton. It might have been different, too, had Gavin Gunning's blistering shot not shaken Celtic's crossbar just moments after Ki's goal, or had Majstorović's clear handball towards the end of the first half not remained unpunished.

As it was, the second half provided the fans at Hampden with a more confident and purposeful performance. On 76 minutes, Motherwell captain Stephen Craigan deflected a Marc Wilson shot past his stranded goalkeeper, and, five minutes before the final whistle, Charlie Mulgrew, another Lennon addition to the squad, this time from Aberdeen, hit a howitzer of a free kick from the edge of the penalty box to clinch a record 35th Scottish Cup win for Celtic.

Lennon danced, hugged his coaching staff, and blew kisses at the fans. His captain, Scott Brown, hoisted aloft the coveted cup. Lennon had endured so much in such a short time of unprecedented hatred but now was his moment to celebrate, to believe it had all been worthwhile.

* * *

5. LENNON ON THE BRINK
KILMARNOCK V CELTIC, 15 OCTOBER 2011
SCOTTISH PREMIER LEAGUE

Turning points in managerial careers are legion and legendary. Perhaps the most famous crossroads moment in British football came at half-time in an FA Cup third round match in January 1990 between Nottingham Forest and Manchester United. The United manager, Alex Ferguson, who had won three Premier Division titles, four Scottish Cups, one League Cup and a European Cup Winners' Cup with Aberdeen in the 1980s, was under the most intense pressure at Old Trafford. Rumours swirled about press rooms and terraces. If Fergie's team, recently supplemented by three expensive signings – Gary Pallister, Paul Ince and Danny Wallace, all approved in the autumn of 1989 by iconoclastic new chairman elect Michael Knighton – departed from the cup at the first hurdle at the City Ground, the Glaswegian firebrand would be handed his P45.

During the break, amid the prawn sandwiches and china teacup conversations, and with the game goalless, the Manchester United majority shareholder Martin Edwards whispered in Knighton's ear, 'If we lose this one, we'll have to be talking.' Thanks, though, to a saving grace goal by Mark Robins, Ferguson went on to win 38 trophies, including 13 Premier League titles and two Champions Leagues.

Another watershed moment, this time at Rugby Park, occurred at half-time during Celtic's autumnal visit to Ayrshire.

Neil Lennon's honeymoon with the fans was over and a brutal divorce from Paradise looked inevitable as the Bhoys were losing 3-0.

The previous league game had seen a dismal 2-0 defeat by Hearts in which the performance was even worse than the result. Celtic collapsed like a house of cards after falling behind and never looked capable of recovery. Lennon had lost the dressing room, it was said, and a club that had looked on the cusp of something special in May now appeared to be floundering towards a season of mediocrity in October.

In the first half against Kilmarnock, disaster followed disaster. On 26 minutes, a long and hopeful diagonal punt from Alex Pursehouse, Killie's English defender signed from Tranmere Rovers, was intercepted by Dean Shiels, an Ulsterman on loan from Doncaster Rovers, who drove the ball past Fraser Forster from 12 yards. It was the way that South Korean defender Cha Du-ri let the ball bounce, however, and the way his colleagues, supposedly on defensive duties, stood still as statues, that was most alarming. It told Killie that Celtic were not at the races.

Five minutes before half-time, Paul Heffernan, another former denizen of Doncaster's Belle Vue stadium, scored a goal that should have been disallowed for offside. Celtic, though, appeared more interested in protesting than defending. Worse followed on the stroke of half-time when Mulgrew misplaced a header intended for the arms of Forster into the path of James Fowler, a defender who would go on to make over 400 appearances for Kilmarnock, and a third goal for the home side ensued. Celtic were booed from the pitch.

The legend of Lennon's half-time team talk, the angry words, the impassioned demands, has grown over the years. James Forrest has admitted the manager told his charges they were 'letting everyone down'. If truth be told, however, Celtic were just as bad for the first half of the second half as they had been before the break. There was no response worth shouting about, no urgency apparent, no concerted effort to find a foothold in the proceedings. Lennon later admitted he thought he would be sacked at the end of the game.

On 73 minutes, however, Celtic were awarded a free kick 25 yards out from Killie's prowling Finnish goalkeeper, Anssi Jaakkola. Anthony Stokes placed the ball and made clear his intent to change the course of the game. His shot cannoned high into the back of Jaakkola's net. Three minutes later it was Stokes once more, from a similar distance, turning and firing a low shot past Jaakkola, who really should have done better. Suddenly everything seemed possible, even Lennon's retention of his job. With a little more than ten minutes left on the clock, in a crowded and frenetic Killie penalty area, Majstorović headed a flighted free kick from Ki Sung-yueng on to Mulgrew's head, and Celtic were level.

Still, it might have been different. With two minutes remaining Heffernan missed an easy chance from close range that cleared the Celtic crossbar. Had the Killie striker's header been a few inches lower then Lennon's record as Celtic manager might have read just one Scottish Cup.

Afterwards, Lennon confessed to puzzlement. 'We're missing something at the minute,' he said, 'whether it's a mindset or a lack of quality.'

It may have aided Lennon's cause that on the same day as the Kilmarnock match Rangers at last showed signs of fallibility in a 1-1 draw at home to St Mirren.

Celtic remained only ten points behind their great rivals. Sometimes, immortals are a mere heartbeat away from being mere mortals.

The Second Nine-in-a-Row: 2011–2020

The Championships

1. TAXING TIMES AND ONE-IN-A-ROW
2011/12

The 14th and penultimate season of the Scottish Premier League's previous incarnation was surely the most extraordinary in its existence and perhaps the most sensational in the entire history of football north of the border.

For Celtic, still basking in the warm glow of their young manager's first trophy, the 2011/12 season began well enough, after a winning tour of Australia in July, with away league victories at Hibernian (2-0) and Aberdeen (1-0), followed by a resounding 5-1 thumping of Dundee United at Parkhead.

It took a decided turn for the worse, however, with a 1-0 home defeat to St Johnstone on 21 August. A missed penalty by Kris Commons in the third minute set the tone for the rest of the match in which chances to score were spurned with the regularity of a shy teenager at a nightclub.

For Rangers, champions for the third consecutive season in 2010/11 but under the new and callow management of Ally McCoist following the retirement of Walter Smith, the season opened with a disappointing home draw with Hearts but then continued with successive victories that saw them open up a one-point lead over Celtic by the end of August.

The Ibrox club were still spending money on new players, though perhaps with a tad less gay abandon than previously, their standout purchase being Lee Wallace for £1.5m from Hearts.

The first Old Firm game of the season was south of the Clyde on 18 September and was a disaster for Neil Lennon's side, who were ahead at the break but fell apart in an orgy of misplaced passes, and in apparent desperate need of an attitude transplant. The final score was 4-2 to the Ibrox team. Rangers had grappled and grasped the opportunity to establish a four-point lead at the head of the table.

Lennon was in the dog house with rumours swirling that he had lost the dressing room, maybe that he never had it, that he was tactically naive, that, like Davie Hay, like Liam Brady, like Lou Macari, like Tommy Burns, like John Barnes, and like Tony Mowbray, he was too young and too inexperienced for a club the size of Celtic.

The one note of potential good cheer was provided by news reports in the run-up to the derby that Rangers might be in trouble with the taxman. There was a delicious swirl of speculation that the old enemy might even be heading for administration with HMRC demanding payment of arrears of £53m.

It was a prospect to cheer even the ragged nerves of fans shredded by a dreadful performance at Ibrox in September.

Still, though, Lennon's team remained inconsistent. In October 2011 Celtic dropped points like confetti at a wedding. There was a hapless 2-0 defeat at Hearts and the month ended with an equally woebegone home draw with Hibernian. At the midpoint of the month came the near aversion of doomsday at Kilmarnock.

At the start of November, Celtic were 15 points behind Rangers. During the course of the next seven league matches in the run-up to the festive season, however, Rangers fell from grace. There was a 0-0 home draw with St Johnstone, and two defeats away from Ibrox, 1-0 at Kilmarnock and, on Christmas Eve, 2-1 at St Mirren.

Perhaps the financial worries, the hurried and huddled negotiations with lawyers, accountants and the taxman, were taking their toll on their tyro manager and his players.

Meanwhile, Lennon's Celtic began to pick up wins, mostly ugly ones, like winos picking up cigarette ends from the gutter. There were victories by hooks and by crooks against Motherwell, Inverness and Dunfermline, and one by skill and panache, 5-0 over St Mirren. It was mostly ungainly football but it was winning football. After the Christmas Eve 2-1 win at Paradise against Kilmarnock, following a dismal first half almost as bad as the first half at Killie earlier in the season, a double from Georgios Samaras saw Celtic only one point in arrears of Rangers.

In fact, the Ibrox club's decline was so vertiginous that a Celtic win at Paradise in the final match of the old year would see the Parkhead side climb to the top of the table for the first time in 2011.

While McCoist was working with the four horsemen of the apocalypse at his back, Lennon was effecting a quiet and youthful revolution at Celtic Park. From the side that faced Rangers on 18 September, only Fraser Forster, Charlie Mulgrew, Scott Brown, Beram Kayal, Georgios Samaras and Gary Hooper survived.

The average age of the Celts in this second Old Firm match of the season was a mere 22 years. Newcomers to the team were Thomas Rogne, a giant centre-back from Stabæk in Norway, signed by Lennon in January 2010; Adam Matthews, a right-back from Cardiff City, signed in July 2011; Joe Ledley, a midfielder signed, like Matthews, from the Principality's capital club in the summer of 2010; Victor Wanyama, another midfielder, signed after a long pursuit from Beerschot for £900,000 in July 2011; and James Forrest, a product of Celtic's youth academy.

By the time of Lennon's permanent appointment in June 2010, Desmond and Lawwell had initiated a clearly defined policy for Celtic's financial survival and self-sufficiency. The founding and fundamental principle was an acceptance that, without income from television rights remotely comparable to the vast riches of the English top flight, the club would only thrive if a profitable transfer strategy could be developed. As former scout David Moss, who worked for Celtic between 2010 and 2017, said in an interview with *The Guardian* after his time in Paradise was over, 'The most we could pay would be around £3m and we had two criteria: did the player have the ability to compete against the likes of Barcelona, Paris Saint-Germain, Manchester City, AC Milan? And did they have the potential to be sold for a huge profit?'

No modern manager could be responsible for both coaching and sourcing these players with such specific qualities of European competence and saleability.

Well before the crucial derby with Rangers in December 2011, Lennon had surrounded himself with a trusted team of assistants to share the coaching duties: Johan Mjällby, his former team-mate under Martin O'Neill, was his deputy; two more erstwhile colleagues, Alan Thompson at Celtic, and Garry Parker at Leicester City, were additional first-team coaches.

The unsung heroes, however, the undercover immortals, were the members of Lennon's scouting setup.

John Park was the head recruitment honcho. He had been chased and harassed by Lawwell from Hibernian where he had worked for nine years as head of youth development and overseen an impressive stream of footballers transitioning from the Edinburgh club's academy to the first team. His graduates included Derek Riordan, a striker who scored 104 goals in two spells for Hibs and who played for two seasons for Celtic under Strachan's management; Garry O'Connor, another striker, who netted 74 times and, like Riordan, also played for the national side; defender Steve Whittaker, another international, whose career initially took a downward turn when signing for Rangers but then progressed to Norwich City before returning, as did Riordan and O'Connor, for a second term at Hibs.

Such was Park's prestige within the football world that he turned down opportunities to become head of football at Tony Mowbray's West Bromwich Albion and a position of youth coach at Chelsea under the powerful Roman Abramovich–Frank Arnesen–José Mourinho axis. That he also rejected Rangers endeared him immediately to Celtic fans worldwide.

Park began work during Strachan's time and his role was clearly defined by the club's chief executive. His primary task was to source players for the first team but with an additional remit to recruit for Chris McCart's academy.

McCart was appointed as head of Celtic's youth development in June 2008, following in the hallowed footsteps of his predecessor, the immortal Tommy Burns, who had overseen the progression of Shaun Maloney, Stephen McManus, Aiden McGeady and John Kennedy, all of whom became Celtic first-team players and full Scottish internationals.

Park proceeded to set up and oversee a revolutionary data and analytics department at the club, where Craig Dunbar and Paul McLeish crunched numbers, merged potential signings' statistics with scouting reports and compared these with the numbers produced by current players. Park was into Moneyball long before it became fashionable in British football. His rigorous methodology produced £97.9m of profit for Celtic during the course of his almost ten years at the club. Players signed on his watch included Virgil van Dijk, Victor Wanyama, Fraser Forster, Tom Rogic, Scott Brown, Gary Hooper, Kristoffer Ajer, Mikael Lustig, Kris Commons, Ki Sung-yueng and Moussa Dembélé.

Park, too, provided steady streams of fresh talent for Lennon and Ronny Deila, only leaving for pastures new when Brendan Rodgers arrived at Celtic in 2016.

In 2012/13 Celtic qualified for the last 16 of the UEFA Champions League while Manchester City and Chelsea failed to do so. Park was asked how this was possible when Celtic's spending was a mere pittance in comparison to that of the English megabuck giants. 'The answer,' he said, 'is astute scouting observations and strong data assessments, a good team of people around you, and then good coaching. It is an entirely possible outcome.'

Park, too, in conjunction with Lawwell, assessed and recruited colleagues within his football development remit. Neil McGuinness was a first-team scout for six fruitful years between 2009 and 2015 and discovered Virgil van Dijk. McGuinness observed the Dutchman weekly at Groningen and was impressed, especially by a physically robust performance against Wilfried Bony of Vitesse Arnhem. 'It's down to watching,' the scout said: 'That's the only way to make a proper decision.' While other top European clubs dithered over Van Dijk's potential, Park took McGuinness's reports to Lawwell, and Celtic signed the centre-back for a paltry £2.6m. Neil Lennon was blessed indeed.

The contrast with the glory days of Jock Stein was stark. The scouting orbit of Sean Fallon was mostly confined to matches overseen by his team of Paradise Irregulars, the priests, the publicans, the holy and the sinners, who watched games on public parks in and around Glasgow. The only member of the Lisbon Lions who was born more than 13 miles from Parkhead was the outsider, Bobby Lennox, who hailed from Saltcoats on the exotic and faraway Ayrshire coast.

Lennon's initial five signings in his first period at Celtic were Charlie Mulgrew from Aberdeen, Cha Du-ri from Freiburg, Joe Ledley from Cardiff City, Daryl Murphy from Sunderland and Efraín Juárez from Club Universidad Nacional. Celtic's scouting net was cast a little wider than in the Stein era. Lennon's time was a shaggy dog story concerning the Scotsman, the South Korean, the Welshman, the Irishman and the Mexican.

From those early signings, listed in the team that faced Rangers on 28 December 2011 were only Mulgrew and Ledley, the Scotsman and the Welshman. Cha was an unused substitute, all of which serves as a reminder that even under the calculating watch of John Park not all signings were equally successful and that scouting can never be a perfectly exact science.

Through the previous night Glasgow had been battered by 80mph winds and freezing temperatures. Still, though, East End hearts were all a-flutter in the morning, agitated in the knowledge that a win, any win, against their great rivals would see Celtic top the league table.

There were fears, though, that the match might be postponed, and some fainter hearts might even have secretly hoped for such an outcome on the basis that if no match was played no defeat could ensue. After all, Celtic had lost comprehensively at Ibrox in the season's only previous engagement.

By the 7.45pm kick-off, the weather had relented sufficiently to allow the match to proceed, and the bitter east winds had condescended to blow at a mere 30mph. Discarded newspaper pages and chip wrappings stolen by the wind, however, still flew about the stadium and littered the borders of the pitch. The faces of the Celtic players were reddened as they faced the first-half winds. The play was unsurprisingly as scrappy as the weather. Fraser Forster, on loan from Newcastle United, made one superlative save, arching backwards to claw back the ball from the goal line's point of no return. A Samaras effort that did cross the line was ruled out for offside. The gale blew and the rain fell.

In the second half, the constant battering ram of the wind had metamorphosed into intermittent bursts of fury, like fire hurled from a besieging army's trebuchet. The rain redoubled its efforts. In the 52nd minute a fierce James Forrest shot, backed by the wind, was tipped over the bar by Allan McGregor. Charlie Mulgrew took the corner and Joe Ledley wanted more than any Rangers defender, putting his side 1-0 in front.

The Ibrox club's players then subsided like the weakening wind, allowing Celtic to dominate the ball for the remainder of the match. It was almost as if Rangers knew that it was not merely the current game of football that was over but that a cataclysmic game being played by their club's directors was also on the cusp of an even greater defeat.

After the victory, with Celtic two points clear at the league's summit, Lennon confessed, 'I was doubting my own position and I'm sure a lot of fans were as well ... Without being brilliant, it was a very good performance against a dogged Rangers side ... I've been waiting three months for this game because the 4-2 defeat really hurt me.'

* * *

Up to the turn of the year and well past Hogmanay and Epiphany, the season had been unexceptional apart from Rangers' collapse from early-season dominance but, on St Valentine's Day in 2012, everything that had gone before was revealed as mere fool's gold, base elements in an alchemist's experiment.

To the bemusement of the world, Rangers, the untouchables, the football club that thought itself immune from the consequences of its actions, went into administration and were docked ten points by the football authorities.

It is important to note, however, that Celtic won the league championship of 2011/12 by 20 clear points and so the first of the second of the club's nine-in-a-row sequences was no title with an asterisk attached or, indeed, any question mark or exclamation mark whatsoever.

The team from Paradise might have won the title as early as 25 March on a visit to Ibrox Park – now renamed 'I Brokes' by Celtic fans – but, in an afternoon of human storms, lost 3-2, and also lost two men and a manager, all sent off.

Celtic, as all too often, were greeted by racist banners and stands overcast with clouds of Union flags.

Lennon was sent off for protesting Cha's dismissal and was told his safety in the stands could not be guaranteed so was forced to watch the second half from the press room. It was a sad commentary on a club unable to control either its finances or its fanatics.

The next opportunity to seal the title occurred on 7 April against Kilmarnock. The match was not without its ghosts, its hauntings from the past. Just three weeks earlier Celtic had lost the League Cup Final 1-0 to Killie.

Lennon, too, would not have been human had he not cast his mind back to Celtic's previous visit to Rugby Park, the fixture in which he might have been sacked at half-time on an October Saturday afternoon.

Fortunately for Lennon, Charlie Mulgrew chose this day as the moment he would play his best match for Celtic. After only eight minutes the manager's first signing headed his team ahead from a corner. In the 17th minute it was the defender's turn to play provider with a cross met by Glen Loovens inside the six-yard box to double the lead. Ten minutes before half-time, Mulgrew chased a ball from Commons along the left flank and calmly slotted past Cammy Bell in the Killie goal. Just before the interval whistle, Mulgrew crossed for Hooper at the far post and, with a 4-0 lead, the championship was surely secure.

Mulgrew, the former Celtic youth player, the club's own prodigal son, was substituted with a quarter of an hour remaining, and was given a standing ovation by the 14,000 travelling fans, allowed by Kilmarnock to occupy three sides of Rugby Park.

Ledley and Hooper completed the scoring, the final score was 6-0 and Celtic had won their first title since 2007/08.

Lennon joined a pantheon of Celtic immortals who have won league championships as both player and manager: Willie Maley, Jimmy McGrory, Jock Stein, Billy McNeill and Davie Hay. It was, according to the Irishman, 'The best day in my professional life.' It was quite a turnaround for the man who was losing 3-0 at half-time just shy of six months previously. 'The last two years,' Lennon added, 'have felt like I've been on probation.' He name-checked both 'Mr Desmond' and 'Peter Lawwell' as providing 'great support'.

It was one-in-a-row.

* * *

2. PROFITS AND LOSSES
2012/13

This was the first season of football since the inauguration of the Scottish Football League in 1890/91 in which the Parkhead club would not be meeting in mortal combat with their Glasgow rivals from across the river.

It was a strange feeling tinged with loss as well as *Schadenfreude*. There was no ghost in the machine; there was no elephant in the room.

The Rangers plc was gone, banished and vanished, only to reappear mysteriously as The Rangers Ltd via a bizarre incarnation as Sevco Scotland Ltd, in the fourth tier of Scottish football.

There were claims and counter claims that the Rangers club inhabiting the lower depths of the footballing pyramid was the very same club that had once challenged for and secured top honours, including 54 league championships, 33 Scottish Cups and 27 League Cups. Unsurprisingly, this resurrection from the dead, this undead state of being, was seemingly supported by Neil Doncaster, chief executive of the Scottish Premier League, who said, 'It is an existing club, even though it is a new company.' Others begged to differ. After all, The Rangers plc was bankrupted when the taxman came calling, the company liquidated.

For the avoidance of doubt, liquidation is a formal process which brings about the closure of a company. All company assets are then sold or liquidated and used to repay, as far as is possible, existing creditors. The company is then struck from the register at Companies House and the former company ceases to exist as a legal entity.

The directors of the oldco, too, were perhaps fortunate not to have been investigated as the company had continued borrowing money, continued taking cash from their customers, when, there was some speculation some may have been aware that the business they were legally responsible for was technically insolvent.

Neither were the assets of the bankrupt club seized and sold to compensate creditors as is normally the case with liquidation. Ibrox Stadium was transferred from the old company's ownership to that of the newco.

Had Celtic been bankrupted in 1994, it is impossible to believe the club would have been treated with equivalent leniency.

By some sleight of hand, the Rangers had not apparently died at all. Somehow, a new football club, owned by new owners of a new company, was to be allowed to compete within the structures of the Scottish Football League. That The Rangers Football Club Ltd was even permitted to compete in the Third Division was due to the generosity of spirit of 29 clubs who voted in favour of granting the new club associate membership of the SFL. Had it not been for the tidal wave of revulsion expressed by fans and owners of smaller but legal, decent, honest and truthful football clubs, the newco incarnation of Rangers might have been granted the absolute continuity they craved through uninterrupted membership of the Scottish Premier League. Had both the SFA and the SFL had their way the newco would have been granted entry into the second tier of Scottish football.

The history of both manifestations of Rangers is littered with overspending, of living beyond the club's means.

The oldco's lifestyle under David Murray was legendary but what was unknown, and even unsuspected until the closing years of his ownership, was that the lavish and habitual prodigality was enabled by dubious tax avoidance schemes. Unsurprisingly, the chairman of Rangers was one of the greatest beneficiaries from the Employee Benefit Trusts, allegedly awarding himself a total of £6.3m in tax-free payments. In total, 63 players, 24 other members of Rangers' staff, and 24 further employees of the Murray Group benefited from trust payments and dual contracts.

Murray, only too well aware of the financial nets of insolvency that were closing around the dysfunctional football club, had been trying to offload Rangers since 2006. At last, in May 2011, Murray sold the oldco incarnation of the Ibrox club to Craig Whyte, a man who claimed to be a billionaire but in fact had a curriculum vitae that majored in collapsed businesses and contained a seven-year ban from company directorships.

That Murray's club was sold for a token £1 says everything anyone needed to know about the way the club had been run into the murk and mire of technical bankruptcy. Following that Rangers' apparent descent into a dizzying whirlpool of moral turpitude continued at an ever greater pace.

In order to complete the takeover from Murray, which also necessitated paying off £18m in debt to Lloyds Bank and to finance the spending spree on new and existing players for the 2011/12 season, Whyte mortgaged the club's future season ticket sales through a disastrous and desperate deal with Ticketus, a London-based company providing working capital for distressed football clubs.

In the summer of 2011, Whyte authorised new and improved long-term contracts for key players including Steven Davis, Steven Whittaker, and Allan McGregor, and the purchases of seven new players at a total cost of just under £4m.

When Rangers exited the Champions League and the Europa League in quick succession in July and August, the club's finances became exposed to an ongoing annual deficit of around £10m and with 60 per cent of season ticket sales already pawned to Ticketus.

Their solution was to withhold from the taxman incomes collected from PAYE and VAT. In total, £9m was retained improperly and used to fund ongoing expenditure.

In May 2012, during the club's administration by Duff and Phelps, Whyte sold the oldco to Charles Green, another man with a business career involving the dissolution of no fewer than nine companies.

One thing, though, never changed, and that was the Ibrox club's extravagance. Just one year earlier, the departing Rangers manager, Walter Smith, had issued a financial rallying cry, demanding that Whyte should spend, spend, and spend again. 'Historically,' Smith said, 'if you look at Rangers over the last 20 years, they have needed a fairly large investment in the team to boost them. When the team has not had that, it has not been successful.' The sheer bloody-minded blinkered blindness of Smith in calling for a continuation of a policy, with which he had been intrinsically complicit, that brought the club he undoubtedly loved to its knees, was staggering in its ignorance.

Whyte responded with a hollow promise to provide £25m to the new manager, Ally McCoist, over a five-year period.

Green felt the same pressures as his predecessor and, in preparation for a campaign in the fourth tier, spent lavishly on players from exotic places on exotic wages: Sébastien Faure, a Frenchman from Lyon; Anestis Argyriou, a Greek from AEK Athens; Emílson Cribari, a Brazilian from Cruzeiro; and Francesco Stella, an Australian from Siena. The money came eventually, neither from Whyte nor Green, but from a share issue in December 2012, which raised £22m of working and spending capital.

In April 2013, Green was hounded from his position as CEO at Ibrox following allegations, which later became a criminal investigation, by Whyte of the existence of a secret deal between the two which cast serious doubts as to the legitimacy of Green's ownership of shares in Rangers. In the autumn of 2013, Green's shares were sold to Sandy Easdale, a man who served one-year of a 27 month sentence in 1997 for a VAT scam. Even allowing for the fact that truth is sometimes stranger than fiction, surely an appropriate response to the ongoing saga of the ownership of the shares would be that you couldn't make it up.

By February 2014, the newco had squandered the entirety and more of the money raised only 15 months earlier, and was forced into borrowing £1.5m from an Isle of Man hedge fund and from the former convict,

Easdale. Money was also flowing into Ibrox in the form of further loans from another source of genuine wealth.

Mike Ashley of Sports Direct and Newcastle United had bought an 8.92 per cent shareholding in Rangers during the short era of Green's control and had installed Derek Llambias on the newco board. He had also negotiated the purchase of naming rights to Ibrox for a mere £1.

Later, too, Ashley engineered a merchandising deal with newco directors desperate for cash that saw the stricken football club entitled to only seven pence in the pound from shop sales. It was claimed that Ashley was using the Ibrox club as a pawn in the magnate's game.

In March 2015, however, at an Extraordinary General Meeting, Ashley and Llambias were ousted by former oldco director Dave King. Under normal circumstances the takeover of a football club by someone with 41 criminal convictions relating to income tax offences in South Africa would be met with universal abhorrence but, such was the hatred of Ashley in Govan, King was welcomed as a saviour second only to Jesus Christ and King Billy.

Remarkably, too, though perhaps unsurprisingly in view of the apparent supine nature of the Scottish Football Association in matters relating to the Ibrox club, King was welcomed by the custodial body as a 'fit and proper person' to assume control of newco Rangers.

This, though, it was important to recall, was a man branded by a South African judge as a 'glib and shameless liar' and as a 'mendacious witness whose evidence should not be accepted on any issue'. King's original indictment in 2013 was on 322 counts including fraud, evasion of both tax and exchange control regulations, money laundering and racketeering.

This man was now the largest shareholder in the newco, he became chairman in May 2015 and stayed until March 2020 when business in South Africa required his personal attention. At the time of writing in early 2022, he is attempting a return to the Rangers boardroom to 'aid the further development of the club'.

While the newco boardroom sometimes resembled a game of musical chairs with the last man standing required to leave, one thing remained constant, and that was expenditure exceeding income in a manner that would have shocked Dickens's Mr Micawber whose dictum was, 'Annual income 20 pounds, annual expenditure 19 pounds 19 and six, result happiness. Annual income 20 pounds, annual expenditure 20 pounds ought and six, result misery.'

The newco's recurring theme of substantial annual losses continued under King's regime and that of Douglas Park, who succeeded the South African as chairman in March 2020.

Accounts lodged with Companies House over a seven-year period show accumulated losses of £112.845m.

For comparison, Celtic's profits and losses for the same period are shown beside those of their Glasgow rivals.

YEAR ENDING	RANGERS	CELTIC
June 2015	LOSS £38.101m	LOSS £3.9m
June 2016	LOSS £2.307m	PROFIT £0.5m
June 2017	LOSS £6.495m	PROFIT £6.9m
June 2018	LOSS £12.268m	PROFIT £17.3m
June 2019	LOSS £10.32m	PROFIT £11.3m
June 2020	LOSS £17.773m	PROFIT £0.1m
June 2021	LOSS £25.581m	LOSS £11.5m
TOTALS 2015–2021	LOSS £112.845m	PROFIT £20.7m

In the Ibrox club's annual reports there is ample talk about financial sustainability but no clear evidence of walking of the sure-footed walk.

Remember, too, that these financial statements emerging from Ibrox are the inevitable results of ongoing spending policies that have continued unabated even after recent and catastrophic bankruptcy.

In Glasgow, since 1994, there has only been one top-tier club that has been run with financial probity and responsibility. By the summer of 2022, incidentally, there may be two well-run clubs in the city, as Partick Thistle are set to become owned and governed by their fans' foundation. The recent history of the Jags provides encouragement and delight for their supporters especially after the ownership by the absentee landlord Ken Bates, and of the financial disasters of the 1990s.

Rangers newco, though, after announcing their most recent and most serious losses, and after citing Covid as the primary reason for the palpably poor results, admitted the club could only survive the rest of 2021/22 by borrowing a further £7.5m.

It seems as if little has been learned from administration and liquidation and, if King returns to the board, alongside Alastair Johnston, the current non-executive director who was in the boardroom from 2004 to 2011 and returned there in 2017, could there be a return to the wayward days when the oldco believed it was immune from both financial rules and realities?

Directors' loans, bank loans, share issues to cover working capital demands, all these ways and means are no ways to create and maintain a stable business structure designed to support a successful football club.

It is just possible that the sale of Nathan Patterson in February 2022 for a reported fee of £12m signifies a belated recognition by Rangers that a continuation of buying and not selling players, of posting unsustainable losses year after year, is an impossible strategy over the longer term, that debts incurred may even have to be repaid. Alternatively, it may be the opening gambit of a long-touted philosophy of copying Celtic's long-standing transfer blueprint of buying or developing young talent and selling players at a profit in order to maintain stability or even profitability.

Rangers' January 2022 deadline day loan of Aaron Ramsey from Juventus, though, smacked of a return to the Murray and Souness magic money tree days of signing expensive of former English Premier League stars. The Welshman's salary was equivalent to almost twice the entire wage bill at Aberdeen. Even if it was true that the Ibrox club were responsible for a mere 30 per cent of Ramsey's wages, £120,000 a week is a shedload of cash.

By the end of the 2021/22 season, Ramsey had hardly kicked a ball in anger for the Ibrox club. The final, humbling moment of this financial gamble came with the Welshman missing the decisive penalty in Rangers' Europa League Final shoot-out defeat to Eintracht Frankfurt.

* * *

Still, at the commencement of 2012/13, the Ibrox club no longer figured in Celtic's calculations for the new season.

Two titles in a row looked an open goal for the club from Paradise. Surely, though, Lennon would never permit his young guns to think like that.

Maybe the players thought differently, however, as they opened the new campaign against Aberdeen in apparently flippant fashion. The immortal Sean Fallon, who as guest of honour a few days after his 90th birthday unfurled the SPL championship flag before kick-off, deserved a better spectacle, one of more honest endeavour at the very least. The crowd of 48,000, too, endured rather than enjoyed their return. It was a turgid affair and Lennon spoke afterwards of a 'flatness' about his team. A Kris Commons goal deep into the second half secured an undeserved three points.

Worse, though, was to follow, with a tame 1-1 draw at Ross County and two more dropped points in a 2-2 home stalemate with Hibernian, then a 2-1 defeat in Perth to St Johnstone. By mid-September, Celtic were treading water, if not quite drowning, in fifth place and four points adrift of leaders Motherwell.

If there was any consolation, or even possible amusement, to be found it was by reading reports of the Rangers newco's struggles in the bargain basement section of the Scottish Football League. The first four away games for the shamed and fallen giant failed to produce a single win. A 2-2 draw at Peterhead was followed by further dropped points at Berwick Rangers, a goalless draw at Annan Athletic and a 1-0 defeat at Stirling Albion.

Still, the Rangers were lucky to be plying their lower-class trade at all. There have been four bankruptcies in Scottish football since World War Two. Third Lanark, founded in the same year, 1872, as Rangers, and league champions in 1904 and Scottish Cup winners in 1889 and 1905, were liquidated under the corrupt ownership of Bill Hiddleston in 1967. Unlike the Ibrox club, they never came back. Airdrieonians were liquidated in 2002 and reformed, at least honestly, as a new club, Airdrie United, and applied for membership, like Rangers, of the Third Division of the SFL. Gretna, however, were preferred to the Airdrie newco, but were reprieved when the league approved a buyout of ailing Clydebank. Like Rangers, Airdrie then reclaimed their original name of Airdrieonians but at least had the decency to wait until 2013. Clydebank, since 2020, have plied their trade in the newly formed West of Scotland League. Gretna, elected to the SFL in 2002, were bankrupt by 2008. The club were reformed as Gretna 2008 by their supporters' trust and now play in the Scottish Lowland Football League.

One or more of these fates could, and perhaps should, have been applied to Rangers newco. Instead, eventually, the Ibrox club's form turned around and, at the end of season 2012/13, they were promoted as champions from the fourth tier.

Celtic, too, needed a recovery, and a turning point occurred in the 2-0 victory over Motherwell at the end of September 2012. It was the second in a sequence of four straight SPL wins for the Celts and saw them head the league table for the first time that season. Gary Hooper drove the ball low and hard past Darren Randolph in the Well goal after half an hour and, five minutes later, the unfortunate goalkeeper turned a Scott Brown cross into his own net to secure Celtic's three points in a dominant performance that might have seen many more goals.

One month and a week later, Celtic hosted Barcelona in a group stage match of the Champions League and gave their greatest European performance and result since the 1967 victory over Inter Milan, the 2-1 win gained through determined defence, especially through the performance of Fraser Forster in goal, and through the goals of Victor Wanyama and Tony Watt. It was somehow fitting that on the previous evening, in St Mary's Church and Hall, there were celebrations including a thanksgiving Mass commemorating the 125th anniversary of Celtic's foundation.

In the league match that followed, however, the Hoops could only play out a desultory draw with St Johnstone.

Perhaps it was inevitable, and understandable, that, with the Rangers newco engaged elsewhere, and with Celtic progressing to the last 16 in Europe, league performances were patchy at best.

Still, by the time of the Hoops' 6-2 rout of Dundee United in February 2013, Lennon's team were 18 points clear at the SPL summit.

Just over two months later, Celtic required just a single point from a home match against Inverness Caley Thistle to clinch two-in-a-row. The only doubt concerning this achievement surrounded the Highlands team's previous visit to Paradise when Terry Butcher's team had won 1-0 in November of 2012. That, though, had been a few days after Celtic's heroics in a 2-1 Champions League defeat at Benfica. This match followed a 4-3 Scottish Cup semi-final victory over Dundee United and, in addition, the players had enjoyed six days of rest and recovery time. The first half was dull and dreary, as if one point would suffice so one point would be the aim.

Just past the hour, however, Commons sparked to life. He played a sharp ball into Hooper, who held off the zealous attentions of Graeme

Shinnie, and drove his shot hard and low from 12 yards past Antonio Reguero, the Caley goalkeeper. The crowd of 55,000 inside Paradise began to stir. This was not Barcelona but it was almost certainly now a 44th league title, and all honestly won.

Five minutes later, a cute ball from Ledley found the overlapping right-back Mikael Lustig, signed the previous summer from Norwegian giants Rosenborg. The attacking defender found Ledley with a return ball and the Welsh midfielder guided it into the corner of the Caley net. It was Hooper again, scorer of 31 goals that season, after 73 minutes who flicked at Commons's cross, and the ball once more bulged the back of the visitors' net.

The celebrations were now in full swing all around Paradise and, with two minutes remaining, Samaras scored a solo special, crashing the ball from a narrow angle on to the Caley crossbar and into the net. A late, late Inverness consolation goal hardly registered amid the wild scenes of celebration in the stands of Celtic Park. At the final whistle, the manager, too, joined the dancing throng on the pitch. For Lennon, a second league title meant more than the first. 'The first time was brilliant,' he said, 'but to do it again, it's your remit and priority at the beginning of the season … it's been a fantastic, memorable season.'

Three weeks later, after an emphatic 4-0 win over St Johnstone with goals from Ledley, Mulgrew, Forrest, and an own goal from Frazer Wright, the Celtic captain Scott Brown, back in the starting XI after three months out injured, lifted the SPL trophy to the skies.

On receipt of his award as the Scottish Writers' Manager of the Year, Lennon said that celebrating a second title at the same time as commemorating '125 years of unique and unbroken history' was special indeed.

* * *

3. CURDLED MILK AND CREAM; LENNON LEAVING
2013/14

Before the start of the new season, the familiar structure of Scottish football was broken up and reorganised.

Among the consequences was the fact that the new authority, vested in the Scottish Professional Football League through the amalgamation in May 2013 of the SPL and the SFL, felt unable to revisit decisions relating to Rangers' accumulation of tainted titles earlier in the century. No points could be docked when the Supreme Court in London handed down its verdict in July 2017 that Rangers had cheated both Scottish football and the British tax authorities for a decade or more. No titles could be stripped because the SPFL was in effect a newco and had no jurisdiction over what had gone on under the aegis of the oldco SPL.

Like Rangers, the powers that be in Scottish football wanted both cakes to be eaten and still to be available for further feasting at a later date. When it suited Rangers to claim continuity of history, the transition, the history, of oldco and newco was seamless and unimpeachable. When it came, however, to honouring debts or acknowledging illegal and immoral actions, well, newco surely could not be held to account for the sleights of hand and mind of oldco.

One further consequence of the restructuring was that Rangers appeared to have been promoted twice in one season. The newco started season 2013/14 in League One, having played in the Third Division in the previous term. It was perhaps more helpful to think and talk in terms of tiers. Celtic remained in the top tier and Rangers had been promoted to the third tier of newco Scottish football.

Even so, it was still slightly surreal to know that once again the sole local derbies in Glasgow would be with Partick Thistle and that this would remain the case for at least another two seasons.

Lennon's task was to keep his players' minds on the job at hand, to remind and reprise, and to ensure, whatever the opposition, that Celtic were ready to win and win again, even if their leading goalscorer Gary Hooper had been sold to Norwich City for £5m and their talented defensive midfielder Victor Wanyama had been sold to Southampton for a Scottish record fee of £12.5m.

In the summer of 2013, significant additions to both defensive and offensive capabilities arrived in Paradise in the shapes of Virgil van Dijk, a £2.6m signing from Groningen, and Teemu Pukki for £3m from Schalke.

Celtic's philosophy for financial stability and profitability was once more unveiled for all to see. Naturally enough, however, buying cheap and selling dear will not always work. Pukki struggled to replace Hooper at the fulcrum of the attack, scoring only seven goals from 33 games. This, too, in a team that scored 102 times in 38 league games in 2013/14. Van

Dijk, by contrast, in spite of remaining at Paradise for a mere two seasons, became an immortal, his footballing class shining as bright as brilliant sunlight in the midst of winter.

It was a curate's egg of a football season for Celtic. There were disappointments, curdled milk among the cream.

After the highs of Champions League victories in the previous season, including the defeat of Barcelona, this time around the Catalan giants dismantled Celtic 6-1 in Spain. In the group stages in 2013 there was a solitary victory over Ajax. The competition by which Celtic wished to be judged proved a disenchantment and a disillusionment.

In the League Cup, Celtic exited at the third round after a 1-0 defeat to Morton. More disappointingly, the Scottish Cup the club had won in such thrilling fashion the previous season against Hibernian at Hampden was relinquished in a fifth-round defeat against Aberdeen. In the previous round, Celtic had beaten Hearts 7-0 in Edinburgh, in Lennon's 200th game in charge, helped by a superb Commons hat-trick.

Disappointment does not begin to tell the tale. Everyone agrees the prime task of any Celtic manager at the start of any season is to win the league championship but the title was already as good as won before winter was out. Celtic were 21 points ahead of Aberdeen after their 1-0 victory over St Mirren at the beginning of February. Retention of the cup should have provided renewed focus on football for the squad. Certainly, the management team of Lennon and Garry Parker took the tie seriously. Lennon had watched Aberdeen in their League Cup semi-final the previous weekend and had been insulted and spat upon for his pains. With the benefit of hindsight, it is not difficult to see this latest example of abuse, followed by the cup exit, as last straws for a manager now perhaps struggling for focus on football in Glasgow and Scotland.

There were highlights, though, aplenty, sufficient, at least, to keep both fans and wolves from Lennon's door.

In goal for Celtic was Fraser Forster, the man dubbed by the sub-editor at *Mundo Deportivo* as '*La Gran Muralla*', the Great Wall, after his match-winning performance against Barcelona in the previous season. The giant goalkeeper was in consistent shot-stopping form throughout the season and on 2 February 2014 claimed a club record of 11 successive clean sheets, beating the previous record held by club legend Charlie Shaw, who shut out opposing forwards for ten games in a row in 1921/22. During the match against Hearts three weeks later, Forster broke the record of Bobby Clark, the Aberdeen and Scotland goalkeeper, of 1,155 minutes without conceding a goal. Eventually, Forster was beaten after 1,256 minutes in Celtic's one league defeat of the season, against Aberdeen on 25 February.

If there were no causes for concern at the back for Celtic, this was far from the case further forward after the sale of Hooper.

In the wake of Hooper's move south, the Celt who stepped up to the plate was a surprise. Kris Commons was an attacking midfielder, a playmaker rather than a goalscorer. There was little in his career in England with Stoke City, Nottingham Forest and Derby County, during which he scored a goal every 4.65 games, to suggest he might in 2013/14 score one more than Hooper had managed in 2012/13. Commons had enjoyed his time with Hooper in the previous season, netting 19 from 46 appearances, but prior to that in his Celtic career had scored 15 goals from 54 games including a drought of biblical proportions in 2011/12 when only one goal was scored in 33 appearances.

Statistics, naturally enough, operate only on the surface of affairs and Commons was always worth his place in Lennon's teams for his hard-working commitment and his ability to knit play and players together in productive patterns. Nevertheless, in 2013/14, it was shocking to see strikers Tony Stokes, Teemu Pukki and Georgios Samaras all failing to discharge their duties, ignoring the basics of their job descriptions, while a mere midfielder scored 32 goals. Commons was not only the leading goalscorer in Scotland, not only the recipient of PFA Scotland and Scottish Writers' Player of the Year awards, but also named by UEFA as one of their 35 Best Players in Europe.

Lennon had played with Commons at Nottingham Forest and understood his value, knew in his bones that acquiring his signature on a contract in January 2011 for a mere £300,000 was a steal.

During Commons's time at Celtic he won five league titles, two Scottish Cups and one League Cup.

On his debut against Aberdeen in a League Cup semi-final at Hampden in January 2011, he collected the ball on the edge of the Dons' penalty area after six minutes, paused for thought, and looped an exquisite chip over Jamie Langfield, Aberdeen's goalkeeper, and into the corner of the net. It was a promise of perfection to come from an unexpected gem of a footballer.

The 2013/14 season, though, was Commons's *annus mirabilis*. In a year when Celtic's strikers mostly ranged from disappointing to dismal, Commons stepped up, pushed himself further forward, and the goals were thunder and lightning among the drear and drizzle when there was no team in Scotland that could push Celtic to the summit of sunlit displays, when motivation had to be provided from within. It is no exaggeration to say that Commons provided the lifeblood and the beating heart of a Celtic team that infuriated and delighted fans in equal measure.

At the close of the season, Lennon said of Commons, 'He is dynamite with both feet,' and added that he was 'probably our best player'. From one immortal to another, the Celtic manager said, 'Kris is writing a very good legacy.'

The league title was claimed on 26 March in Maryhill with a 5-1 thrashing of Partick Thistle. Unusually for Commons, he allowed others to take the lead in terms of goals. Stokes scored twice, while teenager Liam Henderson and Stefan Johansen both also scored before Commons, who left it until the final minute before taking a ball from Samaras in his stride and slotting past Paul Gallacher in the Thistle goal. It was the earliest a championship had been decided since Rangers had won the First Division in 1928/29. At the end of the game, there was spasmodic chanting of 'ten-in-a-row' but Rangers were on their way back, edging closer to a Premiership return with every game. It was all a tad premature perhaps.

Afterwards, Lennon did not appear sated with success, 'We're just an outstanding team and an outstanding club. It's brilliantly run … the strategy is spot on … we've got a fantastic football team …'

Lennon was only the fourth Celtic manager, after Willie Maley, Jock Stein, and Gordon Strachan, to win three consecutive league titles. 'We will be looking to build on that now,' he said.

Two months later, he was gone.

* * *

Lennon's meeting in Dublin on the afternoon of 19 May 2014 with majority shareholder Dermot Desmond confirmed suspicions on both sides.

Lennon was minded to move on, feeling he had achieved all he could with Celtic, although he had nowhere in particular to go, but still felt after four years that the time was right. Desmond was hardly surprised, and had agreed beforehand with Lawwell that he would make no effort to prevent Lennon's leaving. It was agreed that the subsequent announcement would be processed and packaged as an amicable split, a parting of the ways between friends. It was true, however, that relationships between Desmond and Lawwell on the one side, and Lennon on the other, were strained rather than inimical.

From March 2010 Lennon's work at Celtic had been a labour of love, an intense and passionate affair, but, since the ending of the 2012/13 season, rumours of a cooling of that ardour had swirled with the western winds that blew daily about Paradise. As early as May, Lennon had been tipped to take over from David Moyes at Everton. It was an early warning that all was no longer sweetness and light with Lennon at Celtic.

Truth was that Lawwell and Desmond were determined never to put Celtic's careful husbandry of finances at risk. Their strategy was clear. Lennon, before the commencement of the 2013/14 season, had been sent into battle stripped of the spine of his team – Kelvin Wilson, Victor Wanyama and Gary Hooper – and straight into European qualification games against Cliftonville, Elfsborg and Shakhter Karagandy, and almost paid the price of failure when losing the first leg 2-0 in Kazakhstan. In the subsequent group games of the Champions League, Lennon felt humiliated by the footballing lessons handed out by Barcelona and by AC Milan. The manager wanted money spent to prepare for the next European adventure in 2014/15 but the board would not jeopardise stability in order to finance risk.

At the conclusion of the 2013/14 campaign, Samaras was allowed to leave under freedom of contract. No attempt was made by Lawwell to negotiate an extension of his deal. Sammy was a favourite of Lenny's. The manager would have nodded in agreement when the Greek striker said, 'Me and the gaffer, we don't make the decisions – there are people above us who make the decisions.'

Lennon wanted to create a team that would dare to dream of emulating Stein's heroes of 1967. It was all very well winning three league championships but, with Rangers unavoidably indisposed, the domestic challenge was insufficient to fuel the fires of passion the manager needed to stoke his players to further fervour.

There was, too, the constant carping, the venomous diatribes, from friends and foes alike, on the media merry-go-rounds, the hotlines, the forums, the papers. 'Sometimes,' Lennon said in September 2013, 'it really sucks the life out of you.' There was the spitting incident at Tynecastle in February 2014, to say no more of the bombs and the bottles that had gone before. This was no longer the Glasgow of Stein. The closure of the pits and the shipyards and Thatcher and her children had seen to that. It would be fair to say that Lenny had had enough and no one had endured more than this one man in one city.

Still, he might have stayed had Lawwell promised the funds to win the Champions League, but Lennon was not daft. He knew the score and he knew it from day one. Sell high, buy low. It was the law of the jungle in the hierarchy of all those inhabitants of Scotland who did not earn the untold riches of television contracts from Sky enjoyed south of the border. Even Rangers had discovered they were not immune from these iron laws of reality.

Still, he might have stayed if the criticism hadn't harped so much on what hurt most, his professionalism, his abilities as a manager. Without Rangers in close attendance, there was little credit accorded by his critics for winning championships, and there was damnation at each and every cup exit, European and domestic, as if Celtic enjoyed some divine right to lord it over all and sundry, as if an away match in Northern Ireland or Sweden or Kazakhstan, or a home game against Greenock Morton or Aberdeen, were all God-given rights of passage, as if they were somehow easy and the results were preordained.

Lennon had been careless to admit to journalists that he didn't really bother with tactics and so, whenever his team failed to perform to expectations, he was belaboured with criticisms of tactical naivety, especially after the European games in 2013. Lennon was preoccupied with passion, energy and winning mentalities, and, mostly, these fixations worked well. As Kelvin Wilson confirmed in a 2020 interview with Liam Bryce of the *Irish Mirror*, Lennon was loved by his players partly because he trusted them as professionals to understand their roles within the team context, to make it up as they went along, to improvise, to be grown-ups capable of reading the game, taking the initiative, and, ultimately, winning matches. 'No,' he confirmed, tactics and preparation were never prominent under Lennon. 'It wasn't, as well you know, and that's the truth.' Lennon was loved, too, for imposing no dietary requirements on his team. 'We just ate what we wanted,' said Wilson, and the steak and chips was washed down with Irn-Bru.

Perhaps Lawwell and Desmond agreed with the journalists, perhaps they wanted a change of direction, a move with the times. The fact that they appointed Ronny Deila from Strømsgodset as Lennon's replacement rather than the rumoured Henrik Larsson, Roy Keane, Steve Clarke, Owen Coyle or Malky Mackay, suggested they wanted revolution in the coaching of the players rather than mere change or adaptation.

Neil Lennon, however, is a true Celtic original, an immortal to stand alongside Maley and Stein and Strachan in more ways than merely winning three successive titles. If he was a dinosaur in some ways, he was a Tyrannosaurus rex raging against the probabilities of extinction.

The fact, too, that, like Oliver Twist in the Dickens tale, he came back for more in February 2019, at a time when Celtic were in dire need of direction after the resignation of Brendan Rodgers, only adds to the legend, and to the body of work and achievement at Parkhead under his leadership.

* * *

4. RONNY'S BIG SHIP NOW
2014/15

In November 2009, a 35-year-old man began removing his clothes inside the Marienlyst Stadion in the city and port of Drammen in south-eastern Norway. Soon he was seen jogging around the perimeter of the stadium in nothing but his underpants. He was cheered every step of the way by a capacity crowd of 8,900. Finally, he dropped to the artificial surface of the pitch, and completed a series of impressive press-ups.

He had kept his promise. He had told the supporters of Strømsgodset that if the team he managed avoided relegation he would strip to his underwear. His team had just beaten Viking Stavanger in the last home game of the season. Perhaps more importantly he had saved his side without abandoning his principles. 'I would rather go down,' he said, 'than play ugly football.' He was a student of Jürgen Klopp at Borussia Dortmund and of Arsène Wenger at Arsenal. 'Player development,' he added, 'is much more important than my own future.'

This was the coach Celtic appointed as the man to succeed Lennon in June 2014.

It was a left-field selection, possibly the most risk-ridden appointment in the history of the club. Ronny Deila had interviewed well in front of Desmond and Lawwell, and had been considered, it was rumoured, for the position of assistant to Roy Keane or Henrik Larsson, but both favourites for the post had rebuffed Celtic's advances.

Deila had enjoyed a limited playing career, shown early promise, earning nine under-17 caps and two at under-21 level for Norway. He had won the Norwegian Football Cup in 2000 when playing for Odd Grenland in a 2-1 victory over Viking. By comparison, Keane played 154 games for Nottingham Forest, 480 times for Manchester United, 13 games for Celtic under Strachan, and won 67 caps for the Republic of Ireland. He had also won the Football League Championship in 2007 when manager of Sunderland. Larsson played 168 games in two spells with Helsingborg, 149 times for Feyenoord, and made 313 appearances for Celtic, scoring 242 goals in seven seasons under Jansen, Barnes, Dalglish and O'Neill, as well as playing 59 times for Barcelona and 13 times for Manchester United.

Still, famous footballers do not always make the best managers. Stein did, although he was hardly celebrated as a player outside of Albion Rovers and Celtic and his sole representative honour was a solitary cap for a Scotland League XI in 1954. McNeill did, O'Neill, Strachan and Lennon did, but far superior footballers in Davie Hay, Liam Brady, Lou Macari, Tommy Burns and John Barnes did not. Keane's time at Sunderland ended in tears in December 2008 with his team 18th in the Premier League, when both owner Ellis Short and the players celebrated his resignation and the ending of his harsh, authoritarian management style.

Deila, by way of contrast, worked alongside his charges, promoting their welfare, never fearful of loss of status or diminution of ego. In 2010, seeing his Strømsgodset players tense and nervous before a cup final against Follo, he delivered his team talk dressed only in a thong in the shape of an elephant's trunk.

He was perhaps never happier than when encouraging young footballers. At Strømsgodset, before Deila's time in charge, not a single player from the club represented Norway at youth level. During Deila's era, however, no fewer than 179 Strømsgodset players gained youth caps.

His appointment was a brave one, pitching for modernity, for a coach who embraced all the fashionable tenets of 21st-century football, pressing and possession, playing out from the back with a passing, progressive game, all with an emphasis on physical conditioning, diet and lifestyle, for potential, for possibilities, for flair rather than fame.

For track record, too, however, as Deila had transformed Strømsgodset from perennial strugglers and relegation favourites to champions of Norway in 2013, and this with a club that had won only one Tippeligaen title – in 1970 – in its history.

Just in case, two Celtic stalwarts in the shapes of John Collins and John Kennedy were added to Deila's staff, as assistant manager and first-team coach respectively. If the risk of allowing a man with recent success and naked ambition to take care of Celtic's on-field fortunes was not so great, his lack of experience of life in Glasgow and work in Scottish football was a worry for Desmond and Lawwell. Of all the past managers of Celtic only Brady, Jansen, Venglos and O'Neill had no experience of Scottish football, and the latter trio were successful and experienced coaches with pedigrees in Europe and England. Only Brady was a failure. It made sense, therefore, that Collins, who played 229 times for Celtic between 1990 and 1996, had managed at Hibernian and Charleroi, and who had been director of football at Livingston, should assist the new man. Kennedy, while lacking Collins's varied managerial and coaching experience, was Celtic through and through, and had worked at Paradise as scout, first-team coach and assistant manager under Lennon.

It did not start especially well, and then it did, and then it didn't.

Beating Reykjavík home and away in the Champions League second qualifying round was only to be expected but losing home and away in the next round to Legia Warsaw was most definitely not. A 4-0 defeat in Poland and 2-0 in Scotland was a shocking encounter with reality for Deila akin to Strachan's debut humiliation at the hands of Artmedia in Bratislava.

Suddenly, it was obvious to all and sundry that Deila's journey from Norwegian obscurity to Paradise was a step too far for an innocent abroad. His tactics were naive and overly aggressive, leaving gaping holes at the back. Suddenly, too, the parsimony of Lennon's defence, conceding only 25 goals in 38 league games in the preceding season, was appreciated as it never was at the time. It was almost embarrassing when UEFA altered the result of the second leg in Glasgow from a 2-0 defeat to a 3-0 win when it was discovered the Poles had used an ineligible player for the concluding five minutes of the tie. Still, it was considered an omen for

Deila's new regime. Someone, probably sitting in a swanky West End bar, remembered what Napoleon had once said: 'I'd rather have a general who was lucky than one who was good.'

The 2014/15 Premiership campaign opened with a 3-0 win at St Johnstone and a 6-1 demolition of Dundee United at Parkhead. Suddenly the team were world-beaters once more and Deila was the man. Until a 1-0 defeat in the Highlands at Inverness Caley Thistle. The league game fell, unhelpfully, in between Champions League qualifying ties with Maribor. A 1-1 draw in the first leg in Slovenia had been a satisfactory result and Deila decided to prioritise the return leg in Paradise over the run-of-the-mill league game. Ten changes were made from the side that played in Europe. Old-timers wondered what Jock Stein and Sean Fallon would have made of the need to rest players at all, never mind this early in the season, but some younger fans retorted that this was the 21st century and that, if a modern manager is appointed, modern selection tactics are to be expected and accepted.

In the match against Inverness in 2014, it was Charlie Mulgrew who drew the shortest of straws in the team selection game and played against Caley Thistle. The loss would not matter in the grand scheme of things if Maribor were defeated in Paradise.

But they were not. A combination of feckless finishing and reckless defending led to a 1-0 defeat and an exit from the money pot of the group stages of the Champions League.

Even younger voices were now raised against the new manager. Some pointed out inconsistencies. On signing Jason Denayer on loan from Manchester City, Deila called him a '£10m player', yet failed to pick him in Celtic's biggest game of the season so far against the Slovenian champions. He said Leigh Griffiths was the best goalscorer he had ever seen, yet there was no place up front for the former Hibernian man. Anthony Stokes, who had never scored a European goal in three years played in his stead.

Many players looked tired and lethargic after their rest at the weekend. Only the young Callum McGregor, who had scored in Slovenia, and who was man of the match in the return leg, shone brightly, looking every inch a star of the future.

It was the present, though, that troubled Celtic supporters. The club's exit from the top European competition was followed by a dismal draw at Dundee. James McPake, who became manager at Dens Park five years later, scored for the Dee from a set piece in the first minute. Griffiths equalised ten minutes into the second half to claim an undeserved point for the Hoops. What was almost more concerning than the disappointing result, though, was the possession statistics. For a manager who claimed he wished to play from the strength and reassurance of control of the ball, 37 per cent possession was surely unacceptable. Without his new signing from Hearts, Craig Gordon, in goal, defeat would have been inevitable.

The club seemed mired in malaise. Morale among supporters was mirrored in alarming attendance figures. Even on Flag Day, with Fergus McCann as guest of honour and a championship to be celebrated, a mere 44,000 witnessed the opening home game of the season against Dundee United. Four weeks later, 43,600 attended the visit of Aberdeen, and these were the days when gate figures were not amended for tax purposes. Neither was there unity in the dressing room. Virgil van Dijk wanted away to England and was not picked for the away match at Dens Park. It was too early to sack Deila but, in the media, two legendary strikers from the golden O'Neill and Strachan eras, Chris Sutton and John Hartson, were carping from the sidelines.

The first of the turning points, the first balm and a quantum of solace for the beleaguered new manager, arrived on 13 September with that relatively poorly attended game against Aberdeen. In the absence of Rangers, the Dons were the team most likely to challenge Celtic. In the previous season Aberdeen had finished third, two points adrift of Motherwell in second place. There was good news prior to kick-off with Scott Brown returning to the starting XI after a lay-off due to a hamstring injury sustained in July in a friendly against Rapid Vienna.

Brown was signed in 2007 by Strachan, who saw, perhaps, in the feisty midfielder dominating games for Hibernian, images of himself at a younger age. Brown quickly became a commanding presence at Celtic Park, both in the dressing room and on the field of play. When he reinvented himself in the following season as a defensive midfielder, he became indispensable. He had been told by Rangers when he was training with Falkirk as a boy that his lack of height would prevent him from making the grade. John Park, however, saw no problems with Brown's size and took him to Hibernian at the age of 13. Brown signed a professional contract with the Hibees in 2002 and played 135 games for the Edinburgh club. Six months after Park joined Celtic in January 2007, Brown followed suit by signing for £4.4m, a record fee between two Scottish clubs.

On Brown's return against Aberdeen, he played well in the first half before tiring and being replaced by Deila's latest signing, John Guidetti, on the hour, by which time Celtic were 2-1 to the good with goals by Denayer after seven minutes and by Commons just after half-time.

The final half hour was an ordeal for both players and fans. All the early season traumas and torments returned to haunt Celtic's fragile confidence. The eventual 2-1 victory, a first win in five, though, bought the embattled manager some more precious time.

Or maybe it was the distraction of accusations of racial abuse made by Aberdeen's Shay Logan against Aleksandar Tonev, making his debut after signing on loan from Aston Villa, which sidetracked the Celtic board from consideration of Deila's position. Tonev received a seven-match ban from the footballing authorities, Celtic appealed, and the sentence was confirmed for 'use of abusive language of a racist nature'. The standards of proof of such a serious allegation were far from those necessary in a court of law but Celtic eventually conceded in December 2014 they would proceed no further in support of their Bulgarian loanee.

For Deila and his team, though, there was still further to sink. The lowest point of the Norwegian's time at Celtic arrived with October and a home game against Hamilton Academical. Further financial warnings concerning the consequences of Deila's inauspicious start to his career – Celtic were now fourth in the Premiership – were to be laid bare for all to see with another home gate just edging above the 40,000 mark. Peter Lawwell, an accountant by trade, would have been doing the sums, pondering the consequences of appointing a manager apparently out of his depth. The attendance was one fewer than it might have been as the *Daily Record* journalist Keith Jackson was banned after an article had alleged the players were at war with Deila over questions of their fitness and diet.

A goal from midfielder Ali Crawford after 49 minutes sealed Hamilton's first win at Celtic Park since 1938. In a criminal act of defensive negligence, Stephen Hendrie was allowed to run 60 yards with the ball and cross unchallenged for Crawford to drive into the back of the net. Celtic endured a mere 40 per cent possession and slipped to sixth in the league, while Hamilton went top. At full time, those remaining inside Paradise delivered a chorus of boos sufficiently loud to be heard in the boardroom where talk about Deila must have been louder than the polite chink of china teacups. 'It's very disappointing,' Deila said. 'That's not what we want.'

The new manager had delivered seven wins from 17 games and two of those victories were against no-hopers from Iceland in the shape of Champions League qualifiers against Reykjavík.

Still, the board stuck with their man. After the initial gamble of choosing someone with no experience of Scottish football or the top levels in Europe, Desmond and Lawwell rolled the dice once more; they staked their money on the Norwegian turning things around, claiming his day in the sun.

That day arrived on Sunday, 9 November, not that it was a particularly sunny day, the morning in Glasgow a nondescript one of clouds entrenched in the sky. It was also Remembrance Day. In Aberdeen, though, the skies were already clearing, with a full winter's sun ready for the 12.30pm kick-off in the crucial match against title rivals Celtic.

There was tension inside and outside Pittodrie. The Tonev case was still ongoing. The Celtic appeal had been heard and rejected on the Wednesday before the match. The fall-out from the Scottish Independence referendum held in September was still poisonous and divisive. All eight parliamentary constituencies in Glasgow had voted for independence with 53.5 per cent of the vote, whereas in Aberdeenshire the Yes Scotland vote was a derisory 39.6 per cent. Inside the ground, Celtic fans chanted, 'You're just a bunch of Tory shitbags.' The Aberdeen support for the Better Together campaign also provided an additional meaning for the Celtic fans' nickname for the Dons as the Sheep. There was one delicious moment when the visiting fans turned from Aberdonian politics to their opponents' sexual mores. Replacing the commonplace Tory shitbags and scumbags, the cry now was, 'You're just a bunch of sheep shaggers.' One lone voice rang out in reply. 'Don't knock it, Celtic, until you've tried it.'

Humour, though, was in short supply.

Inside the ground, there was the usual militaristic display on view on Poppy Day. Aberdeen shirts exhibited the poppy but Celtic's did not. Many Celtic supporters waited until after the commemorative silence they believed gave succour and support to English militarism, to English imperialism, past English occupations of Ireland, past English genocides, before deigning to enter the stadium. Inside, the silence was not observed in any case, with chanting from both ends of the ground throughout the allotted minutes. Rather than wear poppies that had come to symbolise something so much narrower than sympathy for the slain of all nations in all wars, Celtic gave significant donations to the original cause of remembrance and relief of suffering of former soldiers and their families.

The match itself began with Aberdeen dominant and Celtic sleepwalking on the edge of disaster. Just before the half hour mark, Adam Rooney, the striker signed in January 2014 from Oldham Athletic, scored from close range after unconvincing goalkeeping from Celtic's reserve goalkeeper, Łukasz Załuska. With Craig Gordon absent having sustained a neck injury, it seemed that even good fortune was deserting Deila. Poor keeping at the other end, however, gave Celtic an undeserved equaliser through Stefan Johansen on 38 minutes. The second half meandered, sometimes as slow as water finding its way around an oxbow lake. Celtic earned the majority of the possession but with little ambition and with even less end product.

Until the 81st minute when Scott Brown was sent off for a second bookable offence. And until the 90th minute, when a last-gasp corner was threaded into the Aberdeen penalty area by Johansen, and Virgil van Dijk was on hand with the deftest of touches to score a winning goal that sent Celtic to the top of the Premiership for the first time in the season. The result was pivotal for Deila's survival.

Events after the final whistle were perhaps more lively than the preceding events on the field of play. Shay Logan, reviled by the Celtic support for his accusations of racism against Tonev, and jeered throughout the second half when his play was adjacent to the away section of Pittodrie, was sent off for comments made to the referee at the conclusion of the game.

Deila, meanwhile, was Prometheus unbound, Clark Kent as Superman, his mouth agape, his arms raised, his fists clenched and pumping, running towards the Celtic support. 'It was orgasmic,' he said later, but no clothes were removed. The Ronny Roar was born and, with it, an emotional bond with a significant element in the Celtic support.

The Ronny Revolution was at last on track. Top of the league made all the previous travails seem somehow less important. Deila worked hard, with the players, with the press who sometimes bit the hand that fed them, and with the fans. In the latter times of 2014, Deila engaged with supporters' groups in a series of town hall meetings at which the Celtic manager appeared engaging, open and convincing.

More victories followed: 2-1 at home to Dundee, 4-0 at Hearts, 1-0 against Partick Thistle, 1-0 again at Motherwell, 4-1 against St Mirren, so much so that the 2-1 defeat at Dundee United and the 0-0 home draw with Ross County to bring the year to a close hardly seemed to matter.

The battle with the players over fitness and diet seemed to have been won. Even Leigh Griffiths repaid Deila's faith, in spite of off-field shenanigans, by his dedication to a proper regime of conditioning, for which much credit must go to the assistant manager, John Collins, who was equally committed to the primacy of players' fitness.

In 2015 Celtic pulled away from their championship rivals, finishing 17 points clear of Aberdeen and 27 ahead of Inverness, a triumph set up with a 5-0 win against Dundee on a Friday night in early May, and confirmed on the following day when Aberdeen failed to defeat Dundee United at Tannadice.

The League Cup, too, was sealed with a 2-0 victory over Dundee United and, in an earlier round, there was a sweet but routine win over Rangers newco by a similar score, the first match against this team in Celtic's history.

The sole disappointment was the failure to land a treble after a 3-2 extra-time defeat in the cup to Caley Thistle.

The second half of the 2014/15 season provided fans with the blessings of both style and substance, epitomised by the goals against Dundee, shared between attack and defence, between Griffiths, Brown, Commons, Forrest and Bitton. It was four-in-a-row and Deila was not only Ronny Resilient but also now Ronny Rampant.

Reminiscing about the dog days of the autumn of 2014, Deila confessed in an interview in Norway that his early days in Paradise had been akin to rowing a dinghy single-handed across the Atlantic Ocean. 'We're in a big ship now,' he said at the end of the season.

* * *

5. HOLLOW MEN, STUFFED MEN
AND EXIT DEILA
2015/16

It should have been so good. It was all set up. The ending of the previous season had been so positive.

Perhaps the problem, though, was that only one trophy was won in 2015/16, the league championship, which – in the ongoing absence of Rangers – was assumed by all to be a given.

Five-in-a-row was the bread and butter of the campaign but Celtic supporters wanted jam too. Maybe some strawberry jam and raspberry jam in terms of a Scottish Cup which the club had not won since 2013 and, in fact, had won only three times in the last ten years, and a League Cup victory to repeat Deila's trick from the previous season.

What the men from Paradise really craved, though, was a European feast of Champions League football.

Since 1967, Celtic would be judged by their status and stature within European football, and this remained true in 2015/16, even though the terms of engagement had changed utterly with the Premier League in England hoovering up a lion's share of the mega bucks on offer in the UK from Sky and other satellite broadcasting providers.

The fact that Deila's team had recovered in 2014 from the disaster of Maribor to qualify for the knockout stages of the Europa League in 2015 had only raised the bar of expected success for the forthcoming campaign.

Raised expectations – when objective conditions stay the same or even improve but not as much as the expectations – have seen revolutions occur in England in 1649, in France in 1789, and in Russia in 1917. Kings and emperors, never mind football managers, have lost their heads.

Deila should have been warned.

* * *

The push for qualification for the lucrative group stage of the Champions League began simply enough.

Stjarnan from Iceland and Qarabag from Azerbaijan were dismissed in four displays of competence with relatively few alarms. It looked as if Deila had learned from the previous campaign, had become a tad more pragmatic, and had tightened the defence. The goalless draw in eastern Europe was a masterclass in dealing with a difficult pitch combined with excessive heat and humidity. It was *realpolitik* rather than Ronny razzamatazz and none the worse for that. The play-off round opponents were Malmö from Sweden, a club Deila had turned down on his way to Celtic, and in poor form in their domestic league. Presumptions of progress proliferated.

Reassurances, too, were available from the opening salvo of the Premiership campaign. Ross County were the visitors on Flag Day. There were reminders, too, of 1967 as John Clark was the honoured guest, rescued from his day job as kit man, now tasked to hoist the championship pennant. Clark was the quiet man but certainly not the sleeping partner in that Lisbon Lions defence. Everything in the air belonged to Billy McNeill, everything on the ground was Clark's. In that 1967 side, Clark and Gemmell were the sole ever-presents throughout the season.

In a sport now awash with money – even in Scotland, though to a lesser extent than England – Clark's dignified presence at Flag Day was a reminder of harder times. He was born in 1941 in Chapelhall, a working-class community a baker's dozen miles east of Glasgow, a mining village with a brickworks and 19th-century iron blast furnaces. His father died in a railway accident when the boy was only ten. At 15, Clark worked as a miner and played as a half-back for Larkhall Thistle until signing for Celtic at 17. Like so many other footballers, his career was transformed by the imaginative mind of Jock Stein who shifted his protege from midfield to defence.

Those in the crowd for the season opener who were old enough to remember compared the day's centre-backs with Clark and McNeill. Against Ross County, Celtic's defensive pairing was Virgil van Dijk – soon to be heading for Southampton – and Dedryck Boyata, signed in June 2015 from Manchester City.

With the score a precarious 1-0 to the hosts, Boyata set the tone of much of the match with a misplaced pass latched on to by the Dingwall side's Jackson Irvine. Craig Gordon raced from his line and fouled the Aussie midfielder just outside the penalty box. A red card, had it been shown by referee Willie Collum, might have changed the result. Old-timers struggled to recall ever seeing Clark give the ball away in such careless fashion.

Still, first-half goals by Griffiths and Johansen were sufficient for the day. There was, too, a pleasing first competitive start at Paradise for Kieran Tierney who would be named both Players' and Writers' Young

Player of the Year at the season's close. He had been at the club since the age of seven and, when not playing, was to be found among the most vocal supporters at Celtic Park.

Even Deila's harshest critics could not complain of his record of encouragement of young players. Tierney, James Forrest, Tom Rogic, Callum McGregor and Leigh Griffiths were all young men encouraged and improved by Deila. Links between the academy and first team were strengthened under the Norwegian.

By the time of the Champions League showdown with Malmö, Celtic had won three league games, dropping points only through a 2-2 draw at Kilmarnock.

No alarm bells were ringing. The big ship was on course for destination treble stopping to refuel only in the Champions League port of financial stability.

Neither were there sirens or distress signals in much evidence after the home leg against Malmö. True, the victory was a narrow one, 3-2, and true, the visitors had filched two away goals, annoyingly and embarrassingly scored by a Celtic reject, Jo Inge Berget, who claimed sweet revenge on the manager who had never given him a proper chance. The Swedes, though, had been poor, and Celtic had been cruising comfortably until Berget's second goal in the last minute.

It was the club's first loss in a competitive match against Swedish opposition.

Celtic's Champions League world ended not with a bang but a whimper.

One year ago, it was Maribor, now it was Malmo.

It was tempting to view the club's hierarchy of Desmond, Lawwell, and chairman, Ian Bankier, as TS Eliot's hollow men, and the coaches, Deila, Collins and Kennedy, as men whose commands were meaningless whispers.

That was 25 August 2015. By 12 September, all early-season form forgotten, Celtic paid a visit to title rivals Aberdeen. Their performance was inept and inoffensive – in the latter word's literal meaning. The centre of defence in the charge of Boyata and a Manchester United loanee, Tyler Blackett, was a stumbling shambles. The 2-1 defeat might have been worse, but Aberdeen overtook Celtic at the top of the table, leading by two points and with a game in hand.

There was some consolation off the field of play, at least for those with compassionate political leanings, which is almost all Celtic fans. Hundreds of thousands of Syrian refugees were fleeing war, persecution and starvation and the club sent generous contributions raised through the Jock Stein 30th anniversary remembrance match played between Dunfermline and Hoops legends in June 2015 to refugee charities. The Green Brigade, too, was prominent through both its fund-raising activities and its reminders of the political connections and causes relating to tragedies such as the unfolding Syrian disaster. A banner in the Celtic section at Pittodrie read, 'No one is illegal. Created by immigrants – Celtic FC.'

An opportunity for revenge against Aberdeen presented itself at Celtic Park on the last day of October but the fixture lacked some of its expected cutting edge as the Dons, since that earlier victory, had lost twice in the Highlands – to Caley Thistle and to Ross County – and had surrendered both their place at the top of the Premiership to Celtic and their status as prime challengers to Hearts. Celtic won comfortably with a Griffiths double and a third goal from Forrest.

The goals scored by Griffiths were his 15th and 16th of a prolific season. He told *Celtic View* that his aim was to break his previous best total – 28 – scored for Hibernian in 2012/13. He would go on to score 40 for Deila's Celtic in 2015/16, a figure not attained by any Hoops striker since Henrik Larsson's 41 in season 2003/04 under O'Neill.

The attendance at Parkhead was a miserly 48,000 and a reminder that the loyalty of fans could not be taken for granted. The gate of 52,412 against Malmö on 19 August 2015 was to remain the largest for the remainder of the season. A League Cup tie in September attracted a mere 13,591 people, less of a crowd and more of a stingy huddle.

Meanwhile, the Europa League campaign was increasingly humiliating for Celtic, a club once kings of the continent. As recently as 2012, too, the Bhoys had beaten Barcelona and finished only three points behind the Catalan giants, four-time winners of the premier footballing tournament in Europe, in the group stage of the Champions League.

Before the end of November, Celtic exited European football altogether after a home defeat to Ajax in their penultimate group match. The Bhoys finished bottom of a group containing no other giants of European football and won by Molde of Norway. It was a steep and dizzying fall from grace.

Noises off, once more, provided both distraction and compensation, not that Celtic's hollow men should have permitted themselves a moment's amusement. In December 2015, a court battle between Dave King, the newco Rangers chairman, and Mike Ashley of Sports Direct began in London. Ashley claimed King had breached a confidentiality clause when revealing in July 2015 discussions between Rangers and Sports Direct over commercial contracts relating to merchandising. Eventually, Ashley's attempts to land King with a jail sentence were rebuffed by a high court judge who ruled Ashley's 'muscular, intimidatory tactics' were deplorable. Ashley had bought an 8.92 per cent share of the Rangers newco in October 2014 and retained a vice-like grip on the club through a merchandising deal with Sports Direct, even attempting at one point to obtain a £10m loan using Ibrox Park as security. Just as Ashley was reviled at Newcastle, so he was at the newco. It was amusing, though, for Celtic fans to watch the courtroom drama proceed with one pantomime villain accusing another of villainy. Ashley sold his shares in 2017 but in January 2022 was still battling, and defeating, Rangers in court, as the newco attempted to reclaim £2.8m plus interest and expenses from Sports Direct which the football club believed it was owed from sales of replica shirts.

In purely footballing terms, however, Rangers had won their first 11 Championship matches in 2015/16. A renewed rivalry seemed inevitable in the following season and sharpened desires among those of a Celtic persuasion to see the emergence of a Deila team fit for the challenge.

A 1-1 draw at Tynecastle against Hearts in the final match of 2015 left Celtic only one point clear of Aberdeen at the top of the table. There was work to do.

In the new year there was a freewheeling, cavalier display, an 8-1 win over Hamilton Academical, in which Griffiths scored a hat-trick, and which pushed Celtic six points clear in the chase for five-in-a-row.

Two games later, after another clear-cut home win, 3-1 against St Johnstone, came an eagerly anticipated League Cup quarter-final at Ross County on the last day of January. The game, however, was a disaster from the moment Efe Ambrose, a Nigerian international signed by Neil Lennon from Ashdod in Israel in the summer of 2012, was sent off, leaving his team-mates to struggle for almost 80 minutes with ten men. Griffiths, too, missed a penalty. All this after Gary Mackay-

Steven had given Celtic a first-minute lead and after an opening quarter of an hour when the Bhoys should have made the game safe and sound and been looking forward to a semi-final against Hibernian or St Johnstone. The treble dream was dead once more and Deila looked a dead man walking.

In the Premiership, on 3 February, Celtic lost again to Aberdeen, 2-1, and the men from the Better Together Tory heartlands were once more breathing down the champions' necks. It was Deila's 100th game in charge. Rumours of Ryan Giggs, assistant to Louis van Gaal at Manchester United, pitching up swirled in the winter heartland winds.

Aberdeen faltered, losing 3-1 at Inverness in February and 2-1 at Motherwell in the following month and, by the close of mad March they were nine points in arrears of Celtic. Deila appeared a man reprieved once more.

Europe had been a disillusionment, a disaster, and the League Cup a mischance, a misadventure, perhaps down to a moment of stupidity by Ambrose, but a league and Scottish Cup double was still a possibility that might just, at a stretch, be construed as an improvement on the previous season's league and League Cup double.

In the semi-final at Hampden, on 17 April, Celtic faced a Rangers side recently confirmed as promoted to the Premiership.

The score after 90 minutes was 1-1, Erik Sviatchenko equalising early in the second half after Kenny Miller's opener on a quarter of an hour. There was a worrying lack of intensity to Celtic's play, as if the match might be won with a minimum of fuss, a bargain basement level of effort. In extra time, Barrie McKay returned Rangers to the lead before Tom Rogic levelled the scores in the second period. The penalty shoot-out ended when the Australian Rogic ballooned the ball high and wide.

Either the Celtic players were presumptuous of victory and found it impossible to raise their game when required or they were unfit and, either way, it was a damning indictment of their manager. Physical preparation had been Deila's supposed unique selling point. Celtic had just 37 per cent possession. Tactics seemed to revolve around long balls aimed at Griffiths, a striker only 5ft 9in tall.

Dermot Desmond had travelled from Ireland to watch the game. Days later, Deila announced he would be stepping down from the manager's position at the end of the season.

The league championship was effectively wrapped up with an away win at Hearts on 30 April but mathematical certainty had to wait until 8 May when Celtic entertained Aberdeen in Paradise. The stadium, a monument to Fergus McCann's perspicacity and determination, was bathed in warm sunshine and optimism. Celtic cruised into a 3-0 lead courtesy of a double from Patrick Roberts, loaned from Manchester City in the depths of the midwinter transfer window, and a single from Mikael Lustig.

It was somehow emblematic of Deila's era at Celtic that his time should descend from the sublime to the ridiculous, from the straightforward to the complicated, in the space of one match. It finished 3-2 but Aberdeen probably deserved a draw. By the end of the 90 minutes, Celtic looked drained and exhausted and hanging on like a man on death row waiting for a stay of execution.

It was, though, five-in-a-row. Griffiths won the Professional Footballers' Association Scottish Player of the Year award and Tierney won the young player equivalent.

The subsequent game was at home to Ross County, a 1-1 draw with no meaning to the result. What did matter, however, was the clarity of a significant minority of supporters that Deila was not solely to blame for another Jekyll and Hyde season. In the symbolic 67th minute, a walk-out was staged in protest against the board of directors. A banner, too, was prominently displayed, reading, 'Lawell and Desmond legacy. Empty jerseys, empty hearts, empty dreams, empty stands.'

Still, it was good to end the season on a high with a trophy presentation and, in Deila's final game in charge, to beat Motherwell 7-0 with goals spread between seven different players – Tierney, Rogic, Lustig, Stuart Armstrong, signed in February 2015 from Dundee United, Roberts, Ryan Christie, signed in September 2015 from Inverness, and Jack Aitchison, Celtic's youngest-ever debutant at 16 years and 71 days with his first touch of the ball – a feat not seen since August 1938 when Kilmarnock were beaten 9-1 and the scorers were Jimmy Delaney (two), Willie Lyon, Frank Murphy, Chic Geatons, John Divers Sr (two), Malcolm MacDonald and John Crum.

It was pleasing, too, although only with the benefit of hindsight, to be there at the beginning of something really special. The victory over the men from Fir Park was the first of a run of 69 unbeaten domestic games, a UK record, which eclipsed the previous best sequence held by Willie Maley's Celtic side of 1915 to 1917. Deila will take some pleasure and comfort from his small part in a record unlikely to be beaten any time soon.

There was, in addition, a touching reminder of Celtic's foundational charitable purposes when Syrian refugees were the mascots against Motherwell.

Deila, at the end of the match, became part of the club's history. Like all victims of circumstance, the Norwegian was a casualty of expectations. It was not his fault that sometimes those presumptions were unrealistic. To be perfectly brutal, however, while conquering Europe in imitation of the Lisbon Lions was fanciful in the extreme, expectations of domestic trebles were not. Not only were newco Rangers inhabiting lower levels of existence but, in Deila's first season at least, neither of the Edinburgh giants, Hibs and Hearts, were in the Premiership.

Deila might be blamed for sequences of poor signings whose names need not be named to protect the guilty parties. Many, though, suspected Lawwell pulled these kinds of strings and that the Norwegian was a puppet on one of them. The chief executive, to be fair, denied that he had any input on signings beyond his remit of 'conducting the financial aspects of transfers'.

The Norwegian deserved undoubted praise, however, for the development of young players at Paradise. Tierney, Forrest, Rogic, McGregor and Griffiths all improved and flourished under Deila's tutelage.

Finally, too, he earned his place among Celtic's immortals by dint of being in the right place at the right time and orchestrating the winning of the fourth and fifth titles in the second of the club's nine-in-a-row sequences. From the outside looking in, and with the benefit of hindsight, it appeared easy to win those titles. Deila, though, will beg to differ, and he deserves, at least, due respect for these achievements.

Winning league championships with Celtic was something, after all, that Jimmy McStay, Liam Brady, Lou Macari, Tommy Burns, Josef Vengloš, John Barnes, Kenny Dalglish and Tony Mowbray all failed to do.

With Deila gone, Neil Lennon, whose time at Bolton Wanderers had ended unhappily in March 2016, said, when questioned about the vacant position, that it would be 'difficult to say no'.

Brendan Rodgers, though, late of Liverpool, described Celtic as 'an incredible club', and won the day.

* * *

6. BUCK RODGERS IN THE 21ST CENTURY AND THE INVINCIBLES
2016/17

Brendan Rodgers's career may be divided into two distinct eras. Prior to February 2019, when he upped sticks unceremoniously to move to manage Leicester City in England, Rodgers was lionised by the Celtic support. He was one of their own, claiming at least to have been a lifelong fan of the East End club. It was clear, though, the Northern Irishman was ambitious, had never stayed too long at any club, appeared always to have one eye on a main chance.

Youth team management at Chelsea under José Mourinho in 2004 became reserve team management in 2006, until Watford called in 2008, and until Reading offered Rodgers an opportunity to return to the club he had played for until knee problems forced him into early retirement at the age of 20. There was sentiment as well as pragmatism and ambition in the move, together with an apparently better chance of promotion to the Premier League. It did not work out and Rodgers was sacked after six months with Reading deep in the relegation mire.

Possibly, some of the manager's sentimentality died with that dismissal. He stayed at Swansea for two highly successful years, gaining promotion to the English top tier and then stabilising the club in mid-table the following season. Liverpool called, and Rodgers was a mere two points adrift of a first league title for a quarter of a century. His appointment at Celtic in May 2016 was a coup for Desmond and Lawwell, but also for the new manager. For Rodgers, there was a familiar blend of romanticism and realism. 'I've just landed my dream job,' he announced, 'with the team I've supported all my life.'

It was a marriage, if not made in heaven, a union at least manufactured in mutual need. Celtic, although champions of Scotland, were in need of root-and-branch reform, reorganisation, and a revitalisation of the fanbase. 'I've come to Celtic to build something special here,' Rodgers claimed. There was, though, an equal necessity for Rodgers to rebuild his career and the powerbrokers at Paradise had provided him with just such an opportunity.

So, perhaps, there should have been less surprise in February 2019 when Rodgers jumped ship to join Leicester even if the English club's pedigree was far less impressive than Celtic's.

In Shakespeare's history play, *Julius Caesar*, the Roman dictator, addressing Mark Antony, said:

> *Let me have men about me that are fat,*
> *Sleek-headed men and such as sleep a-night.*
> *Yon Cassius has a lean and hungry look...*
> *Such men are dangerous...*

In Celtic's history, Willie Maley, Jimmy McGrory and Jock Stein, all were 'fat', in the sense that they were solid, loyal to the last, even though Stein, at least, could never 'sleep a-night'. Rodgers, though, always had a 'lean and hungry look'.

BBC journalist Tom English, commenting upon Rodgers's departure from Glasgow, said, 'Sentiment nearly always gets trumped by ambition in football.'

The Green Brigade were less polite. Their banner, in block capitals, read, 'YOU TRADED IMMORTALITY FOR MEDIOCRITY. NEVER A CELT. ALWAYS A FRAUD.'

Rodgers's betrayal cut deep, his abandonment of his unfinished building project. It defied belief to leave Celtic on the cusp of an unparalleled treble treble. Could it really be true that Rodgers's two and two-thirds seasons in Paradise had always and only been about one man's career? Questions, though, are impossible to answer.

Rodgers remains, to borrow Churchill's words about Russia in 1939, 'a riddle, wrapped in a mystery, inside an enigma'.

It would not be a surprise to see Rodgers soon depart from the King Power Stadium, his allotted span of time now passed, a soul as restless as a hungry ghost awaiting rebirth.

This is not, however, to deny Rodgers his moments of magic, his reinvention of Celtic as an irresistible force in Scotland and as a serious competitor in Europe, his gifts of joyous and joined-up football, his blarney that made us all smile, as long as he was *our* Brendan Rodgers.

His first season at Celtic Park was one to rival the very best of times, perhaps the greatest since 1966/67 but, if not then at least on a par with and probably greater than the seasons of the centenary double, the stopping of the ten, and Neil Lennon's 2012/13 when Celtic won the league and Scottish Cup double and defeated Barcelona in the Champions League.

During those domestically invincible months of 2016/17, Rodgers was Buck Rogers, the swashbuckling adventurer, the comic book hero whose first incarnation was in *Amazing Stories* in 1928, an adventurer into outer space.

It began properly, not with the improbable 1,000-1 defeat to Lincoln Red Imps of Gibraltar in the qualifying round of the Champions League, but with the opening game of the Premiership at Tynecastle on 7 August 2016.

Hearts had finished the preceding season in third place and the Edinburgh club's supporters always provided a hostile and often volatile environment for Irish Catholic visitors. Rodgers could hardly have chosen a more difficult fixture in which to make his bow in Scottish domestic football.

The match began as it intended to continue with fast and furious helter-skelter football, with corners to the Jam Tarts, a missed opportunity by Hearts striker Conor Sammon, and a goal by Celtic. McGregor, playing composed football amid the mayhem, played in Forrest whose left-footed shot found the corner of Jack Hamilton's net.

Hearts equalised after 36 minutes through a penalty awarded by referee John Beaton. Later, the player who won the spot kick, Jamie Walker, was suspended for two matches for simulation. It was not the only mistake Beaton made. Eleven players were yellow-carded during the match although it was a frantic rather than a dirty encounter.

With half an hour to go and a draw looking increasingly likely, Celtic's most recent signing, Scott Sinclair, replaced Stuart Armstrong. He had been Rodgers's most urgent target in the transfer window and arrived and signed from Aston Villa for £3.5m only hours before kick-off. The manager had known Sinclair since their time together at Chelsea. With less than ten minutes to go, the new Bhoy scored the winning goal from a low cross by Griffiths and the celebrations began in the visiting fans' section of Tynecastle. Rodgers, speaking later to *Celtic View*, said the victory provided a 'really special feeling for us all', and was a consequence of 'all the hard work throughout the season so far'. Rodgers had already won his first three points of the season and mastered the art of the cliché required in interviews for the official organ of the club.

The first meeting with Mark Warburton's newco Rangers occurred on 10 September at Parkhead. Celtic were already two points clear of Hearts in second place and with a game in hand. The initial victory over the Jambos had been followed by further league wins, 4-2 at St Johnstone, and 4-1 at home to Aberdeen. The Ibrox club had already dropped four points through two 1-1 draws, at home to Hamilton Academical and away to Kilmarnock.

In the build-up to the match, there had been reminders of the scandal still engulfing newco Rangers concerning oldco's use of employee benefit trusts. In a BBC documentary, *Scotland's Game*, Alex McLeish admitted that without the tax avoidance scheme his club would never have been able to lure top-class players and would never have been able to compete with Celtic. McLeish, who managed Rangers between 2001 and 2006, himself received £1.7m from the Murray Group Remuneration Trust. During his spell at Ibrox, McLeish's side won two league titles, two Scottish Cups and three League Cups, all tainted triumphs. The league championships of 2002/03 and in 2004/05 were won by the slimmest of margins, on goal difference by one goal only, and by one point, respectively. As McLeish confessed, 'If we didn't pay the money on wages Celtic were paying we'd have been behind them.'

Between 2001 and 2010, a total of 72 directors, players and coaching staff received a total of £47m in tax-free income from Murray's trust.

In the Celtic dressing room, before the match, Rodgers spoke of Jock Stein. It was the 31st anniversary of the great man's death, pitchside, on national duty. 'It's all about the guy looking down,' he said, 'the man who set the tone for this club, the template ... make sure we do him proud.'

Rodgers may have been excused, too, of thinking of his own father, who died five years ago to that day.

If anyone in the dressing room needed any further reminders of the Celtic history they represented every time they pulled on a green and white hooped jersey, they had only to study the commemorative badges sewn into their shirts. Around a Celtic cross were the words 'National Famine Memorial Day'.

It may seem harsh to carp about such apparently admirable sentiments but it is important to insist that the Irish Potato Famine or Great Hunger was no such thing. Famine suggests an event beyond human ability to prevent. The Holocaust of 1845–1850 was genocide pure and simple and evil.

As the teams entered the field of battle, Rangers fans were chanting from their sectarian songbook. There is an especially unpleasant incantation aired on that day and still sung today, 'The famine is over, why don't you go home?'

The match itself, as Scott Brown said, was 'men against boys'. An injured Griffiths was replaced by Moussa Dembélé, signed in June 2016 from Fulham, who scored a hat-trick, the first in a league game against Rangers since Stevie Chalmers hit a threesome in 1966. Or, if you prefer, the first hat-trick scored by a Celtic player against newco Rangers. Sinclair and Armstrong scored the remaining goals and a 5-1 stroll was a fair reflection of the play in which Celtic enjoyed 57 per cent possession and 20 shots to Rangers' six. Still, Warburton thought there was 'no gulf' between the teams.

The Ibrox manager was a former City trader turning over somewhere between £1.5bn and £2bn on a daily basis. As an odds man, he might have been expected to know the differential probabilities of victory between one team having nine shots on target and the other just two. Such stats were likely to produce just such a scoreline as the 5-1 at Paradise on that day. The 'gulf' between the two clubs was a mere 39 points at the close of the 2016/17 season.

After the game, it was discovered Rangers fans had trashed toilets inside Paradise to the tune of £40,000 of damage.

The second meeting in the Premiership – Celtic had beaten their city rivals 1-0 in the semi-final of the League Cup – took place, bizarrely, on Hogmanay, although concessions to the celebrations came in the form of a 12.15pm kick-off at Ibrox.

Prior to the game, Celtic already held a 16-point lead at the head of affairs, so pride and bragging rights rather than a league title were the bones of contention. Maybe complacency and condescension, therefore, accounted for a lazy, half-witted performance by Celtic in the first half an hour. The home side took the lead after 12 minutes through Kenny Miller, who thus became, according to the bookmakers, Coral, 'the only man in history to score for all three teams in the Old Firm derby'. The tweet was delicious in its wickedness and many Celtic fans forgave the error referencing the Old Firm when that particular institution had died in 2012 with oldco Rangers.

Celtic fans had already reminded their opposite numbers of this sad fact with a banner that read, 'No history, no money, no trophies.'

Celtic equalised after 33 minutes through Dembélé after Brown had rallied and galvanised his troops, and they gained their 15th straight league victory via a Sinclair winner with 20 minutes to play. Rodgers said he was 'disappointed' his team had not scored more.

One curiosity concerning the game was the insensitive appointment as referee of Steven McLean, whose brother Brian was a former Rangers youth and reserve team player. It was widely believed, too, that the official was an Ibrox season ticket holder. McLean, in addition, had been the subject of fury among Celtic fans for his refusal to award Ronny Deila's team a penalty for blatant handball during the first half of a Scottish Cup semi-final against Inverness in April 2015. A second goal for Celtic at that stage would have killed the tie stone dead and, instead, Caley Thistle went on to win 3-2 in extra time, and rob the Norwegian manager of a treble triumph in his first season at the club. That season, Celtic lost five times in domestic competitions and McLean refereed on three of those occasions. Sometimes, in dealings with the Scottish Football Association and the Scottish Premier Football League, Celtic must have felt like Alice at the Mad Hatter's tea party when she was moved to say 'curiouser and curiouser'. But, even with McLean as referee, Rangers still could not win the game.

In the following month, Warburton was dismissed. Rumours abounded that the Rangers manager was canoodling with Nottingham Forest of the English Championship. In the event, he was not offered the post he had apparently coveted and, instead, he was dismissed by Rangers, although the Ibrox club claimed it had accepted the resignations of the manager together with his assistant, David Weir, and the head of recruitment, Frank McParland.

In February, after a 5-2 away win against St Johnstone, and another Dembélé hat-trick, Celtic were 27 points clear at the top of the league. Winter had hardly started and the league title was already impossible to lose.

On 29 April, Rodgers got his wish for more goals in another Glasgow chicken shoot when a second 5-1 demolition derby occurred, this time at Ibrox. No victory of similar substance on enemy territory had occurred since the 19th century.

Five different players scored the goals: Sinclair, from the penalty spot, Griffiths, McGregor, Boyata and Lustig.

Pedro Caixinha, a left-field appointment of a man last seen as manager of Al-Gharafa in Qatar, was in charge of newco Rangers in good time to oversee the home humiliation at Celtic's hands.

Six-in-a-row was accomplished on Sunday, 2 April in a return to Tynecastle. The opening match of the season had been a tight 2-1 affair, but this was different class.

Griffiths, with a bad back, and Dembélé, with a hamstring problem, were unavailable, so Celtic had no recognised principal striker on the field. There was, though, no problem, and no shortage of goals.

Sinclair scored a hat-trick, with supporting goals from Roberts and Armstrong. There was no response from Hearts, who finished a disappointing season in fifth place. Scott Brown became the first player in Celtic history to lift the league championship trophy under the auspices of four different managers.

Celtic's captain and talisman was perhaps the greatest beneficiary of Rodgers's man-management skills. Many had written off Brown's future at the beginning of the season. He was widely regarded under the latter days of Deila as one for the scrap heap but was revitalised under the Northern Irishman. Rodgers sought out Brown on his arrival, put a reassuring arm around the midfielder, assured him of his good opinion, and promised him he was relying upon his leadership of the club and of the players under his charge on the field of play. Brown responded with a renewed commitment and renewed dominance of midfield battles in 54 appearances throughout the season.

Brown and his team-mates that day – Craig Gordon, Mikael Lustig, Jozo Šimunović, Dedryck Boyata, Kieran Tierney, Stuart Armstrong, Callum McGregor, Scott Sinclair, Patrick Roberts and James Forrest, with Cristian Gamboa, Kolo Touré and Gary Mackay-Steven coming on as substitutes – were history makers. Only one other European team – Paris Saint-Germain – had won a 38-game league after a mere 30 matches. It was, too, just the third time Celtic had won six titles in a row. They were reaping the rewards of their appointment of an elite coach.

By the end of the league campaign, Celtic had won more games, 34, and gained more points, 106, than any team in Scottish history, the previous record of 103 points held by Martin O'Neill's side of 2001/02. The number of points was also a European record, with only Juventus, Barcelona and Real Madrid winning more than a century in a major footballing nation's league competition. Rodgers's team, too, had repeated the feat of Maley's invincible predecessors of 1898, although the 19th-century side had only to negotiate 18 rather than 38 matches. Only Preston North End, in the inaugural season of the English Football League in 1888/89, and, in the modern era, Arsenal in 2003/04 and Juventus in 2011/12, had remained unbeaten in league championship campaigns.

The fighting spirit engendered by the manager and his captain was evident in the fact that Celtic had fallen behind on four occasions during the 2016/17 season and had won each time.

There was, though, one more record to fall. There was a Scottish Cup Final against Aberdeen to win to conclude an 'InVIncible' domestic campaign.

The afternoon of 27 May was dark and damp but still history beckoned. Aberdeen, under the astute management of Derek McInnes, had finished as runners-up in the league and had lost to Celtic in that season's League Cup Final and were clearly the second-best team in Scotland.

The Dons dominated the first half and took the lead after nine minutes when Jonny Hayes half-volleyed a deep cross from Niall McGinn high into the Celtic net. The shot was as unstoppable as Aberdeen appeared to be in the opening exchanges. Celtic were out of sorts in a one degree under sort of way. Still, though, against the run of play, Rodgers's men equalised two minutes later through Armstrong whose shot from outside the box zipped and fizzed past Joe Lewis in the Aberdeen goal. It was the former Dundee United man's 17th goal of a stellar season. Throughout the final Armstrong drove forwards and deep into the Dons' defence, encouraging his colleagues to follow suit. Just after the 25-minute mark, however, Jayden Stockley's assault on Kieran Tierney left the young Celtic defender with a fractured cheekbone, weakening the Bhoys on their left flank.

Earlier murk and mizzle turned to rain. Turbulence on the pitch was matched in the skies above Hampden Park. Gradually, however, the Aberdeen storm was subdued and, in the second half, Celtic looked the team more likely to snatch a winning goal. Fans, though, were biting nails to the quick. One breakaway goal might still ruin a season's work. There was, too, the possibility of another refereeing mistake by Bobby Madden, a man with an unenviable track record of errors. The official had already failed to send off Stockley for eliminating Tierney from the contest.

With every minute that brought the game nearer to its close, jeopardy increased, extra time loomed larger. Two minutes into added time, however, Tom Rogic, who had replaced the wounded Tierney, began a dizzying solo run, rounded an Aberdeen defender, and persuaded the ball across the goal line and into the net from the most impossible of angles. The Australian midfielder was the hero of the moment. Understated, he said, 'I think the way it ended made it a little bit more sweet.'

If Rogic was the hero of injury time, Tierney was the hero of singing-and-dancing-in-the-rain time, as he returned from hospital in time to pick up his winners' medal.

In truth, though, all of Brendan's men were heroes and, not just on the day, but throughout the InVIncible, VI-in-a-row season.

Rodgers, too, was the man of the moment. 'I was born into Celtic,' he said, and he may be excused the hyperbole and the hostage to fortune as he had earned his moment of delirious celebration.

If it was impossible to replicate the triumphs of the Lisbon Lions, whose 50th anniversary had been celebrated throughout the week prior to the cup final, these Celtic immortals had given the Bhoys of 1967 a run for their money.

* * *

7. RODGERS'S RECORD BREAKERS
2017/18

In some ways, Rodgers found himself in a comparable situation to that of Jock Stein at the beginning of the 1967/68 season.

It was a case of where do you go from here? Nothing could top winning five major competitions including the European Cup. The answer in Stein's case was downhill, inevitably, winning only three trophies in the following season, with first-round exits in both the Scottish Cup and European Cup.

With Rodgers, it seemed impossible to replicate an invincible domestic campaign, never mind improve upon it. Of course, the Northern Irishman had not won the European Cup or its reincarnation as the Champions League, but his team had restored some Celtic pride with two draws against reigning English champions Manchester City, and a battling performance for a further draw in Mönchengladbach.

Domestic trebles had only come around three times previously in the 70 years since the inauguration of the Scottish League Cup: twice under Stein and once under O'Neill.

Rodgers and his 2017/18 team, however, managed the impossible and somehow trumped the untrumpable by extending their unbeaten domestic run deep into the new season.

When Celtic defeated Hamilton Academical 3-1 on 13 December, with goals from Olivier Ntcham, Forrest and Sinclair, 69 games in the Premiership, in the Scottish Cup and League Cup, had been played since a 2-1 defeat at the hands of St Johnstone in Perth on 11 May 2016 in the dying days of Deila.

The previous British record of 62 unbeaten domestic games had been surpassed on 4 November in a 4-0 revenge romp over the Saints at McDiarmid Park, after which Rodgers confessed his motto had 'always been about to win the next game', which was at Victoria Park in Dingwall, and was duly won 1-0.

Sometimes, Rodgers's post-match comments belied his keen footballing intelligence and, so it was, after a devastating 4-0 defeat at Tynecastle one week prior to Christmas Day, he admitted, 'It was always going to happen,' adding, 'It is never nice when it does.' He was spot on, however, when he said, 'The players will go down in history,' and continued later, 'I don't think it will be done again, certainly in our lifetimes, it won't be done.' The run spanned 585 days during which the world had moved on and changed beyond recognition. In the UK, the Brexit referendum result had pitched prime minister David Cameron into the political wilderness and his job had been taken by Theresa May; in the US, Barack Obama was president in May 2016 but, by November 2017, the man at the White House was Donald Trump.

The defeat by Hearts that ended the run was comprehensive and brutal. In truth, Celtic had not been playing as well as the previous season for some time. Outside of the domestic game there had been the humbling 7-1 annihilation in the Champions League in Paris in November and an earlier defeat by three clear goals in Munich. There had, too, been some narrow squeaks, none more so than at Motherwell on 29 November when an 88th-minute penalty tucked away by Sinclair saved the day. After the record ended, Celtic were only two points clear of Aberdeen at the top of the table. The previous season, at the same stage, the Parkhead club were an almost unassailable 11 points clear at the summit.

For some older fans of a romantic and nostalgic bent, whose grandfathers fought in World War One and who watched Willie Maley's Celtic when on leave from the mud and blood of the trenches, it was perhaps consoling that one of the immortal Maley's records remained intact.

In terms of league championship games only, Rodgers's team had thrived and survived for 56 matches, the record of 69 swollen by 13 domestic cup matches. Maley's men held firm for 62 league games from 1915 to 1917. Rodgers, too, might have smiled if he had studied the world records of unbeaten league games, a list headed by Steaua Bucharest, European Cup winners in 1986, who survived 104 games unbeaten between 1986 and 1989. Amusement might have been prompted, however, by the team in second place in the list, Lincoln Red Imps of Gibraltar, who stayed unbeaten for 88 between 2009 and 2014. Clearly, these European minnows were not even at the peak of their powers when they defeated Rodgers's Celtic in the manager's first game in charge. For the record, in this numbers game, Maley's Celtic are in fourth place behind Sheriff Tiraspol of Moldova.

The first match after the defeat at Hearts saw Celtic beat Glasgow rivals Partick Thistle 2-0 at home, and order appeared to have been restored.

However, close challengers Aberdeen were the visitors to Celtic Park just two days before Christmas, and were expected to provide a much sterner test than the Jags. Hearts had shown one way of ruffling Celtic feathers with their unrelenting physicality in the 4-0 mauling of the champions. Derek McInnes's side set out to follow the Edinburgh side's template for success.

Fergus McCann

He might have been mistaken for a bank clerk or a minor official from the ministry, a man deputed to bear bad news to grieving widows that their pensions had been lost or misplaced in some disastrous financial scandal

McCann and Tommy Burns with the Scottish FA Cup 1995: happy times before Burns was sacked in 1997

It was not easy being Tommy Burns… Nothing was easy with McCann

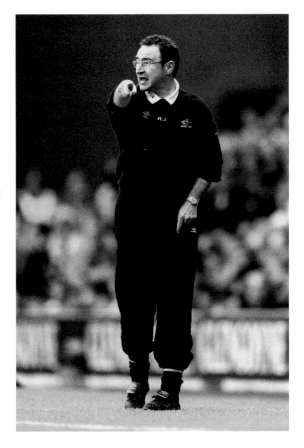

Martin O'Neill at Ibrox, November 2000

O'Neill, like his mentor, Clough, made no condescension to either smartness or fashion. His tracksuit bottoms spoke of a man who cared only for his work and these were his working clothes, and fuck you in the nicest possible way if you thought them inappropriate

Martin O'Neill flanked by Neil Lennon and Paul Lambert after retaining the league championship, April 2002

O'Neill, a footballing genie and genius, was at the peak of his powers

Gordon Strachan pointing the way at Celtic Park, October 2006

Strachan took the club to two consecutive last-16 ties in the Champions League against Milan and Barcelona, not to mention three consecutive league titles, one Scottish Cup, and two League Cups, in spite of bearing the brunt of Celtic's return to a policy of sound money, of balancing books, of McCann's principles

Calm down! Strachan and his first team coach, Neil Lennon, at Ibrox in May 2009

Neil Lennon as player, as manager, and as Celtic fan

Lennon heads clear, April 2004, El Madrigal, Villarreal, UEFA Cup

'Neill had his favourites … his best signing was Neil Lennon, who might not have been the most talented player at Celtic Park, but was certainly the most influential

Lennon celebrates victory, November 2019, Stadio Olimpico, Rome, Europa League

Lennon wearing the hooped scarf, May 2019, Hampden Park, Scottish Cup Final against Hearts

Ronny Deila in roaring, congratulatory, and celebratory poses

The Ronny Roar, February 2015, Hampden Park, celebrating victory against Rangers in the League Cup semi-final

Deila was Prometheus unbound, Clark Kent as Superman, his mouth agape, his arms raised, his fists clenched and pumping. 'It was orgasmic,' he said

Ronny Deila congratulates Leigh Griffiths on his hat-trick against Kilmarnock, April 2015

Deila celebrates with players, including Aleksandar Tonev, Nir Bitton, and Scott Brown, after a Scottish Cup victory against Hearts at Tynecastle, November 2014

Brendan Rodgers, new Celtic manager, with scarf, May 2016

'I've just landed my dream job,' he announced, 'with the team I've supported all my life'

Manager and captain, January 2017, after a 4-0 victory over Hearts at Celtic Park breaks the Lisbon Lions' record for consecutive unbeaten domestic matches in one season

Rodgers sought out Brown on his arrival at the club, put a reassuring arm around the midfielder, assured him of the manager's good opinion, and promised him he was relying upon his leadership of the club

Ange Postecoglou celebrates winning the Premiership, and provides a riposte to the doubters: *'How do you know I wasn't fifth choice, mate?'*

Players, and manager, including Kyogo Furuhashi, David Turnbull, Stephen Welsh, Joe Hart, Cameron Carter-Vickers, Anthony Ralston, Matt O'Riley, Postecoglou, Jota, Callum Mcgregor.

'I'm really proud of the players, the staff, the supporters,' Postecoglou said. 'Nobody gave us much of a chance at the start of the year. To do what they've achieved is unbelievable. Our football has been outstanding.'

Four Celtic Geniuses: Larsson, Moravcik, Nicholas, Furuhashi

Henrik Larsson celebrates his 30th goal of the season against Dundee United, Tannadice, March 2004

Lubomir Moravcik, December 1999, Celtic Park, is fouled by the current Rangers manager, Gio van Bronckhorst

Charlie Nicholas, August 1992, enjoys the moment at Tynecastle against Hearts

Kyogo Furuhashi in balletic pose, December 2021, Hampden Park, League Cup Final v Hibernian

The first half saw raw red meat football from Aberdeen but no goals to back up their dominance. In addition, after 40 minutes, Celtic scored a freak goal to break the deadlock. Mikael Lustig essayed a speculative punt towards the Dons' goal. It was the equivalent, perhaps, of placing the last fiver of the rent money on a 100-1 no-hoper in a last race of the day handicap at Ayr. Even Jock Stein would not have gambled on that long shot coming home a winner. Lustig's hit-and-hope effort cannoned off defender Dominic Ball and deflected past a stunned and rooted Joe Lewis.

Midway through the second half, with the home team looking increasingly comfortable in spite of the frenzied efforts of the visitors, a Sinclair cross pinballed between defenders and was bundled into the back of the net by Jonny Hayes, signed by Rodgers in June 2017 for around £1m from Aberdeen, for his debut goal in green and white. With 15 minutes remaining, Ntcham pounced on an appalling back-pass by Kenny McLean and completed a reassuring 3-0 victory that provided an eight-point Christmas cushion at the top of the league.

Two wins and two clean sheets since the heartbreak at Hearts and Rodgers was emboldened to claim this second win on the bounce was 'all part of the culture we have here', and nothing to do with his opposing manager's claim that 'the luckiest team won'. It was, too, Celtic's 25th consecutive league victory over Aberdeen in Glasgow's East End.

In truth, it was all too easy through the winter and spring months of 2018. Celtic continued to hold the hex over Aberdeen, with a comfortable 2-0 win at Pittodrie towards the close of February, after which they were nine points clear at the top of the table.

Rangers were in disarray financially and off the pace in footballing terms. Caixinha was sacked in October 2017 after a 1-1 draw against bottom club Kilmarnock, his appointment a disaster from start to finish, and the shortest-lived 'permanent' manager in their history, both short and long.

As 2018 dawned, Graeme Murty, a former youth team coach at Southampton and Norwich City, was enduring a second period of caretaking for Rangers, although he was nominally appointed as manager until the end of the season in December 2017. He was utterly out of his depth, not waving but drowning. He enjoyed one brief spell of relative success in the build-up towards the Glasgow derby on 11 March. After defeat at home to Hibs at the beginning of February, Murty's men won four consecutive league matches, and thoughts turned to reclaiming the Premiership title from Celtic. At 1-0 up after three minutes and at 2-1 up after 26 minutes, their fans were in full voice at a full Ibrox Park. Twice, though, Celtic equalised through Rogic and Dembélé.

On 57 minutes, however, Šimunović was handed a straight red card by Willie Collum following injudicious use of an elbow against Rangers' provocative Colombian striker, Alfredo Morelos. It was possibly the referee's one incontrovertibly correct decision of the entire match. The game, if not the title, was in serious jeopardy. Then, with 20 minutes remaining, a Celtic counter resulted in substitute Odsonne Édouard, on loan from Paris Saint-Germain, curling a shot from just inside the penalty box past a despairing dive from Wes Foderingham. It was a fitting reward for an adventurous substitution in replacing a wideman in Forrest with a second central striker to partner Dembélé. Afterwards, Rodgers claimed it was 'definitely my most satisfying win over Rangers'.

The brouhaha prior to the match involving posters on programme sellers' stalls stating 'THE TIME IS NOW', and a provocative poster produced by the Union Bears showing a Celtic fan being kicked as he lay on the ground, and inciting Rangers fans to march to Ibrox for 'the match against the Fenians', was put into perspective by the Celtic captain, Scott Brown, who said, 'We did our talking on the pitch.'

Before the season concluded, there were further crushing defeats of Rangers in the month of April: 4-0 in an FA Cup semi-final and 5-0 at Paradise, a victory which clinched the league title for the seventh consecutive time. Murty was subsequently sacked.

After the Parkhead rout, Rodgers said, 'We wanted seven but we'll take five.' In truth, it might have been ten. Jak Alnwick, in goal for the Ibrox club, made three top-class saves. Celtic were five goals to the good before the hour at which point they simply oozed class and confidence but stopped any serious pursuit of further goals. Édouard scored twice and was silky, serene and sublime. Every single Celtic player, though, from Gordon in goal to Forrest on the wing and through Lustig, Boyata, Ajer, Tierney, Ntcham, Brown, Rogic, McGregor and Édouard, and to the substitutes, Hendry, Sinclair and Griffiths, all played their parts, with a thrilling combination of subtlety, pace and physicality. Lustig stole a policeman's helmet in the celebrations and stole the show in the post-match party. No Rangers players or members of the coaching staff were permitted to speak to the media after the game.

Back-to-back trebles were secured at Hampden in May through the 2-0 defeat of Motherwell in the Scottish Cup Final.

It was the first time in Scottish football history that a clean sweep of domestic trophies had been completed in consecutive seasons. Even the great Stein side of 1968/69 and 1969/70 fell at the final hurdle, losing to Aberdeen 3-1 at Hampden, although the Celtic players might have been partially excused as they were a mere four days away from the second leg Battle of Britain European Cup semi-final against Leeds United. Had they despatched Feyenoord in the final in Milan in May, the team would have been forgiven utterly for their lapse against the Dons.

Walter Smith's 1994 Rangers team, too, slipped up, like Devon Loch in the Grand National of 1956, when it seemed impossible not to beat Dundee United in the Scottish Cup Final. Just as the racehorse was spooked by shadows 50 yards from the finishing line, Smith's haunted players failed to turn up at Hampden for the final leg of an expected double treble. United had finished the league campaign in sixth place, 16 points behind Rangers and with a negative goal difference of -1 to Rangers' +33. The team from Tannadice won 1-0.

Celtic's 2018 victory over Motherwell was their 18th straight win in domestic cup ties and Rodgers's merry men had scored 60 goals, conceding only six in the process.

Rodgers was ecstatic, claiming the second treble was a greater achievement than the first and, on the basis that it is often harder to stay at the top than to climb to the top in the first place, that may even be true.

* * *

8. JUDAS'S BETRAYAL AND PARADISE REGAINED
2018/19

If, as Buddhists claim, the only permanence in life is impermanence, the radical changes witnessed inside Paradise during the season 2018/19 were proof positive of such a philosophy. As a precursor to that momentous change, something happened during the summer of 2018. Or some things.

The difference between the demeanours of Brendan Rodgers after winning the double treble in May and at the beginning of a new season in August was subtle but profound.

After the Scottish Cup Final celebrations at Hampden in 2018, Kris Commons, an immortal presence for the six-in-a-row from 2011 to 2017, although playing no active part in the sixth, speaking to the BBC, said, 'Brendan Rodgers will stay for ten-in-a-row … I think probably when he first came up, he's probably thinking two, three years top, and then try and get back to the English Premier League, but now.'

Rodgers said himself, 'You know, I've got three years left, we're up to seven.' Clearly, the man imagined his immortality, the manager who delivered ten-in-a-row. Clearly, Rodgers was as happy as a pig in shit. So, what changed?

Primarily, Rodgers's relationships with Desmond, but especially with Lawwell, shifted sufficiently for the boss to have been looking for a way out of Paradise, possibly as early as late summer 2018.

His press conferences no longer seemed freewheeling or face value occasions. There were coded communications to his bosses, to the public, and to the press.

Once upon a time, the subliminal messages whispered, 'I was a manager of Celtic, an architect, a creative man who designed and headed a project to conduct a root-and-branch transformation of this football club, but now I am a mere coach, a menial servant who executes decisions made elsewhere that are above my pay grade.'

If it is reasonable to accept Rodgers's interpretation of the causes of the changed atmosphere at Celtic Park through the short summer that followed seven-in-a-row, who was responsible for this revolution? Whose fault was the breakdown in relations between boardroom and manager/coach inside Paradise? Two press conferences, in particular, provide historians with clues, with evidence for both defence and prosecution.

Before the Champions League qualification game at home to Rosenborg on 25 July, Rodgers was asked about a possible incoming player, Daniel Arzani, an Australian prodigy owned by Manchester City. 'Not my job,' Rodgers responded. There was an edge to his voice, a sneer to his smile. 'I work with the players that are here, develop them, improve them, that is my job.'

After the fine 3-1 win in which Odsonne Édouard, a man recently signed on a four-year contract costing a transfer fee north of £8m, scored a brace of goals, Rodgers returned to face the press once more. He seemed a happy man, a relieved man, after a good result marred only by an away goal banked early in the game by the Norwegian visitors. His good mood, however, was punctured by persistent questioning on Arzani. 'I can't tell you anything about him,' he said, 'or anyone else … I think he's been one that has been identified.'

One minute, Rodgers was a prime mover at Celtic, but now he seemed to have nothing to do with transfer targets. All of a sudden, was Rodgers being given signings without consultation, even ones he did not know or want? It seems barely credible, but the code the manager was using was hardly understated.

By January 2019, there was no subtlety left whatsoever. When the Ukrainian international Marian Shved was signed on a four-and-a-half-year contract and loaned back to Karpaty Lviv, Rodgers was beyond patience: 'I can't say I know a great deal about him … We've got about a million wingers and don't need another one.'

In the interim, Celtic missed out on a signing Rodgers was undoubtedly desperate to see over the line. John McGinn had been on the radar since he debuted for St Mirren in 2012. During the course of the summer six years later, Celtic made repeated offers for the midfielder, all rejected, but still there was an assumption – a presumption by the board perhaps – that they had only to whistle a little harder and the grandson of the club's former chairman would put pen to paper.

As the saga lengthened and the days shortened Rodgers's brow became more furrowed. On 8 August, as Celtic struggled to negotiate a way through the massed ranks of AEK Athens defenders in a European qualifier at Celtic Park, Aston Villa unveiled their new signing from Hibernian, John McGinn. Rodgers was apoplectic and, at the AGM in November 2018, let slip his frustrations with the board of directors who had failed to deliver players he had wanted during the summer recess. The failure to sign McGinn was 'disappointing', as was the inability to strengthen Celtic's central defence, where the manager had been forced to play the callow Jack Hendry in both legs of the lost European tie against the Greek champions.

Moussa Dembélé, scorer of 51 goals in 94 appearances, was sold to Lyon for almost £20m to be paid over a five-year term. Rodgers had tried to block the move.

Incoming players in January 2019 provided no indication of either long-term planning or of input from Rodgers. The rule of thumb appeared to be the reign of the quick fix. Oliver Burke, Timothy Weah and Jeremy Toljan appeared and later disappeared without much trace.

In November 2017, Lawwell had said he would not swap Rodgers for any other manager in the world. In February 2019, just two months distant from an unprecedented treble treble and eight consecutive league titles, Rodgers walked out of Paradise on a Monday lunchtime, after supervising morning training, and without saying goodbyes to his players.

Leicester City paid a rumoured £9m compensation for his release from his contract.

Later, Rodgers explained his conduct, 'What is hard for a supporter to understand is that this is my job, football management is my career and my life, and unfortunately at times you have to make a professional decision.' He might have been less condescending.

What is not hard to understand, however, is that Rodgers doubled his salary from around £45,000 a week to £90,000, and that this figure was doubled again when Leicester upgraded his contract in December 2019.

The English club, too, engorged with TV money, and with funds taken from Thailand in contravention of an agreement with the Thai government by the club's owners, paid average annual player salaries of £2.71m, compared to Celtic's £865,000. Leicester had spent around £300m on transfer fees in the previous four years. Celtic's record fee paid was to Paris Saint-Germain to secure the services of Édouard for beyond £8m.

Rodgers said it was a 'tough call,' but felt he had left Celtic 'in great shape'.

Most would agree with both those claims. 'Hopefully,' he added, 'in time, people will respect the work I did there.'

* * *

It was all change across the city of Glasgow too, although the revolution at Ibrox Park took place in the space between the seasons rather than the dangerously disruptive mid-term makeover at Celtic.

Three was the number at Rangers in the preceding campaign: third place and three managers. Caixinha was sacked in October 2017 after only 229 days in charge; Murty, dismissed on 1 May, not even making it to the conclusion of the league programme; Jimmy Nicholl was a temporary appointment pending the arrival of Steven Gerrard at the beginning of June.

Dave King, the convicted South African criminal, was still at the helm at Ibrox, and was joined in April 2018 by vice-chairman Douglas Park, the car dealer who, once, locked a referee in his dressing room when on the board at Hearts.

These were colourful times across the river and the men in charge at Ibrox now took a punt on the unproven Gerrard, recently manager of Liverpool's under-18 side.

By the time of the first Glasgow derby of the season at Parkhead on 2 September, Rangers had already dropped four points in away draws at Aberdeen and Motherwell. Celtic had accrued maximum points from wins against Livingston, Hearts and Hamilton.

It was a midday Sunday kick-off and Celtic dominated from start to finish but failed to finish a plethora of chances. Dembélé was missed, replaced by Édouard, who was later replaced by Griffiths. Forrest, Lustig, Ntcham and Griffiths all hit or scraped the woodwork, before the deal was sealed with a goal on 62 minutes, an irrepressible move begun by Rogic and continued and complemented by Édouard, Forrest and Ntcham.

Paddy Power, the Irish bookmakers, tweeted it was 'a disappointing result but a huge day out for a small club like Rangers'.

Rodgers was now unbeaten in 12 games against the new Ibrox club. In the return fixture at Ibrox, however, there was an utter reversal of form and fortune. At the end of December, Rangers won 1-0 and bossed the game from start to finish.

The Celtic performance was unacceptable and shambolic and perhaps a reflection that all was now no longer well in Paradise. Craig Gordon saved the Celts from a hiding. Still, they were top of the league but only on goal difference from Gerrard's revived Rangers.

By the time of Rodgers's departure, however, Celtic had regained the initiative with an eight-point lead in the league after Rangers' defeat at Kilmarnock and a home draw with St Johnstone.

The manager who delivered beautiful and successful football and beautifully successful football for over two and a half seasons at Celtic will remain a divisive figure. By the time of his departure, Lawwell and Desmond were probably glad to see the back of a demanding man who wanted more and more but who, like all managers, was only too happy to spend other people's money, and other people's money in an irresponsible and unsustainable manner too.

Rodgers, though, felt he had earned more, delivering not just back-to-back trebles but also back-to-back Champions League group stage qualifications worth up to £60m. He was right, too, that he left the club in better shape than he found it. Once it was clear, however, that Lawwell and Desmond were not prepared to gamble with Celtic's finances to chase the dream of a return to European greatness, it was inevitable Rodgers would leave.

It was no one's sole fault. Elite managers and coaches deliver results but come with strings attached: the twin needs of control and of constant evolution and advancement. Once barriers are erected to these goals, even when manifestly in the long-term interests of the football club, a parting of ways becomes inevitable. Everyone, fans included, has to move on.

Remember, though, that Rodgers, while at Paradise, delivered on both the quality of the football and the quantity of the trophies. There had been no one since Stein who had done that as successfully. It was because it had been so good that it hurt so much.

* * *

Lawwell and Desmond, with some relief as well as regret, turned once more to an old soldier, a veteran at 47, a man who knew the ropes, who knew the men who pulled the strings, who knew the boundary lines, the ties that bind, and those that loose.

For the second time, Neil Lennon was called to a temporary position, to rescue Celtic from embarrassment. The first occasion followed the resignation of Tony Mowbray after the Englishman's disastrous term in charge. On neither occasion did it appear that Lennon was a man to be wholly trusted by the board of directors.

Lennon's time with English Championship club Bolton Wanderers was an unmitigated disaster. Bolton faced the most serious of financial difficulties throughout Lennon's 17 months in charge, the extent of which was not revealed to him at the time of his appointment in 2014. A total of £172.9m was a considerable burden of debt even if it was mostly borrowed from previous owner Eddie Davies, who did not wish for repayment. In Lennon's second season at Bolton, his team won just four out of 37 matches prior to his exit and were 11 points adrift at the bottom of the table.

Back in Scotland, appointed manager of Hibernian in June 2016, Lennon secured a return to the Premiership for the Edinburgh club in his initial season and a fourth-placed finish and a return to Europe for the Hibees in his sophomore year at Easter Road. He had put the failure at Bolton Wanderers, where lack of finances had made the job impossible, firmly in its place.

The man's volatility, as well as his bravery, however, meant it was never going to be a smooth ride to ongoing success at Hibernian. On 31 October 2018, at the end of a ferocious Edinburgh derby, Lennon was felled by a coin, thrown from the Hearts crowd, that struck his face. Two days later he spoke of the abuse he had suffered throughout his career in Scotland:

'You call it sectarianism here … I call it racism … I get called a Fenian, a pauper, a beggar, a tarrier … These people have a sense of entitlement, a superiority complex, and all I do is stand up for myself.'

In January 2019, after a 1-0 defeat at Motherwell, which consigned Hibs to a fifth successive game without a win, there was a stormy exchange of views in which Lennon took no prisoners, and in which he particularly targeted striker Florian Kamberi. The Swiss took exception to the ferocity of the criticism and stormed out of the meeting. Lennon and his assistant, Garry Parker, were told to stay away from work by chief executive Leeann Dempster. Later, the Edinburgh club issued a statement which concluded that it was in the 'best interest of all parties to part amicably'. Lennon had not been sacked, nor had he resigned, but still he was gone from Leith.

Lennon, like Rodgers before him, had a managerial career to rehabilitate, and was eager to return to Paradise: 'I have given everything to Celtic as a player and a manager already in my career and I am ready to do the same again.'

For better or for worse, Desmond and Lawwell had regained an unchallenged control over football operations at Parkhead.

A needy manager, even one with a reputation for turbulence, was a doctor's prescription for steady as you go at Celtic. It seemed counter-intuitive that the bravest man in Scotland should be regarded as undemanding and a safe pair of hands, a tractable, even compliant manager, one to play it straight and true towards eight-in-a-row and a possible treble treble. That this was the truth of the situation, was one reason Lennon was not universally welcomed back to Celtic Park.

It was the most difficult of briefs for Lennon. Rock no boats but steer the club to the impossible heights of a third consecutive treble.

Lennon was regarded, too, by some fans, as a cheapskate appointment and further evidence of skinflint tendencies in the boardroom. In addition to winning matches, Lennon had to win over his critics in the stands at Parkhead, some of whom were still smarting from his abandonment of the club in 2014.

The man himself was only too aware he was on a hiding to nothing. Win the title, win the treble, and it would be said it was Rodgers's team, handed to Lennon on a plate. Lose it all and, heaven forbid, his past successes would be forgotten, his career on Skid Row. Still, the opportunity was too close to his heart to turn down.

Over the years, he must have thought time and time again about what he had thrown away when exchanging Paradise for a mess of potage in a soulless modern stadium in the middle of a car park on the outskirts of nowhere in particular in Lancashire, England.

Neither was it the easiest of beginnings. Lennon's second tenure commenced with a must-win game at Tynecastle against Hearts.

The home side ripped into the match like a North Sea storm and Celtic were all out to stay afloat. Against the run of play, however, after 36 minutes, the visitors launched a lethal counter. The ball was passed with bewildering speed from Ewan Henderson to Sinclair to Burke to Forrest and the winger tapped home an opening goal that the interim manager celebrated with manic abandon.

When Jeremy Toljan was elbowed in the face just before half-time and Hearts were reduced to ten men, it seemed Lennon's stars were aligned for victory. The Jambos, though, continued to press in the second half and were awarded a penalty for a desperate scything tackle by Kristoffer Ajer after a Scott Bain clearance had placed the Norwegian defender in mortal peril. It was scored.

Just after the hour, Lennon took off Henderson and brought on Édouard. A draw against ten men, even at Hearts, would not have been a good look for the returning manager who was animated on the touchline, urging his men forward and, with added time draining away, Édouard volleyed home a Brown cross, and all was well. Celtic remained eight points clear at the head of affairs.

Those looking for differences between the Rodgers regime and the Lennon leadership detected a more direct approach from the temporary appointment. Nothing much needed to change but it was important for the new man to imprint and implement his own ideas, if only for his own self-esteem. He said, 'I think we overplay a little too much ... We just need to get the ball forward a little bit quicker because we've got players who can hurt teams.'

At the end of March, Lennon's Celtic had the opportunity to end Rangers' challenge for the title. A win at Celtic Park would put the home side 13 points clear with a clearly better goal difference to boot. An Édouard opener had been cancelled out through an equaliser by Ryan Kent.

In a tempestuous match, Alfredo Morelos, Rangers' headbanger of a striker, elbowed Brown in the face, and was dismissed just after the half hour. With 20 minutes to play Celtic were reduced to ten men too when rash substitutions by Lennon combined with an injury to Boyata. It was 1-1, and all to play for but, with five minutes left, an untimely loose pass from Tavernier allowed McGregor to steal the ball and pass to Édouard, who found Forrest to slide his shot into the net.

The league championship was all but over. It was formally won on 4 May via a 3-0 win at Pittodrie to cap an emotional recent time for Celtic during which two Lisbon Lions, Billy McNeill and Stevie Chalmers, passed away.

Later in the month, when Hearts were beaten 2-1 at Hampden Park in the Scottish Cup Final, it was mission accomplished for Lennon.

He had done everything expected of him and was rewarded with an opportunity to take the club forward on a permanent basis. Lawwell said no one else had ever been under consideration.

When all the changes that had marked the season had been reviewed and remarked upon, when acceptance of the supremacy of impermanence had been acknowledged, there was still one matter that remained unchanged, unchallenged: once more, Celtic had claimed a league title and, once more, too, a treble had been achieved.

What had once seemed impossible, was now apparently commonplace, and, in dreams at least, potentially perennial.

Lennon admitted his goal was now nine-in-a-row and a quadruple treble.

* * *

9. PANDEMIC POLITICS AND NINE-IN-A-ROW
2019/20

While it is certainly true no one, at the commencement of the previous season, could have predicted a Rodgers' runner or a Lennon restoration, this transition, this spinning of the wheel of fortune at Celtic Park, was not beyond the wildest realms of fantasy.

Rodgers had always been a restless soul, driven by the need for continuous revolution, constant improvement and ceaseless challenge. Lennon, too, ever since 2014, must have cast envious eyes over the work of his successors inside Paradise, longing glances in the direction of Glasgow's East End.

Still, it would have been absolutely impossible, when Celtic kicked off a new Premiership programme on 3 August with a 7-0 rout of St Johnstone, to have foreseen the way the nine-in-a-row would be decided on 18 May at a meeting of the SPFL board rather than on the football pitches of Scotland.

* * *

If the season began well for Celtic with that thrashing of the Saints, followed by a 5-2 romp at Motherwell, it soon went some way downhill for Lennon's side, with two lamented exits: Kieran Tierney's expected departure to Arsenal and an unexpected home defeat in the Champions League qualifier against CFR Cluj, the Romanian title holders.

There were compensations, however. Farewell to Tierney meant a transfer fee of £24m which, in turn, meant Lennon was given funds to remodel the team. Christopher Jullien arrived for £7m from Toulouse and Fraser Forster returned on loan from Southampton. Both were crucial, statement signings. There were less successful transfers including Patryk Klimala from the Polish side Jagiellonia Białystok for £3.6m, and Boli Bolingoli from Rapid Vienna for £3m but, overall, Lawwell's wheelings and dealings on Lennon's behalf brought the club a net profit of over £6m and a team well worth watching. This was now the established Celtic way, the prudent way, the financially stable way, the only realistic way.

A second successive failure to reach the lucrative group stages of the Champions League, however, brought recompense in the form of a brilliant table-topping Europa League crusade culminating in a home and away double over Lazio.

Celtic's league form remained good, too, throughout the early autumn months. The highlight was a visit to Ibrox on 1 September. The build-up to the derby was all about the home team – how the appointment of Steven Gerrard had brought about a transformation at Rangers and how a seismic shift of the tectonic plates underpinning the power structure of football in Glasgow had been wrought by the genius of the man from Liverpool. Of ten pundits located in the offices of the *Daily Record*, six predicted a Rangers win – one, Mark McDougall, by a margin of 4-0 – two guessed at a sharing of the spoils, while only two argued for a Celtic victory.

The visitors started on the front foot, playing football with purpose and precision. Rangers, by contrast, appeared lethargic and without a clear plan of action. It was no surprise, therefore, just after the half hour, when Mikey Johnston latched on to centre-back Connor Goldson's error, threaded a pass to the nimble feet of Édouard, and the French striker slipped the ball precisely past Allan McGregor.

There might have been more goals in the first half but Celtic had to wait until the third minute of added time at the end of the match before victory was confirmed. A lightning counter-attack saw passes flash between Ntcham, Édouard and Jonny Hayes, with the former Aberdeen winger applying the final touch. It was an afternoon of vindication for Lennon:

'We were an afterthought coming into the fixture ... It was all about the opposition and what they were going to do to us. We didn't listen. We stayed strong and we played brilliantly.'

The classic spine of the team from Forster in goal, through Jullien at centre-back and Brown prowling in front of the back four, to Édouard up top, was in large part a Lennon creation. The team had won its first four league fixtures and was three points clear of Rangers.

It had not been a good week at all for Gerrard's club, Rangers learning they had been charged twice by UEFA for racist chanting in Europe.

It was, though, a good week for Pope Francis, who was late for his Sunday address in St Peter's Square. The official excuse that the pontiff had been stuck in a Vatican lift due to a power cut was denied by insiders who said he had been anxious not to miss the Glasgow derby on television. Perhaps the Pope was wearing the Celtic shirt presented to him in Rome by the mother of Paul the Tim, a social media man, who had 'POPE FRANCIS' printed on the back of a replica top in 2014. There had, after all, been a long-standing connection between the papacy and Celtic. As early as 1889, the club sent a telegram to Leo XIII informing him the newly formed club had won its first trophy by beating Cowlairs 6-1 in the final of the Glasgow North East FA Cup.

There was, though, a blip and a dip in Celtic's league form as autumn deepened and first leaves and first points began to be tossed to the winds. A 1-1 draw at Easter Road with Hibs on 28 September and a 5-0 Rangers newco victory over Aberdeen cut Celtic's lead to one point. Worse was to follow with a 2-0 defeat at Livingstone on the horror of a plastic pitch at Almondvale, which allowed the Ibrox club to go two points clear at the top of the Premiership.

The welcome news was that Celtic's latest financial figures showed the club with £38.9m in the bank, an increase of almost £12m from the year before. Fans were pleased, of course, although some wondered whether a little less anal retention of pounds and pence might have provided a better autumn statement of intent on the field.

It was now nip and tuck between the two Premiership teams from Glasgow. By the beginning of Advent, Celtic led the league once more but only on goal difference. Every aggregation of every margin, however small, might make the difference in the determination of the location of the season's premier prize.

So it was good news at the beginning of December that a fragile peace deal had been brokered at Paradise between the club's authorities and the most vocal supporters. The Green Brigade had been locked out of the recent home victory over Rennes in the Europa League and it was presumed an indefinite ban on tickets had been imposed but, prior to the League Cup Final and to the Glasgow derby at the end of the month, it was announced the embargo had been lifted. A cup final or any home game without the presence of the club's political conscience and most colourful and vocal supporters was a diminished context in which to play and support football.

After the home tie against Lazio on 24 October, Celtic had been fined £15,000 by UEFA for a display of banners by the Green Brigade. Those regarded as offensive included one 'BRIGATE VERDE' with a white cross which resembled emblems of the Brigate Rosse, a revolutionary grouping from the 1970s who were responsible for the kidnap and assassination of the Italian prime minister, Aldo Moro, in 1978. Equally, though, the banner might have referenced Italy's World War Two Catholic resistance movement, the Green Flame Brigade.

Less subtle banners included 'FUCK LAZIO', 'LAZIALE PARTO ANALE', and 'FOLLOW OUR LEADER'. The latter was accompanied by a cartoon of a hanged Benito Mussolini.

For further context, however, it is important to note that Lazio's cultural attachment to fascism was every bit as deeply entrenched as the commitment of Rangers' supporters to Unionism, right-wing politics, and to anti-Irish racism. Prior to the match, Lazio's ultras had marched through Glasgow city centre – without police intervention – singing fascist songs and making Nazi salutes, for which the Italian club were fined £10,000.

On 8 December, the Bhoys won the League Cup at Hampden by defeating Rangers 1-0, their tenth successive domestic title. The performance, however, left much to be desired and much to be feared concerning future meetings with their rivals. Christopher Jullien's goal was their sole shot on target and for most of the match Rangers swarmed around Celtic's goal like bees about their hive, although they lacked a harmful sting in any of their 16 shots. Forster was as much a wall as he had been all those years ago against Barcelona.

A 2-1 win at St Mirren on Boxing Day sent Celtic two points clear at the top of the league after the newco drew 2-2 with Aberdeen ahead of showdown shoot-out day with the Ibrox side, at 12.30pm three days later.

Celtic fans were anxious that a similar performance to that of League Cup Final day would lead to a different result. Better, though, would be a better performance.

Fears, however, were well founded. It was as if the final whistle at Hampden had never sounded, as if play had continued to flow, with Rangers on the front foot playing the same coherent and composed football, while Celtic played with lead in their boots, with dread in their bones.

It took almost 20 minutes for the Hoops to essay a hopeful but no-hoper shot off target, when Ryan Christie's effort sailed over the crossbar. Ryan Kent, on 35 minutes, gave the Ibrox club a deserved lead. Approaching half-time, however, an equaliser arrived alongside the gods of good fortune, as a Callum McGregor shot deflected off an Édouard hand and past a wrong-footed Allan McGregor. The game was won after 56 minutes through a disputed corner, lax defending, and a towering header from Nikola Katić, Rangers' Croatian centre-back.

Although Gerrard was still without a trophy halfway through his second season with Rangers, the final game of 2019 provided final confirmation that the club he managed was alive and well and once more a serious force in Scottish football. It was Rangers' first win in the major Glasgow derby since 2010.

At the dawning of 2020, Lennon's Celtic remained at the head of the Premiership, two points clear of Rangers, but Gerrard's side now held both a clear advantage from their game in hand and the most important ascendancy of momentum. The nine-in-a-row and the fabled ten were in jeopardy.

In response, Lennon took his players for a new year break in Dubai and, on their return, strung wins together like pearls on a necklace, eight in total before a 2-2 draw at Livingston broke the sequence. Rangers, by contrast, appeared dizzied and dazed by their proximity to greatness, stumbled and fell into a black hole from which no escape was possible.

The world, too, hovered on the event horizon of an existential calamity. On 9 January, while Celtic supercharged their batteries with bright Arabian sunlight, the World Health Organization announced a cluster of cases of a 'mysterious viral pneumonia' in the Chinese city of Wuhan. Two days later, the first deaths from Covid-19 occurred. By the time Celtic returned to Premiership action at Kilmarnock on 22 January, the WHO had confirmed evidence of human-to-human transmission of the new virus and had convened an emergency meeting to decide on whether events in Wuhan constituted an emergency of international concern.

All this was barely whispered in Scotland and the rest of the UK. Four days after Rangers lost 2-1 at Tynecastle and five days after Celtic had beaten Ross County 3-0, the first UK cases of Covid were reported, with two Chinese nationals hospitalised in York. On 1 February, Rangers dropped more points with a 0-0 home draw against Aberdeen. By this time, the WHO had reported 7,818 cases worldwide, with 82 cases outside China in 18 countries. Still, there was more interest in football than in a pandemic.

The first case of Covid in Scotland was announced on 1 March, a Tayside resident recently returned from Italy, by which time Rangers had lost 2-1 at Kilmarnock and drawn 2-2 in Perth. On 4 March, Rangers were defeated 1-0 at Ibrox by Hamilton Academical and, three days later, Celtic beat St Mirren 5-0 and moved a momentous 16 points clear of their Glasgow rivals.

Next up was to have been a local derby at Ibrox on 15 March but the game was postponed two days after the first confirmed death in Scotland from the virus.

The Premiership programme was never resumed and, on 18 May, Celtic were declared nine-in-a-row champions by the SPFL.

It was not how anyone wanted it to be but the worthiness of Lennon's team to be title winners was indisputable by anyone bar bigots south of the Clyde.

It has been suggested that because season 2019-20 was unfinished an asterisk should be placed next to Celtic's league title, denoting a doubt as to its worth. Celtic fans might just accept that in return for a series of asterisks placed against Rangers' tainted titles won through many years of enhanced wages and inducements paid to their serried ranks of mercenaries through employee benefit trusts.

Lennon, though, was in no doubt as to his team's credentials. It was his own ninth title, five as a player and four as a manager. 'It's the best,' he said, 'no question it's the best.

'I can safely say it now after a long time – we're going to go for the ten.'

EXTRA TIME

Other Celtic Stories

The Curse of the Ten

1. HISTORICAL CONTEXT

Celtic were not the first club to fail to win ten successive league championships and nor will they be the last.

In 1963, a year in which Jimmy McGrory's Celtic won nothing, losing the Glasgow Cup Final 2-1 to Partick Thistle and the Scottish Cup Final 3-0 to Rangers in a replay, the Bulgarian army club CSKA Sofia failed in their bid to become the first club in the world to win ten championships in a row, finishing third and six points behind Spartak Plovdiv.

Next to strive for immortality were Stein's Celtic in 1975 and disarray and disappointment was their fate too.

Rangers, under David Murray and Walter Smith, next suffered the curse of the ten in 1998, stopped by Celtic under the mercurial management of Wim Jansen.

Dynamo Kiev looked set for ten in 2002 but were pipped at the post by Shakhtar Donetsk by a solitary point, having scored 13 more goals and conceded one fewer than the new champions. That was a season in which Celtic won their second title under Martin O'Neill and in which King Henrik Larsson scored 35 goals.

In 2021 two great European giants failed to make the transition from single figures to double. Juventus, under head coach Andrea Pirlo, faded to fourth place in their bid for immortality, in spite of Cristiano Ronaldo scoring 29 Serie A goals. Celtic, too, under Neil Lennon, were to stall on nine consecutive titles.

The ten-in-a-row may be unrealistic in competitive, major European leagues, but is by no means beyond the bounds of possibility in smaller nations and in countries where finances have been so skewed by the intervention of nation states or by television money and worldwide sponsorship deals.

Bayern Munich wrapped up the first Bundesliga ten in the spring of 2022, also the first time such an achievement had been accomplished in a major European competition. Surprisingly, Paris Saint-Germain, since their takeover by the sovereign wealth fund Qatar Sports Investments in 2008, have only won eight titles, and potential long-running sequences have been interrupted by Monaco in 2017 and by Lille in 2021.

The world record of 15 consecutive championships, set between 1994 and 2009, is held by Tafea from the South Pacific. Other clubs to have broken into a double-figure sequence of titles are MTK Budapest of Hungary (ten, 1914–1925), Dinamo Tbilisi of Georgia (ten, 1990–1999), Sheriff Tiraspol of Moldova (ten, 2001–2010), Pyunik Yerevan of Armenia (ten, 2001–2010), Ludogorets of Bulgaria (11, 2012–2022), Dinamo Zagreb of Croatia (11, 2006–2016), Rosenborg of Norway (13, 1992–2004), BATE Borisov of Belarus (13, 2006–2018), Skonto of Latvia (14, 1991–2004), and the inimitable Lincoln Red Imps of Gibraltar (14, 2003–2016).

Of the teams that failed to crack the code of ten-in-a-row, Celtic are the only team to fail twice, and that is a record unlikely to be broken any time soon.

* * *

2. THE BLAME GAME
STEIN'S FAILURE, 1974/75

The September 1974 annual meeting of shareholders was not a difficult one for Jock Stein. Nine-in-a-row was in the bag and there was an assumption right through the club from directors' box to the North End terracing known as the Jungle that the world record would be Celtic's at the end of the season. Ten-in-a-row were words imprinted in East End hearts like words inside a stick of Blackpool rock.

The Big Man smiled as he faced the lights and the audience. He tried not to overthink or plan these occasions. He wished he had nothing but soothing thoughts to impart, knowing his people, understanding what, to a man, they wanted to hear. He stood to warm applause, opened his mouth to speak, and gagged slightly on the acrid smoke and the alcoholic stench that merged with outpourings of affection and gratitude for the manager's presence, for his achievements.

Results so far that season had been satisfactory, but performances were a patchwork of light, dark and indeterminate greys. In his heart, Stein knew all was not as it should be inside Paradise, no longer as it once was at Celtic Park.

He reviewed a quick succession of images, turned the pages of an album of snapshots stored in his head, and reappraised some of the early-season matches.

The friendly defeats by Preston North End, Hamilton Academical and Schalke 04 were warnings. So, too, was the Drybrough Cup Final, won on penalties against Rangers. Three times his team had come from behind: first half, second half and in the shoot-out. Jock Wallace might have been a bigot but he deserved more than his public reputation as a mere disciplinarian and devotee of running up and down sand dunes on the beach at Gullane on the Firth of Forth. Celtic had also negotiated the group stage of the League Cup in spite of a 3-2 defeat at Ayr United.

On the other hand, the Division One campaign had opened with a 5-0 walloping of Kilmarnock and a claw-back 4-2 win at Clyde after falling two goals behind.

Stein closed the book of memories, not yet willing to confront the loss to Rangers at Celtic Park on 14 September.

Instead, he spoke. He knew his role here was to reassure, to offer platitudes if necessary, but he could not resist his primary role as a prophet of doom. Before the bromides, the banalities, some truths had to be told.

The transfer of Davie Hay, after an embittered and protracted contract dispute, to Chelsea for a record £225,000, was a blow, he said. He recalled Sean Fallon's pearls of wisdom. 'If you sell Davie,' his assistant had said, 'you might as well sell George too.' Now, Stein reported to the massed ranks of shareholders, the club had lost George Connelly, too, 'through his own decision'. No team, he said, could afford such losses and mount a serious European challenge. Bile rose in his throat as he still reckoned another tenner a week might have stayed Hay from his ugly exit. Bob Kelly would have seen the sense of that but not the bean counters under Desmond White.

He was genuinely more optimistic, though, about maintaining domestic dominance. 'God willing,' he said, and raised his voice, 'we intend to make it a full decade of Celtic supremacy.'

310

Raucous hurrahs reverberated, dispersed the clouds of smoke and doubt about the room. With Stein at the helm, everything was possible.

* * *

Until it wasn't.

The opening blow to belief arrived with the initial whisperings of autumn and with the first Old Firm clash of the season. George Connelly, bereft without his pal Hay, walked out on Celtic on the eve of the game. It was not the best preparation for Stein and his team.

The match was as tetchy as the weather, clouds tackling clouds, summer colliding with autumn. Jim Brogan was sent off after a clash with Derek Parlane. The Rangers striker followed eventually but not until after the game was won and lost. The referee, J.R.P. Gordon, was no more in control of the players than the argumentative clouds.

Dalglish opened the scoring after the half hour with a thunderous shot from the edge of the penalty area but Ian McDougall equalised just prior to the hour. Then Colin Jackson, with a quarter of an hour remaining, was offered a free header inside the Celtic box, and Denis Connaghan, who should have claimed the ball, watched as it sailed serenely into the back of his net.

Stein was apoplectic, disconsolate, sleepless, after the Ibrox club's first win at Celtic Park since 1968.

By the end of November, however, Rangers had failed to take any clear advantage from their Old Firm victory. Wallace's men shared top place with Stein's, both teams on 24 points, and both with a goal difference of +26.

By then, too, Stein's gloomy prognostications on European football had come true, with his team exiting the European Cup in the first round to the Greek champions, Olympiakos.

In December 1974, Celtic compiled a run of four consecutive victories in the league, and a 1-0 win at Kilmarnock three days prior to the turn of the year provided Stein's side with a two-point cushion combined with an improved goal difference worth, in theory, an extra point's superiority over Rangers.

Ten-in-a-row seemed both possible and probable.

* * *

Stein spent Hogmanay pondering. Drinking was out of the question, as was relaxation. There was a home match against Clyde the following day and then a pivotal fixture at Ibrox three days later. Stein was always reluctant to think beyond the next 90 minutes but, if sleep was impossible, what else was there to do but relive the past and plan for the future?

The Killie game had been a tricky one. It had only just turned out to be all right on the night – although, of course, it had been a Saturday afternoon kick-off. If it hadn't been for Ally Hunter and the former Kilmarnock goalkeeper's two fine saves in the second half, there might have been a wasteful spurning of the opportunity provided to put clear daylight between his team and Rangers. If it had not been for a watertight defence held together by George Connelly playing as a sweeper behind a back four of McGrain, Brogan, McNeill and Callaghan, the recent defeat of Rangers by Airdrie would have counted for nothing. If it had not been for the genius of Dalglish and his winning goal …

Stein was worried. He understood that was nothing new, but this was a set of worries of a different quality from normal, everyday Celtic worries.

He wondered how long it would be before the circling vultures from south of the border, the ones with money and spies, came for Dalglish, like they came for Hay. This was a new game, a different game from how it was with the Lisbon Lions. They had only wanted to play for Celtic. He knew McNeill had been tempted but once it was clear he was wanted by Celtic, wanted by Stein, he was never crossing the border. In those days, too, Stein could bark and never need to bite. Well, not much anyway, except with Johnstone.

And 'Jinky' was drinking again. Later, Stein confessed the errant and whimsical but explosive and outlandish footballing genius that was Jimmy Johnstone 'took five years' from his life.

The never-ending supply of young Celtic players who had filled his teams full and overflowing with talent, the Lions, the Quality Street Gang, appeared to be ending after all.

The exits of McNeill and Johnstone signalled the end of an era. There was no one to replace them, no way of replacing them, save buying players, and that had only occasionally been the Celtic way, and Stein was averse to spending money, whether it was his own or anyone else's.

It had not been the same since Bob Kelly's death. There were people to talk to but there was no-one like his former chairman.

Even Sean Fallon didn't come close.

Scarred by betrayals of family and boyhood friends when he crossed the sectarian divide to play for Celtic, viewed by father and friends as an apostate, a traitor, Stein always found it difficult to trust. Fallon was good for finding players, placating those upset by Stein; good, too, as a companion at the races, a fool for love, a foil for the manager's detailed knowledge of the horses, their handicap ratings, an honest, open book to Stein's darkness, secrecy, and demons.

By the winter of 1974/75, Stein's closest friend was still Tony Queen, the Glasgow bookmaker. The pair had been inseparable in the previous summer during the World Cup finals but, even so, at bottom, Stein was still a loner.

* * *

The Clyde game was a stroll, a 5-1 walk in the Celtic Park, but it was not without its concerns. Connelly suffered a deep laceration of his leg that required three stitches and it was improbable he would be fit to face Rangers which, in turn, meant there could be no reprise of Stein's tactical masterstroke of employing the young man as a sweeper against the men from Ibrox.

Stein, too, could not help thinking about Scotland. In many ways, too many ways perhaps, his life had been altered irredeemably by his work as a pundit at the 1974 World Cup in West Germany for the BBC. Stein was a proud nationalist, but a rational analyst, without apparent need for speaking without something worthwhile to say. His profile and opinions were much more highly valued than those of the Scotland manager Willie Ormond, whose sole previous coaching experience was at Perth in charge of St Johnstone. During the tournament, players sought out Stein for advice rather than their manager, and complained to him about Ormond's inability to handle indiscipline within the national squad. As a teetotaller, Stein had no time for the drinking culture that stymied Scottish achievements on the field. Still, he trod a fine line; he had no desire to undermine Ormond, but his very presence did so.

Stein had managed both Scotland and Celtic once before in the spring of 1965. Thoughts of doing so once again niggled him, pained him, like small stones in a shoe. There were rumours he might be offered charge of the national under-23 squad.

It was not that he had taken his eye off the ball of managing Celtic. It was, though, more like his eyes had been opened to a wider world.

It had been nothing but Celtic now for almost ten years and the responsibility, without Kelly, without a working relationship with White, was a burden, and a lonely one at that.

* * *

The day of the Old Firm derby dawned as bleak and as blear as a night without sleep.

Heavy rain reduced the Ibrox pitch to a muddy field, too wet even for ploughing. Both Johnstone and Connelly were omitted from Celtic's starting line-up.

An early Rangers goal from Derek Johnstone added to the gloom and doom. Hood missed his shot from barely three yards out and Dalglish hit a post. Stein seethed. In the second half, Tommy McLean added to the Ibrox crowd's delight with a second goal in the 50th minute and the game was dead and buried by a third goal from Derek Parlane with a quarter of an hour to play. Stein bemoaned bad luck, missed chances, missed defending.

'Jinky' was invisible when he was called from the subs' bench in place of Hood. The wee man could do that sometimes, throw a sickie, make a 'fuck you, Stein' point in return for his initial exclusion.

In truth, Celtic had not played that badly, just badly enough to lose a critical match in the race for ten-in-a-row, just badly enough to make Jock Wallace look a tactical genius for instructing his captain, John Greig, to stop Dalglish from playing, just badly enough to make Rangers' rookie goalkeeper Stewart Kennedy look world-class.

The following Saturday, Stein's side compounded derby day errors by losing at home to Motherwell. Just as at Ibrox, Celtic started well, playing attractive football in spite of the atrocious conditions, and fell behind early when Willie Pettigrew scored with aplomb, running straight through a slack defence in the 12th minute. Bobby Graham added a second for the Well ten minutes later. Hood scored a brace to level the scores but Pettigrew, providing Celtic with a devastating masterclass in the taking of chances, stole the points with a winner after 76 minutes.

February 1975 proved no more palatable to Celtic supporters than the previous disaster of a month. More slack defending meant more points thrown away; a 2-2 draw at Arbroath after goals from Hood and Dalglish had given Stein's side a lead but a Derek Rylance equaliser ruined the result. Celtic had spent the majority of the match inside the home penalty area but still failed to win against the bottom team in Division One. Rangers, though, were still only two points clear at the top after their own disappointment in a 1-1 draw at relegation-bound Morton.

Three days later, 11 February, a home fixture against second-bottom Dumbarton provided an opportunity for atonement, and a two-goal lead before half-time should have been insurance enough against any fightback by the Sons of the Rock. It wasn't, and Celtic left the field to a barrage of jeers after another 2-2 draw. The effective end of Celtic's challenge for the world record ten-in-a-row ended in Edinburgh on 22 February with a 2-1 defeat to Hibernian.

This time around, there was no lead to throw away. On ten minutes, Peter Latchford, making his debut in goal for Celtic after his loan move from West Bromwich Albion, came for a cross, missed it, and Arthur Duncan scored for the home side. The winger scored again five minutes later and a consolation goal for Paul Wilson proved meaningless in the grand scheme of things. Rangers enjoyed the view from the top with a four-point lead and with a superior goal difference too. This time there were no excuses. The Celts had been comprehensively outplayed by a team that would finish the season above Stein's side in second place.

It was the end of an era. The lights were going out all over the East End of Glasgow. In his report on the Hibernian game, Ian Archer, the *Herald* journalist, recalled a 1950s hit song by Nat King Cole, 'The Party's Over'. For Stein, the dreams were over and it was almost time to call it a day..

If most people thought it was all over by the end of February, it most certainly was by mid-March after the 3-2 defeat at Aberdeen. This was Celtic's game in hand over Rangers who climbed six points clear. Billy Williamson scored a hat-trick (17, 57 and 77) for the Dons and Andy Lynch (53 and 62) scored for the Celts. The game was hard-fought but pointless, leaving the rest of the league season aimless for Stein.

A Scottish Cup triumph, a 3-1 win over Airdrieonians, was barely consolation. The legendary Celtic manager was exhausted, tired of being a father figure to Connelly, to Johnstone, to Dalglish, tired of the burdens of finance, the wheelings and the dealings of wages, tired of the weight of sectarian history, the hatred of Protestants, the Celtic fans he called 'wreckers' who 'chanted about things that have nothing to do with football', and tired of dressing room intrigue and his own attempts to divide and rule, to 'keep the six players who hate you away from the five who are undecided'; tired of it all without Kelly, just over two and a half years since his death, and fearful, too, of the future without his captain, McNeill, who had taken his advice to retire at the top, with a cup final trophy in his hands and another medal in his pocket, and without his favourite son, Johnstone, who he knew he would free in the summer.

For years now, though, like the anonymous man in the Stevie Smith poem, Stein was 'not waving but drowning'.

Two months later, Stein and his buddy Tony Queen, returning from a family and friends holiday on the island of Menorca, were fighting for their lives in the Dumfries and Galloway Royal Infirmary following a head-on collision with a car travelling on the wrong side of the A74 near Lockerbie.

There would be one more bright blaze of glory for Stein when his team completed an emphatic league and cup double in season 1976/77.

Afterwards, there was the unbearable sadness of decline, and farce, as the greatest manager in Celtic's history, and possibly the greatest in the entire history of football, was offered a job in the summer of 1978 by chairman White as a salesman of the club's lottery tickets.

To have accepted this new role would have been as near to death for Stein as his road traffic accident two years earlier.

During his time at Celtic, the Big Man had accumulated 25 major trophies, including a European Cup, ten league championships, eight Scottish Cups and six League Cups.

It was crucial not to permit the bitter disappointment of 1974/75 to overshadow or eclipse the extraordinary achievement of nine-in-a-row that preceded the time of sorrows.

* * *

THE CRUCIFIXION OF NEIL LENNON
LENNON'S FAILURE, 2020-21

It was a penalty kick, an open goal. It was easy, this ten-in-a-row business.

The original plan for this book was a celebration of a perfect sequence of league championships. I was a part of the culture of arrogance and entitlement and complacency that overtook Celtic at some point during the earlier years of simple dominance of Scottish football.

What we failed to take account of in the years of Rangers' exile from the top table were the inevitable consequences of hubris, of overweening pride. There was also the small matter of events, happenings, beyond our control. When the former Conservative prime minister Harold Macmillan was asked by a journalist what he feared most, he replied, 'Events, dear boy, events.'

Celtic, then, in 2020/21, were simply overtaken by events. That is not to say, however, that no one in particular was to blame.

What does need insisting upon, straightaway, though, is that Neil Lennon, while needing to shoulder some of the blame, was as much the victim of that fatal combination of arrogance and events. In some ways, Lennon was the fall guy, the patsy, the frontman who faced the blame and the shame. He was the only man to lose his job. It is easy to sack a manager, impossible to sack two dozen footballers.

* * *

If the origins of the disease of complacency lay in the period of facile supremacy of Scottish football, perhaps during Brendan Rodgers's time as manager, when Desmond and Lawwell refused to contemplate the manager's desire to take on Europe as Stein had done so many years ago, when the board of directors refused his requests to sign Timothy Castagne from Genk and James Justin from Luton Town in 2017, then the idiocy of the behaviour of newco Rangers in spring 2020 offered too many assurances of further easy triumphs, reinforced a treacherous superiority complex.

First, Rangers voted against the season's end. Next, the Ibrox club wanted the entire 2020/21 season declared null and void. The stench of desperation to avoid conceding Celtic's ninth consecutive league championship oozed from every pore of chairman Park's body.

Naturally enough, Rangers would dream dreams in which nothing happened between 22 January and 7 March 2020, during which time the Teddy Bears seemed to think it was picnic time and let slip a new year's advantage of a game in hand over Celtic and a mere two-point deficit. By the end of the shortened season the Gers were 13 points behind with a mere nine games to play.

The Ibrox club's counter proposal to the Scottish Professional Football League's advice to end the season was, though, deemed 'not competent' by the league's legal advisor. At which point, Rangers decided they wanted to bring the whole playhouse down, demanding the suspension of the SPFL chief executive, Neil Doncaster.

To those with exceedingly long memories, it was reminiscent of the behaviour of Rangers in their early days when the result of almost every lost match was challenged by the club's irascible secretary, John Mackay, so much so that an editorial in the influential *Scottish Athletic Journal* in 1884 suggested that Rangers' fielding of ineligible professionals in cup matches against Third Lanark constituted 'one of the biggest scandals that ever disgraced the annals of football', and that it would be better that 'Rangers should die' rather than 'a noble pastime be dragged in the mire'.

In the 1884/85 edition of the Scottish Cup, in addition to the doctoring of documents to permit the mugging of the Thirds, in the following round Rangers lost 4-3 against Arbroath but then protested the pitch at Gayfield had been too narrow and a mere 'back green'. A replay, which Rangers won 8-1, was ordered by the Scottish FA when the field was found to be 11 inches short of the legal minimum width. Rangers were vindicated but sour tastes were left in many mouths. When the Glasgow club eventually exited the competition in the semi-final at the hands of Renton, the *Scottish Athletic Journal* noted, 'So far there has been no protest from Rangers.' These were happy 19th-century days of an innocence now lost.

It should be added at this point that while Rangers were eager to have the season called null and void, Celtic always wanted it to be played to a finish.

* * *

The summer of 2020 was dominated by the transfer strategies of the Old Firm giants. For both Glasgow protagonists in the Premiership, it was as much about hanging on to players under contract as it was about adding to their collection of stars.

For Rangers, Alfredo Morelos was the key component in manager Steven Gerrard's approach. By the middle of July, it was difficult to tell whether the Rangers hierarchy wanted to stick or twist with the Colombian striker. Morelos had not been easy to manage. His mounting collection of red cards, his propensity to go absent without leave, had both made Gerrard impatient and angry. In March 2019, after the striker's fifth dismissal of the season during a 2-1 defeat by Celtic, his manager said, 'I can't defend Alfredo anymore.' More recently, in June 2020, Gerrard had admitted, 'Every player has his price.'

Morelos's goals – 29 in the previous season although only one after the midwinter break – were probably irreplaceable. Gerrard, though, might well have been mindful of his former club Liverpool's sale of their best player, Philippe Coutinho, in the summer of 2018 which allowed a rebuilding of the team and which, arguably, led to their first Premier League title in 30 years.

For Celtic fans, though, Morelos was the perfect pantomime villain, and many would have been sad to see him depart the Glasgow hothouse. At this time Morelos had famously never scored in an Old Firm match.

For Celtic, there was no dilemma, merely too much drama. The club was desperate to have Odsonne Édouard as striker in chief throughout 2020/21. French Eddie had already scored 62 goals in his three seasons at Parkhead and the very biggest birds of prey were circling in the louring skies above the East End of Glasgow. The striker had represented and scored goals for France from under-17 to under-21 level, and was selected on many occasions in preference to Kylian Mbappé, a global superstar with Paris Saint-Germain. The previous season alone, Édouard netted 11 times in six appearances for the France under-21 side. The hovering raptors included Arsenal, who stole Kieran Tierney for a mere £24m one year previously. Success, naturally enough, breeds persistent suitors.

Fans of Celtic would judge their football club and its determination to hoist the league championship pennant for a tenth successive year by their success or otherwise in keeping hold of Odsonne Édouard.

It was not just about strikers, however. Some of the spine of Celtic's 2019/20 team seemed at risk of not being available for the ten-in-a-row season.

With Fraser Forster in goal, the defence looked impregnable. Single-handedly, it seemed, the Wall won the League Cup and, after the final against Rangers in December 2019, his manager Neil Lennon commented, 'I've not seen a goalkeeping performance or a goalkeeper like

Fraser for a long time.' In 28 matches for Celtic in his second spell at the club, 50 per cent resulted in clean sheets.

The stumbling block, though, was that Forster was contracted to Southampton. At first, Celtic fans believed the problem was no problem. How could Forster not want to be part of the historic ten-in-a-row team?

As time spun its web of emerging events, however, it seemed he might prefer to stay on the English south coast and fight for his place in a battle against relegation from the Premier League. Some people, it seemed, had no understanding of the superiority of the status of a European Cup-winning team from the East End of Glasgow.

Those same people might have thought similar thoughts when Brendan Rodgers jumped ship in the middle of the 2018/19 season to manage Leicester City, a club without a European title, who had won a solitary league championship and three League Cups.

Southampton, the team so admired by Fraser Forster, won the FA Cup once in 1976. And the Southern League in 1897.

In addition to being the first British club to win the European Cup in Lisbon in 1967, Celtic's hoard of honours include 52 league championships, 40 Scottish Cups and 20 Scottish League Cups.

When Celtic Park was redeveloped in the 1990s, its capacity permitted the attendance of over 60,000 fans, and became, at the time, the largest club stadium in Britain. When Southampton opened their new ground, St Mary's, the stadium catered for a mere 32,500 souls.

Goalkeeping became a serious problem for Celtic throughout 2020/21. It had been a grave error of judgement to let the excellent and experienced Craig Gordon leave for Heart of Midlothian in June 2020. Neither new Greek international signing Vasilis Barkas, nor the callow Scott Bain and Conor Hazard, proved reliable replacements for Forster and Gordon.

There was a potential problem at centre-back, too, where Kristoffer Ajer was being courted by English Premier League clubs.

No Forster, no Ajer, no Édouard, no ten-in-a-row?

* * *

Still, Lennon spent much of the summer searching for strikers, just in case the unthinkable and unbearable happened, and Peter Lawwell accepted an offer for the transfer of Odsonne Édouard. As Chris Sutton said on

BT Sport, however, 'The Celtic fans would burn the house down if the ten was lost because of that.'

In the end, both Morelos and Édouard stayed with their respective clubs. For one that was a triumph, for the other it was an unmitigated disaster.

By the conclusion of the 2020/21 season, Morelos had scored 17 goals, even though he conceded top scorer status to Kemar Roofe on 18. Édouard scored 18 league goals and 22 in all competitions and yet it was the Frenchman and not the Colombian who was the devastating disappointment.

Rangers won the league title, and stopped the ten, by an astonishing 25 points. Someone had to be to blame.

* * *

THE BLAME GAME/THE PLAYERS

Prior to the season, Neil Lennon had reiterated that it was 'pivotal' to keep hold of Édouard, saying, 'We don't want him to go anywhere,' and describing the striker as a 'special talent'. Édouard had scored 28 goals the previous season and his class had been demonstrated in almost every game through his intelligent movement off the ball and his sinuous movement on it.

Against Hamilton Academical, on the first day of the league season, Édouard scored a carefree hat-trick in a 5-1 win. This was in the days before the transfer window closed and imprisoned the Frenchman inside Paradise, in the days when he was still trying to impress his suitors from the Premier League and beyond.

Édouard should have been a shoo-in for immortality among Celtic fans but his attitude during the majority of the season was a damning disgrace. Édouard played 40 games in 2020/21 and gave his best for the cause perhaps for as little as 40 minutes in total throughout all those matches. It is a testament to his sublime talent that he continued to score goals when he put half a mind to the task but, for most of the time, he was uninterested and apathetic, so anonymous he might have died and been replaced by his insubstantial ghost. In Celtic's second match, an anaemic 1-1 draw at Rugby Park against Kilmarnock, Édouard made not one touch of the ball inside the opposition's penalty area in the first half.

Shortly before the crucial home leg of the Champions League qualifier against Ferencváros in August, the Frenchman declared himself unfit to play, something about a tight thigh, but more likely a head that was by now utterly disconnected from any desire to represent his employers. The next day, after defeat by the Hungarians, a game in which Lennon was forced to field a team without a recognised striker, the manager suggested the medical department inside Paradise were far from convinced Édouard was injured in any way whatsoever. It was unforgivable.

As Gerrard said, in relation to his own striker's disaffection, 'I only want players who are hungry for the shirt.'

On the substitutes' bench for the game against the Hungarian champions was Albian Ajeti, a £5m striker signed from West Ham who was not considered fit enough to replace Édouard, and Patryk Klimala, a £3.5m Polish striker not considered good enough or experienced enough.

Leigh Griffiths was another case altogether. He had reported back to Lennoxtown for pre-season training a stone overweight, and a shocked Lennon complained, 'He needs to get his head down and get fit because that's what we pay him for.' Chris Sutton, legend and immortal and scorer of 86 goals for Celtic, utilised his mastery of understatement and suggested Lennon 'will feel let down'.

The 2-1 home defeat by Ferencváros was Celtic's earliest exit from Europe's premier competition since Gordon Strachan's humiliation at the hands of Artmedia in 2005. It was played out before an eerie and echoingly empty stadium due to Covid restrictions. Celtic did not play that badly and, on a night of different fortune, might have coasted through the tie. The Hungarians, though, were sharp as drawn swords, counter-attacked with relish, made the most of defensive errors, and deserved the win.

For the bean counters in the boardroom, the result may have cost the club as much as £30m. For the manager, it prompted Lennon to call out his players.

The post-match pressers were even more dramatic than the events on the field of play. Grizzled hacks were stunned by the manager's strategy. Lennon, brave as ever, began by claiming that some players contracted to Celtic – unnamed and unnumbered – 'may want to leave' and 'have made inroads into that in the last six months or so'. There was a pregnant pause before Lennon continued, 'So, if they don't want to be here, we have to do something about it. If they are making waves to leave the club they are obviously not committed.' The manager shaped his mouth to smile but what emerged was a snarl, 'We want players who are committed to the club … I am putting it out here because it has been bugging me for some time.'

What planet was Lennon on? Was he employing the classic distraction ploy favoured by managers time out of mind? Was he messaging the chairman, Peter Lawwell, and the board? Or was he simply telling the truth?

Whatever the motive, managers have been sacked for less, and the following morning Paddy Power, bookmakers in love with drama and publicity, published odds of 1-4 on that Lennon would be gone by the close of the season.

Lennon's staunch lieutenant on the field of play, Scott Brown, felt compelled to defend the players. 'For me,' he said, 'the players want to be here.'

The manager, meanwhile, merely added more grist to the mill. The players had only themselves to blame for their defeat. When asked if he had a further message for the dressing room, Lennon said, 'Get your mentality right, get your attitude right. If some of you don't want to be here, leave.'

Battle lines were drawn and criss-crossed throughout the club. Chris Sutton said the manager now had to name names. He was beaten to the punch, however, by Anthony Joseph of Sky Sports who named and shamed Kris Ajer and Olivier Ntcham.

Was that it? Just two wantaway rebels? All Celtic fans knew all about these two already. Surely, Lennon, was referring to Édouard as well?

The striker's agent, Lasana Koita, said, 'Odsonne is happy here at Celtic,' but he would not be the first representative to speak with forked tongue.

The following day peace broke out and all was sweetness and light in the Celtic camp. Suddenly, the restless players were 'great lads' who the manager wanted to 'settle down and do what they do best'. It was the biggest U-turn since any one of the 17 performed by Boris Johnson's English government in the previous fortnight. Had Lennon been invited upstairs by Lawwell and the board of directors and warned about depreciating values of players who are criticised? Had Scott Brown warned him about losing the dressing room?

Whatever the reason, Lennon picked the same team, and the same formation, with the same lack of a striker as against Ferencváros, for the weekend game against Motherwell.

On Sunday, 30 August, with Rangers nine points clear of their bitter rivals having beaten Hamilton 2-0 and having maintained clean sheets in all six of their league matches, the 'great lads' trotted sheepishly on to the Paradise pitch. For 40 minutes they were dismal, disjointed, not exactly dilatory but not exactly dynamic either, and the first half drifted towards its downbeat conclusion. Suddenly, though, Callum McGregor picked up the ball halfway inside his own half, surged forward, shrugged off the attentions of two opponents, and fed a slide-rule pass towards James Forrest who picked out the far corner of the Motherwell net. In the second half, too, Lennon reverted to the winning formula from the previous season, played 3-5-2, and Klimala nearly scored twice, Ajeti did score once, and Celtic strolled to a 3-0 victory.

All was well with the world once more. Especially since David Turnbull, a sublime and youthful midfielder with a goalscoring habit, had been signed from Motherwell on a four-year deal for around £3m.

Rumours, too, were increasingly strident that a loan deal for Brighton's biggest Celtic fan, Shane Duffy, was on the point of being signed. The centre-back with 33 caps for the Republic of Ireland would solve all Celtic's defensive woes with a stroke of his pen on the contract.

The much maligned board were not doing too badly in this transfer window so far: a new goalkeeper, a new centre-back, a new midfielder and a new striker. Crisis? What crisis?

It was time indeed for perspective as well as passion. Neil Lennon had done a superb job since his return to Parkhead. Two league titles, numbers eight and nine in a row, in the most testing of circumstances – Brendan Rodgers's disappearance and Covid-19. So far, in this current season, he had had to cope with juvenile delinquents in Griffiths and Bolingoli, who had broken every pandemic restriction in the book by flying faway or a Spanish holiday, as well as those players who seemed uncommitted to the goals of the club, and who appeared unwilling or unable to share the passion of the fans, their desperation, for the achievement of ten-in-a-row.

The truce between the club and its supporters lasted until 17 October when Celtic hosted Rangers with the visitors two points clear at the top of the Premiership but with the home side having a game in hand.

There were excuses available: Paradise was empty of spectators once more and Celtic were missing six members of the first-team squad, mostly Covid-related. Having said that, however, when Connor Goldson put the league leaders ahead before the first ten minutes were out, there was little response from Celtic. First, Ajer conceded a needless free kick for a foul on Ryan Kent in a dangerous position. Next, Duffy stepped backwards as the ball was swung in by James Tavernier and played Goldson onside. Barkas failed to strong-hand the downward header away from the goal. Three errors by three Celts implicated in the dismal decline of 2020/21: Ajer, with his head turned by interest from AC Milan, and Duffy and Barkas both signings made with the best of intentions but the worst of outcomes.

In the second half, Goldson scored a second with a tap-in. Sutton described Celtic's display as 'gutless' and suggested the 'scoreline flattered Celtic'. For the first time in 11 years, Celtic did not have a single shot on target throughout the entire match. The historian and chronicler of all things Celtic, David Potter, wrote that the performance was 'unacceptable, unbelievable, unforgivable'.

Lennon said Celtic could not continue to 'live off the past'. The manager was up front as always but his players skulked inside dressing rooms and behind the walls of Lennoxtown. It was time to name names.

Édouard, the sublime magician with a football, was a deserter, a man who had gone AWOL while still ostensibly around and about the club. By the following season he was a Crystal Palace player, but sold for a fraction of the fee that might have been available a year earlier.

It was never a good idea to cling to players who wished to ply their trade elsewhere. Ntcham sulked through the season. In 2021 he played on loan at Marseille and now plies his trade in the English Championship with Swansea City.

Andy Walker, a Celtic striker in the McCann era, and now a truth-telling commentator for Sky TV, said, 'Some players are not really interested in ten-in-a-row ... their culture is to get a move to a bigger club, bigger wages.'

Ajer was disappointed no move to Italy materialised but he did give his all to the Celtic cause, although prone to avoidable defensive errors. He now plays for Brentford in the English Premier League.

Ryan Christie blew hot and cold throughout the season but was a shadow of the powerhouse player from 2019/20 when he netted 21 goals in all competitions. He was allowed to leave Celtic in 2021 and now plays for Bournemouth.

Boli Bolingoli appeared once for Ange Postecoglou's side in 2021/22, and that was probably once too often.

Griffiths never recovered form or fitness after eating his way through lockdowns in 2020 and his contract was cancelled in 2021, a sad decline for a man who scored more than a century of Celtic goals and, at his best, was a mercurial genius, a player blessed by the gods.

Most dressing rooms contain a small handful of malcontents, players who believe they have been mistreated, misjudged by management, who cannot find a place in the first team for love nor money. They are the mutterers in quiet corners, the conspirators in cahoots with self-delusion, and they are generally relatively harmless. When they become a vocal minority or even a rebellious majority, the manager's days are doomed.

Quite simply, they become unmanageable, and no team, under these conditions, can withstand their assaults on team cohesion, and no team can maintain a sustained attempt at ten-in-a-row.

From the time Lennon lost the Glasgow derby in October 2020, and probably from the time the manager attacked his wantaway players, his so-called professionals, in August, he was a dead man walking.

Equally, from the time Desmond and Lawwell decided not to cash in on Édouard and his fellow rebels, Lennon was a dead man walking.

The majority shareholder and his chief executive were not sacked, although Lawwell retired in June 2021. The players, 'the good lads', were rewarded with the transfers they mostly wanted. Lennon was sacked for failing to do what was impossible, to play a winning hand from a bum deal.

THE BLAME GAME/THE BOARD OF DIRECTORS

Celtic's Green Brigade are not only the club's political conscience but also provide regular and pertinent reminders to the club's directors about their responsibilities.

As early as August 2019, a banner produced by members of the North Curve fan collective showed Lawwell, Lennon and Desmond in a car with the headline 'DON'T SLEEP AT WHEEL'. It appeared after an early exit from the Champions League at the hands of Romanian champions CFR Cluj, and after a narrow extra-time squeak of a League Cup victory over Dunfermline.

One year later and counting, even though nine-in-a-row was achieved and, belatedly, a scarcely credible quadruple treble, still there were alarming intimations of mortality in the performances of Lennon's squad.

In August 2020, Celtic, for the third consecutive season, were eliminated from the Champions League, by Ferencváros. Once again they were utterly unprepared in terms of transfer business done and undone.

In the summer of 2021, with Ange Postecoglou eventually installed in place of Lennon, the Aussie was sent into European battle against the Danish champions Midtjylland without either guns or ammunition. No one was killed, but it was not dissimilar to Russian soldiers in 1914 at the Battle of Tannenberg who were supplied by horse-drawn carts, while the advancing Germans were provisioned by motorised vehicles. Many Russians, too, fought this major battle with only one boot per soldier. Postecoglou must have known how they felt.

AEK Athens, Cluj, Ferencváros and Midtjylland is not a roll call of Celtic honour in Europe.

In fact, complacency had probably taken root inside Paradise the moment Rangers were removed from the battlefield. With Celtic's only serious rivals out of the picture, it could and should have been a decade to build a modern European powerhouse of a club. Desmond and Lawwell, instead, saw no need for investment in a director of football. Midtjylland, by way of contrast, had offset their lack of turnover and lack of broadcasting millions by investing in data analytics. At Celtic Park, vision was needed but found lacking. Continuance of balance sheet economics was also needed, but times had changed within the football industry, and more and more of mere McCann philosophy was no longer the route to continued success.

McCann was and will always remain the immortal saviour of Celtic, but stories of his penny-pinching seem quaint in the third decade of the 21st century, when the club's annual wage bill is now £53m. McCann's legendary querying of chief scout Andy Ritchie's lunch receipt for a chicken kiev sandwich purchased at Zürich airport is indicative. McCann was reported to have told Ritchie he should have chosen the chicken without the Russian embellishment because it was four francs cheaper.

Brendan Rodgers left Celtic because he perceived the board's careful husbandry as parsimony, because of a lack of prescience, because of an apparent lack of ambition beyond mere domestics. Lawwell's failure to sign John McGinn from Hibernian in the summer of 2018 may have been the last straw.

Under the watch of Desmond and Lawwell, a precipitous decline in the quality of players employed by Celtic was permitted in the four years from 2017 to 2021. Compare and contrast Postecoglou's line-up against the Danish champions with Rodgers's squad for Champions League group games in 2017. Against Anderlecht at home in December 2017, Craig Gordon – still, in 2022, performing miracles for Hearts – was in goal; the back four was Lustig, Boyata, Šimunović and Tierney, three of whom played in the following summer's World Cup; in midfield was a still dominant Scott Brown, Stuart Armstrong, now a regular in the English Premier League for Southampton, Callum McGregor and James Forrest, at the peak of his powers; Scott Sinclair and Moussa Dembélé were the strikers; on the bench were Édouard, Ajer and Griffiths. In Denmark, there was a callow defensive line-up of Scott Bain, Anthony Ralston, Stephen Welsh, Dane Murray and Adam Montgomery. Further up the field, Postecoglou was forced to include the inexperienced Soro and Abada, and the apparently indifferent Édouard and Christie.

'Obviously,' the new Celtic manager said after the club's Champions League exit, 'I haven't done a good enough job convincing people we need to bring people in.'

With new signings galore since then, including four Japanese internationals, it is difficult to recall just how dismal prospects were for Celtic and Postecoglou in late summer 2021.

Books are still – rightly – balanced, but there was a clear sense by the end of the winter 2022 transfer window of drive and vision restored to the club.

It is not easy, however, being asleep or awake at the wheel of Celtic. In the summer prior to the disastrous season of 2020/21, the board did its best to do what supporters wanted: no sales of star players prior to ten-in-a-row. It is easy to forget how desperate the fans were to keep Édouard. That policy of keeping the Frenchman and Ajer, Christie and Ntcham was wrong, wrong, and wrong again and again. These players were not all bad apples but some were.

McCann, by the way, would never have stood for Édouard's nonsense. He would have recognised the opportunity to garner as much as £30m for

Celtic's treasury and handed the striker a one-way ticket to a destination of the owner's choosing.

The world, though, was a simpler place in the McCann era. There was more dithering and indecision, too, over the sacking of Lennon.

In hindsight, it probably should have happened earlier, maybe as early as the manager's rant against players who were unhappy and underperforming. If not then, perhaps after the humiliating exit from the Europa League at the hands of Sparta Prague. Losing one match 4-1 might be considered a misfortune, but to lose a return leg by the same score looked like carelessness. If not then, perhaps three days later, after the 2-0 home defeat in the League Cup by Ross County, which brought to an end any remaining dreams of a quintuple treble. As Chris Sutton said, Lennon had been 'badly let down by his players', but still the buck always stops with the manager on these desperate occasions.

In fact, Lennon was not relieved of his duties until after another defeat by Ross County in late February 2021, which left Celtic 18 points behind Rangers in the Premiership. It was too little – some of the players should have been offloaded earlier, too – and too late.

More hesitation and confusion was to follow with the wasted months waiting for Eddie Howe to decide the role was not for him.

Maybe more by luck than judgement, the current board, with Michael Nicholson eventually replacing Peter Lawwell, via the interim appointment of Dominic McKay, had at last got something right with the judgement call on Ange Postecoglou and then with significant financial backing of the new manager's assessment of players from Japan.

For the time being, at least, the Green Brigade could concentrate on their role of moral and political crusader.

Nicholson, a sports law specialist and former company secretary and former director of legal and football affairs at Celtic, and Postecoglou, a coach with an enviable track record of success in Australia and Japan, have been a transformative and restorative double act for the foreseeable future at Celtic.

THE FINAL WHISTLE

Quadruple Treble 2016–2020 and Scottish Cup Winners 2016–2020

TWO RECORDS IN ONE AFTERNOON

Hampden Park, 20 December 2020

The final curtain fell on the old era of Lennon, Deila, Rodgers and Lennon again, five days before Christmas 2020.

It was celebrated, not inside a football stadium, but mostly inside houses, by families reduced in so many sad and tragic ways by the global pandemic. By Celtic supporters, the result was received mostly joyously, although not without sadness, wistfulness about what might have been.

In the end, two records were at stake in one match on one afternoon.

An eerie and empty Hampden Park was the venue for the Scottish Cup Final postponed from the previous season during the ongoing Covid pandemic.

When the 2019/20 league season remained uncompleted except by decree, it seemed unlikely the outstanding cup semi-finals between Hearts and Hibs and between Celtic and Aberdeen would ever take place. That these matches, together with the final, were played amid lockdowns and thousands of pandemic deaths in Scotland, is a minor miracle, and something not approved by everyone. In the week prior to the final, there were 203 Covid-related deaths in Scotland including 31 in Glasgow. On the day itself, there were 934 new cases confirmed. The original plans of the SFA were to play these matches in front of capacity crowds but the virus and the Scottish government put paid to such wild ideas.

* * *

It was a Glasgow morning, westerly winds shifting clouds across the sky and presaging rain later in the day. In spite of a heavy police presence, hundreds of Celtic fans travelled Southside to support their team from outside the stadium. Covid masks and green smoke from flares were the order of the day. It was a change of venue for many Green Brigade Bhoys who had been protesting outside Celtic Park for weeks at the ongoing inactivity of the board in the face of increasingly disappointing results in the ten-in-a-row season. Earlier in the month, Celtic recorded a third consecutive defeat in the Europa League and a tame home draw with St Johnstone that left the team from Paradise 13 points behind Rangers.

Optimism before the final was confined to the hope and the promise that it would be inconceivable to lose against Hearts, a team from the Scottish Championship, albeit one relegated by proclamation rather than through performance on the field.

It was a Glasgow Sunday too, with an early Hampden start at 2.15pm. Some of the fans outside the stadium might have made it to early morning Mass but probably not too many. The days when Celtic players, as well as supporters, were regular attenders of Catholic churches were long gone. The power and influence of both church and kirk had been diminished, for good or evil, by the scandal of paedophilia.

Even the visit of Pope Benedict XVI to Scotland in 2010 seemed historical rather than almost contemporary. The atheism that the German Pope complained of had stormed the ramparts of Scottish Catholicism, aided and abetted by the resignation of Scotland's top Catholic, the Archbishop of St Andrews and Edinburgh, Cardinal Keith O'Brien, in 2013, as a consequence of his sexual misconduct.

No more would Celtic's Catholic players attend Mass before a European Cup Final. The days in the old stadium in the late 1970s when black-frocked priests seemed as numerous as laymen were past and dead and buried. The days of Artur Boruc, Celtic's Holy Goalie, and his revelations of his love for Pope Benedict in April 2008 seemed like a relic of a bygone age.

If Celtic were to win the Scottish Cup for the 40th time, they would also break a record held by Queen's Park since 1876, when the Hampden club won their third successive Scottish Cup, beating Third Lanark 2-0 in front of 10,000 spectators at Hamilton Crescent in a replay after an initial 1-1 draw.

If Celtic were to defeat Heart of Midlothian in the 2020 final, the club would become the only team to have won four successive Scottish Cups.

At stake, too, of course, was the almost inconceivable quadruple treble, clean sweeps of 12 consecutive domestic trophies. It was the final game in a series of 180 fixtures.

The odyssey began on 7 August 2016, Brendan Rodgers's first league match in charge of Celtic, and the opponents were Hearts, the first and the last team in the sequence. On that faraway day, James Forrest netted the opening goal of the quadruple treble. In a frenzied opening, before a packed and ferocious Tynecastle crowd, McGregor found himself clear on the right flank, drove towards the Hearts penalty area and was blocked by Brazilian midfielder Igor Rossi, but the ball fell to Forrest, who curled a trademark left-footed shot past Jack Hamilton. There was an element of good fortune, as required in every human enterprise, in the Celtic goal, as Stuart Armstrong was in an offside position, apparently in the sight line of the goalkeeper.

All records have to start somehow. This one had begun with a 2-1 win in a hard-fought match in Edinburgh.

The 2020 final, however, opened with warning shouts from Robbie Neilson, the Jam Tarts' manager, as Celtic swarmed like birds in the Hitchcock film around the Hearts defence. Neilson's voice echoed in the empty stands. No player could be excused from hearing instructions in the absence of a crowd.

After 19 minutes, Celtic's attacking intent and prowess was rewarded when Ryan Christie brought down a clearing header and fizzed a curling shot past Craig Gordon's right hand and into the net. Ten minutes later, Christophe Berra's arm made contact with a David Turnbull corner and Celtic were blessed with an opportunity to take a two-goal lead from the penalty spot. Odsonne Édouard, even in his previous season's pomp and circumstance, could not have conceived of such an audacious shuffle and chip over Gordon's flailing arms.

Whatever Lennon had to say at half-time, surely it could not have been relax, it's all over, but clearly Celtic's players had been dozing while their manager talked as Brown and co sleepwalked out of the Hampden dressing room and dreamed of a comfortable second half. Or maybe Lennon's words inspired the chill of fear into his troops; perhaps he placed too much emphasis on the powers of Hearts to stage a recovery. Neither scenario, given the manager's passion, seems likely.

When ten minutes after the break, with the Celts seemingly bemused and becalmed in a fool's paradise, Ajer was beaten too easily, Shane Duffy misjudged a cross from former Rangers stalwart Andy Halliday and Liam Boyce headed home to bring the underdogs right back into the match, still Celtic seemed unconcerned. Boyce, the shaven-headed, bearded Northern Ireland striker turned away calmly and crossed himself, as if to say, amid all these empty spaces, surrounded by ghostly silence, and enveloped by an arrogant assumption of agnosticism, there is a God after all. Watching the Celtic players on TV, there appeared an alarming lack of reaction. There was no rage, no bollocking from Brown, merely a subdued resignation, a hint of dropped heads.

In truth, it was the end of an era, a group of players on borrowed time, hoping rather than believing in destiny.

Celtic's defence was a shambles with Ajer and Duffy as calamity cousins. Brown, though, was at the heart of the decline. In former times he strutted about the field of play, demanding, cajoling, controlling every player that shared his stage, whether friend of foe. 'Why, man, he doth bestride the narrow world like a Colossus.' Shakespeare's words spoken by Cassius about Julius Caesar might have been written just as aptly about the Celtic captain. He was simply invincible, but not on this day, not on this stage without an audience at Hampden Park.

Perhaps Lenny and Broony were too close, maybe the manager could not bring himself to drop his old friend. Certainly, a mostly ineffective Brown remained on the pitch for 105 minutes of this extended cup final.

Just after the hour, a sheer shambles of defensive errors following a Hearts corner resulted in an equalising goal headed just over the line by Stephen Kingsley. The young Celtic goalkeeper Conor Hazard, with a bare handful of appearances to his name, was badly at fault in failing to deal with the inswinging ball from Josh Ginnelly.

In extra time, another fading legend, Leigh Griffiths, scorer of a century of Celtic goals and counting, replaced the precious genius of Édouard, and scored what appeared to be a winning goal, hooking the ball into the net from half a dozen yards after Gordon had blocked a Brown header. To be fair to the Celtic captain, the elder statesman's charge into the box to meet Ryan Christie's corner was a moment of greatness, and a fleeting but crucial return to the past, the days when sheer determination seemed to result in the granting of Brown's every footballing wish. The ball powered from the captain's shaven head and was parried by Gordon into the path of Griffiths. Lennon danced and

Brown was replaced by Ismaila Soro. Surely the cup was now returning to Paradise.

It was Scott Brown's last great hurrah. In March 2021, it was announced Brown had signed a pre-contract agreement to play for and to coach Aberdeen. In his time at Paradise, Brown had won ten league titles, six Scottish Cups and six League Cups. One year later, when Brown at last conceded his aching bones could no longer endure the playing of top-class football, his former Celtic manager Gordon Strachan said, 'When it comes to being a giant of the game, there can't be a conversation. Absolutely not … the genius is a guy who can make people around him great players. That is a gift.'

Strachan, as a conversationalist, meandered through his thoughts just as he zigzagged through defenders in his prime, but eventually he made his point, 'Scott has the ability to make the people around him great. That's what he has done over the last 15 years or so.'

In the final, however, there was more comedic defending to endure for Celtic. Once again, Hazard failed to deal with an in-swinging ball and Ginnelly bundled it into an open net for 3-3 and penalties to come. Sporting history was in the lap of the gods.

First up for Hearts was Steven Naismith, a wily veteran of campaigns with Kilmarnock, Rangers, Everton and Norwich City, prior to his arrival at Tynecastle, who would surely not fail in his duty, and he did not.

Griffiths, another tried and trusted goal machine, replied for Celtic.

To follow, Michael Smith restored the advantage to Hearts, and McGregor, calmness personified, brought Celtic level once more.

Olly Lee, a denizen until recently of English lower-league clubs Barnet, Birmingham and Luton, sent Hazard the wrong way and planted the ball into the bottom-right corner of the Celtic net.

Ryan Christie looked uncertain in his run-up, and placed rather than belted the ball to the Hearts goalkeeper's right. Gordon had undoubtedly moved early but Christie's tame effort deserved to be saved.

Kingsley, signed from Hull City earlier in the year, and scorer of Hearts' equaliser in normal time, failed to capitalise on Christie's error. His shot, too, was weak, and Hazard smothered and mothered the ball near his right-hand post.

Mikey Johnston, a product of the Celtic youth system, appeared calm in spite of nerves raging and roiling, and shuffled in his approach, deceived Gordon, and placed the ball into the bottom-left corner.

Craig Wighton was next in line to be the fall guy to hand the Scottish Cup to the opposition. The former Dundee man, overcome by the occasion, shot weakly straight towards Hazard, who saved easily.

If Kristoffer Ajer slotted home the subsequent penalty, Celtic were home and hosed and men of history. The worry was, however, that the Norwegian central defender had been cramping badly throughout extra time. In the end, though, Ajer struck the ball cleanly and firmly and high into the back of the net and the quadruple treble was Celtic's to keep forever and ever, amen.

In the final analysis, it did not matter that Celtic had played poorly, and it did not matter they had enjoyed only 36 per cent possession against a team from a lower tier. As Lennon said after the match, it was a 'monumental achievement', one that it is hard to imagine will ever be equalled or surpassed.

***

THE ANGE REVOLUTION
2021/22

When Ange Postecoglou presided over his inaugural press conference, he was asked how it felt to be Celtic's second choice as manager. 'Mate,' the Australian quipped, 'how do you know I wasn't fifth choice?'

Anyone with that kind of perspective, with that lack of ego, with that dry sense of humour, had to have a good shot at immortality, never mind a fighter's chance of turning around the fortunes of a troubled football club in the East End of Glasgow.

The journey had been long and hard but riven, in his adult days, with success.

When he was five years old, Postecoglou's family upped sticks from Greece, endured a month-long boat trip in cramped, sordid conditions, and arrived in Australia without accommodation, without work, without friends or extended family, and without any words of English. He tells the story about his father who heard of a mattress left outside a house in Melbourne shortly after his family's arrival in Australia, 'My dad set out in search of this bounty, this free mattress but, unfortunately, got lost on his way home.' There is not the slightest hint from Postecoglou of self-pity or of anything but admiration for his father. 'He couldn't ask anyone for directions so he lugged this heavy mattress around for hours until he found his way again.' It was life and life only, just the way it was, the way things were.

Just as it was how it was at Celtic.

In spite of finishing the previous season 25 points behind Rangers, in spite of their star players being sold to raise funds for renewal, even though replacements were far from found, let alone brokered and signed, in spite of losing the first three away games in the Premiership and suffering the usual demotion from the Champions League, in spite of Rangers being six points clear at the top of the league at the turn of the year, in spite of serious injuries throughout the first three-quarters of the league season, it was just the way it was, and a no complaints, no excuses culture was created. As the new manager said in a film of an early training session, 'We never stop.'

Postecoglou's personal stories, his tough upbringing, his uncompromising manners of speaking and of playing football all resonate with Celtic supporters.

At the funeral of Bertie Auld in November 2021, the manager said, 'Irrespective of whether you've been at this football club five months, like some of us, or ten years, like some, we're putting on a shirt that represents something.' It was reminiscent of Stein's comment about not shrinking the shirt to fit inferior players.

Postecoglou gets Celtic, understands its values and shares them with the fans. In an interview early in 2022 with Stan Sports, an Australian media outlet, he referenced 'Celtic's whole background and why the club was actually formed to feed the Irish immigrants'. For good measure, he added, 'There was a purpose behind this club that's stayed with it right to this day. For me that obviously resonates strongly being an immigrant in our own country. South Melbourne Hellas, Melbourne Croatia, Sydney Croatia – all these clubs were set up the same way. They weren't set up solely to be football clubs, they were set up to actually help people adjust to life in a new land.'

Postecoglou does loyalty too. He joined South Melbourne Hellas at the age of nine, staying with them for two decades and four more years as a manager.

Even more importantly, the Australian does winning too. Postecoglou captained his Melbourne side to the league title, won two more as manager in consecutive years and, in 2000, took South Melbourne to the FIFA Club World Championship after winning the Oceania Championship the previous year. More titles followed, too, with Brisbane Roar in the A-League and with Yokohama F Marinos in the J1 League in 2019.

Once his 17 new signings at Celtic in 2021/22 began to settle, to integrate, to understand the manager's demanding footballing philosophies and practices, Postecoglou's Bhoys began to play, and the wins flowed too. The League Cup returned to the Celtic trophy cabinet with a 2-1 victory over Hibernian. The first win in a Glasgow derby for more than two years arrived at Celtic Park in early February 2022 with a 3-0 victory that showcased almost perfect precision football and which was marked by a stunning performance including two goals from Reo Hatate, one of Postecoglou's four signings from the J1 League. In the first half of the season, another of his signings, Kyogo Furuhashi from Vissel Kobe, who suffered from vile racial abuse on social media from Ibrox fanatics, scored 14 goals in his first 23 matches and, in doing so, drew comparisons with the immortal Henrik Larsson.

Key to Postecoglou's overwhelming and unexpected success in returning the league title to Paradise – and in the League Cup triumph too – has been his impeccable recruitment. If Dermot Desmond is to be believed, moreover, the revolution in staffing at Celtic has been primarily the Australian's doing, both the clearout of dead wood from the botched ten-in-a-row and the majority of the new signings. In a major interview in April 2022, the Celtic majority shareholder stated unequivocally, 'Ange is chairman of the board as far as recruitment is concerned.' If this is true – and it rings true at least as far as the Japanese signings are concerned – it constitutes a major shift since the latter days of Rodgers and Lennon.

It was not just in recruitment, however, that Postecoglou excelled. Upon his arrival, it was expected that staff hung over from the Lennon era would be ditched, with the Australian bringing with him his own trusted coaches. Instead, Postecoglou embraced the existing setup, briefed Gavin Strachan, John Kennedy and Stevie Woods, and trusted them to deliver his footballing philosophy on the training pitches. The man's lack of ego was breathtaking.

The sole staffing recruit was Anton McElhone, a new head of sports science, who systematically improved fitness through gruelling training sessions.

Existing players, too, soon bought into the Postecoglou methodologies. Anthony Ralston was an early and dedicated convert to a new role as an inverted wing-back. Greg Taylor, too.

Within weeks of the rest of the players returning from international duties, Postecoglou had a core group of unquestioning devotees: captain Callum McGregor, Josip Juranović, Ralston and Joe Hart, who said, 'He makes me want to come into work every day,' later adding, 'I can't wait to play the system.'

A team ethos was crucial but the season did not start well. Celtic dropped 11 points from the first seven games and were sixth in September.

Postecoglou, though, showed no sign of wavering, no signs of doubt in his playing style based on constant attack, constant creation of space through rotation of positions.

'You call things early here, don't you?' he quipped in response to journalists suggesting a second consecutive Rangers title was already in the bag.

At the time of the winter break in season 2021/22, Rangers were six points clear of Celtic at the top of the table.

By the time of Celtic's stirring 2-1 victory at Ibrox at the beginning of April, however, they had reversed the situation, and pulled half a dozen points and a superior goal difference ahead of their great rivals.

By the time of the split in the Premiership in April 2022, with five league games remaining, Postecoglou was in possession of a squad of players from which two first 11s might be selected of almost equal standing. Substitutions in the spring matches against Rangers and St Johnstone make the point. At Ibrox, there was no diminishment of either commitment, intensity or skill when Anthony Ralston replaced Greg Taylor, when Matt O'Riley replaced Tom Rogic, when O'Riley, in his turn, was replaced by David Turnbull, when Reo Hatate was replaced by Nir Bitton, or when Jota was replaced by Liel Abada. In the subsequent 7-0 dispatch of St Johnstone, when Giorgos Giakoumakis pulled a hamstring, there was no weakening of resolve or technical ability when he was substituted for Kyogo Furuhashi.

Postecoglou's mastery of his Lennoxtown domain, too, was illustrated in the way that the athletes under his command peaked in the spring of 2022 in perfect time for the run-in to the title.

The return of the league championship to Paradise, the club's tenth in 11 years, formally occurred on Wednesday, 11 May at Tannadice with a 1-1 draw against Dundee United.

In fact, because of Celtic's vastly superior goal difference, the 52nd league title had been won, in effect, at Paradise the previous Saturday with an exhilarating 4-1 romp over Hearts. The four goals were all scored by Postecoglou recruits. After Ellis Simms had caused Celtic nerves to jangle with a third-minute – probably offside – goal, Celtic reasserted their authority with strikes from Daizen Maeda after half an hour and Furuhashi eight minutes from half-time, and with second-half goals from O'Riley and Giakoumakis.

'I'm really proud of the players, the staff, the supporters,' Postecoglou said. 'Nobody gave us much of a chance at the start of the year. To do what they've achieved is unbelievable. Our football has been outstanding.'

He might have said the football and the footballers were *immortal*.

Personal and Political: A Celtic Prospectus

TWO FUNDAMENTAL QUESTIONS

1) How to respect and honour the political culture of Celtic – and Rangers – without resorting to bigotry and hatred?

This is the most intimidating of all the questions that demand answering.

I have one more personal tale to tell. By November 1998 I had long since left Glasgow, called by a love affair to a second marriage. I was, though, still an innocent abroad, at least with regard to the specifics of Glasgow geography.

It was my son's 16th birthday and I decided to treat him to the gift of a match at the new Celtic Park against Motherwell.

This time, it was before the game that fear struck once again at my heart.

'I'm hungry, Dad!'

Without those words, there would have been no trouble, no alarm.

I could never eat before a football match. My nerves were always taut as bowstrings, but my son had no such qualms.

'All right,' I said, 'we'll find a fish and chip shop somewhere.'

I was still relocating my bearings along London Road but Paradise could not have been more than a further five-minute walk away.

'There's one, Dad, down that street.'

We were in Bridgeton, near the Orange Lodge, but still I didn't clock the problem. We were in full Celtic regalia, replica shirts and scarves, birthday presents, now within sight of the stadium. There was no one else in the chip shop but the man behind the fryer refused to serve us.

'This,' he explained, as if it were the most obvious thing in the world, 'is a Protestant chippie.'

'What?' I said.

'Look,' he said, 'just fuck off and be thankful I warned you.'

Still bemused, I didn't move. An element of the old stubbornness that had almost landed me into serious trouble back in 1979 still persisted.

'You'll not get out alive,' the fryer said, 'if they find you in here.'

My son stayed hungry.

* * *

For the record, November 1998 was in the last days of Fergus McCann and the brief time of Dr Jozef Venglos̆.

Celtic were unbearably inconsistent then, having lost to St Johnstone 2-1 and beaten Rangers 5-1 on the previous two Saturdays. The 2-0 win over Motherwell was a tonic and took Celtic within four points of Rangers but was in vain as the Ibrox club romped to the league title by six points.

For the record, too, I understand now that I had trespassed on the former territory of Billy Fullerton's Brigton Billy Boys, Glasgow's most notorious gang of the 1920s and '30s, who provided muscular support and protection for Scottish Tories, who broke up and beat up any left of centre political meetings in Glasgow, and who stood side by side with the Orange Lodges in marching seasons.

I appreciate, of course, that my personal stories are from bygone ages – my son is now approaching his 40th birthday – but, even so, the anger, the bitterness, the repressed sectarian violence is only a heartbeat away from resurfacing at any moment.

As it did on the Saturday evening of 22 May 2021 when Rangers supporters celebrated stopping Celtic's ten with sectarian songs and violence to both people and property in George Square and beyond. The glass front doors of Celtic's Argyle Street shop were shattered; memorial benches were set alight; police were attacked with missiles and five officers were injured. Eventually, the mob was dispersed around 9pm but not before significant damage was done to the tattered remnants of the Ibrox club's reputation. The country's first minister, Nicola Sturgeon, complained of 'thuggish behaviour'. There was, she said, 'vile anti-Catholic prejudice on display'.

Almost one year later, too, in early April, at half-time in the crucial Premiership fixture between Rangers and Celtic, broken glass was thrown into Joe Hart's goal area and another bottle struck a member of the visitors' backroom staff requiring the unnamed Celtic employee to receive stitches to the resulting head wound.

On display to the worldwide television audience, too, was a Union flag overprinted with the stark word 'CULLODEN'.

In case anyone is unaware, the Battle of Culloden was the final conflict in the Jacobite Rebellion of 1645–1646 when Catholic and nationalist Scots attempted to overthrow the German Protestant monarchy ruling Britain from London. The government forces were led by the Duke of Cumberland, the son of George II, who earned the soubriquet 'Butcher' for the brutality of his troops, for the murdering of wounded Jacobites, and for the ruthlessness of his administration of the occupation of rebellious Scotland.

Most of the bigotry and hatred in Glasgow appears to linger at Ibrox and envelops the club, even in the 21st century, like a smog of evil-smelling murk. The long-standing sectarian employment policy at Ibrox, although that particular iniquitous practice is now dead and buried, appears to have left its indelible mark. Sadly, it is still true that a small minority of Ibrox supporters continue the tradition of violence and racist behaviour in public.

* * *

The madness – and the celebration of madness – has to stop. How, though, to preserve the identities and cultural heritages of the Glasgow footballing giants without the hatred and the bile and the fists and the knives, is a question of apparently insurmountable difficulty.

One way these intractable problems may disappear is through natural wastage or through the passage of time.

Attending Celtic–Rangers matches in 2021/22, with the absence of most visiting supporters, has sanitised the matchday experience, has eliminated the prospects of violence and disorder, but it has, too, diminished and impoverished that experience, and is not a long-term solution. Expressions of racism, sexism, homophobia and religious bigotry may now be unacceptable in public and inside football grounds but that does not mean the culture that spawned these evils has disappeared altogether.

The concept of the natural wastage of enmity, however, is an interesting one. It presupposes that one side of a footballing rivalry becomes so superior to its former antagonist that hatred becomes of increasing irrelevance.

For years, Manchester United were so superior to their rivals City that the club from Moss Side were no more thought of than wasps at a Christmas party. Now, the situation is reversed.

The irrelevance of Rangers is not impossible in Glasgow. With Ange Postecoglou's Celtic denying the Ibrox side a repeat league championship in 2022, there was an accompanying denial of desperately needed guaranteed finance from automatic participation in the Champions League group stages.

By the summer of 2022, there was an increasing divergence in terms of financial viability of the two clubs. Rangers' model of spending and spending and relying on the pockets of directors maintaining their current depth of resources is a fool's paradise. Even with qualification for the Champions League, the money would merely provide a temporary respite from the precipice of further insolvency.

Every home game, in the SPL or in Europe, too, widens the gap between Celtic and Rangers. A full Paradise provides income from 60,000 paying customers whereas a full Ibrox contains a mere 51,000. As the Americans say, you do the math.

Natural wastage may occur as suddenly as a heart attack or it may occur over an extended period of time as a debilitating disease. In the meantime, however, some gesture, some kind of reaching out across the divide is needed urgently.

After the Ibrox disaster of 1971, Celtic extended the hand of friendship and compassion, which was greatly appreciated by Rangers, but some such similar gesture does not have to wait for the next calamity.

I have in mind a revival of the Glasgow Charity Cup, perhaps renamed the Friendship Cup, but still raising funds for charity, perhaps reviving the old idea of a Glasgow Select or a Glasgow United team playing against visitors, alternatively at Paradise or at Ibrox or at Hampden.

There is often more in common between enemies than seems possible.

When Billy Fullerton's Billy Boys fought bitter pitched battles in Glasgow's East End against Catholic gangs from the Calton, it was all too easy to forget both sides were neighbours and equally exploited and abused by the Glasgow ruling classes, the owners of the shipyards and the mines and factories that kept their workers at no better than subsistence and sometimes starvation wages.

It is easy to forget, too, that when Celtic were formed in 1888, there were years of friendship that followed between the new club and its established older Glasgow cousin, Rangers. Neither were there sectarian employment policies adopted by either club in the latter years of the 19th century.

It was the arrival of shipbuilders Harland and Wolff in Glasgow that may have influenced Rangers, in need of finances, into becoming a narrow and bigoted institution, and, in the following years, it was the Scottish press and the Scottish Church that aided and abetted the shipbuilders in their unpleasant practices. It may, too, be possible to borrow more from the past than a reborn Charity Cup.

Brother Walfrid's original determination was that Celtic would be a *Celtic* club, one that unified Scots and Irish rather than divided them. It was this resolution that formed the basis of the club's open employment policies continued to this day.

It is right and proper to celebrate Irish and republican roots in Celtic's political culture but not improper to celebrate its Scots roots too.

Rangers fans will also rightly never forget the club's loyalist and Protestant 20th-century history and heritage.

Both clubs, however, enjoy a common Glasgow and Scots heritage, and both sets of fans were formed mostly of working-class Glaswegians, divided and ruled by the masters of capital.

The history of workers' protests and strikes in Glasgow has seen the involvement of both Catholics and Protestants often standing shoulder to shoulder in solidarity. The first recorded industrial action in Scotland occurred in 1787 in the Calton when six weavers protesting against a 25 per cent wage cut and an employers' lockout were shot by soldiers in Duke Street.

Glasgow weavers were once more prominent in the 1820 Radical War when a national strike and a Committee of Organisation for the Formation of a Provisional Government was declared in Glasgow in protest against the hardships that followed the Napoleonic Wars and the mechanisation of industry.

In February 1915, Glasgow women formed the Women's Housing Association in protest against the relentless exploitation by landlords of their city tenants, and the first rent strike took place three months later.

In June 1919, Clyde's engineers and shipbuilders, predominantly Protestant, organised the Forty Hours Strike to shorten the working week to alleviate the mass unemployment prevalent after the demobilisation of soldiers at the conclusion of World War One. Winston Churchill, the secretary of state for war in David Lloyd George's government, declared war on the workers by sending tanks to George Square.

Red Clydeside has a long history of industrial action, from the apprentices' strike in 1937 to the work-in in 1971 at Upper Clyde Shipbuilders. Two Glasgow firebrands of the trade unionist movement from the 1960s and '70s, Alex Ferguson and Jimmy Reid, were both Protestant but both married Catholics. Unity is possible.

For those who are unwilling to compromise, unwilling to move forwards, these men will live in what poet, Emily Berry, calls *unexhausted time.*

It is a sad place and time in which to live but, eventually, the bigots will all be dead, hopefully before passing the sins of the fathers on to children and grandchildren. Education will help, as will an emphasis on what unites rather than on what divides.

If Celtic's current financial and footballing supremacy does not result in terminal woes for the Ibrox club, both teams could do worse than come together in symbolic fashion and, once a year, play a genuine friendly match for good Glasgow causes.

The past may be a foreign country but there may still be lessons to be learned from its strange wisdom, if we search in the right places in the past.

Celtic's first matches were all friendlies. Remember, too, the opening show was against Rangers. A report in the *Scottish Umpire* from 5 June 1888 had this to say:

'The match was a capital one, fast and friendly. After the match, over 70 gentlemen sat down to supper in the Hall, East Rose Street, where a pleasant evening was spent. Dr Conway occupied the chair, and on the platform also Messrs. M'Fadden (Hibs), McCulloch (Our Boys), Grant (Rangers), and the Reverend Brother Walfrid.'

If only it had stayed that way. There was a peaceable kingdom at that moment in the past. Is it too much to ask for more of the same in the future? Do we not have more in common than that which divides us?

If soldiers in opposing trenches at Christmas 1914 could lay down their arms and play football matches in no-man's land and sing carols of peace together, surely an agreed truce could be arranged between the warring Glasgow tribes? If we could enjoy our heritage, and abandon the hatred, Brother Walfrid would look down from his place in heaven and smile the smile of both the just and the justified.

In 2022, Ange Postecoglou has shown the way. He has embraced and celebrated Celtic's origins, the club's history and culture. He has, though, not been afraid to embrace Rangers manager Gio van Bronckhorst, to meet him in Glasgow restaurants, and to talk about these contacts as if they were the most natural things in the world. In doing so, he has issued an important and subtle but persuasive challenge to bigotry.

* * *

2) How to become good Europeans?

One result of an abandonment of the old obsessions, the old hatreds, might be an ability to focus on both Celtic's and Rangers' – if the latter survive their suicidal financial practices – restoration to the forefront of European football.

The true measure of Celtic will always be in Europe. With one classical and solitary star, signifying one European Cup win, imprinted on shirts, the club has nailed its colours firmly to the mast of continental club football. Custodians should not sleep at night until Celtic once more becomes a force in the European game.

In each of the three previous summer European qualifying campaigns, from 2019 to 2021, the board have sent, first a returning Neil Lennon, and then an arriving Ange Postecoglou naked, to borrow Aneurin Bevan's phrase from the 1957 Labour Party Conference, into the conference chamber, devoid of preparation, devoid of proper players.

There must be a way of combining financial prudence with adequate preparation. At least, in the summer of 2022, there will be no high summer, high noon, qualifying matches to negotiate.

The previous occasion when Celtic qualified for the group stages of the Champions League was in 2017 under Brendan Rodgers. The last time Celtic qualified for the knockout phase of Europe's major competition was 2013 under Lennon.

If Scotland achieves independence from London's imperial outreach and if that enables the nation to return to membership of the European Union, this might be a signal for Celtic to return to the latter stages of the Champions League and even to win a second star on their shirts.

This is no time to wait, however, for politicians to deliver the goods. With Postecoglou's Celtic winning the 2021/22 Premiership and thereby earning automatic qualification for the group stages of the Champions League, now is the time to be determined on progression.

It is possible. As John Park said in a 2021 interview with The Athletic, with 'astute scouting observations' and 'strong data assessment ... and good coaching', participation and progress in the later stages of the Champions League 'is an entirely possible outcome'.

Celtic already have a footballing and financial model before them in Ajax of Amsterdam, another European club with sound finances, another club that buys and sells well. The Dutch club has won the primary European trophy four times in 1971, 1972, 1973 and 1995, but has also proved it is possible to win again, even in times when TV revenue is hogged primarily by English clubs, and even when playing outside of the major European leagues.

Borussia Dortmund, too, another leading European club, have adapted and survived and prospered with an economic model of buying to sell similar to Celtic and Ajax. It is possible to be good Europeans.

In 2022/23, in particular, with automatic qualification to the group stages of the Champions League, it is eminently feasible. With estimated earnings of at least £35m, Celtic's accustomed policy of making one big sale a year to balance the books may be abandoned. As long as participation in the Champions League continues, player sales become a choice rather than a necessity.

In the future, too, Celtic might prefer playing in a European league to a resumed pursuit of ten-in-a-row.

Leading clubs from Scotland, Scandinavia, the Benelux countries, and even from former Soviet states in northern and eastern Europe might come together in this project to provide greater competition for Celtic even to add a second star to their shirts.

In addition, or instead of a European League, a *Celtic* knockout competition involving leading clubs from Scotland, Wales, Ireland, Cornwall, the Isle of Man, Brittany, Galicia, Asturias and Cantabria would provide further and wider horizons.

The club from Paradise could still compete in the Scottish Cup and in UEFA competitions. The focus, though, would shift from narrow parochialism – and its dependent bigotry – to a European perspective.

Scotland, as a nation, has always looked to Europe, and its foremost football club needs to learn to be good Europeans too.

The immortals of Celtic's past, present and future all demand and deserve it.

Select Bibliography

ONE OF the most important sources for this book – and a constant companion – has been the truly wonderful website www.thecelticwiki.com. This is a labour of love by fans, on behalf of fans, and contains detailed information and reports on every match ever played by Celtic. It also contains biographies of players, managers, coaches, directors: all the immortals. There is even a comprehensive list of all published books on Celtic, helpfully divided into numerous categories.

Another useful website for research purposes is Google News on which may be found free archived editions of both the *Glasgow Herald* and the *Evening Times*.

Listed below is a selection of books that are recommended reading for all Celtic fans and which have been used in the research process for this book.

Corr, M., *Invincible* (The Celtic Star, 2020)
Fogarty, C., *The Perfect Holocaust* (Fogarty Publishing, 2014)
Gordon, A., *Billy McNeill* (Black & White Publishing, 2018)
McCarra, K., *Celtic: A Biography in Nine Lives* (Faber & Faber, 2012)
Kelly, L., *Take Me To Your Paradise* (Independently published, 2019)
Kelly, L., Potter, D., Corr, M., *Walfrid and the Bould Bhoys* (The Celtic Star, 2020)
Kelly, Sir R., *Celtic* (Hay Nisbet and Miller, 1971)
Low, D., Shennan, F., *Rebels in Paradise* (Mainstream, 1994)
Macpherson, A., *More Than A Game* (Luath Press, 2020)
Macpherson, A., *Jock Stein* (Highdown, 2004)
McColl, G., *Tommy Gemmell* (Virgin Books, 2004)
McNee, G., *The Story of Celtic* (Stanley Paul, 1978)
Moynihan, L., *Gordon Strachan* (Virgin Books, 2005)

Moynihan, L., *The Three Kings* (Quercus, 2019)

O'Donnell, S., *Tangled Up in Blue* (Pitch Publishing, 2019)

O'Donnell, S., *Fergus McCann v David Murray* (Pitch Publishing, 2020)

Potter, D., *Celtic v Rangers* (Pitch Publishing, 2019)

Sullivan, S., *Sean Fallon* (Back Page Press, 2012)

Wilson, B., *Celtic* (Arena Sport, 2017)

In-house Celtic publications, such as *Treble Treble* and *The Official Story of Nine-In-A-Row* are useful reference books and include post-match interview quotes previously published in *Celtic View*.

The author's personal collection of Celtic programmes has been mined for nuggets of information.

Celtic fanzines such as *Not the View* provide both wonderful entertainment and alternative and irreverent perspectives, as have fan-based websites Celts Are Here, The Celtic Star, The Celtic Underground, and many others.